A History MANITOBA 125

VOLUME TWO

GATEWAY TO THE WEST

GREAT PLAINS
PUBLICATIONS

WINNIPEG, MANITOBA
1994

GATEWAY TO THE WEST

© Copyright 1994 Great Plains Publications Ltd.
All rights reserved
ISBN 0-9697804-2-7
Printed in Canada

CANADIAN CATALOGUING IN PUBLICATION DATA

Main entry under title:

Manitoba 125: a history

    Edited by Gregg Shilliday.
    Includes bibliographical references and index.
    Partial contents: v. 2. Gateway to the West
    ISBN 0-9697804-2-7 (v. 2)

1. Manitoba – History.   I. Shilliday, Gregg.
II. Title: Gateway to the West.   III. Title: Manitoba one
hundred twenty five

FC3361.M35 1993   971.27   C94-920003-4
F1063.M35 1993

THE WRITERS AND EDITORS OF **MANITOBA 125 – A HISTORY** DEDICATE
THIS SERIES TO THE RESOURCEFUL PEOPLE, OF ALL RACES AND CREEDS,
WHO BUILT THIS PROVINCE.

TABLE OF CONTENTS

LIST OF MAPS AND CHARTS

VOLUME ONE RUPERT'S LAND TO RIEL
(PRE-1870)

VOLUME TWO GATEWAY TO THE WEST
(1870–1940)

VOLUME THREE DECADES OF DIVERSITY
(1940–1995)

STAFF

<table>
<tr><td>PUBLISHER
AND EDITOR</td><td>**GREGG SHILLIDAY**   Over the years, Mr. Shilliday has worked for a wide range of news organizations including the *Winnipeg Tribune*, the *Winnipeg Free Press*, the *Ottawa Citizen, Western Report* magazine, and *CBC Newsworld*. He was also contributing writer to *The Great West Before 1900*, a journalistic history of Alberta.</td></tr>
<tr><td>DESIGN
DIRECTOR</td><td>**PAT STANTON**   A graphic design consultant and teacher, Ms. Stanton has shifted her interest and expertise to the areas of book design and publications. Her projects have gained both national and international recognition, including winning a silver medal at the International Book Fair in Leipzig, Germany.</td></tr>
<tr><td>MARKETING
DIRECTOR</td><td>**TREVOR KENNERD**   Mr. Kennerd operates a successful marketing and communications company in Winnipeg. Before that, he was a key member of the Winnipeg Blue Bombers football club, spending his off-seasons working in the advertising industry.</td></tr>
<tr><td>ASSOCIATE
EDITOR</td><td>**LLOYD FRIDFINNSON**   Mr. Fridfinnson was a principal in Probe Research Consultants before joining Great Plains Publications. Mr. Fridfinnson has a Master's degree in Political Studies, with an emphasis on Manitoba's role in international affairs.</td></tr>
<tr><td>HEAD
RESEARCHER</td><td>**MAUREEN COUSINS**   After spending several years as a reporter with the *Portage la Prairie Daily Graphic*, Ms. Cousins returned to school, graduating from Brandon University in 1991. She is now pursuing a Master's degree in history at the University of Manitoba.</td></tr>
<tr><td>CONSULTING
HISTORIAN</td><td>**J. EDGAR (ED) REA**   One of Manitoba's most respected historians, Prof. Rea has written extensively on the province's history. A past president of the Canadian Historical Association, Prof. Rea teaches at the University of Manitoba.</td></tr>
<tr><td>COMMUNITY
ADVISOR</td><td>**WILLIAM NORRIE, C.M., Q.C.**   Since retiring from his lengthy term as mayor of Winnipeg, Mr. Norrie has been active in many volunteer and charity organizations. A former Rhodes scholar and lawyer, he recently helped establish the William Norrie International Centre for Environmental Research and Education.</td></tr>
</table>

CONTRIBUTING WRITERS

DON BAILEY   Mr. Bailey is one of Manitoba's best known writers, having published five novels and numerous other works of fiction and non-fiction. He has also written for *Saturday Night,* the *Globe and Mail* and the *Toronto Star*. His most recent collection of short stories is called *Window Dressing*.

INGEBORG BOYENS   After several years as legislature bureau chief for the *Winnipeg Free Press*, Ms. Boyens joined the CBC where she worked as a political reporter and as a producer for *The Journal*. She is now a producer for CBC's *Country Canada*.

LUCIEN CHAPUT   Mr. Chaput has worked an an archivist, and as a journalist for St. Boniface's *La Liberté*. He also edited *Histoire de St. Boniface: A l'ombre des cathedrales*.

CHRISTOPHER DAFOE   A columnist and editor, Mr. Dafoe's work has appeared in newspapers across the country. He has also been published in the *London Times, Manchester Guardian* and *Jerusalem Post*. He is currently editor of *The Beaver* magazine.

GARRY ENNS Mr. Enns has produced a series of Manitoba Day publications for Manitoba Culture, Heritage and Citizenship. He is also author of *Gretna: Window on the Northwest.*

NELSON S. GERRARD A local historian and genealogist, Mr. Gerrard specializes in the history of Icelandic settlement in North America, and lives at 'Eyrarbakki', near Hnausa, in the heart of "New Iceland" on Lake Winnipeg.

STELLA HRYNIUK Dr. Stella Hryniuk is a professor of history and Slavic studies at the University of Manitoba. Her most recent book is *Multiculturalism and Ukrainian Canadians.*

LARRY KROTZ One of Manitoba's best known freelance writers, Mr. Krotz has published articles in many of Canada's national magazines. His documentary film work has been shown on PBS, CBC and Vision Television.

DON LANGFORD A graduate of the University of Manitoba, Mr. Langford has written extensively on native issues for the *Winnipeg Free Press* and has worked for the Manitoba Aboriginal Justice Inquiry and the Royal Commission on Aboriginal Peoples.

ALLAN LEVINE A prolific writer with several books and numerous journalistic articles to his credit, Mr. Levine teaches history at St. John's Ravenscourt. His most recent book, *Scrum Wars,* was an examination of the relationship between Canada's prime ministers and the news media.

JAKE MacDONALD Mr. MacDonald has written several books dealing with native and white cultures in Canada's north country. His most recent novel is entitled *Raised by the River.* His journalistic work has appeared in many national publications.

FRED McGUINNESS Mr. McGuinness is a popular writer, lecturer and broadcaster with a special interest in the development of rural communities. He lives on a farm near Brandon; he lectures in journalism at Brandon University.

JIM MOCHORUK A professor of history at the University of North Dakota, Prof. Mochoruk has written extensively on Manitoba's North. He has also contributed to the Manitoba Labour History series and many other scholarly publications.

TERENCE MOORE An editorial writer for the *Winnipeg Free Press*, Mr. Moore has a particular interest in civic affairs. He is the author of *Joe Doupe: Bedside Physiologist.*

MORRIS MOTT Prof. Mott, a former professional hockey player, teaches history at Brandon University. He is co-editor of *Manitoba History* magazine.

WILLIAM NEVILLE A professor of political science at the University of Manitoba, Prof. Neville is a former Winnipeg city councillor. He writes a weekly column for the *Winnipeg Free Press.*

BYRON REMPEL A journalist and writer, Mr. Rempel was born in Steinbach. He now lives in Key West, Florida, where he is completing a novel.

DAVID ROBERTS As the *Globe and Mail*'s Manitoba correspondent, Mr. Roberts has interpreted the province to a national audience for several years. He has also written for many other magazines and newspapers.

MARGARET SWEATMAN An author and playwright, Ms. Sweatman has been widely published. Her novel *Fox*, an account of the effects of the 1919 General Strike, was turned into a play and performed by the Prairie Theatre Exchange.

STUART JAMES WHITLEY, Q.C. Mr. Whitley has published numerous legal articles and two textbooks. He has also written an historical novel, *Climates of our Birth,* based on the early settlement of Manitoba. Mr. Whitley is presently assistant deputy minister in Manitoba's Justice Department.

PREFACE

Manitoba in 1870, even in 1940, was a very different place from the Manitoba of today. Perhaps a key difference was that the people of those times were not tentative in proclaiming their pride in being Manitobans. The new settlers looked around and saw limitless potential: the rolling beauty of the Pembina Valley, the blue-green immensity of Lake Winnipeg, the rich abundance of the Portage Plains, the timbered vastness of the North. They saw their new home as being different, and in many ways better, than the places they had come from—whether it was Ontario or Poland or Holland.

Early Manitobans were also very possessive. They didn't appreciate interference, especially from eastern politicians or businesses. At that time "western alienation" was more than just political rhetoric—it was a heart-felt reaction to eastern Canada's treatment of Manitoba as a hinterland. For example, the Canadian Pacific Railway's monopoly seemed designed to benefit the railway's eastern investors and customers. Freight rates, especially, favoured the eastern shipper of finished goods over the western supplier of raw materials. National political decisions, weighted by sheer population numbers, almost always gave way to eastern interests. Even the western provinces' powers were less than eastern ones as the federal government insisted on keeping control of the West's natural resources.

Manitobans didn't like being treated as second-class citizens and clashed frequently with eastern power structures. Premiers like John Norquay and Thomas Greenway demanded the right to build railways to compete with the CPR. The struggle for provincial rights escalated during the 1890's as Manitoba politicians fought with Ottawa over how education should be administered. As Manitoba grew, its leaders flexed their muscles on the national stage. Clifford Sifton developed into a powerful voice in the federal cabinet; Portage la Prairie's Arthur Meighen became Prime Minister of Canada.

Our province became a place of firsts. Social reformers like Nellie McClung gained the vote for Manitoba women—the first province to do so. New kinds of wheat were developed here—wheat that would turn agriculture into the engine of the Canadian economy. Even in war, Manitobans distinguished themselves: more Manitobans per capita gave their lives in World War I than any other Canadians. Later, James A. Richardson would create the first national airline, and the *Winnipeg Free Press* would feature the first commercial radio broadcasts in the nation.

Manitobans often forget that our province—unlike any other in Confederation—was born of armed insurrection. The mixed-blood people of this region rejected distant masters in a battle for control over their own affairs. Louis Riel was defending the rights of the Métis in 1870, but he was also articulating the later resentment of westerners generally at being treated as colonists. Even after the Métis had been swept away by a tide of immigration, the new homesteaders shared the independence of Riel. They had travelled great distances and worked long days to shape a new society. They were proud of what they had created.

In the era covered by this volume—1870 to 1940—our province grew from a backwoods fur trade colony to a powerful partner in Confederation. Driven by the metropolitan engine of Winnipeg and wearing proudly the agricultural designation "Breadbasket of the Empire", Manitobans were a confident, even cocky, lot. They saw their province as a place of unlimited potential, with room for people of all backgrounds to make a fresh start.

Millions of settlers passed through Winnipeg in the early decades of this century. Winnipeg quickly became a supplier for the entire West, growing so quickly that land would triple in value overnight and boomtown millionaires became commonplace. Towns and farms spread west and north as new waves of immigrants—many from eastern Europe—took to the soil. The population of the province jumped from 12,000 in 1870 to 730,000 by 1940. The other Prairie provinces were also booming. Manitoba truly had become Gateway to the West.

With the **MANITOBA 125** series, we are trying to make history enjoyable. We believe history can and should be relevant, for both students and the general public. In an effort to improve the telling of history—to make the stories of our past come alive—we have utilized hundreds of colourful paintings, photographs and maps. We have also used a journalistic writing style that concentrates on people rather than dates.

The year 1995 marks the 125th anniversary of Manitoba. It is a time to remember—with pride —the triumphs and sorrows of the resourceful men and women who built our province. This series is our birthday gift to them.

—Gregg Shilliday

EDITOR'S NOTE

One of the more obvious observations to make about history is that things change: place names change, demographics change, attitudes about race change, even methods of measurement change.

The careful reader may notice, for example, references to "Negro" or "Galician" in contemporary accounts quoted in the book. Clearly, we can't change quotes, so the references (however outdated) are left intact. Readers may also note the text switching back and forth between metric and Imperial measurements. We have generally converted information to metric, except when it leads to silly or inappropriate complications. Railway measurements like Mile 312, for example, are left in Imperial, as are human heights and weights. We have also left farm measurements in Imperial.

On the issue of native nomenclature, we have used tribal names where possible. In other cases, we use the terms *native, aboriginal* or *Indian* depending on the circumstances. None of these terms are pejorative.

Finally, please remember that the three-volume **MANITOBA 125** series is intended as an overview. If we have piqued your interest in Manitoba's fascinating history, please consider reading the more detailed books and articles suggested in the back of this volume. ❧

ACKNOWLEDGMENTS

Many people have helped with the production of **GATEWAY TO THE WEST**. In particular, we would like to thank Thora Cooke of the Western Canada Pictorial Index, Elizabeth Blight and Lynne Champagne of the Provincial Archives of Manitoba, Gary Essar of the Winnipeg Art Gallery, Dan Ring of the Mendel Gallery in Saskatoon, Sharon Reilly of the Manitoba Museum of Man and Nature, Anne Morton of the Hudson's Bay Company Archives, John Lohrenz of the Department of Education and Training, Brian Cole of the *Winnipeg Free Press*, Bruce Cherney of the *Winnipeg Real Estate News*, Michael Czuboka of the Manitoba Historical Society, Ludek Stipl of the Canadian Pacific Archives in Montreal, Dave Barber at the Winnipeg Film Group, George Lammers and the volunteers at the Western Canada Aviation Museum, Gord Crossley and Larry Lajewness of the Fort Garry Horse, Gerry Oliver at the Seton Centre in Carberry and Jack Templeman of the Winnipeg Police Museum.

Grateful thanks are also extended to Phil Romaniuk, Craig Wiwad, David Wolinsky, Doug Allen, Ron Robinson, Murray McNeill, Dale Cummings, Caron Hart, Jim and Beth Shilliday, and as always, David Friesen and the dedicated staff at D.W. Friesen in Altona. ❧

CHAPTER ONE

The Transformation of Manitoba

BY INGEBORG BOYENS

Manitoba in 1870 was an anomaly within Confederation—a tiny postage stamp province populated mainly by Métis and Indians. Created in response to armed insurrection, the new province was a rough and ready place, still dependent on the fur trade and the buffalo hunt. Its citizens had a fierce pride in their unique society—a society that protected the rights of Catholic and Protestant, French and English. Over the next 15 years, however, Manitoba underwent a remarkable transformation. A flood of Protestant immigration, mainly from Ontario, changed the province from a bi-cultural outpost of the fur trade into a solidly British, anti-Catholic, agricultural society. In little more than a decade, without time to even mourn its loss, the old order of the plains was permanently swept away.

With additional material by
DON LANGFORD, GARRY ENNS, NELSON GERRARD, LLOYD
FRIDFINNSON, JAKE MACDONALD AND STUART JAMES WHITLEY

The Forks by W. Frank Lynn

Ontario immigration sweeps away the old order

The Transformation of Manitoba

Thursday, May 12, 1870, was unusually hot and humid in the Red River settlement. Otherwise, the old colony on the banks of the Red and Assiniboine rivers was slipping into the routine rhythms of spring. Mosquitoes were stirring. Métis plains hunters, loaded with buffalo robes, were returning from a winter in the Northwest. The Hudson's Bay Company's steamboat *International* had arrived the previous week after a winter in dock. And local wagonmen were preparing for the spring Red River cart brigade to St. Paul. Merchant Alexander Begg summarized the day's events in his journal: "Nothing of importance happened today."

For Louis Riel, president of the settlement's self-declared provisional government, May 12 was also an uneventful day. The Métis leader was eager for news from delegates who had been dispatched to Ottawa in March to lobby the Canadian government for provincial status. But the evening mail, once again, brought no word from points east.

Yet on that same day, across more than 2,000 kilometres of swampy muskeg and tangled forest, the future course of the residents of Red River was being cast. The Parliament of Canada passed the Manitoba Act—legislation which carved a tiny province out of the vast stretch of land once ruled by the Hudson's Bay Company. Manitoba was now Canada's first western province.

However, it would be June before the delegates returned to Red River with details of the settlement's step into provincehood. And it would be longer still before it became clear that the Manitoba Act had launched an inevitable process that would transform a frontier society dependent on the fur trade into a complicated new world where settlers from foreign lands forged an economy based on the cultivation of wheat.

In 1870, the Red River settlement was still part of the fur frontier. Almost all of its 12,000 residents were tied in some way to the Hudson's Bay Company or its former rival, the North West Company. For two centuries, The Hudson's Bay Company had been the paternalistic administrator of the entire Northwest, a tract that stretched across much of present-day Western Canada.

The Red River settlement was divided between English Protestants and French Catholics. Both groups were largely bound by native blood and both were built on the old fur trade ethic. The French Métis made up the largest segment of the population. When the HBC agreed to transfer control of the Northwest to the Dominion of Canada, the Métis feared—with good reason—that they could be swept aside by English-speaking settlers from Canada.

Louis Riel shaped that apprehension into a united political and military force. In the fall of 1869, the Métis rose up under Riel's leadership, took control of the HBC's Fort Garry and declared themselves the provisional government of what they called Assiniboia. Mindful of the duality of the settlement, the Métis government deftly addressed the concerns of both French and English speakers, winning the support of many English residents. It was a bloodless uprising—until the execution of Ontario Orangeman Thomas Scott. Scott was among the agitators who challenged Riel's provisional government. He was court-martialed according to the old Métis discipline of the buffalo hunt. His death provoked outrage in English Ontario and later proved to be the undoing of Riel.

The Manitoba Act encompassed virtually all the demands the delegates of the provisional government put before Canada. It acknowledged the long co-existence of French and English in the Northwest by declaring that both languages and Protestant and Catholic educational rights would be protected. It recognized the land rights of the Métis by granting 1.4 million acres of land to the children of mixed-blood families. Also, the new province would be governed by a lieutenant-governor appointed by the Dominion, a nominated upper house of seven members and an elected assembly of 24 members.

But Prime Minister Sir John A. Macdonald and his Conservative colleagues were not blindly generous. The new province would be tiny, only 28,500 square kilometres. The rest of Rupert's Land, the vast bulk of the British Northwest, would become a territory governed by Ottawa. And contrary to Canadian precedent, the Dominion would control public land inside the province for purposes of railway building and land settlement.

Nonetheless, it was relief and satisfaction that greeted Father Noel Joseph Ritchot, the principal delegate to Ottawa, when he returned to Red River in June. On June 24, the "legislative assembly" of the provisional government of Assiniboia enthusiastically endorsed the Manitoba Act. Riel himself had nothing but praise for the legislation. One key matter—a general amnesty for the Métis insurgents—had not been resolved. Ritchot assured Riel he had been told the government would forgive all crimes. Bishop Alexandre-Antonin Taché, who had long played the godfather to the Métis efforts at self-determination, echoed the belief that an amnesty would be forthcoming.

So Riel continued to lead the government, preparing to hand over the reins of power to the newly appointed lieutenant-governor, Adams G. Archibald, when he arrived. Convinced the Red River settlement had finally achieved harmony, Riel disbanded the provisional government troops. Indeed, it appeared as if the settlement was on the brink of a peaceful transference of power—until the arrival of a military expedition threw the colony into turmoil once again.

Prime Minister Macdonald had authorized

Louis Riel

Colonel Garnet Wolseley

The Wolseley Expedition, lacking access to a railway, was forced to follow the old voyageur route on their arduous journey to Red River.

the military force weeks before Parliament considered the Manitoba Act. It was a political move designed to placate Ontarians incensed by the execution of Thomas Scott. A force of 1,200 men—British Imperial troops augmented by volunteers, most of them from Ontario—was assembled under the leadership of Colonel Garnet Wolseley. But Macdonald also had to appease Quebec francophones who viewed a military force as unfair punitive action against their kin in Red River. With that in mind, Macdonald told Parliament on May 12: "Her Majesty's troops go forth on an errand of peace, and will serve as an assurance to the inhabitants of the Red River Settlement and the numerous Indian tribes that occupy the Northwest, that they have a place in the regard and counsels of England, and may rely on the impartial protection of the British sceptre."

Impartial or not, Wolseley's expedition was beset by problems. It was forced to take the old North West Company canoe route from Lake Superior to Lake Winnipeg over a huge expanse of rock, water and forest. Instead of smartly marching into action, the British Imperial forces had to cut a road through primeval forests and hoist tonnes of military gear over countless portages.

After more than three months of grinding labour, the troops—exhausted and dispirited—finally moved into Métis-held territory. Their only consolation was the hope that Riel and his supporters would give them a good fight. Forgetting they were "on an errand of peace", the Ontario-based militiamen were particularly eager to exact revenge for the execution of Scott. Wolseley himself seemed to share the bloodlust. He wrote his wife: "I have such a horror of rebels and vermin of his [Riel's] kidney, that my treatment of him might not be approved by the civil powers."

On the morning of August 24, in drenching rain, the bedraggled army approached Fort Garry. As the men plodded through the mud, their spirits dropped even more as they realized none of the guns at the fort were manned. There would be no glorious battle against the half-breed rebels. Soon after, the Imperial troops, rifles at the ready, marched in and secured the empty fort.

The Métis had long since abandoned any notion of resisting the military force. Riel and his supporters had been assured the expedition came on a mission of peace. Riel waited patiently for some conciliatory gesture from Wolseley. It never came. On the morning the troops advanced, Riel finally realized his life was in danger. A Hudson's Bay Company

> **"I have such a horror of rebels and vermin of his [Riel's] kidney, that my treatment of him might not be approved by the civil powers."**
>
> **Colonel Garnet Wolseley, leader of the troops authorized by Prime Minister Macdonald**

employee rushed into his house, breathless from a breakneck ride. "For the love of God, clear out," he gasped to Riel. "The troops are just outside the city and you are going to be lynched."

Riel ran out, leaving his uneaten breakfast on the table. He collected two of his colleagues; they slid down the nearby Red River's muddy bank and pulled themselves across the Red on the ferry. As they cut the ferry cable on the other side, they watched helplessly as the green-coated Imperial riflemen marched through Fort Garry's main gate.

Riel made only one stop as he fled the Red River settlement—at Bishop Taché's house to tell his mentor he had been deceived. Ever philosophical, Riel apparently said: "No matter what happens now, the rights of the Métis are assured by the Manitoba Act; that is what I wanted. My mission is finished."

When Wolseley marched into Fort Garry and took control of the colony, he swept away all vestiges of the provisional government. In the eyes of Canadian law, the Hudson's Bay Company was the only legal authority in Red River. Until Archibald arrived, HBC commissioner Donald A. Smith was pressed into action as the reluctant head of a reconstituted Company government.

The citizens of Red River were soon helpless in the face of a lawlessness unseen before, even at the height of the Riel uprising. The trained British troops—after securing the fort—departed almost immediately for Ottawa. But they left behind the undisciplined Ontario militia volunteers. These rowdy "peacekeeping" forces overran Winnipeg saloons, draining all the liquor in the community in a matter of days. A captain in the troops described the alcohol-induced pandemonium this way: "Indians, half-breeds, and whites in all stages of intoxication, fighting and quarreling in the streets with drawn knives, and lying prostrate on the prairie in all directions, like the killed and wounded after a sharp skirmish."

On September 2, 1870, in the midst of this havoc, the best hope for order in Red River appeared in the person of Adams Archibald. As the new lieutenant-governor's canoe drew up at Fort Garry, Commissioner Donald A. Smith offered these words of greeting: "I yield up my responsibilities with pleasure." Well aware of the challenge before him, Archibald replied, "I don't anticipate much pleasure on my own account."

Adams Archibald was a well-considered choice for the job of lieutenant-governor. The tall, quiet Nova Scotian was perhaps the only Canadian statesman who could fulfill the difficult mandate of creating a functional democracy from the ferment of the Red River settlement. It was Archibald's assignment to keep the peace, establish the institutions of executive and representative government, negotiate with the natives, and through it all, avoid the trap of favouring one side or the other.

While Red River's Scottish and half-breed residents generally supported Archibald, the rest of the colony was perilously divided—on one hand were the leaderless and embittered Métis; on the other were the Ontario volunteers who wanted Riel to pay for the death of Thomas Scott. Encounters between the Canadians and the Métis were frequent and ugly. Archibald said beatings were so endemic that the Métis lived virtually in "a state of slavery". Sometimes the confrontations were fatal. Eleazar Goulet, who had been with Riel in Fort Garry, was drowned as he tried to escape an angry mob by swimming across the Red River to St. Boniface. A month later, an English half-breed, who had fallen in with the Ontario Orange faction, was killed by a fall when his horse was deliberately frightened by his enemies. Andre Nault, who had commanded the Scott firing squad, was chased south to the American border, kicked, stabbed and left for dead.

Archibald immediately set about establishing a parliamentary government and administration. The lieutenant-governor began with the appointment of his executive council. He selected moderate men, affiliated neither with Riel nor the extremists of the Canadian movement. This executive council (essentially Archibald's cabinet) issued commissions to magistrates, recruited a small police force, and organized an official census. Twenty-four electoral districts were drawn from the parishes along the rivers and in the outlying settlements. Care was taken to ensure 12 were French and 12 were English.

In December, 1870, the first election to the Manitoba legislative assembly was held and in March, members of the upper chamber were appointed. The first session of the Manitoba legislature was heralded with as much pomp and ceremony as could be mustered. Legislators met in the home of A.G.B. Bannatyne, a well-established trader, as no public building was available. One hundred members of the Ontario Rifles provided

Indians and Métis were frequent targets of drunken militiamen after Wolseley's regular troops returned east.

Unruly mob violence was commonplace in early Manitoba. In 1871, a jeering mob reduced the province's attorney general to drawing his revolver in self-defence.

the ceremonial guard.

When the session of the legislature came to an end six weeks later, the Province of Manitoba was equipped with a system of courts, a school structure, and 43 statutes to serve the needs of a small community. Peace gradually began to temper the lawless brawling that had marked the first months of provincehood.

Louis Riel still moved on the periphery of the Métis society, attempting to exert his leadership from a careful distance by slipping in and out of St. Boniface, St. Vital and other supportive communities. Canadian politicians had not yet dealt with the issue of an amnesty, and they were loath to do so, knowing they could not satisfy both Ontario and Quebec. But finally, in 1872, they found a compromise: they granted full amnesty to most of the participants in the troubles, but banished Riel from the country for a minimum of five years.

Over the next few years, Riel remained a

Steamboats on the Red River

Paddlewheelers carried goods and people before the arrival of the CPR

"STEAMBOAT COMIN'!" was a cry frequently heard on the Red River between the years 1859 and 1912. Once the American government allowed Hudson's Bay Company goods to be carried through the United States, the bulk of west-bound traffic shifted from the Hudson Bay route to the railhead at St. Paul, Minnesota. The Chamber of Commerce there offered a reward of $1,000 to anyone who would launch a steam vessel on the Red River and sail it to Fort Garry.

Anson Northup, a Minnesotan hotelier and speculator, agreed to do it for double the reward. He owned at the time a small vessel named the *North Star,* which he took apart and dragged overland. Sixty men, 13 yoke of oxen and 17 horses sledged the equipment the 240 kilometres between the headwaters of the Mississippi and the Red River. In 1859, the new boat, vaingloriously named the *Anson Northup,* sailed to "Garry," consuming wood at the rate of one full cord each hour.

To handle the shallow waters of prairie rivers, steamboats were frequently equipped with spars and tackle forward of the mast. Aground, a spar would be lowered through rings on the side of the hull, with a tackle

The *Marquette*

attached to the top, leading down through a turning block to the capstan. The hull was lifted an inch or so, and engines were run either to clear or back off the obstacle. Steamers were usually loaded most heavily at the head, so that when the bow cleared, the craft would not hang up amidships. In this way, the craft might literally "walk" or "grasshopper" over obstacles.

The HBC steamer *International*

brought many hundreds of settlers to Manitoba. On July 31, 1874, 50 families of Russian Mennonites were landed; in 1875, she brought more than 270 Icelandic settlers. At 137 feet long, 26 feet in the beam, and 20 feet from waterline to hurricane deck, she was the largest of the Red River steamers. But even when fully loaded with passengers and freight, she drew less than 42 inches of water.

In 1871, the United States gov-

mythic force in Manitoba, even in exile. He was elected twice to Parliament as a member from Manitoba during his absence, but he was never able to assume his seat. Riel's banishment ensured he had little real influence on the dramatic events that were about to transform the embryonic province.

Garnet Wolseley spent only a short time in Manitoba. But the natural wealth and beauty of the land captivated him. He wrote in *Blackwood's Magazine* soon after he returned to the East from Red River: "Gallop out alone in the evenings a few miles towards the southwest, and the least impressionable of mortals will experience a novel sensation. A feeling of indescribably buoyant freedom seems to tingle through every nerve, making the old feel young again."

Wolseley's discerning eye captured an essence that was to lure thousands of men and

First-class riverboat lounge, c. 1881

The *Selkirk*

River was Norman Kittson, a St. Paul businessman. Under the name of the Red River Transportation Company, Kittson put the *Dakota,* the sidewheeler *Cheyenne* and the *Alpha* into service.

By 1874, a syndicate of Manitoba and St. Paul businessmen formed the Merchants International Steamboat Line, hoping to drive freight rates down. The following year, they launched the *Manitoba* and the *Minnesota*. But after a year these ships were sold to the Red River Transportation Company, which was now backed by the Hudson's Bay Company.

In 1877, the *Selkirk* brought by barge, Manitoba's first locomotive—the *Countess of Dufferin*. The arrival of the railway was to signal the end of the steamboats on the Red. While traffic continued for a few years, railways were now the preferred method to move goods and people.

ernment decided that only ships of American registry could carry freight on American waterways and across the border. The *International,* of British registry, was put out of business for the time being. James Hill, the Canadian-born transportation baron who made his fortune in the American Northwest, decided to get into the burgeoning Red River trade. He commissioned the construction of a new ship, the *Selkirk,* which was a smaller version of the grand Mississippi riverboats.

Red River shipping had come of age. In the next few years, the king of the Red

The last steamer to make the run for commercial purposes was the *Grand Forks,* arriving in Winnipeg on June 7, 1909. By 1912, extraordinarily dry weather had lowered river levels to make passage impossible for even the shallow draft steamers. Though freighters and pleasure steamers were to continue for decades on Lake Winnipeg and the lower Red River, the glory days of the Manitoba riverboats were effectively over.

A Simple Handshake

Archibald and Riel fell victim to Protestant rage

A SIMPLE HANDSHAKE BETWEEN two prominent Manitobans in 1871 spelled the political end for one and hastened the exile of the other.

The two men were Manitoba's first lieutenant-governor, Adams Archibald, and the controversial Métis leader Louis Riel. A gesture that would have been commonplace in polite company set off a storm of protest from Ontario Protestants who saw Riel as a criminal—hardly the sort of man deserving of recognition by the province's vice-regal officer.

Archibald came to Manitoba determined to favour neither the Red River Métis nor the Ontarians who demanded Riel's head. But his efforts at forging harmony in the fledgling province were threatened in the fall of 1871 when American Fenians attempted to invade the province.

William O'Donoghue, a former colleague of Riel, was the instigator of the invasion plot. He had support for the plan from the Fenian Brotherhood, an Irish-American organization which aimed to overthrow British rule wherever it might be found. O'Donoghue was counting on additional help from the Métis, whom he knew to be disillusioned with life in the new Manitoba.

But he neglected to consider Louis Riel's influence. Working in the shadows of the Métis society, Riel made it clear he would not support the Americans. He even went to the length of warning Archibald of the Fenian plot. Not sure of the strength of the Fenian assault, Archibald called on Red River residents to assemble a defence force.

He was surprised when the Métis agreed to take up arms against the threat. When Archibald went to St. Boniface to thank them, he was even more surprised to see Riel amongst the Métis force. The lieutenant-governor shook hands with all the men, including Riel, then returned to Fort Garry.

The Fenian threat turned out to be a farce. O'Donoghue and 35 men crossed the frontier at Pembina on October 5, 1871 and took possession of the Hudson's Bay Company fort. No Métis arrived to bolster the effort and, after a few hours, American authorities arrested the would-be invaders.

The Fenian threat was suppressed but Archibald found he could not withstand the political outrage his brief encounter with Riel provoked. Under a barrage of criticism, he resigned from office. And instead of being thanked for his support against the Fenians, Riel was hounded even more aggressively until, banished by the federal government, he left Manitoba for a life in exile.

Lt. Gov. Adams Archibald was instructed to govern Manitoba as a "benevolent despot".

women from Ontario to Manitoba from 1871 to 1874. Everyone in Ontario had heard of the vast, fertile prairie—free of stones or trees to impede the plough. Entire Ontario farming communities made the decision to move for the heralded land of opportunity.

The trip west required fortitude and a sense of adventure. Most of the early settlers came by way of the United States, by railroad to Minnesota and then on to Manitoba by steamer or Red River cart. Some ventured along the more difficult Dawson route—the water and road trek the Canadian government opened from Fort William to Red River in its eagerness to have an all-Canadian approach to the West.

The newcomers found a series of established Scots, half-breed and Métis settlements in an unbroken line along the Red and the Assiniboine Rivers. Virtually no settlement had taken place on the open prairie where wood for fuel was scarce and water was not readily available.

The new settlers were eager to acquire a piece of the West for themselves, but there was little political machinery to accommodate them. The first order of business was to ensure they would not be confronted by angry Indians who claimed the land for themselves. Already, Yellow Quill's band of Saulteaux (Plains Ojibway)

Cartier's Young Men

The eastern Canadian elites, who had grudgingly granted Manitoba provincial status in 1870, could not conceive that the citizens of Red River, especially the leaderless Métis, could govern themselves.

Sir George-Etienne Cartier (Sir John A. Macdonald's French lieutenant) in concert with Bishop Taché of St. Boniface, convinced several members of the Québec élite to go West and take up the challenge of governing the new province. Often referred to as "Cartier's young men", Marc-Amable Girard, Joseph Royal and Joseph Dubuc arrived in Manitoba and were elected by acclamation to the first provincial Legislature.

The three men had much in common. They were all lawyers and all conservatives. Marc-Amable Girard had helped Cartier first get elected in 1858. Joseph Royal had articled under Cartier in the early 1860's. He had also been the editor of *La Minerve*, principal voice for the Conservative party in Lower Canada. Joseph Dubuc, who had met and befriended Louis Riel at the Collège de Montréal, was a contributing editor for the same newspaper while studying law.

During the 1870's, all three men would hold a number of important political offices. Elected in the riding of St. Boniface East, Girard was asked in 1874 to choose a cabinet and form a government. Girard effectively became Manitoba's first premier (although some historians call his predecessor Alfred Boyd the first premier). Girard's tenure as premier was short-lived. Recognizing that the French were rapidly becoming a minority he declared: "I am the first Francophone to become Premier of this province and I fear I shall be the last."

Joseph Royal, as member for St. François-Xavier, served successively as speaker, provincial secretary, minister of public works, and attorney general. From 1879 to 1888, he represented Provencher in the House of Commons. He later returned to Montreal to resume his career in journalism.

As for Joseph Dubuc, the youngest of the young men, he would give up active political office in the late 1870's after serving as attorney general and speaker. Named to the Manitoba Court of Queen's Bench in 1878, he became Manitoba's sixth chief justice in 1903. He was knighted in 1912 and died in St. Boniface in 1914.

had turned back settlers who tried to go west of Portage la Prairie. To guarantee the land rush would be orderly, Ottawa hastened to negotiate Treaty 1 with the Saulteaux and the Crees. Under it, all of Manitoba and the lands to the north and west of the existing boundaries were ceded by the natives to the Queen in return for reserves, annual presents and money payments.

The Red River uprising had interrupted the first teams of surveyors, halting the Dominion's early plans for the allotment of land. The surveyors returned in the summer of 1871. In just two years, all of Manitoba was divided into a grid of sections one mile square with road allowances between all sections. The river lots of the settlement belt survived—an anomaly in the patchwork of squares.

The Dominion survey system also reserved land for the children of mixed-blood families, for schools and for the Hudson's Bay Company. As well, every odd numbered section was reserved to finance a transcontinental railway. Of 36 sections in a township, 16 were available for homesteading. According to the policies of 1872, set-

FIRST LEGISLATURE - MANITOBA

Treaties 1 and 2

IN THE TINY POSTAGE STAMP province of Manitoba, the Cree and Saulteaux watched apprehensively as Ontario settlers began pouring into the new province.

Although past British practice had been to seek the surrender of Indian lands in return for reserves and compensation, in 1870 the Dominion of Canada had no formal plan on how to deal with the Indians of the Northwest.

Saulteaux Chief Yellow Quill

But when Yellow Quill's band of Saulteaux (Plains Ojibway) turned back settlers who tried to go west of Portage la Prairie—and when other bands of Saulteaux and Cree began to insist upon a treaty respecting their claims to the land—Manitoba became the focus of the West's first treaty negotiations.

Treaties 1 and 2 marked the beginning of the treaty process in Western Canada—a process that would last much of the 1870's and pave the way for an attempted new native economic order based on agriculture.

"God intends this land to raise great crops for all his children, and the time has come when it is to be used for that purpose," Indian Commissioner Wemyss McKenzie Simpson told about 1,000 assembled Indians at Lower Fort Garry in the summer of 1871. "White people will come here to cultivate it under any circumstances. No power on earth can prevent it."

Under orders from the Canadian government, Simpson was to negotiate a treaty with the Indians of Manitoba that would not only extinguish their title to land in the province but open the door

for peaceful settlement as well. Treaty 1—or the Stone Fort Treaty as it is sometimes called—would establish the pattern.

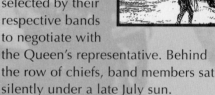

Seated on chairs across from the splendidly-attired Indian Commissioner were Saulteaux and Cree chiefs who had been selected by their respective bands to negotiate with the Queen's representative. Behind the row of chiefs, band members sat silently under a late July sun.

"I have turned over this matter of a treaty in my mind and can not see anything in it to benefit my children," elder statesman Ay-ee-ta-pe-pe-tung said gravely. "This is what frightens me. After I showed you what I meant to keep for a reserve, you continued to make it smaller and smaller... Let the Queen's subjects go on my land if they choose. I give them liberty. Let them rob me. I will go home without treating."

Newcomers to Winnipeg were told if they saw a hat floating in the mud of the streets, they should throw in a line —there could be a man underneath it.

tlers were allowed to stake a claim for a free grant of a quarter-section of property as long as they improved it over three years, residing there at least six months of the year. The requirements for homesteading changed over the years, but as a rule half of the claims were dismissed because landowners failed to build a shanty or cut a field.

Homesteads could be filed only on land already surveyed. So settlement followed the Dominion Land Survey as it made its way across the Red River, westward beyond the limits of Manitoba as then described, and down the Pembina escarpment. The "true prairie" of the southwest, as defined by Palliser and Hind, was

surveyed last on the assumption that it would not be favourable for farming.

The new settlers were openly dismissive of their Métis predecessors. For example, a group of Ontario land seekers was attracted to a tree-lined stream that wound through the meadows, marshes and bluffs north of the Pembina Mountains and south of Portage. They ignored signs that spoke of Métis occupation, set up their homes, and named the stream the Boyne. The Métis returned from their annual buffalo hunt to the area they called Riviere aux Ilets de Bois to discover their land occupied. Only the intervention of Lieutenant-Governor Archibald prevented open warfare.

Natives gather at Fort Garry to consider treaty.

With his body smeared with white earth and his only clothing a breach cloth, Ay-ee-ta-pe-pe-tung stood before Simpson waving an eagle wing as he criticized the government's refusal to consider larger reserves for the Cree and Saulteaux. Under his proposal and the proposals of other chiefs, two-thirds of Manitoba would remain under Indian control.

Instead, Simpson stood firm on his offer of 160 acres for every family of five. The Cree and Saulteaux did not have to accept the treaty, Simpson said. But when the flood of settlers began taking up land in Manitoba, Indians without a treaty could eventually find themselves with no land. Accepting the treaty and adapting to an agricultural way of life was the only way the Cree and Saulteaux could survive in a rapidly changing world, he said.

"How are we to be treated?" Saulteaux Henry Prince asked Simpson. "It is said the Queen wishes Indians to cultivate the ground. They can not scratch it—work it with their fingers. What assistance will they get if they settle down?"

Prince, whose father Peguis had taken treaty in 1817 with Lord Selkirk, believed the only way the Canadian government could compensate Indians for the loss of their lands was to ensure their future economic security. If the Cree and Saulteaux were to become farmers, any treaty must provide farm equipment, supplies and instruction.

Throughout the course of seven days, the Cree and Saulteaux negotiated the best deal possible. While they were unable to get everything they wanted, they succeeded in obtaining more than Simpson was originally permitted to offer. On August 3, 1871, the Cree and Saulteaux of Manitoba signed Treaty 1.

The object of Treaty 2—or the Manitoba Post Treaty as it is sometimes called—was to extinguish Indian title to the rich timber lands to the north and east of Manitoba, as well as to a vast tract of agricultural land to the west of Portage la Prairie.

Unlike Treaty 1, negotiations for the second treaty went smoothly. Having heard of the treaty signed at Fort Garry, the other Cree and Saulteaux bands were content to sign if they received the same terms as their brethren to the south.

On August 21, 1871, Indian title to land three times the size of 1870 Manitoba was extinguished with the signing of Treaty 2.

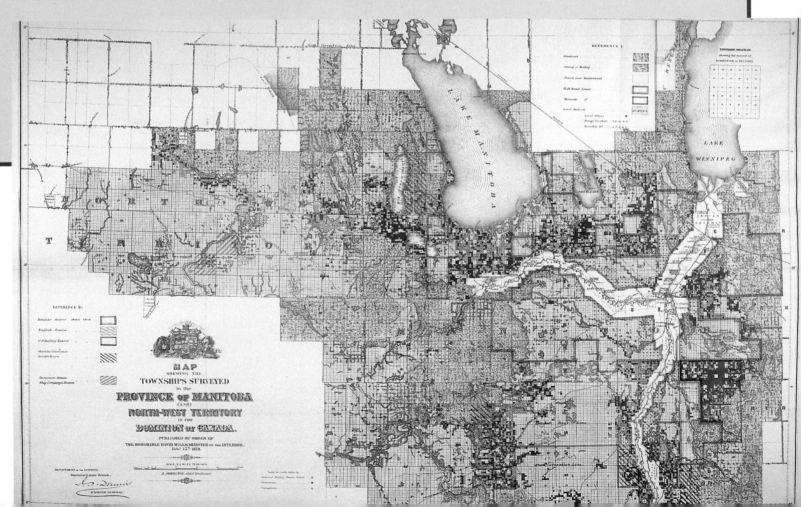

Treaties were necessary to facilitate settlement as early settlers and aboriginals clashed over desirable lands.

The first Mounties made an arduous march into history

IN THE EARLY 1870'S, reports from the West indicated that whisky traders and other riff-raff from the United States were causing trouble on the plains. These troubles culminated in 1873 when a party of Montana wolf hunters murdered 20 Assiniboines in the Cypress Hills.

Prime Minister Sir John A. Macdonald decided that it was time to establish a western police force, both to protect native tribes and to deter any American thoughts about annexing Canada's Northwest. Macdonald envisioned a police force along the lines of the Royal Irish Constabulary—mounted police officers, "hardy and well-trained, men of courage and good physique, good riders and good shots, capable of meeting the difficulties facing any force penetrating that wild and virginal land".

During the recruitment drive in Toronto, the prospect of wilderness adventure attracted far more applicants than there were openings. The officer candidates tended to be well-born former army officers and the recruits were a mixture of working-class clerks and farm boys.

The officers were men like Cecil E. Denny. Born in England and educated in colleges in France and Germany, Denny was 24 years old when he accepted a captain's commission with the North-West Mounted Police. An aristocratic and vigorous man, Captain Denny observed the punishment dished out by the bucking horses and screaming drill instructors with approval, noting that "much weeding out of bad characters among the men is needed".

After two months, thousands of applicants had been sifted down to 150 men, and those first "Mounties" left for Fort Garry by the old North West Company route to Red River. They arrived in the fall of 1873. The recruits trained through the winter, but without proper uniforms or equipment. Finally, reinforcements were sent the following spring, bringing horses, guns and the new scarlet uniforms that were soon to become the Mounties' trademark.

The Fort Garry contingent rode south to meet the reinforcements at Fort Dufferin

The future of the Métis was supposed to be secured through the provisions of the Manitoba Act. The act provided that 1.4 million acres should be distributed in "scrip"—certificates for parcels of 240 acres to each child of a half-breed family. Later, the heads of half-breed families were themselves provided with 160 acres of land or $160 in scrip. But many of the Métis felt uncomfortable in this new agrarian world; they were not interested in the sedentary life of agriculture. The newcomers exacerbated the divisions by treating the mixed-bloods with ill-disguised contempt. As their scrip was transferable, many Métis simply sold it, often for a fraction of the face value. They retreated from the Red River settlement, moving west in search of the ever-diminishing buffalo herds. Through the sale of scrip, thousands of acres passed into the hands of speculators.

With the constant influx of newcomers from Ontario, the balance of the population soon turned against the French-speakers. The old principles of duality in the settlement began to fade. In 1874, there was an attempt to alter the electoral districts to give more representation to the new settlers. There were also protests against the dual Catholic-Protestant school system and the official use of the French language. The

The 49th parallel marks part of the world's longest undefended border. From 1872–74 it was formally demarcated. Iron markers or stone or earth mounds were placed at one-mile intervals to mark the border.

The Red Coat Trail

(Emerson). After setting up camp, the greenhorn Mounties experienced the full force of a prairie thunderstorm. On June 20, the storm exploded onto the camp, and amidst the pounding rain and terrifying flashes of lightning the horses stampeded, knocking down tents and trampling the men inside. Several half-dressed Mounties leaped bareback onto charging horses and pursued the runaways. Although most of the horses were recovered, several died in the stampede and 25 were never seen again. After that, the police adopted the proven Indian practice of hobbling their mounts when setting up camp for the night.

The NWMP now consisted of about 300 men organized into six troops under the command of Lieutenant-Colonel George French. On July 8, 1874, the force was finally assembled for the "Great March West". The Mounties made a stirring spectacle—the men dressed in scarlet tunics and white helmets, their prancing horses precisely assigned by color: "A" Division on dark bays, "B" Division on its horses of brown, "C" Division on bright chestnuts, "D" Division on greys, "E" on jet-black mounts and, bringing up the rear, "F" Division on its light bays. Accompanied by Métis packers, beef cattle and oxen carts, the whole procession made a jingling, clattering, red-tunicked parade several kilometres long.

The Mounties presented an impressive sight, but they knew little about the country they were entering. Tornadoes, quicksand, tainted drinking water and tales of bloody Indian battles to the south soon dispelled any lingering sense of romantic adventure. Colonel French might have been wiser to purchase supplies and food from natives en route. But in true British military fashion he insisted on self-sufficiency for his troops. The fancy

Greenhorn Mounties lost several of their mounts as they got their first taste of a prairie electrical storm.

Ontario horses were ill-suited for work as pack animals and, with the blazing sun and poor forage on the arid southern prairie, they began dying.

The Mounties forged on, with mouths blistered by the sun and faces black and "smutty" from the blowing ashes of prairie fires. To add insult, hordes of grasshoppers descended on the troops and began eating up tents and uniforms. "If the people of Canada could see us now," wrote Sub-Constable James Finlayson "with bare feet, not one half-clothed, half-starved, picking up fragments left by the American troops, I wonder what they would say of Colonel French."

Finally, 251 troopers and 24 officers arrived at the junction of the Bow and Oldman Rivers, 60 kilometres west of the present day site of Medicine Hat. They built two fortified detachments, went to work arresting the whisky traders and, in a short time, won the respect of the local Indians.

In this, the NWMP experience was very different from the situation south of the border, where the average U.S. Cavalry soldier faced the prospect of capture and death by hostile Indians if he was ever separated from his troop. In contrast, a lone NWMP officer could ride into a formidable camp of 200 Blackfoot warriors, arrest a lawbreaker, and lead his prisoner away without mishap.

Although poorly equipped and ill-supplied (many of the men worked the entire first year without a paycheque) the NWMP worked hard to gain the trust of the Plains tribes. They were surprisingly successful. In 1876, the Sioux war chief Sitting Bull sent a message to Chief Crowfoot of the Alberta Blackfoot asking for support against the U.S. Army. In return, Sitting Bull offered to give Crowfoot some captured white women and to send his own warriors north to wipe out the "weak soldiers" of the NWMP. Crowfoot replied disdainfully that if it came to war, his tribe intended to fight alongside the North-West Mounted Police.

complaints went unheeded for the time being, but they would become more persistent over the years.

Winnipeg in 1874 was a very different place from the tiny collection of shanties that clung to the junction of the rivers just four years earlier. Fort Garry, now transformed into Winnipeg, was growing quickly. The fur trade remained the chief business of the community, but none of the

A British con man hid out in Winnipeg after notorious New York swindle

The Ignoble Lord Gordon Gordon

AS LORD GORDON GORDON strolled along Main Street's wooden sidewalks in October 1872, the citizens of Winnipeg had no idea that this dignified aristocrat, resplendent in kilt and tam, was a world-class con man whose alleged crimes would soon jeopardize Canadian-American relations.

In the spring of that same year, Gordon was in New York mixing with the city's social elite. To famed American financier and railway tycoon, Jay Gould, the appearance of Gordon was a godsend. Gould was on the verge of losing control of the Erie Railway when Gordon came forward with a plan to save the day. In an opulent hotel suite—befitting a nobleman with claimed estates in England, Ireland, and his native Scotland— Gordon explained that he controlled $50 million in Erie Railway stock. Gordon offered to use his stock in a manner advantageous to Gould. The New Yorker quickly demonstrated his appreciation: he gave Gordon $200,000 in cash and several thousand shares in various companies.

Soon after the deal was struck, doubt was cast upon Gordon's character. The two men next met in a New York courtroom. After fielding some tough questions from Gould's lawyer, the mysterious British lord waited for an adjournment, then disappeared. Over the next few weeks, Gordon embarked on a jour-

ney that brought him, literally, to the end of the line—Winnipeg, Manitoba.

Still maintaining his aristocratic guise, Gordon boarded at the home of Mrs. Abigail Corbett in Headingley. He did little to bring attention to himself other than an occasional display of skill as a sportsman. Gordon reputedly bagged 1,500 partridge while hunting near the Brokenhead River.

He did, however, catch the eye of a visiting Minnesota merchant familiar with Gordon and his trail of

swindles across the continent. A few days later, Gordon was visiting James MacKay when a party of five armed Minnesotans burst in and abducted the startled "lord". Word of the abduction was telegraphed to a Canadian custom's official at Pembina and the kidnappers were themselves seized and returned to Winnipeg.

There was outrage on both sides of the border. Newspapers in the United States cried that Manitoba should be "wrapped in flames" for thwarting the exercise of American justice. Manitobans replied that the sovereignty of Canadian soil had been violated. It wasn't long before Prime Minister Sir John A. Macdonald and President Ulysses S. Grant were pulled into the matter. High-level political pressure culminated with the Americans receiving a symbolic one-day sentence. A potentially explosive international incident was defused.

Throughout the excitement, Gordon retained the confidence of many local residents and remained at Mrs. Corbett's house in Headingley. But Jay Gould's vengeance had not been appeased and he soon sent a second group to arrest Gordon—this time with a Canadian warrant.

Confronted at Mrs. Corbett's home, the master swindler cheated Gould one last time. On the pretext of needing a warmer coat, Lord Gordon Gordon went into his bedroom and shot himself in the head.

Rescue on the Red

In June 1874, the *Dakota*, a Red River sternwheeler, was churning its way downstream from Moorhead, North Dakota, headed for Fort Garry. The passenger manifest listed 140 on board, including the wife and six children of Captain George White. He had come out the previous year to begin a homestead near Teulon.

Among the passengers were several prisoners in chains, bound for trial at Pembina. One of the prisoners was an unemployed ironsmith by the name of George Bellhymer. With a wife and infant son to support, and no means, he had broken into the store at Fort Seward, stealing food and clothing. Now chained hand and foot, he sat with the other prisoners on the upper deck, under the watchful eyes of armed deputies.

Below, four-year-old Emma White was trying to pull leaves off boughs which trailed over the slow-moving ship. Having missed a few, she climbed onto the rail and seized a branch. Instantly, she was tugged off balance and fell into the torpid current.

Bellhymer saw what happened, stood up immediately and leapt into the water more than six metres below. As he did so, a deputy fired at him, unaware of the girl's plight. Swimming laboriously with a sideways scooping motion, Bellhymer made his way back to where Emma had disappeared. He then dived, coming up more than a minute later with Emma, her dress grasped in his teeth.

As he manoeuvered her onto his back, she struggled and the two of them sank. Bellhymer came back to the surface with just a piece of Emma's dress in his teeth. Coughing and spitting, he then tried to slip his hands from the manacles. Onboard ship there was near pandemonium as the vessel tried to back toward the bank. A small boat was unshipped, and a chorus of voices called out advice.

Suddenly the little girl's arm surfaced about six metres away and Bellhymer dove again. He managed to seize her dress again with his teeth, and held her in this way until the small boat pulled them out of the water. Emma was quickly revived and returned to her distraught mother.

At Bellhymer's trial, the heroic event was related and he was acquitted with strong praise by the judge. George Bellhymer and his family later moved to Winnipeg where, with the assistance of Captain White, he set up shop as a blacksmith.

---

fur firms—not even the Hudson's Bay Company—limited their operations to the enterprise that had defined the Northwest in the previous two centuries.

The farm frontier was spreading, and as it did, Winnipeg merchants became wholesalers and manufacturers. As the gateway to the rapidly expanding agricultural hinterland, business-minded immigrants were attracted to the newly incorporated city. Builders, real estate and insurance agents, lawyers and bankers quickly found a place in the increasingly diversified city. Professional associations like the Manitoba Law Society and the Manitoba College of Physicians and Surgeons were established. Membership in the newly founded Manitoba Club became an expression of leadership in the commercial community.

The social structure of the community also diversified: the first public school opened in Point Douglas; the Presbyterians' Manitoba College, a precursor to the University of Manitoba, was launched; and the first telegraph link was established with the East. The *Manitoba Free Press,* which began publication in 1872, enthusiastically announced the establishment of a new entertainment—a billiard room, complete with six tables and a sidewalk from Main Street.

Winnipeg still had the look of a frontier town. Main Street and the Portage Trail were broad avenues, not out of any great foresight, but to accommodate side-by-side Red River cart traffic. Patches of wooden sidewalks "floated like barges" in the gumbo that made up the thoroughfares of the fledgling community.

> "...He flies into your face, he climbs up your garments, he sits upon your food, he lets you walk upon him, drive over him, slay him by the thousands, but still he forms a thick covering over your palings, and darkens the air with his devouring presence. He has but one merit—no, two: he does not bite you, and the Professor declares he is good to eat."
>
> **The Countess of Dufferin commenting on the proliferation of grasshoppers on the Prairies**

Past and present were captured as a Red River cart stood in front of newly-constructed shops on Winnipeg's Main Street.

The influx of immigrants, many of them single men of the roughest kind, made Winnipeg a "Wild West" frontier town. Winnipeg saloons were notorious for their rowdiness, and the police court was regularly crowded with drunks and prostitutes. It was noted in Ontario that "Winnipeg and Barrie are the two most evil places in Canada". Both communities were prayed for at the YMCA convention that year.

Winnipeg was still administered like a village, with the province dispensing minimal ser-

vices. If the community hoped to grow and gain such amenities as sidewalks and sewers, it felt it had to govern itself. In 1872, a popular movement began to incorporate the settlement as a city. But incorporation would mean the introduction of property taxes and the weight of those would fall most heavily on the community's largest land owner—the Hudson's Bay Company. As a result of its agreement with Britain, the HBC owned 500 acres around Fort Garry—one-third of all of the taxable property in the proposed city limits. The company was understandably not eager to pay the taxes proposed and it was speculated that it managed to convince the province to hold off dealing with the incorporation proposal.

There was open hostility to the company and the legislature. Citizens held "indignation meetings"—apparently a favourite form of entertainment in early Winnipeg—throughout the summer and fall of 1872. In February, 1873, they submitted another demand to the legislature for incorporation. Legislative action was taken this time, but there were drastic revisions to the citizens' bill, including a substantial drop in the tax rate, a clause to prohibit the city from borrowing money, and a requirement that revenue collected for licences be handed over to the province. As if to add insult to injury, the name Winnipeg was

The presence of prostitutes occupying the best seats in the Princess Opera House generated controversy. In 1883, the manager announced he would not sell tickets for the better seats to these women. The problem persisted and in 1886 he resolved the matter by screening off a corner of the theatre to make a special section for prostitutes.

French Fact Drowned in Ontario Wave

 The growing number of Ontario and British settlers coming to Manitoba and the Northwest after 1870 was a cause of much concern to Bishop Taché of St. Boniface. If the Franco-Catholic population was to maintain its place in the new province, its numbers would have to increase substantially.

Mass recruitment in the province of Québec was met with stiff opposition. Father Albert Lacombe reported to Bishop Taché in 1876 the following summary of his meeting with the premier of Québec. "Far from encouraging us in our emigration project, [the premier] assured me that he would do all in his powers to prevent the French Canadians of his province from emigrating to Manitoba. He told me to recruit those that are in the United States. End of conversation."

Repatriation of French Canadians from the United States was seen as a good solution for a number of reasons. It was estimated that 200,000 French Canadians had left Québec for the United States from 1860 to 1870. In 1874 there was an economic recession in the textile mills of the New England states. Federal immigration agents estimated that many families would emigrate if the Canadian government paid the transportation costs.

Dozens of French Canadian families did leave and settle in the Red River Valley (in what is today the region of Letellier—St. Jean Baptiste). However, by the mid-1880´s, the numbers dropped off after an end to subsidized transportation.

In the following decades, new francophone settlers would come from Québec and after 1890 from Europe (France, Belgium and Switzerland). But there were never sufficient numbers to maintain the English-French duality of the Manitoba of 1870. By 1886, the French-speaking element had already plummeted to only 10 per cent of the population of Manitoba.

changed to Assiniboia.

Winnipeg residents responded with predictable anger. They stormed the legislature, demanding their bill be reinstated. When the Speaker of the House, Dr. C.J. Bird, ruled the citizens' proposal out of order, he was targeted for frontier justice. He was lured from his house in the middle of the night on the pretext of seeing a sick patient, and then at the north end of Main Street, the unfortunate man was tarred and feathered.

In the face of this resolve, the legislature backed down and redrafted its bill. On November 8, 1873, the former fur trade station and settlement colony officially became the City of Winnipeg. Francis E. Cornish, a staunch incorporation proponent, became Winnipeg's first mayor. The council was drawn from both the old Red River community and the new settlers, and it was defiantly business-oriented. In the first year, council used the new tax dollars to pay for sidewalks, roads, and bridges. Five hundred dollars went to help develop the new Winnipeg General Hospital.

Winnipeg's civic optimism was tested in 1874 when the community discovered that the new Canadian Pacific Railway was planning to put the mainline of the much-anticipated transcontinental railway through Selkirk, not Winnipeg. A Citizen's Railway Committee was set up, a petition protesting the decision circulated, and a delegation sent to Ottawa. During the next seven years, until the route was resolved in Winnipeg's favour, the railway question preoccupied council at the expense of local improvements. Finally, in the spring of 1881, the CPR—presented with numerous financial inducements—relented and agreed to direct the mainline through the city. Selkirk, instead of rivalling Winnipeg, was fated to remain the river port onto Lake Winnipeg.

Have Ballot-Box, Will Stuff

 Francis Evans Cornish, Winnipeg's first mayor, probably had more criminal charges laid against him during his political career than most of the inmates in the city jail.

Before coming to Winnipeg, Cornish was mayor of London, Ontario, but had to leave after being accused of ballot box stuffing. He also assaulted the commander of the British troops stationed there, whom he believed was having a tryst with his wife.

Cornish, a lawyer, arrived in Winnipeg and soon continued his rabble-rousing ways. Disgruntled over the 1872 federal election coverage in local newspapers, a mob led by Cornish ransacked the offices of the *Manitoban*, the *Gazette* and the *Métis*. Thereafter Winnipeg was dubbed "the graveyard of journalism".

During the first civic election in 1874, Cornish ran for mayor, receiving 383 votes, compared to 179 for opponent William Luxton. Interestingly, there were only 382 eligible voters. Property owners could vote in each ward in which they owned property, and many Cornish supporters voted for him more than once.

One story has it that when the ever-unpredictable Cornish was mayor, he sat in as police magistrate. Suffering a bad hangover, he laid a charge against himself for driving his horse and buggy while intoxicated. Stepping down from the bench, he stood humbly before the court and pleaded guilty. He then fined himself five dollars, but suspended the fine as it was his first offence.

Cornish left civic politics and created more mischief when he ran for the Legislature in 1878. He arranged to have his opponent delayed on voting day, and as a result, Cornish was charged with kidnapping. His death at age 47 prevented his hearing on that charge.

The transcontinental railway guaranteed Winnipeg would become the hub of commercial activity in the Northwest. This prospect sparked Winnipeg on the wildest 16 months in its history. Immigrants began pouring into the city in search of opportunity and the 2,000 jobs the CPR had just announced for its new shops. In 1882, the population of the city leapt to 14,000. There were so many immigrants coming in that hotel space, even in canvas-roofed hotels, was not available; newcomers slept in hallways, in stairwells, under billiard tables. The city was dotted with tents and there were so many prospective home buyers that houses were built literally overnight.

In a river city such as Winnipeg, ferries played an important role in moving people and goods before the proliferation of bridges.

Ever-increasing traffic, including a street railway, led to the city of Winnipeg paving Main Street in 1882.

During the boom winter of 1881-82, Winnipeg hired a wagon driver to pick up all the drunk men, unconscious from a night of revelry, and trundle them off to jail so they wouldn't freeze to death in the night.

weeks, he sold $1 million worth of lots from his auction mart near the corner of Portage and Main. He sold so many lots on unpaved Main Street he became known as the "Marquis of Mud". He wore a sealskin coat worth $5,000 and was reputed to celebrate a profitable sale with a champagne bath.

By 1882, there were eight chartered banks, seven private banks and 12 mortgage and loan companies with headquarters in Winnipeg. In keeping with the flush times, entrepreneurs installed telephones and a two-mile horse drawn street railway. And the city finally paved Main Street.

Churches, society meeting halls and mansions all rose in tribute to the boom of 1881-82. Wagon factories, breweries and food processing plants added to the city's industrial diversity. The machinists, fitters and foundrymen who worked at the CPR yards formed the Boiler Makers' Union, the first labour union in Manitoba.

The boom, and the frantic speculation that went with it, collapsed suddenly in the spring of 1882 when real estate tycoons overreached themselves and unsuccessfully tried to sell lots in distant Edmonton. Confidence ebbed and the banks tightened credit. More than 100 businesses failed. The city's population actually dropped and so did property values. But the major business houses of Winnipeg survived. And to those people, who had

Real estate speculation was feverish; Winnipeg soon had more than 300 real estate offices. Building lots in the city were sold at high prices and resold at ridiculous prices. A lot in Winnipeg cost more than one in Chicago or New York. Speculators held property auctions anywhere, anytime, often off the back of a buckboard on a street corner. Canvas-topped wagons, painted with golden pictures of proposed cities, patrolled the streets with barkers announcing the auctions. Lots were brazenly advertised in non-existent towns, even swamps.

Jim Coolican, known as the "Real Estate King", was one of the top speculators. In two

the faith and the energy to sustain early Winnipeg, fell the responsibility for its economic future.

Until 1874, almost all of the immigration into the province was from Ontario, skewing the balance of the population in favour of the English tongue and the Protestant faith. In 1874 and 1875, the federal government agreed to put aside reserves of land to encourage the entry of other groups. The government saw the settlement of the Prairies as a priority and feared losing European immigration to the United States.

The first to take advantage of the strategy were Franco-Americans who Quebec authorities hoped would help safeguard the language, faith and rights of the Métis. A French Colonization Aid Society was set up in St. Boniface and in Montreal. But few groups left Quebec for Manitoba, subtly discouraged from doing so by the Catholic Church. The promise of land did, however, prove attractive to groups of French-Canadians who had been lured to the textile mills of Massachusetts

in the 1850's. They established colonies which later became the towns of Letellier, St. Pierre-Jolys and St. Malo.

In 1874, a new group came to join the ethnic quilt that was developing in Manitoba. Pacifistic Mennonites, deeply disturbed by the Russian government's new requirement of military service, sent emissaries to the United States and Canada. The Canadian government promptly offered the German-speaking Mennonites religious freedom and large tracts of prairie similar to their homeland on the Russian steppes. Soon after, the first Mennonites arrived by steamer from St. Paul. They quickly showed their mettle as the first pioneers on the open prairie. Ignoring the square survey system, they imposed the familiar pattern of the agricultural village they had left behind.

"Extravagance was in the air. We swaggered, and boasted, and puffed until we were busting with happiness. Nothing was too good for us, and the more it cost the better."

The *Winnipeg Times* describing the boom of 1881-82

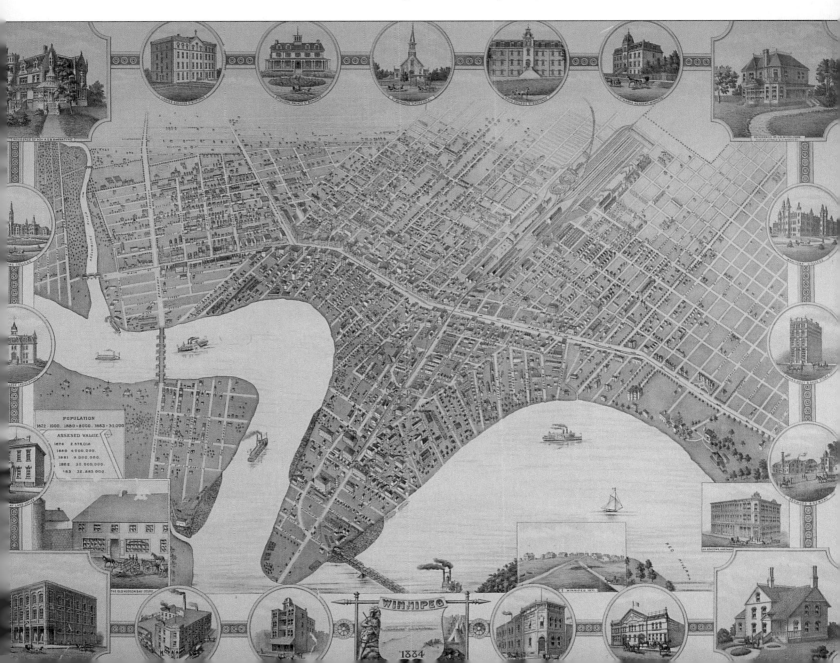

The Search for

AT THE SAME TIME THAT MANITOBA entered Confederation, thousands of Mennonites—considered among the best farmers in Europe—were preparing to leave Russia. The Protestant sect had enjoyed more than a century of prosperity and religious tolerance in that country. But enforced military service threatened that freedom.

The first Mennonite settlers travelled to Winnipeg by steamer from St. Paul, Minnesota.

Military service challenged the Mennonite pacifist faith. Also, proposed legislation making Russian mandatory in Mennonite schools endangered educational control. Tensions between German-speaking Mennonite settlers and Russian patriots were further heightened by the creation of a unified Germany by Bismarck in 1870.

Mennonites were looking to the New World as a new home but Manitoba was not at the top of their list. They had heard about America, its freedoms and its republican system of government. The nationalism sweeping Europe did not seem to exist in America. America was also attractive because new wheat varieties that could mature in the short growing seasons of northern climates were now flourishing in the American Midwest.

When Manitoba was created in 1870, the federal government took a keen interest in attracting Mennonites to its newest province. Ottawa knew that Mennonites were successful pioneers familiar with farming on the

steppes. They were ideal for the job of opening up the treeless prairie.

But Manitoba needed to be marketed. The Canadian government asked Jacob Y. Schantz to inspect Manitoba and prepare a report on its suitability for settlement. Schantz was a Mennonite farmer and businessman

from Berlin, Ontario. On his first trip to Manitoba in 1872 he was joined by another Mennonite, Bernhard Warkentin. Warkentin liked Manitoba's possibilities but decided Kansas held more promise. The new province's

mosquitoes, restless natives, long cold winters and lack of railways were just too much to outweigh the exceptional quality of the land.

Based on his trips to Manitoba, Schantz prepared a *Narrative of a Journey to Manitoba* to promote the new province and its agricultural po-

They also introduced innovations like summer fallow. Through hard work and self-sufficiency, they soon prospered in their new land.

Things were not quite so straightforward for the next ethnic group to venture to Manitoba. When Mount Hecla erupted in 1873, it buried vast stretches of Iceland. The Icelanders, descendants of Vikings, hoped to find a new land that reminded them of what they had left behind; broad stretches of meadow for grazing and wide waters for fishing. In 1875, the first parties of 235

were drawn to a spot beyond the northern boundary of Manitoba on the west shore of Lake Winnipeg. It was to be dubbed Gimli, Icelandic for "paradise". But it was hardly paradise during that first bitter winter, with few rations and poor shelter. It was only stark pride and stubborn resolve that allowed the Icelandic newcomers to set the roots for a continuing immigration.

The West's original inhabitants did not fare as well in adapting to an agricultural lifestyle. In the space of a few years, the Plains tribes were trans-

Freedom

tential. The Department of Agriculture translated the 19-page booklet into several European languages and distributed thousands of copies as part of their settlement promotion. The Mennonites in Russia sent out their own delegation to inspect conditions in Canada and the United States in 1873. The delegation came up from Fargo, North Dakota and arrived in Manitoba during one of the Red River Valley's wet years.

The wet and the mosquitoes, and a run-in with a hostile Métis band at White Horse Plains convinced the majority of the delegation to return to the U.S. before completing the tour. The remainder recognized Manitoba's drawbacks but they also saw some clear advantages.

For example, the American government's offer of military exemption on religious grounds was ambiguous. Settlement in the traditional large blocks favoured by the communal Mennonites was not possible in the U.S. The Canadian government's commitment was clear and firm. A large reserve of land south-east of Winnipeg was set aside for settlement. A

This thatched-roof barn is an example of the unique architecture imported by the Mennonites.

similar reserve could be established west of the Red River bordering on the 49th parallel.

The first Mennonite immigrants arrived in Manitoba in 1874. They came from St. Paul on the steamship, the *International,* and disembarked near Ste. Agathe. They quickly discovered conditions were not as good as they had been led to believe. Soil conditions did not live up to promotional claims. Land was poorly drained, roads and railways were non-existent, and much of the land needed to be cleared of brush and rock.

Dissatisfied, many joined a second group of Mennonite settlers on the West Reserve in 1875. The move

from the east to the west side of the Red River created splits in communities, families, and churches. Even today, Manitoba Mennonites will ask which side of the Red River is home—*Ditseed auda Jantseed*—(This side or that side).

Whether this side or that side, Mennonite farmers applied lessons learned in Russia (like summer fallow) to growing good quality wheat for the export market. The Mennonite success story soon became part of the European marketing campaigns of the Canadian Pacific Railway and the federal government.

Of the 18,000 Mennonites who arrived in North America, one-third came to Manitoba. They felt confident their pacifist beliefs and their German culture would be secure under Canadian law. They also came to Manitoba because the price was right: free land and subsidized travel. Through hard work and innovative farming techniques, Mennonites were able to find new freedom in a new land and, at the same time, help transform Manitoba into an agricultural breadbasket.

---

formed from the masters of a vast land to isolated outcasts in an increasingly white society.

Many of the Plains tribes had kept gardens long before the treaties, but they were not equipped to make the transition to an export-based economy. They did not share the white settlers' appetite for acquisitiveness. As well, close ties to family and clan discouraged individual enterprise. Perhaps the single most important cause for their difficulties was the woeful inadequacy of the farming tools they were given—two

hoes, one spade and one scythe for each family; a plough for every ten families; one bull and four cows for every band.

To the north of the existing boundaries of Manitoba, the relationship between Indians and the fur trade continued undisturbed by the innovations on the southern plains. Bands of Cree still came to the Hudson's Bay Company posts to trade and the York boats still ran the rapids of the northern rivers. But the North had, in many ways, become a backwater, untouched by the drive of

A second major influx of Mennonites to Manitoba took place in the 1920's, following the Russian revolution. Many moved into villages which were created in the 1870's but which stood vacant after the 1916 Manitoba Public School Act prompted some disgruntled Mennonites to move to Mexico.

Confederation, the railways and the farming frontier. This vast and rich area, however, would later become the base from which a new frontier in lumbering and mining would spring.

The arrival on the southern prairies of strangers from foreign lands deflated the old notions that Manitoba was a dualistic society. Mennonite and Icelandic migrations and other individual immigrants from Europe furthered the evolution of a new multi-ethnic society. In the early 1880's, the first Jewish immigrants arrived in

Winnipeg, fleeing the Tsar's pogrom in Russia. By the late 1870's, there were already enough Germans in Winnipeg to form a German Society. The old Red River society, where French and English were deftly balanced, was quickly disappearing.

Whatever their backgrounds, the courageous settlers who ventured out from Winnipeg onto the open prairie shared the same struggles—the need to cut the stubborn soil, to survive the winds of

A harsh utopia on Lake Winnipeg

New Iceland

FOR THE FIRST PARTY of Icelanders who ventured onto Lake Winnipeg in 1875, the poplar forests and mosquito swamps that ringed the inland sea were a stark contrast to the crags and fjords of their homeland. At the same time, however, these Nordic pioneers were heartened by the fish-filled waters of the great lake and the grazing meadows that extended far back from the shore line.

An Icelandic exploratory party led by Sigtryggur Jonasson and immigration agent John Taylor had arrived in Manitoba from Ontario in the summer of 1875 to select a site for settlement. Fleeing poverty, volcanic eruptions and oppressive living conditions in their homeland, the Icelanders envisioned a New World 'utopia' on the shores of Lake Winnipeg, where the best aspects of Icelandic

culture could be preserved within the framework of British Canada.

The new province of Manitoba —with free 160 acre homesteads available—appeared ideal for their purposes. Finding the Red River Valley ravaged by grasshoppers and deeming open prairie unsuitable for Icelanders, the group voyaged by York boat north to the unsurveyed shore of Lake Winnipeg—beyond Manitoba's

winter in a sod hut or a log cabin and, in the spring, to plant and raise a crop. From 1873 to 1875, the old plague of Red River agriculture—the grasshopper—struck with devastating severity. But the pioneer spirit triumphed and in 1876, the first load of export wheat—857 bushels—was shipped to Ontario.

In the late 1870's, prairie farmers and the fledgling wheat economy benefited from the development of the mechanical drill, the sulky and gang ploughs, the self-binding reaper, the steam thresher and barbed wire. A valuable new strain of wheat was developed: Red Fife yielded well, ripened before the Manitoba frost, and produced a white, smooth flour, perfect for baking.

Before the transcontinental railway joined Manitoba to the East, transport of the harvest was cumbersome—by ox cart and steamer to Winnipeg or Emerson and from there to the railhead in the United States. (In 1878 the provincial government financed a short line—the Red River Valley Railway—that connected Winnipeg to

When 1881 rains slowed new Birtle MLA Stephen Clement on his way to the Legislature, he decided to abandon the muddy roads and try his luck on the Assiniboine River. The Liberal sailed a home-made raft from Brandon to Portage where—discouraged by the river's ice—he gave up and caught a train to Winnipeg.

boundary. A sea-faring people (descended from Vikings), the Icelanders rejoiced in the vast Lake Winnipeg waters teeming with fish, as well as stands of valuable timber, grassy meadows and bountiful game. Upon the party's return to Winnipeg, an "Icelandic Reserve" was established after consultation with the Canadian government.

Nyja Island, as New Iceland was called in Icelandic, stretched 90 kilometres along Lake Winnipeg's west shore—from Boundary Creek north to Hecla Island. As a part of the District of Keewatin in Canada's Northwest, this self-governing territory would fall directly under Ottawa's jurisdiction.

Despite a lengthy train journey from Eastern Canada via Grand Forks, spirits ran high as 235 Icelanders left Winnipeg on a flotilla of flatboats in October, 1875 and drifted down the Red River to Lake Winnipeg. Lofty visions of prosperous farms and a free society in New Iceland fired the creative energies of these literate people, and the name Gimli ('gold thatched hall' of the Norse gods) won approval as the name for an envisioned capital of the settlement.

The group was soon confronted, however, with sobering realities. Towed out onto the stormy waters of Lake Winnipeg by the Hudson's Bay Company steamer *Colvile*, the little flotilla battled icy winds and two-metre waves on its way north, and the captain—fearing for the safety of his charges—aborted the voyage in the lee of Willow Island (a few kilometres

south of Gimli). There, on October 21, 1875, the first Icelandic pioneers waded ashore and established a temporary camp. That night—in a tattered buffalo hide tent anchored to a massive white rock—26-year-old Sigridur Olafsdottir gave birth to a boy, as the wind howled and the year's first snow descended.

Initially, a spirit of adventure and discovery prevailed amongst the settlers. In a race to see who could fell the colony's first tree, Flovent Jonsson demonstrated his prowess, and Kristmundur Benjaminsson won a cash prize for the first fish caught. Difficulties quickly set in, however, as the highly independent settlers balked under John Taylor's leadership and thwarted efforts at communal building. Plans to bring in cattle were abandoned, as promised hay had not been put up, and provisions bought in Winnipeg proved insufficient and poor in quality. As winter tightened its grip on the fledgling log village, scurvy reared its head, and virtually all the young and elderly at Gimli perished.

Though optimism waxed anew with the spring sun and the arrival of 1,200 new settlers direct from Iceland (under the guidance of Sigtryggur Jonasson), New Iceland's trials persisted. The reserve faced an outbreak of smallpox in September, 1876 (picked up at immigration sheds in Quebec) and by late winter this virulent plague had spread from Boundary Creek to Hecla Island, claiming 102 lives. Unsympathetic Manitoba authorities established a quarantine along the

southern border at Boundary Creek.

Wet weather hampered early agricultural attempts, hordes of mosquitoes bedevilled settlers, and isolation intensified the hardships. In 1878, divided religious loyalties (between choices for Lutheran ministers) hardened into factional feuding. Disaffection with the settlement became endemic when Lake Winnipeg's waters, driven by a north gale, flooded low-lying homesteads in November, 1880.

The trickle of fed-up settlers leaving New Iceland (for North Dakota) in 1879 now became a torrent, and by 1881 only a handful of families remained—mostly at Icelandic River where a sawmill established by Sigtryggur Jonasson and Fridjon Fridriksson provided employment. It seemed as if the 'utopia' on Lake Winnipeg had failed.

New Iceland, however, rose from its ashes in 1883 with a fresh influx of settlers direct from storm-battered Iceland. Reassured by the example of those who had remained in the settlement, hundreds of new pioneers reoccupied abandoned homesteads—and with time, the settlement flourished.

At this time, Sigtryggur Jonasson, steadfast champion of the settlement over the years, became the undisputed leader and earned the title "Father of New Iceland". And Sigridur Olafsdottir's son—born in the shelter of the white rock on Willow Island—grew to manhood and became the forefather of many who today still regard Gimli as "God's country".

American railroads.) The grain trade, soon to redefine Manitoba's economy, had started. The leading business houses of Winnipeg, many of which were still dealing in furs, advertised they would pay cash for wheat. Four flour mills opened in the city—the largest of which was the Hudson's Bay Company's mill.

The ultimate success of the grain trade and of agricultural Manitoba depended on the coming of the transcontinental railway. But ironically, the railway also limited farm settlement. In 1881, the CPR was awarded most of the odd numbered sections in a belt extending for 40 kilometres on either side of the mainline, plus two other reserves. More stretches of land were provided as subsidies for pro-

posed branch lines. Altogether, the railway appropriations, along with the other settlement reserves, locked out much of Manitoba's public land for homesteading.

When the CPR made its way across Manitoba in 1881, it spawned towns along the route. Branch lines were established to Manitou, Minnedosa, and Elm Creek. But not all towns flourished in the boom of 1881-82. Emerson, for example, suffered

Manitoba's first woman doctor

Charlotte Ross

CHARLOTTE ROSS HAD an unusual ambition. She wanted to be a doctor. She followed the traditional course of a Victorian lady, studying subjects like French and music at a convent school, marrying at 18 and moving from Ontario to her husband's home in Montreal. All the while, however, she secretly studied medical textbooks. She diagnosed her chronically-ill sister's condition as tuberculosis and, when she nursed her, applied Pasteur's and Lister's new ideas about the role of cleanliness in the prevention of communicable diseases.

After her sister's death in 1870, Ross decided to act on her long-time ambition. Because no Canadian medical school would accept female students, she enrolled at the Woman's Medical College of Pennsylvania. In spite of her father's disapproval, the birth of her fourth child and the hos-

tility of the medical community, she graduated in 1875 and returned to Montreal determined to practise medicine.

The Quebec College of Physicians and Surgeons was equally determined not to license a woman, regardless of her qualifications. So Ross practised without a licence, risking arrest. Attempts at intimidation failed. When an attempt was made to shut down her practice by hiring carriages to block both ends of her street, she charged one of the carriages with her own buggy, forcing its panicked horse and driver out of her way.

In 1880, Ross became the first

female doctor in Manitoba. The next year she and her children joined her husband in Whitemouth, where she began a practice that continued for 30 years. Among the railway workers, lumbermen and homesteaders in the area, communicable diseases and accidental injuries were common. Once Charlotte amputated a homesteader's leg, using his kitchen table as an operating table and his saw as a surgical instrument.

Charlotte Ross continued to practise medicine in Whitemouth—without a licence—until 1912, and died in Winnipeg in 1916.

Indispensable to early life on the prairies were the sod hut and the plough.

an intense bout of land speculation fever. The newly incorporated city was convinced it would rival Winnipeg as the gateway to the west. In fact, it built a bridge across the Red River to tie into the anticipated Emerson and North-Western Railway. The bubble burst in 1882 when the charter for the rail line was disallowed.

In 1870, the Métis earned provincehood for Manitoba in their fight for what they believed to be their rights. The new residents of Manitoba continued the fight for "a better deal" from Canada. The biggest constraints to the province were its tiny size and frugal financial support from Ottawa.

In 1881, the boundaries of the province were extended to grant Manitoba an additional area of almost 190,000 square kilometres. This was not, however, enough to placate the citizens of the aggressive new West. Under Premier John Norquay, the province sought the right to grant charters for the construction of railways within its own borders. That was denied and the CPR was given a monopoly to build railways south of its mainline for 20 years. The CPR monopoly frustrated Manitoba farmers and politicians for many years. The otherwise indomitable John Norquay left office without winning the railway concessions he thought were so vital to the province's self-determination.

The outbreak of the second Riel Rebellion in 1885 (in what is now Saskatchewan) interrupted life in Manitoba and breathed fresh vigour into old controversies. With the influx of settlers and the retreat of the buffalo farther and farther west, many of the Métis who once lived in Manitoba were now established along the South Saskatchewan River. But the relentless Canadian surveyors, pushing ever westward, soon arrived there and the Métis were convinced they were about to be, once again, pushed off their land.

The Métis in desperation turned to their old champion—Louis Riel. The leader of the Red River uprising of 1869-70 was living a quiet life in Montana, where he taught school. The terms of his banishment from Canada had long since been fulfilled, and he was persuaded to return in 1884 to his homeland to take up the cause of the Métis. Much as in Red River, his strategy for the North-

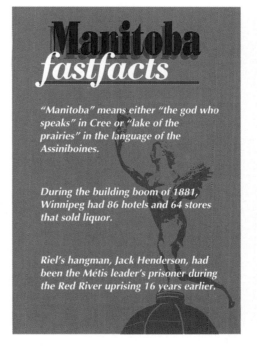

Manitoba
fastfacts

"Manitoba" means either "the god who speaks" in Cree or "lake of the prairies" in the language of the Assiniboines.

During the building boom of 1881, Winnipeg had 86 hotels and 64 stores that sold liquor.

Riel's hangman, Jack Henderson, had been the Métis leader's prisoner during the Red River uprising 16 years earlier.

west was to use persistent but peaceful entreaties to the Canadian government. A "Bill of Rights" followed, as did a provisional government. But Sir John A. Macdonald, the same prime minister Riel dealt with in 1870, refused to negotiate.

In March, 1885, Riel ran out of patience. He formed alliances with discontented native leaders,

"Manitoba's climate is superior, on account of its steadiness, dryness and purity of air, both in summer and winter... The temperature should not be measured by the thermometer, but by the humidity... the severest cold is less felt than even a milder cold in the damp atmosphere of the Eastern province, U.S.A. and England."

Geologist G. M. Dawson, with the first recorded "It's a dry cold" rationalization

The Ontario-Manitoba boundary dispute

Anarchy in Rat Portage

AS THE CPR PUSHED THROUGH Northwestern Ontario in the early 1880's, Rat Portage (now Kenora) became the headquarters for "Section B" of the railway construction contract. The Rat Portage Chamber of Commerce described the town as "the future Saratoga of North America," but it was probably the roughest place along the entire rail line.

One correspondent said that Rat Portage seemed to have been "laid out by a colony of muskrats". The town was inhabited by an army of gamblers and whisky peddlers, who preyed upon the railway workers. In the summer of 1880, the *Winnipeg Times* dolefully announced that Rat Portage was in "a state of degradation... intensified by the appearance of a number of demi-mondes (prostitutes) with whom these desperadoes hold high carnival at all hours of day and night."

Law and order in Rat Portage was preserved by a rough-and-ready police force made up of individuals with names like "Charlie the Bull Pup" and "Haggerty the Hard Case". These lawmen were paid by the railway contractors, who built the jails, collected the fines and sent the proceeds to the provincial government. For several years, however, there was some question as to which government was actually in charge.

Both Manitoba and Ontario claimed the country between Lake of the Woods and Lake Superior. A member from Northwestern Ontario actually sat in the Manitoba Legislature while, at the same time, the Ontario government installed its own judiciary in Rat Portage. Eventually, the town boasted two complete and antagonistic systems of judges, jails and police. And each justice system was determined to carry on as if the other didn't exist.

The Dominion of Canada tended to side with Manitoba, but Ontario fought tirelessly through the courts. Meanwhile, the administration of law in Rat Portage crumbled. After a disputed election, the police forces of both jurisdictions began arresting each other. When the cops of one province were imprisoned, their brothers marched across the street, broke them out of jail, and arrested the police who were responsible. After one particularly inflammatory incident where the Manitoba jail was burned down, an enraged Premier John Norquay personally led a detachment of the Manitoba Provincial Police to Rat Portage to arrest the perpetrators.

In 1884, the Privy Council finally ruled on the boundary. But the dispute smoldered on through one appeal after another, and many years passed before Manitoba admitted defeat and the vast, rich territory between Lake Superior and the Lake of the Woods finally became part of Ontario.

placed himself at the head of an armed force, and—with the help of the Métis field general Gabriel Dumont—took a number of government officials prisoner. The Métis irregulars were then buoyed by a victory at Duck Lake where they lured a North-West Mounted Police force into a trap.

An infuriated Macdonald ordered the Canadian army into action. A force of 8,000 was assembled under General Frederick Dobson Middleton. The bulk of the force was made up of Westerners, although volunteers and regulars also came from the East. The army, gathered together at Winnipeg, waited only long enough for more rail cars to be delivered before pushing on to the Qu'Appelle Valley. From there, Middleton and his men marched north towards Batoche.

At Fish Creek, they were ambushed by the wily Dumont and 150 Métis buffalo hunters. This encounter set back the indecisive Middleton by two weeks. On May 12, finally confident of his force's overwhelming superiority, Middleton advanced on

Three hundred pounds of fighting Conservative
John Norquay

UNDER THE FLEDGLING provincial party system, Manitoba Liberals battled "300 pounds of fighting Conservative" in the person of Premier John Norquay.

Born in 1841 in a log house at the St. Andrew's settlement, Norquay was Manitoba's first native-born premier and the only one able to claim some Indian heritage. As a boy he hunted buffalo with his family. After being orphaned, he learned Greek, Latin and French as the protégé of Bishop David Anderson. The study of classical languages complemented his knowledge of Cree, Saulteaux and Sioux and provided enough of an education to start a teaching career.

Far from bookish, "Big John" Norquay regularly attended community dances. To these he took along an extra pair of moccasins, to replace the pair he invariably wore out.

Elected to the Manitoba legislature in 1870 at the age of 29, Norquay became a cabinet minister one year later. Although he never lost an election, he once won his seat by a single vote. Years later he still thanked the escaped bull that treed a Liberal voter on his way to the polls.

Upon the retirement of R.A.

Davis in 1878, Norquay was chosen premier. He was a skilled orator and called for understanding between Catholics and Protestants, old-stock settlers and new. His most memorable cause, however, was the fight to connect Manitoba with American rail lines. Norquay's government granted railway charters only to have Ottawa disallow the legislation. The result was the establishment of the provin-

cial government's own company—the Red River Valley Railway. Only after Norquay's government was ousted by Thomas Greenway's Liberals did Ottawa put an end to disallowance (the policy which allowed the CPR to maintain its monopoly).

Norquay's administration was also significant because party politics emerged in a meaningful way as Tom Greenway's Liberals increasingly challenged Norquay's leadership. Although candidates for office could run under a party banner, there was general agreement that provincial politicians should place Manitoba's interests ahead of the desires of federal party policy. The fight against Ottawa for control of railway development was not enough, however, to hold together groups and individuals with disparate ideas of how Manitoba should be governed.

After his defeat by the Greenway Liberals in 1887, Norquay continued to lead his party until his death at age 48. As a mixed-blood descendant of the original Selkirk settlers, Norquay was the last political link between the old Red River society and the new Manitoba. With his death, Ontario settlers were in firm control of the province.

the Métis stronghold at Batoche. The poorly armed Métis held off the might of the Canadian army for three days until they were reduced to using nails for ammunition. Then, with even the nails gone, they fled into the woods.

A few days later, Louis Riel gave himself up. On November 15, after a lengthy trial in Regina, the man later to be honoured as the founder of Manitoba was dropped through the hangman's trap to his destiny. The death of Riel marked a sea-change in Canadian politics: it ended French-Canadian aspirations for a flourishing presence in the West; it destroyed the Tories as a political

force in Quebec; and it killed forever the dream of nationhood for the Métis.

Once the Lords of the Plains—and the people who forced Canada to recognize Manitoba as a province—the Métis had no place in the new order. Manitoba was now a largely English-speaking society of 110,000 people who earned their living mainly from the soil—a soil shaped into a neat patchwork of ordered, fenced fields as far as the eye could see. Manitoba was a place transformed, and continued immigration in the coming decades would change it almost beyond imagination. ✒

The rapid and successful deployment of troops by railway to fight the North West Rebellion finally persuaded Parliament to free up funds to complete the CPR.

Riel's Last Stand

The Métis force ambushed Middleton's troops at Fish Creek and set back the Canadian army's advance on Batoche by two weeks.

"He shall hang though every dog in Quebec bark in his favour."

Sir John A. Macdonald in November, 1885, when presented with clemency pleas for Louis Riel

Despite the jury's recommendations for clemency, the Canadian government proceeded with Riel's execution.

The Métis field general Gabriel Dumont was reduced to performing in Buffalo Bill's Wild West Show after the collapse of the Métis resistance.

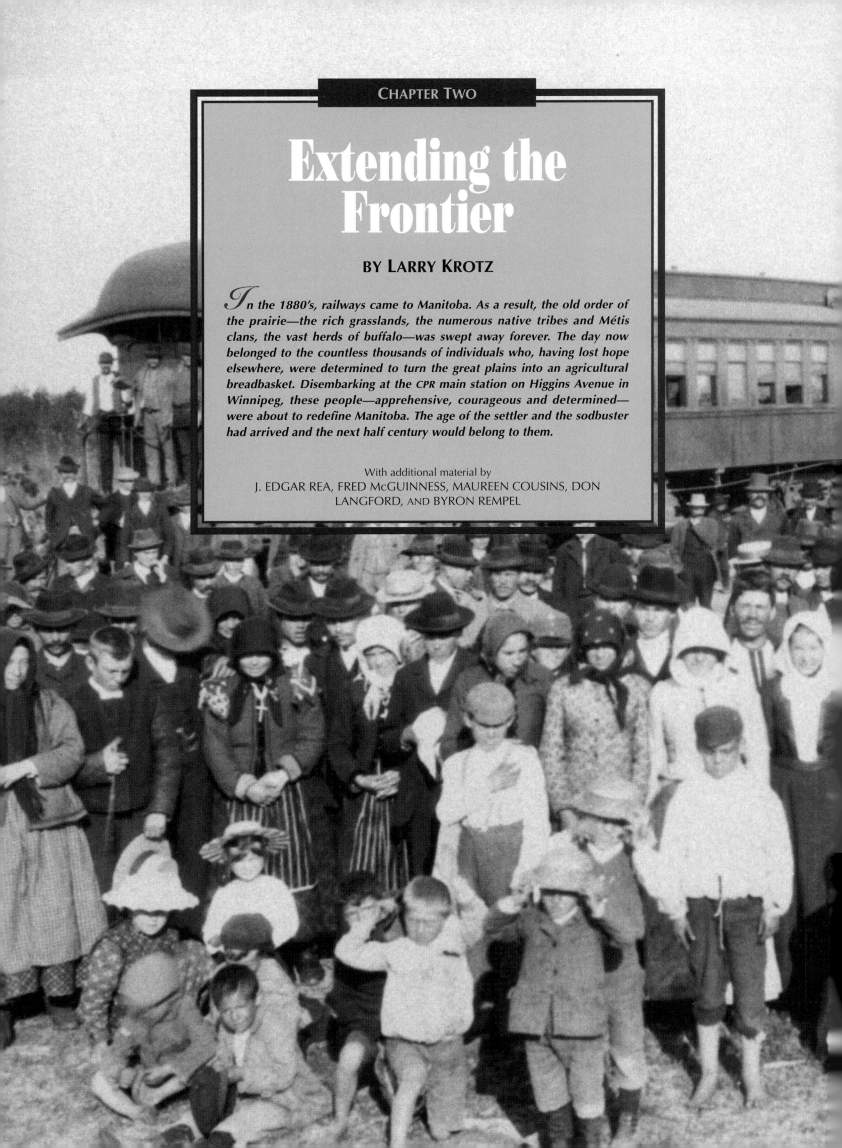

CHAPTER TWO

Extending the Frontier

BY LARRY KROTZ

In the 1880's, railways came to Manitoba. As a result, the old order of the prairie—the rich grasslands, the numerous native tribes and Métis clans, the vast herds of buffalo—was swept away forever. The day now belonged to the countless thousands of individuals who, having lost hope elsewhere, were determined to turn the great plains into an agricultural breadbasket. Disembarking at the CPR main station on Higgins Avenue in Winnipeg, these people—apprehensive, courageous and determined— were about to redefine Manitoba. The age of the settler and the sodbuster had arrived and the next half century would belong to them.

With additional material by
J. EDGAR REA, FRED McGUINNESS, MAUREEN COUSINS, DON
LANGFORD, AND BYRON REMPEL

Edward Roper's
A Settler's Home Near Carberry

Railways open up the West to settlement

Extending the Frontier

If ever there was a time built on dreams, it was the settlement of the Canadian West in the latter part of the 19th century. Looking back a century later, it is hard to fathom the audacity, the stunning arrogance, the unwavering determination required to push through one of history's great movements of people, and—by the humble plough— affect Hone of its most profound alterations of landscape.

It was a time of grandiose national dreams and modest individual dreams: politicians saw a nation stretching from sea to sea, with Manitoba as the gateway for agricultural settlement; the settlers themselves had a vision of new opportunity in a new land. Taken together, these shared dreams re-defined Manitoba and its future.

Imagine what it must have been like to make the trip from the Old World. The average voyage was 12 days from Liverpool, or 14 from Hamburg. Most of the time was spent heaving about in the smelly, rocking depths of steerage. The immigrants were political and economic refugees fleeing over-crowding, oppression and poverty. Their simple belongings were roped into crates and trunks. In every corner of the ship, their children played quietly together, bored and apprehensive. Even

idea of what this place called Manitoba would look like.

Imagine the farmer in old settled Ontario, restless in middle age or full of bravado in youth. He wanted more land, better land, and he knew there was an endless acreage on the other side of the Canadian Shield. Manitoba was a magic word. The rich soils of the Red River Valley were already attracting people like him—British, Protestant and hard-working. With the blessing of the Dominion government and the new railway, he might become rich. He might even have a town named after himself.

Imagine being in the boardroom of the Canadian Pacific Railway in Montreal, or the Cabinet room of the great grey buildings of Parliament in Ottawa. The map on the wall in either place showed two horizontal black lines running toward the left, clear into the blue of the Pacific Ocean. One mark was the border separating the still youthful Dominion of Canada from the United States. The other, slightly above it, was the route of the Canadian transcontinental railway. The railway was the spine which carried the nerves and the energy for both a political and an economic dream. But for these dreams to work, all the pink on either side of the railway line had to be filled in. Settlers—men, women, producers, consumers, entrepreneurs and farmers—were needed to fill that vast space.

Imagine a member of the Board of Trade in rapidly growing Winnipeg. He had triumphed in one battle—the new railway. Its tracks, yards, and warehouses had been lured by money and deft

One method of making the West appear more attractive to railway passengers was to plant lush flower gardens and shrubs at Canadian Pacific Railway stations. The idea came from CPR employee David Hysop of Killarney who argued, "If you want to show how good the soil is, why not have gardens at the railway stations in which flowers and vegetables can be grown."

after landing in Canada, few had any idea of the length, in either time or distance, of the rattling train journey that awaited them; and absolutely no

Although easier than building through the Rockies, CPR engineers soon discovered that Manitoba's terrain was not completely flat.

manoeuvre away from rival towns to both the north and south. All traffic into a newly opened half-continent passed through Winnipeg. Businesses sent out their salesmen, a veritable army with sample cases and order books, fanning out to the ends of the continent, to the ends of the line. Winnipeg, even though its streets were still muddy and its gas lamps barely up, would not be a simple provincial capital, but a continental metropolis on the scale of a Chicago or a St. Louis. Halfway between old Montreal in the East and the brash little seaport on the Pacific, Vancouver, there would be Winnipeg—"Bull's Eye of the Dominion".

Handling grain on Pacific Avenue

Canada's first transcontinental railway was built through Manitoba in 1881-82. Compared to earlier construction over Lake Superior and later construction in the Rocky Mountains, the building of the Canadian Pacific Railway through Manitoba was almost effortless. Politically, however, the CPR's directors faced many headaches as they sought the best route across the province.

Before the mainline even entered Manitoba, a heated fight had broken out between proponents of a northern route through Selkirk and the Interlake and boosters of a prairie line anchored by Winnipeg. The CPR's own superintendent of engineering, Sandford Fleming, recommended crossing the Red River at Selkirk because its higher river banks precluded spring flooding. But polit-

IT WAS THE "NATIONAL DREAM" that determined the location of Brandon. And it was the community's rapid growth as an outfitter for settlers that led it to incorporate in 1882.

An earlier attempt to establish a community at what is known as Grand Valley was not successful. This location, only four kilometres east of present-day Brandon, was on low-lying land subject to the floodings of the Assiniboine River. Railway surveyors knew that the CPR's

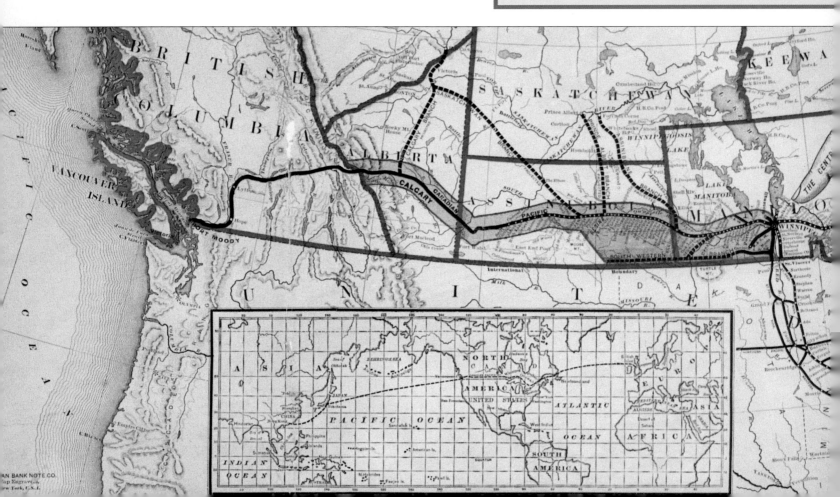

Brandon became a city almost overnight Wheat City

right-of-way had to follow high ground and Grand Valley's dream of cityhood soon evaporated.

When Brandon was in its infancy, there wasn't a single tree to provide a stick of wood. One early settler writing home to his parents in England described this shortage with a terse but telling phrase, "there isn't a tree in sight large enough for a cow to rub against".

The first shelters that would keep out the elements and the hordes of mosquitoes were made of canvas. Those scores of tents gave way to frame structures when the fleet of steamships, the *Alpha,* the *Marquette* and the *Manitoba* began to deliver loads of lumber. The first permanent residence was that of D.H. Adamson, near the site of present-day St. Augustine's Church.

The first passenger train arrived on October 11, 1881. The community was incorporated May 30, 1882. Brandon never knew life as a hamlet, village or town; it sprang into life fully fledged, at least in legal terms, as a city. According to the *Brandon Sun:* "It had been discovered that a charter for incorporation as a city would cost the same as that for a town, and therefore, economically, let alone any other reason, it would be wiser to ask incorporation as a city, especially as there was no population requirement, and anyway, sooner or later, a city charter would be required."

The first Brandon city directory, published in September of 1882, reported that this tiny community on the agricultural frontier "possessed all the elements of a growing city, and could boast of possessing a railway depot, a river boat landing, a post office, an express office, three temporary places of worship for the several denominations, a branch banking house, a planing mill, a saw mill, an engineer's office, a lawyer's office, about two dozen general stores, two hardware stores, about a score of real estate offices, several temporary hotels and boarding houses, and several livery and feed stables, all in full swing."

Early residents were not noted for their modesty. In their promotional literature they spoke of Brandon as "The Pearl of the Prairies". This sobriquet eventually gave way to "The Horse Capital of Canada", and this in turn yielded to "Wheat City", a nickname that was to endure for more than a century. Early photographs gave proof to the validity of Wheat City as a secondary name; they show scores of horse-drawn carts lined up at elevators on Pacific Avenue, filled with grain in sacks, the first bounty of the land.

Due to its growth as a transportation centre and a hub for western Manitoba's grain-and-cattle industry, Brandon soon dismissed other challengers and became Manitoba's second largest city.

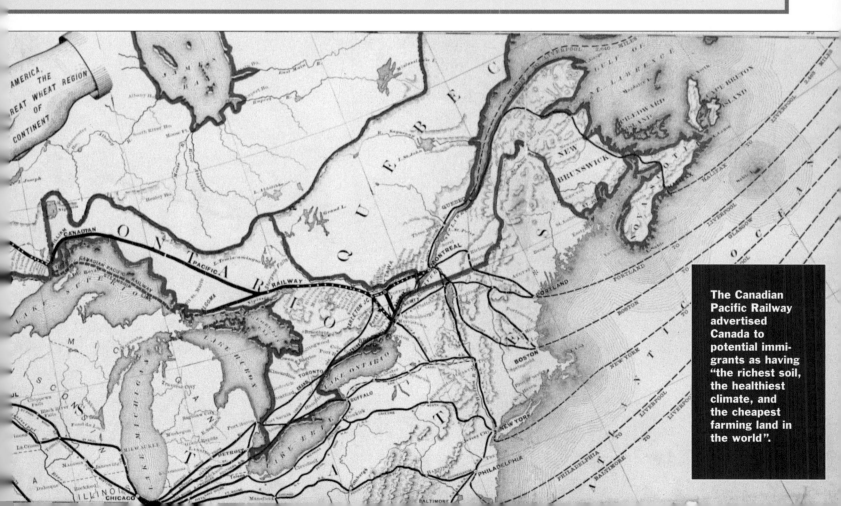

The Canadian Pacific Railway advertised Canada to potential immigrants as having "the richest soil, the healthiest climate, and the cheapest farming land in the world".

ical and economic power was wielded by the fledgling metropolis of Winnipeg. By 1880, Winnipeg had won the political fight and a terminus was established in the Manitoba capital. The mainline reached Brandon by 1881, and extended into the flat plains of Saskatchewan (still part of the North West Territories) by 1882.

Three years later, on a soggy November morning in 1885, the "last spike" of the transcontinental railway was driven by a sometime Winnipegger, Donald A. Smith, into the jagged rocky earth at Craigellachie, British Columbia. Smith, as chief commissioner of the Hudson's Bay Company, had seen the HBC through its last great days as a fur empire. Now this most successful of Canadian businessmen had neatly side-stepped into the next grand continental enterprise, the Canadian Pacific Railway.

The "spine" image for the CPR was appropriate. It would be the nerve running through the west of the country, and its placement was critical to everything else. The railway route determined where settlement would go; the choices made in 1881 and 1882 shaped the future development of the province. It guaranteed the success of some towns while dashing the hopes of others. It made Winnipeg and embittered Selkirk, by-passed Emerson and ensured Brandon. In some cases, towns

General T. Lafayette Rosser

Many colourful characters found their way into the employ of the Canadian Pacific Railway, including the rapacious and aristocratic General Thomas Lafayette Rosser.

Rosser, a southerner who had fought in the American Civil War against West Point classmate General George Custer, eventually became the CPR's head engineer. Rosser was responsible for establishing the CPR's first divisional point west of Winnipeg. He initially struck a deal with the McVicar brothers to acquire their 320 acres of Grand Valley area property for $30,000. However, the McVicars held out for $60,000. Rosser, advised that the site was prone to flooding, crossed the Assiniboine and chose a site four kilometres west that he named Brandon.

During his time with the CPR, Rosser flagrantly sold his privileged information to speculators. Railroader J.J. Hill complained, "It looks as though everyone from Genl. Rosser down has been engaged in townsite operations. It is openly advertised that Rosser is a promoter of the town of Raeburn."

Joining one's relocated family in Manitoba often proved an arduous task. One Belgian woman travelled alone as she tried to be reunited with her husband at Swan Lake. The woman, who spoke no English, wore tags on her clothing detailing her name, travel plans and destination. The trip took 23 days, and she was unable to speak to anyone.

Tired of Rosser's antics, CPR general manager William Van Horne fired him on February 1, 1882. That summer, a still angry Rosser confronted Van Horne in the Manitoba Club. He launched into a vitriolic diatribe against his former boss, then stomped out. Shortly after, an alarmed club member scurried over to Van Horne and warned him that Rosser was brandishing a gun and vowing to shoot Van Horne.

Thomas Lafayette Rosser

William Van Horne

The threatened assassination never materialized, and a sheepish Rosser later made an "ample apology" to the Manitoba Club. It is not recorded whether he also apologized to Van Horne.

created in anticipation of the railway's arrival were forced to move—lock, stock and barrel—to new locations nearer the actual route of a rail line.

But the CPR mainline was still only the spine. If the eastern dream was to turn the West into an agricultural hinterland for its interests, the ribs were still needed. Branch lines had to extend out so they could haul back to the middle. Shipping rates had to be affordable for pioneer grain farmers. As well, a whole infrastructure had to be built; stations, platforms, warehouses, water tanks, elevators and grain handling facilities. A lot of work was still to be done, and quarrels over railway rates and the construction of branch lines would dominate politics at least until the end of the century.

The CPR had been chartered only after convincing the federal government to guarantee it a 20-year monopoly on east-west traffic and the setting of freight rates. The 20-year holiday had barely begun when both the monopoly and the rates became irritants in a number of quarters. Everyone from grain farmers to Winnipeg businessmen to provincial politicians began to chip away at them. Winnipeg business succeeded in getting a preferential rate for merchandise shipped from eastern Canada, a deal which gave it a lasting advantage over potential rival western centres.

But what many people really wanted, including Manitoba politicians of every political stripe, was an end to "disallowance" of competing railway charters. Provincial governments attempted to challenge the CPR monopoly, using government influence and funds to sponsor local railway projects in the same way Sir John A. Macdonald had used the national government to support the CPR. These schemes, too numerous to itemize, lurched through the 1880's and 1890's with varying degrees of success and folly. Some built short stretches of track, others got mired in petty scandals and bankruptcies.

When rival companies were able to build branch lines to feed freight to the mainline, the CPR—absorbed as it was with its east-west work—seemed to welcome them. But when farmers and politicians became impatient with high rates or the shortage of grain-moving box cars and pushed for a competing east-west line (specifically one heading to Lake Superior by going south to the U.S. border and then hooking up with the Northern Pacific to Duluth) relations soured.

The hostility boiled over into outrage in 1887 when a bumper crop of wheat had to be heaped in huge rotting mountains at every siding. The next year, Macdonald and the CPR gave in to the new Manitoba premier, Thomas Greenway, and "disallowance" was formally ended (in return for a cash bond which allowed the CPR to pur-

Battle at Fort Whyte

The Canadian Pacific Railway did not take kindly to the end of its railway monopoly, and in 1888 it got into an armed standoff with a competing Manitoba company over a right of way.

Conflict was inevitable because the new Northern Pacific and Manitoba Railway proposed to cross the CPR's mainline on its way to Portage la Prairie. This did not sit favourably with William Van Horne and William Whyte, the CPR's top officials in the West, who balked at the notion of competition in freight rates.

Whyte was sent to take control of the disputed crossing spot, a site ten kilometres southwest of Winnipeg. The spot was immediately dubbed "Fort Whyte" by Winnipeg newspapers. An angry provincial government asked Winnipeggers if they would like to "put the CPR in its place". In response, three flatcar loads of volunteers hustled to Fort Whyte, but the Northern Pacific's track layers had not yet arrived. When the angry Winnipeggers returned two days later, they were galled to see that the CPR had built a fence around its property and had ditched an engine in the track layers' path.

Undeterred, the attackers tore up part of the CPR's tracks and installed a "diamond" to allow the Northern Pacific to cross the CPR's line. Whyte's crew then arrived and, after facing down the Winnipeggers, ripped out the diamond and traipsed off to the city with it, claiming victory.

Thereafter the CPR installed 200 men to guard Fort Whyte. Van Horne provided sleeping cars and meals for the crew, and a Sunday church service was held. Each evening, the two factions faced each other over a blazing bonfire, guns at the ready.

The standoff did not resolve the matter. Instead, the Supreme Court ruled that the Manitoba government had the right to pursue alternatives to the CPR, and so ended the "battle" of Fort Whyte, without a single shot fired.

chase two American railroads). The farmers and the provincial politicians had won a victory in a battle they were destined to have to fight over and over again.

The railway was called the National Dream then, and still is by myth-makers now. But the dream was not the railway itself. The dream was everything that was to follow on those long ribbons of steel.

For those who sat in Winnipeg waiting for the dream, waiting to make their fortunes, things were not happening quickly enough. After the incredible boom of railway building and the land grab that went with it, the economy during the last half of the 1880's fell into recession. Land prices and values, inflated in the early 80's, collapsed. Business and immigration slowed. A sort of desultory mood, unusual for optimistic Winnipeggers,

Origins of the Chinese Cafe

Coolies helped build the railway and introduced a new cuisine to the Prairies

As the railway neared completion, bitter feelings against Orientals began to surface. The British Columbia government passed the Chinese Regulation Act in 1884, which declared the Chinese "are not disposed

THERE'S ONE IN NEARLY every town across the Prairies, in every little nook and cranny from Killarney to Medicine Hat: a Chinese cafe.

The anomaly of Oriental cuisine on the bald prairie is explained by the great railway construction of the 1880's. The CPR hired thousands of Chinese workers (or coolies as they were called) to help push the new transcontinental rail line across the Prairies and through the mountains of British Columbia. It was assumed that any race that could build the Great Wall of China could also build a railway—and the assumption was right.

Paid $1 a day for work for which others earned $1.50, the Chinese offered the railway magnates an enormous saving. They cooked their own food and carried everything they needed on their backs. Two thousand coolies could be moved 40 kilometres in one day while it took a week to move a similar camp of whites.

to be governed by our laws; are governed by pestilential habits; are useless in instances of emergency; habitually desecrate graveyards by the removal of bodies therefrom and... are inclined to habits subversive of the comfort and well-being of the community."

After the railway boom was over, the Chinese were discharged and left to scratch for a living in the turn-of-the-century bars of British Columbia and Alberta. Others tried to make a new start by pooling their meagre capital and establishing restaurants, hotels and laundries in the Prairie towns farther to the east.

Most of the original coolies came from Kwangtung province in southern China, not far from Canton. This perhaps explains why, until recently, Cantonese has been the dominant Chinese restaurant cuisine in places such as Brandon, Neepawa, Winnipeg and scores of other Prairie places where Chinese workers settled after their release from the railway.

set in. The railway was here; where were the waves of new Manitobans? The *Manitoba Free Press* as early as 1873 had stated bluntly, "the two great wants of this country are railroads and settlers. The former is necessary to secure the latter." They now had the former, but the latter weren't following quickly enough—even though millions of acres of free homestead land were being offered by the federal government.

From some perspectives, the breathing time provided by the slow growth of the 1885-1895 period was important. It permitted a kind of cultural consolidation which turned out to be critical to the flavour Manitoba would maintain for decades. Most historians say that this was the time Manitoba acquired its prevailing rural, British and Protestant culture, a culture that broke substantially from the past, and was solid, prosperous, and tenacious enough to withstand other influences for a long time into the future.

These cultural changes were reflected in the province's politics. W.L. Morton wrote that the provincial election of 1888 definitively "marked the triumph of Ontario over Quebec in Manitoba. The decision of 1870, the work of Riel's daring and Taché's diplomacy, was tacitly undone."

The election of 1888 was the end of the trail for Premier John Norquay, the lumbering 300-pound mixed blood descendant of early Kildonan settlers. Norquay had been the first, and for a long time only, native-born premier. After a brief transitional period during which a Minnedosa businessman named David Howard Harrison enjoyed the role of "the three-week premier", Thomas Greenway acceded to the premier's chair. Greenway exemplified everything Norquay wasn't: he was a Liberal and, more importantly, a new arrival who wanted Manitoba to be recreated as a more westerly Ontario.

Greenway's dream was already coming true. By 1886 the province boasted a population of 110,000. The ethnic composition—half French-speaking Métis 15 years earlier—had been radically altered. Only seven per cent, by this time, were French speaking, the proportion of Roman Catholics had shrunk from one-half to one-eighth, and the Ontario-born were the largest single group. So when Greenway and fellow Liberals like Clifford Sifton, Joseph Martin, and James Smart (all of them with close connections to Brandon and the newly developing southwest of the province) swept into power, it was as if they were held by no memory of the past and were driven only by a very pragmatic view of the future.

Everybody seemed to want to forget the days of Rupert's Land, with its ties to the old order of fur, Métis and the Hudson's Bay Company. In Winnipeg, the stones and framework of old Upper Fort Garry were pulled down so that Main Street could run straight. Only the gate was left, a lonely memento. Gas lights, electric trolleys, and some newly paved streets were changing the frontier nature of the city, which by 1886 had jumped to 20,000 citizens.

The premier who banned French in Manitoba

Thomas Greenway

THOMAS GREENWAY—THE FIRST Liberal premier of Manitoba—would steer his party through a number of difficult issues, including the Manitoba School Question. He became best known, however, as the premier who banned the use of French in Manitoba institutions.

In 1878, hoping to take advantage of the western land boom, Greenway moved from Ontario to Manitoba. He filed a homestead claim and began developing a townsite for the future Crystal City. Greenway immediately became active in provincial politics, sitting as an independent for the Mountain riding. He lobbied for better railway connections and competitive freight rates. In 1883, he led a group of Provincial Rights candidates in the provincial election campaign. His four elected candidates quickly joined forces with the Liberals to become the opposition.

By 1887, Norquay's Conservative government faltered under the weight of the railway debate and allegations of misuse of government funds. Early in 1888, Greenway was asked to form a government. At the same time, the CPR surrendered its monopoly. Greenway claimed credit for this and he swept into power, as a Liberal, in the July, 1888 provincial election.

Greenway continued to lobby for an alternative to the CPR, but with little success. A deal was struck with the Northern Pacific whereby the Red River Valley Railway would become the Northern Pacific and Manitoba Railway. It had no intention of competing with the CPR—its interests lay elsewhere—and Greenway's policy was soon in shambles.

A more contentious issue then arose—the Manitoba School Question. Although he wanted the support of French Catholic voters, Greenway argued the province couldn't afford the existence of both Catholic and Protestant schools. In 1890, his government abolished the use of French in the legislature, civil service and courts and ended denominational schools. Six years of constitutional battles followed, as Catholics tried to regain their education rights. In 1896, the Liberals won power federally, and an irritated Prime Minister Laurier ignored Greenway, dealing with Clifford Sifton in negotiating the so-called Laurier-Greenway compromise.

The decline of Greenway began thereafter. He was unable to provide railways to compete with the CPR. Nor was he able to secure financial aid for the province from the Laurier government. Unable to find a popular issue on which to wage an election, he underestimated the popularity of Conservative leader Hugh John Macdonald, and the Liberals lost the 1899 provincial election.

Greenway stayed on as provincial Liberal leader until 1903. Out of financial need, he ran as the Liberal candidate in Lisgar in the 1904 federal election. Later he was appointed to the federal Railway Commission. However, he died before he could assume the position.

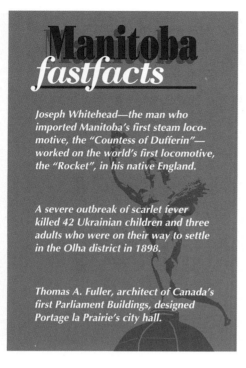

Across the province, the very landscape was being altered, not just by the railway's roadbed, but irrevocably by the plough, axe, and saw of the farmer, and the transit of the surveyor and road builder. The park belt originally had a flowing beauty where meadows encircled poplar bluffs, willow runs edged creeks, wetland marshes spread out through hollows. Indian trails and animal tracks followed the contours of a subtle undulation. Now the whole land was being overlaid with a pattern of strict rectangles; ploughed fields and quarter-section farms. Fences and road allowances broke abruptly the meander of traditional trails. The geometric grid was inflicted with little bend on nature's landscape.

Studies showed that a farmer could efficiently transport his grain by horse and wagon for a distance of about 16 kilometres; so that became the distance between depot sites and elevators along the rail line. And since a depot was where people and business should gather, it was at those locations that the new towns were laid out. Often, towns were named on the spot by the railway contractors; Rosser after the CPR's chief engineer, Ethelbert after railroader William Mackenzie's daughter Ethel Bertha.

Some of the immigrant settlements, those of the Icelanders on Lake Winnipeg or the Mennonites in the two southern reserves, showed Old World influences in their design. The Mennonites built central villages where they all lived, while their farms stretched back into the surrounding distance. A herdsman came through the village in the morning to take everyone's cows to a common pasture.

But the British towns were built on geometric patterns, every 16 kilometres. Even when they were only a station and a few houses, they were saddled with ambitious names like Rapid City, Dominion City and Crystal City as if merely willing it could set them on the road to an eventual London or San Francisco.

New institutions sprang into being. If eastern Canada saw the West as the grand, faraway hinterland for their business and political purposes, Winnipeg identified everything west of it as a more immediate version of the same thing. The grain trade was making Winnipeg its headquar-

More than a million settlers passed through Winnipeg on their way to new homes in the West.

ters, with the Grain Exchange formed in 1887 and 26 thriving grain companies by the end of the century. Winnipeg had a new centre of higher learning, the University of Manitoba; a haughty businessmen's club, the Manitoba Club (as formal and exclusive as any you might find in Montreal or London); a busy Historical and Scientific Society; a couple of home-grown militia regiments which had flexed their muscles during the North-west Rebellion in 1885; and some of the biggest wholesalers in the country.

Winnipeg merchants like J.H. Ashdown saw themselves as wholesalers for the continent, with the whole of the territory to the end of the rail line

as theirs to supply. An army of salesmen with their sample cases packed and their families waving good-bye set off weekly on the new trains to take their wares as far as the mountains. What they needed, though, was an ever-growing list of customers, and they were panicked when, after 1882, immigration slowed from a rush to a comparative trickle.

Concerned but resolute, Winnipeg's civic and business leaders stepped into the breach. If more people were good for their business, then more people was what they would get. As the *Manitoba Free Press* explained: "Of what avail is it that there are in western Canada millions of acres

---

Mennonite sod huts provided ingenious shelter from the elements

Semlins on the Prairie

WHEN JACOB BARKMAN AND HIS wife Katherina led 18 Mennonite families into the settlement of Steinbach in the early fall of 1874, they hardly had time to build adequate shelters for the approaching winter. And while the wealthy Barkman— *eltester* (bishop) of the church group, and thus also the mayor of the village—was used to the brick houses of the Russian steppes, money could not buy time or supplies that first fall. Instead the group turned to the natural resources at hand for shelter: poplar trees, soil, grass and sod.

Using the same design the Mennonites had used 100 years earlier when they emigrated to Russia from Prussia, Barkman oversaw the building of "semlins", or sod huts. The men first dug holes in the prairie one metre deep, four metres wide and 12 metres long. Then the natural insulator of sod, one-half metre thick, was piled one metre high around the cavity. A roof was created from poplar logs, smeared with clay and covered with more sod. The whole creation resembled nothing more than a bump in the vast flatness of the prairie. Winter blizzards and even

prairie fires raged over the cramped but secure quarters.

Barkman tramped from hut to hut that winter, encouraging the settlers that God had directed them to the promised land. In some huts he found families sharing the space; in others, families had taken in four-legged occupants during the bitter snowstorms: their cattle. It was a truly symbiotic relationship, for while the livestock certainly added a sharp pungency to the tiny room, they also provided body heat to help keep their owners warm. When hay ran out, the close relationship was taken one step further. Both people and cattle ate bread to survive.

Barkman's faith in his God must have been tested that first winter, for first his four-year-old daughter Mar-

garetha died, followed a month later by his nine-year-old daughter Anna. When a blizzard buried the family inside the hut after Margaretha's death, Barkman had no choice but to put the body of the young girl in a cradle and hang it from the rafters of the hut. The semlin, with its dirt walls and floor, turned into a crypt for three days until Margaretha could be buried in the frozen ground.

With the promise of springtime and the chance to build a permanent home, Barkman made the plodding ox cart trip to Winnipeg, intending to buy supplies for a permanent wooden house. But the ferry carrying him over the Red River capsized, and the persevering leader drowned in the chilly waters, weighted down by his long beaver coat.

In later years, Lord Dufferin would comment on the pacifistic group's struggles to make a life in the new country. They fought a successful war, he said, "not against flesh and blood, a task so abhorrent to Mennonite religious feeling, but against the brute forces of nature".

The semlin version of the prairie sod hut was dug one metre into the ground.

of the finest land that lays open to the sunshine, awaiting only settlement and development to give its cultivators comfort and competence, unless the advantages they offer to the home-seeker are made known to the people their possession would benefit?"

Civic leaders wanted Winnipeg to be more than just a gateway for immigrants. They believed prosperity was rooted in growth and wanted as many immigrants as possible to settle in the city. They were particularly concerned about new arrivals moving on from Winnipeg south into the United States. As early as 1877, Winnipeg's city council supported Alexander Begg in publishing

Canada's first electric transit system Winnipeg Street Railway

horses from Ontario. Headquarters were established on Assiniboine Avenue between Fort and Garry streets. The inaugural run took place on October 20, 1882. A ride cost 10 cents, or 15 tickets for a dollar.

The operation was a success from the start, and soon new track was laid from City Hall north to the CPR station at Higgins, and west on Portage Avenue to Kennedy Street. During the winter, the cars were outfitted with runners, turning them into sleighs to cope with the inevitable building up of ice and snow on the tracks.

The city continued to expand in all directions, and Austin realized that the horse drawn system would be unable to keep up with the increasing demand. Reports of an electrical street railway in Richmond, Virginia, prompted Austin to travel there in the spring of 1888. He returned to Winnipeg convinced that electric trolley cars were the way of the future. Nervous about the prospect of "dangerous aerial wires" city council hedged, but finally agreed to allow Austin to test the new system across the Assiniboine River in sparsely populated Fort Rouge.

After successful tests, the first electric street car manufactured in Canada arrived via CPR flatcar in November, 1890. Austin was so confident of this system that he did not wait for spring to test it, and on January 27, 1891, before a large crowd of curious onlookers, the car made its first run from the south side of the Main Street Bridge, up River Avenue to Osborne Street, and back again, without a hitch. The next day, the first commercial electric street railway system in Canada went into regular service.

LIKE ALL SUCCESSFUL ENTREPRENEURS, Albert W. Austin was quick to recognize opportunity. The son of James Austin, one of Toronto's wealthiest businessmen, Austin arrived in Winnipeg in the spring of 1880, at the age of 23. After surveying the spring quagmire on Main Street, Austin decided that Winnipeg needed a horse-drawn street railway system, such as had been in operation in Toronto for more than 20 years.

One year later, on April 28, 1881, Austin organized The Winnipeg Street Railway Company. Prominent local investors included J.W. Ashdown and Hugh Sutherland. After lengthy negotiations with city council, the company was awarded a 20-year franchise to own and operate a street railway system.

The first track was laid along the west side of Main Street, north to the new City Hall at William Avenue. Austin ordered four 24-passenger rail cars from New York, and imported 20

and distributing 10,000 copies of *A Practical Handbook and Guide to Manitoba and the Northwest*. Countless pamphlets and pieces of propaganda followed, sponsored by the city. Their efforts got wide distribution. Some publications were sent, for example, to every library in Great Britain, or every library in eastern Canada, as well as many locations in the United States.

Civic support for the effort was widespread, with only labour leaders failing to agree. The fledgling Winnipeg Trades and Labour Council feared the competition of cheap immigrant workers and "most emphatically objected to the taxation of labour in order to flood the labour market against the wage earner". These objections, and those of the Knights of Labour, were ignored; after 1885 civic leaders and the business community redoubled their efforts, and through publications, agents, and conferences became inextricably involved in a relentless search for immigrants.

By the mid 1890's, the federal government decided to mount an aggressive immigration campaign. The new Liberal government under Wilfrid Laurier assigned responsibility to Manitoba cabinet minister Clifford Sifton. The vigorous Sifton moved quickly—in 1896, 65,000 pamphlets extolling the virtues of the Canadian west were sent into the U.S. and Europe. The marketing hyperbole knew no bounds: prairie streets were paved with gold; Mounties were mythologized to assure immigrants of a peaceful country; the free aspect of the homestead land was emphasized; and rarely did they use the word "cold".

Pierre Berton quotes a British immigrant recalling years later that the propaganda claimed Canada "to have a healthy climate guaranteed to be free of malaria.... It was said that while the prairie summers were hot, the heat was delightfully invigorating and while it got cold in the winter the cold was dry and not unpleasant." The pioneer admitted with some rue, "I used to recall those glowing words as I pitched sheaves with the temperature at 95 in the shade, and as I ran behind a sleigh at 30 below to keep from freezing."

The CPR mounted its own campaign in Britain, northern Europe and the United States. Free tours were conducted for trainloads of farmers, newspaper editors and even such international notables as David Lloyd George (who would later become Prime Minister of Great Britain).

After 1896, the immigrant rush started again, although not as quickly or in as great numbers as Manitoba boosters might have wished. There were not yet many of the "sturdy peasants in sheepskin coats" who would arrive in droves after the century turned and Clifford Sifton's policies really took hold in eastern Europe. Some groups had arrived in the 1870's: Mennonites from Russia to settle the east

By 1872, the federal government had immigration sheds in Winnipeg. Immigrants were allowed seven days free shelter.

CPR immigration pamphlets often presented an idealized view of Prairie farming.

and west, Mennonite reserve blocks in southern Manitoba, Icelanders for Gimli, and French Canadians from New England who settled as a group around St. Malo. The first Jewish settlers came to Winnipeg in the early 1880's, refugees from the Tsar's pogroms in Russia.

But the clearly stated preference pre-1900 was still for the British and the Ontario born. These made up an ever-growing majority, enough

The CPR built dozens of third class carriages dubbed "colonist cars" to carry immigrants to their new homes in the West.

Tragedy at Bonnie Doon

Written by Interlake pioneer Major J. Proctor and recorded in Woodlands Echoes, *a history of Woodlands municipality. Prairie fires were a frequent threat on the grassy plains, especially before large-scale cultivation. The Bonnie Doon fire was one of the worst in Manitoba's history.*

to set a solid cultural base for the province well into the next century—Protestant, conservative, and very British—and to overwhelm the French and Catholics who became an aggrieved minority.

On a hot summer's afternoon in August of 1889, an Ontario Conservative Member of Parliament named Dalton McCarthy made a whistle stop in Portage la Prairie in order to make a speech to a crowd of recent Ontario settlers. In it, he lashed out against French-speaking influences in the country. As head of the Equal Rights Association, he had been making the same speeches throughout Ontario and in Parliament. But in Portage that day, he had a particularly receptive audience—including Manitoba Attorney General Joseph Martin—who, when he rose to thank McCarthy, promised legislation for Manitoba that would put

Perhaps the greatest single calamity which befell any part of the rural municipality of Woodlands was the great Bonnie Doon Fire, which occurred on October 2nd, 1897. This fire left such a train of devastation and destruction behind it, that the district never fully recovered from the effects. Many of the residents lost all their possessions and moved away the following spring. Others struggled bravely to make a fresh start, but they had no heart left and they too, moved away a year or two later....

The morning of October 2 dawned bright and clear, unusually warm, even hot, for the season with a strong south-west wind, and around noon, smoke was seen low down on the southwestern horizon, and soon the smell of prairie fire was noticeable...

Slowly at first, the smoke and smell of fire spread before the wind, but soon the air became thick with smoke. It became difficult to breathe. The cattle around the farm yards became restless and uneasy. Horses whinnied with fear. Even the people seemed stupefied, they well knew what was coming. Yet they made no effort to save their stock and possessions. Perhaps none knew as well as they how futile any effort would be, for the wind which had been steadily rising had, by two o'clock, become a gale...

The smoke was now suffocating. Objects could be seen only a short distance. Flocks of birds were seen flying past the farm houses. Rabbits in thousands were busy hurrying by, and an occasional wolf or deer. Presently the roar of the approaching fire could be heard. The heat and smoke

became unbearable. Ashes, cinders and burning tufts of grass and limbs of trees were falling thickly. The herds of cattle and horses which had been showing every sign of fear and terror, now broke away in a mad stampede..... With a roar like that of a cyclone, the fire struck each farm home in succession, and in a twinkling, houses, barns and stables were all alight. To save anything now was impossible. Every building and hay stack seemed to burst into flame in a hundred places at once.

How any human being escaped seemed miraculous. Most of them took refuge in wells, others lay on plowed ground, face down, until the wall of flame had passed. These had their clothes burned from their bodies, and many were terribly burned on the face and hands. One man, Hamilton Upjohn, was dead, suffocated with smoke while attempting to reach a neighbour's house to render what help he could. The other man who lost his life, Walter Allan, attempted to get through the fire from Woodlands to his home in Lake Francis, where his wife and family were alone. His team was burned to death. His load of goods was destroyed, but he himself got through the three miles of burning woods to the nearest settler, Mr. Harris Bates, making the last part of the distance on his hands and knees, as blinded by the fire, he had felt for and followed the road with his hands. Mr. Allan was so terribly burned that recovery was impossible, and he died in the hospital three days later in terrible agony...

Little did we who were watching the swiftly rolling clouds, have any conception of the tragedies being enacted beneath. Like all pioneers, we all knew something of bush and prairie fires, but never of any in which human life was in danger, or even where livestock was seriously threatened, and when the reports began to come through, the whole community was shocked and stunned.

The writer, in the company of A.J.H. and Walter Proctor and G.H. Broadfoot, drove over part of the burned area on Sunday, October 10, and followed the same road taken by Mr. Allan, in his brave attempt to reach his family. Of his wagon and load nothing remained but the twisted ironwork, even the barrels of a shot gun were melted apart. The horses had evidently been unhitched from the wagon and were lying about one hundred feet away—literally roasted....

The horrors of what we saw that day were indescribable.... Coming back by the shores of Swamp Lake we passed where the rabbits had been caught between the fire and the lake and had perished in thousands. Three years afterwards, their bleached and whitened bodies could be followed for two miles along the shore.

Clifford Sifton

At the turn of the century, Clifford Sifton provided Manitoba's strongest voice on the federal political stage. His key contribution was opening the West to hundreds of thousands of Eastern European settlers who forever changed the ethnic composition of the Prairies.

Sifton was born in Ontario, but came to Manitoba to seek his fortune in 1880. He quickly compiled an impressive resumé: called to the Manitoba Bar in 1882, elected Liberal MLA for Brandon in 1888, appointed attorney general of the Manitoba government in 1890. Along the way, he became an enthusiastic promoter of the West, intent on convincing Ottawa that the future of the nation depended on the development of the Prairies.

In 1896, he ran for federal office, won, and found himself the only western MP appointed to Sir Wilfrid Laurier's cabinet. His assignment was relatively minor: minister of the interior and superintendent of Indian Affairs. But Sifton attracted notice beyond the portfolio when he devised an aggressive immigration policy unabashedly designed to benefit Western Canada.

For years, Canada had seen settlers overwhelmed by the rigours of prairie life pack up their belongings and move to the United States. With missionary zeal, Sifton set out to reverse that migration. He offered free land to American immigrants. Agents were appointed in key cities to seek out settlers. Advertisements appeared daily in 7,000 American newspapers. The strategy paid off. In 1896, records show there was no immigration from the U.S.; in 1897, after just one year of Sifton's aggressive promotional campaign, 2,500 Americans made their way to Canada.

Once American immigration began to move into the West, Sifton turned his attention to Eastern Europe. He was convinced the "stalwart peasants in sheep-skin coats" had the necessary grit for life on the Prairies. His campaigns said it all—"Only farmers need apply."

Sifton's strategy to promote Canada as the "golden land" was often controversial. For example, the North Atlantic Trading Company, a group of shipping agents, was promised a bonus for every agricultural immigrant delivered to Canada. Sifton even considered banning the publication of prairie temperatures lest they frighten off prospective immigrants. The campaign worked: hundreds of thousands of settlers came in search of new opportunities.

Many Canadians, however, didn't appreciate the flood of Poles, Ukrainians and Russians. One paper greeted the immigrants as "Mr. Sifton's Grand 'Round Up' of European Freaks and Hoboes." But Sifton persisted, paying only lip service to efforts to recruit from Britain, saying labouring "city folk" were "undesirable from every standpoint".

Sifton resigned from office in 1905 following a dispute with Laurier over school policy for Alberta and Saskatchewan. Although he was highly secretive about his business affairs, he was obviously successful. Upon his death, his estate was valued at nearly $10 million. His most public and prized acquisition was the *Manitoba Free Press*. Sifton was knighted in 1915, but his most lasting monument was the rich and varied population he encouraged to settle Canada's West.

A provincial dispute escalated into a symbolic national issue

THE MANITOBA SCHOOL Question went to the heart of the Canadian dilemma. What began as a dispute over the funding of the public schools of the province in the 1880's became the vehicle of many other long-simmering resentments, often injected from beyond Manitoba: questions of Protestant-Catholic animosities; minority rights; English-French relations; constitutional guarantees; Ontario-Quebec rivalries, and so on until it became the leading issue in the national election of 1896. By this time, however, Manitoba had reached its own decision.

Until the Red River colony entered Confederation in 1870, education had been in the hands of the churches; Anglicans, Catholics and Presbyterians ran their own schools. Denominational education was confirmed by the Manitoba Public School Act of 1871. This first school law created a dual, public system funded by the province—thus protecting the denominational rights of Protestants and Catholics as guaranteed by the Manitoba Act of 1870. The population of just over 12,000 people was evenly divided between English-speaking Protestants and French-speaking Catholics, so the new school law, reflecting this balance, simply continued a familiar system. Twenty years later, things were radically different.

Catholics, mostly French but now with a significant English minority, made up only 13 per cent of the population. The overwhelming Protestant majority, mostly from Ontario, had brought with them their distinctive attitudes to public education. Pragmatically secular, they saw the public schools as an instrument of social policy, the means of securing a British and

The Manitoba School Question

Protestant future for the Prairies.

But there were practical difficulties as well. As the frontier expanded there was chronic underfunding of schools in the newly settled (and English) areas of the province. Complaints began over the distribution of the school grants. Despite periodic adjustments, the older settled areas where most of the French lived seemed to receive a disproportionate share of education funds. Understandably, if inaccurately, the new majority began to associate Catholic schools with French schools and the old issue of

> **There is no "right" answer to such a question, there is only politics.**

ethnic hostility was rekindled. The increasing criticism of "separate schools"—a term peculiar to Ontario—pressed the beleaguered Liberal government of Thomas Greenway to action.

Under the insistent prodding of Cabinet ministers James Smart and Joseph Martin, Greenway determined on a sweeping revision of Manitoba society. Early in 1890, the Assembly was presented with bills ending the printing of documents in French; creating a new government Department of Education and establishing a system of "national" schools, by which was meant non-denominational schools teaching in English. The Catholic schools were not proscribed, but parents who chose to send their children there would have to pay for them as well as pay taxes to support the new public system.

The Catholic minority felt doubly aggrieved. The guarantee of de-nominational rights in the Manitoba Act was apparently useless, and worse, the new public school system was in reality the old Protestant system with the same buildings, books, teachers, inspectors and religious exercises. For Manitobans, the question had been reduced to its essence; in creating the kind of public school system they desired, was the majority obliged to honour the constitutional guarantees on education clearly set out in both the Manitoba Act and the British North America Act? There is no "right" answer to such a question, there is only politics.

For Prime Minister Sir John A. Macdonald,

Minister of Public Works James Smart

the political prospects were bleak. In responding to the minority's request that he disallow the new school law, he risked alienating either Quebec or Ontario, so he prudently sought a judicial resolution. J.K. Barrett, sponsored by the federal government, refused to pay his Winnipeg school taxes on the ground that the school act of 1890 had violated his constitutional rights. The Manitoba court upheld the new school law but this decision was overturned by the Supreme Court of Canada. Before appealing to the Privy Council in London, Manitoba arranged another challenge to the law, this time by an Anglican named Logan. When both cases went to the Privy Council, Manitoba argued that if Barrett and Logan were both sustained, the ability of Manitoba to provide an adequate system of public education would be fatally undermined. It was a clever ploy and it worked: Barrett and Logan were turned down.

Now there was only politics. Under another clause of the Manitoba Act, the Catholic minority sought federal remedial action. The Cabinet tried to duck the issue, but the Privy Council, in the Brophy decision, concluded there was indeed a right of appeal. So Manitoba schools became a central issue in the national election of 1896 won by the Liberals under Wilfrid Laurier, who promised to resolve all the difficulties with "sunny ways". The outcome was the Laurier-Greenway compromise of 1897 which made minor concessions to religious and language concerns. But the 1890 school act was maintained; there would be one public school system—English and non-denominational—and the Catholics of Manitoba would be taxed to support it whether they sent their children there or not.

Contradictory policies assured natives of failure

Aboriginal

DURING THE NEGOTIATIONS of Treaties 1 and 2 in the early 1870's, Indian Commissioner Wemyss Simpson told the assembled Cree and Saulteaux (Plains Ojibway) of Manitoba that their one hope for survival was to adopt an agricultural way of life— to become farmers instead of hunters. Under the new reserve system, native people received 160 acres of land for every family of five and promises of agricultural assistance.

Many Crees and Saulteaux, having watched the buffalo disappear from Red River and their traditional economy severely disrupted by settlement, agreed with Simpson. Adaptation was nothing new for First Nations people in Manitoba. During the fur trade, many Cree successfully went from being woodlands hunters to middle-men traders, trading European goods to other tribes. Native tribes were more than willing to accommodate themselves to a new way of life. Given their lack of economic options in southern Manitoba during the early 1870's, the tribes initially viewed farming positively.

Unfortunately, policies aimed at making the Cree and Saulteaux self-sufficient farmers were sabotaged almost immediately by contradictory policies. The first problem was the land itself. Not being familiar with farming, many bands chose reserves with lands poorly suited to raising crops. When bands did manage to find good farmland, their requests were often ignored or overruled by federal Indian agents. The second factor that worked against the tribes was inadequate financing. On the one hand, the government wanted to help the Cree and Saulteaux become successful farmers; but at the same time they wished to do it as cheaply as possible.

Under the treaties, Indians in Manitoba were promised agricultural assistance in the form of implements and instruction. While the instructors seemed to have been adequate, the implements provided were not. Many bands had to wait years for the tools promised under treaty. When they did arrive, there were not enough to go around and they were of such inferior quality that many a farm instructor protested bitterly to the reserve's Indian agent.

On some reserves, band members were forced to harness themselves to a plough to work their fields because they had no oxen. On other reserves, threshing machines were not purchased because they cost more than the crop was worth. And if a band did manage to raise a successful crop, grain often rotted in bins as there were few mills or markets located close to the isolated reserves.

In 1889, Indian Commissioner Hayter Reed announced a new system of farming. Aboriginal farmers were to emulate "peasants of various coun-

an end to the inconsistency of public tax money supporting Catholic schools, most of which were French.

In 1890, Martin and the Greenway government duly brought in the Manitoba School Act which ended publicly financed denominational schools for both Catholics and Protestants. The act set up a public school system, told churches that if they wanted to run schools they would have to pay for them themselves, and curtailed the official use of French.

French-speakers and Catholics in Manitoba believed that the Manitoba Act of 1870 (which allowed parallel Protestant and Catholic publicly funded schools) guaranteed their culture and their language. But that was back when they represented half the population. In the interim, demographics had changed dramatically and both French and Catholics were now a distinct minority.

With the shift of demographics, so shifted the public mood. Editorials in the *Brandon Sun* argued that "the unwisdom of allowing separate schools was universally recognized". Other editorials throughout the province criticized the dual system of denominational schools as expensive, inefficient, a barrier to the creation of a united—

Farming Sabotaged

tries" by keeping their farm operations small and self-sufficient, eliminating the need for expensive machinery and large herds of cattle. The intent, Reed asserted, was "to make each family cultivate such quantity of land as they can manage with such implements as they can alone hope to possess for long enough after being thrown upon their own resources".

Reed was strongly opposed to aboriginal farmers purchasing machinery, and particularly going into debt to do so. Merchants were informed that Indian Affairs would not be held liable for aboriginal farmers' equipment debts. Reed believed it was "unnatural" for aboriginal farmers to make the leap to mechanized farming.

Indian agents criticized Reed's machinery policies, arguing that using hand implements resulted in lost yields at harvest time, thus preventing Indians from earning extra income and becoming self-supporting. Reed countered that if grain was being lost during harvest, they had planted too much.

By 1891, the Oak River Dakota (Sioux) had 540 acres under cultivation, expanded cattle holdings and modern machinery. However, that year a new farm instructor was placed on their reserve to see that no grain left the reserve without a permit. Grain buyers, when given a permit,

The federal government discouraged aboriginal farmers from purchasing modern farm equipment. The use of such machinery was the exception rather than the rule.

were asked to pay the implement dealers to whom some of the Indians were indebted.

The Dakota, who had been handling their own finances for years, loathed the interference. Marketing their grain without permits, they tried to maintain their independence. Oak Lake grain buyers were fined by Indian Affairs for buying grain from Indians. Many area residents supported the Dakota, and the *Virden Chronicler* claimed that the Indians, through the "obnoxious order are not allowed the full benefit of the fruit of their labour".

The protests continued until

1894, when an investigation into their complaints was conducted. Inspector T.P. Wadsworth concluded the evidence favoured the permit system and the farm instructor, and blamed the Dakotas' problems on their debt problem and several poor crops. He called the Dakota lazy and informed them the permit system was in their best interests.

By the early 1900's, the initial enthusiasm of Manitoba natives for farming had been replaced with deep disenchantment. Although some reserves experienced success with agriculture, most did not.

To speed assimilation, aboriginal children were relocated to distant residential schools such as this one at Elkhorn.

Red River steamers did not normally dock on Emerson's Main Street. However, this boat made an exception during the 1897 flood.

read British—community, and "an iniquitous special privilege to one religious sect".

For Manitoba's Catholic, and particularly its French, minority this was a bitter pill. It confirmed what Archbishop Taché had feared 20 years before—that Protestant immigration would outflank and crush his flock. Combined with the outcome of the Northwest Rebellion in 1885 and the hanging of Louis Riel, the Manitoba School Act gave a clear message to the French. It told Quebec that the West was lost to them; they had really no safe home outside their province. And it told the French in Manitoba that they had little choice but to protect themselves in whatever small ways they could; theirs would always be a struggle to survive.

Other traditional Manitobans were squeezed to the outside in these years as well. Cree and Saulteaux bands,

worried about starvation after the disappearance of the buffalo herds, had signed treaties across the Prairies—starting with Treaty 1 at Lower Fort Garry in 1871. These treaties set aside reserve lands and placed native people squarely under the care of the federal government. The native chiefs had originally wanted to provide railway and settlement corridors through their land, but Canadian

One of Winnipeg's most spectacular fires was the destruction of the Manitoba Hotel on February 8, 1899. Built in 1892 by the Northern Pacific, it was called the grandest hotel between Montreal and Vancouver.

Manitobans enthusiastically volunteered to join the British in their fight against the rebel Boers in South Africa in 1899.

Because of the treaty obligations, about 60 per cent of Indian Affairs budget was destined to be spent in Manitoba and the Northwest, so it was here that the spending cuts were most felt.

By the late 1880's, the federal government was actively involved in the schooling of natives. Ottawa's education policy had many goals, including "Canadianizing" and "Christianizing" the aboriginals, protecting them from the evils of white society and preparing them to enter a different type of work force. In the operation of the schools, the government continued to be assisted by various churches and missionaries.

Three types of schools evolved: day schools located on the reserves, boarding schools and industrial schools. Children enrolled in industrial schools were away from home for months at a time, the idea being that they would forget their traditional way of life and adapt to white society. Students were taught English and the European work ethic, and were expected to conform to the practices of the prevailing culture. Time was split between the classroom and learning various trades.

Due to their high cost of operation and their failure to substantially alter the aboriginal way of life, the industrial schools were phased out early in the 20th century. The boarding, later called residential, schools continued for years, but were also frowned upon by natives for their goal of ending native traditions. Indeed, when aboriginal children went home for the summer months, they were again exposed to their traditional way of life, and government attempts to eradicate powerful native customs such as sun or thirst dances were less than successful.

Notre Dame Des Prairies, Our Lady of the Prairies, the Trappist monastery in St. Norbert, was founded in 1892 by the Abbot of Belfontaine, France. He had received a proposal to extend his order from Archbishop Taché and Father Ritchot. The Trappists were offered 1,200 acres of land, to which Ritchot added another 300 from his own estate.

negotiators insisted on full ownership of the Western plains. Faced with a food-gathering crisis, the tribes reluctantly accepted Ottawa's terms.

Education and altering of native culture were declared to be priorities, but the federal government seemed ambivalent about both. In 1879, a report recommended the government hire well paid, qualified teachers for Indian education. To economize, the government instead opted to hand the responsibility to churches who paid teachers less than half the going rate. In doing this, they also ignored the report's recommendation against allowing religious denominations a free hand on the reserves. The government seemed committed to self-sufficiency on the reserves, and lamented having to give handouts. J.A.J. McKenna, Sifton's right-hand man at Indian Affairs, argued that "the Indians can only be advanced through labour—growing grain and raising cattle—and I propose doing what I can to hasten the day when ration houses all cease to exist".

Natives, however, were not a great public priority after 1885. Whenever the government was in a penny pinching mood, Indian Affairs was an easy target. During Sifton's tenure at Interior, his departmental budget nearly quintupled and the national budget more than doubled, but that of Indian Affairs increased by less than 30 per cent.

"Smart clean girls can do better here than men."

Mrs. Mary Lowe of St. Agathe quoted in the 1896 Canadian Pacific Railway pamphlet, *What Women Say of the Canadian North West*

In 1886, both rural Manitoba and the city of Winnipeg looked like blueprints of what they would become over the next 30 years. In that year, only 18 per cent of the four million acres occupied by homesteaders had been cultivated. But a decade later, the farms and villages to the south and west of Brandon—Hartney, Killarney, Deloraine and Souris were already prosperous and settled. The same was true in the area north of Brandon—Minnedosa and Neepawa, Birtle and

Russell were solidly established. By 1890, the Interlake was already filling in, with towns like Woodlands, Stonewall, Teulon and Arborg attracting new settlers.

At mid-decade, it was generally agreed that the post-railway recession had ended and boom times were on the horizon, this time on a scale previously unimagined. The long wait of Winnipeg's boosters and merchants was over, their patience was to be rewarded. It is probably fitting that this was the year, 1896, that the Winnipeg Victoria's hockey team went east to win the recently minted Stanley Cup, and the year a Manitoban, Clifford Sifton, took on the job of federal Minister of the Interior.

In 1896, the most successful competitors to the CPR, Sir William Mackenzie and Sir Donald Mann, obtained a grant from the provincial government to start on the Manitoba and North Western Railway. This new line was to run up from

The Only Woman Hung in Manitoba

Orphan Hilda Blake was executed for shooting her employer's wife

POLITICS AND INTRIGUE SHROUDED the case of a young British orphan, Emily Hilda Blake, the only woman ever executed in Manitoba. She murdered her employer's wife, a crime she argued was perpetrated at the request of her employer, who allegedly promised to marry her.

Blake's tale began in Norfolk County, England. Her parents died when she was nine, and she was sent to a workhouse. Under an arrangement between Britain and Canada, Canada agreed to supervise "state" children who emigrated to the country. In 1888, Emily was placed with a farm family at Elkhorn, and she eventually went to work as a domestic for Brandon businessman Robert Lane and his wife Mary.

Tragedy befell the Lane household on July 5, 1899, when the pregnant Mary was killed by a shot to the back of the head. Blake steadfastly maintained that Mary had been murdered by a tramp with a foreign accent. A mob of vigilantes roamed the streets seeking a likely suspect. However, when faced with the "killer", Blake had to admit that he was not the man.

The next day Blake assisted police in locating the murder weapon under a barrel behind the Lane home. The investigation continued, with Blake now the likely suspect. A Winnipeg gun shop owner reported selling a gun to a woman matching Blake's description and on July 9, the 21-year-old Blake was arrested for murder.

Faced with the evidence, Blake confessed. She claimed that she had planned to kill herself, but in a fit of jealousy had killed Mary instead. At the preliminary hearing she stated, "I am guilty, and I want the severest punishment you can inflict." The case was set over for a fall trial and Blake was placed in Brandon Gaol.

Public opinion flared. Some labelled British orphans in Canada "villainous and criminal", and demanded

> **"Forsaken by friendship, kith and kin.**
> **I lie in my lonely cell;**
> **It seems but a dream that I've crossed that dark stream.**
> **And descended from heaven to hell."**

"My Downfall" appeared in the Brandon Sun on December 14

that Britain stop sending the children. Others could not understand how a woman so seemingly intelligent and hard-working had committed such a heinous crime.

At her trial, Blake refused legal counsel and confessed once more, ignoring warnings that she would be executed. Judge A.C. Killam did not recommend mercy and sentenced her to hang. The case was sent to the federal cabinet for review.

In the meantime, a movement arose to have the sentence repealed. Dr. Amelia Yeomans visited Blake and concluded that she was a "moral lunatic" who bore no moral responsibility for her actions and hence should not hang. The Brandon Women's Christian Temperance Society circulated a petition asking that the death sentence be changed to life imprisonment.

Blake herself fanned public opinion when her poem "My Downfall" appeared in the Brandon Sun. In it she claimed that she had sinned because she had been tempted by a man.

In Ottawa, politicians debated the case. Prominent officials argued strongly for a deferral of the execution. Canada's Governor-General was convinced that Robert Lane had indeed played a role in his wife's death.

In the end, Prime Minister Laurier's cabinet maintained the court's decision. Blake went to the gallows without protest on December 27, 1899. The hanging was a distasteful conclusion for many. The Regina Standard went so far as to claim that Blake was "lawfully murdered".

Gladstone into the as yet untouched Dauphin country. Settlers followed the track, pouring in to homestead this virgin fertile plain, and pushing on to pioneer the towns not only of Dauphin, but Gilbert Plains and Grandview.

Again, many of these pioneers were from Ontario or Britain. Significantly, however, the Dauphin settlers included the first Polish and Ukrainian immigrants (whose numbers would increase so dramatically after the turn of the century). Also, this new migration saw the first real signs of Americans moving up from their Midwest. The American influx was due, in part, to cheap land disappearing at home; but also because the Canadian advertising campaigns were starting to pay their dividends. When Clifford Sifton took office in 1896, his department had six immigration agents working south of the border. By 1899, it had 300.

These campaigns were necessary because a sizable percentage of settlers attracted to the Manitoba did not stay. Sifton wanted hardy farmers from Eastern Europe but, whether Ukrainian, Irish or Ontarian, large numbers of immigrants gave up on Manitoba after a couple of years and moved farther west or south. One analysis showed that less than half the immigrants who poured into the Prairie region from 1890 to 1920 actually stayed.

Beyond the Dauphin country and the Swan River Valley lay the Saskatchewan River, the fur post town of The Pas, and the old fur trade connections of the North. Here the trapping and trading of Rupert's Land days still went on. The Cree and Dene still moved from their camps to the missions and the trading posts of the white man.

The main trader—the Hudson's Bay Company—was developing a new transportation system to replace the old York boat system. Specialized steamboats were purchased for use on Lake Winnipeg, a tramway was constructed at Grand Rapids on the northwestern corner of the lake and river steamboats were assembled at Grand Rapids for use on the Saskatchewan River.

These innovations caused great economic dislocations. Hundreds of seasonal tripmen from York Factory, Norway House, Grand Rapids and other such northern transportation centres of the HBC were thrown out of work. Indeed, the natives of Norway House asked for a treaty, which would include a reserve farther south, specifically so that they could take up farming in order to escape the unemployment caused by the HBC's southern-oriented transportation system.

Most of the North, however, was not experiencing the radical change evident in the south of

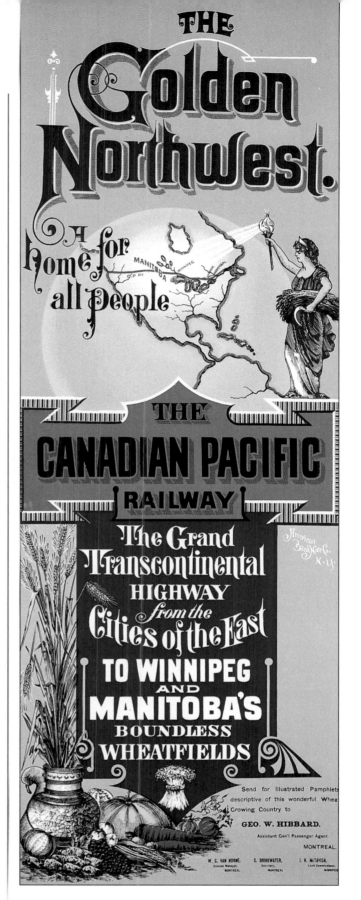

the province. Perhaps, looking to the overheated flurry going on through the Prairies and parklands, they welcomed their calm.

Manitoba was being redefined. The old fur-based economy was gone forever. New people and new ways of producing wealth would now dominate the province. And the engine of that new wealth would be the old centre of the fur trade—once called Red River, now known around the continent as Winnipeg. 🐾

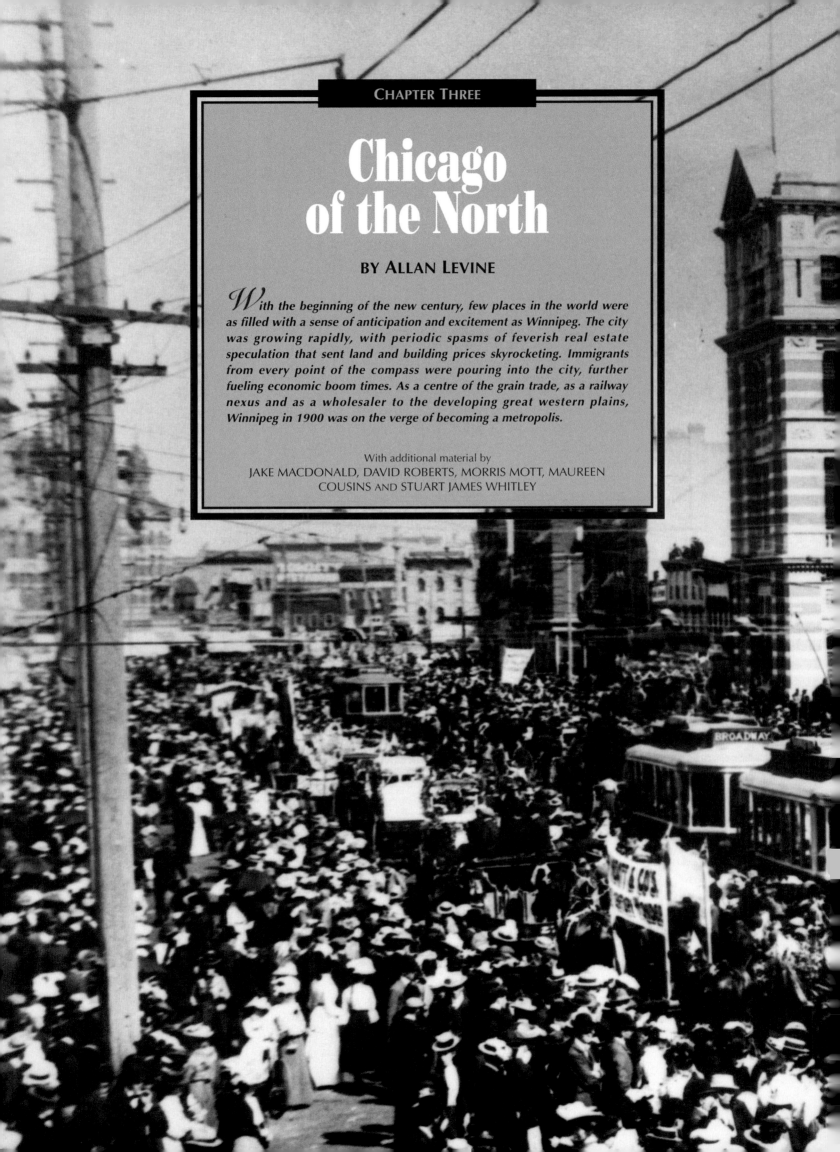

CHAPTER THREE

Chicago of the North

BY ALLAN LEVINE

With the beginning of the new century, few places in the world were as filled with a sense of anticipation and excitement as Winnipeg. The city was growing rapidly, with periodic spasms of feverish real estate speculation that sent land and building prices skyrocketing. Immigrants from every point of the compass were pouring into the city, further fueling economic boom times. As a centre of the grain trade, as a railway nexus and as a wholesaler to the developing great western plains, Winnipeg in 1900 was on the verge of becoming a metropolis.

With additional material by
JAKE MACDONALD, DAVID ROBERTS, MORRIS MOTT, MAUREEN
COUSINS AND STUART JAMES WHITLEY

Chicago of the North

Booming Winnipeg becomes a metropolis

"All roads lead to Winnipeg," declared Chicago journalist William E. Curtis after visiting the city in September, 1911. "It is the focal point of three transcontinental lines of Canada, and nobody... can pass from one part of Canada to another without going through Winnipeg. It is a gateway through which all the commerce of east and the west, and the north and the south must flow... It is destined to become one of the greatest distributing commercial centres of the continent as well as a manufacturing community of great importance."

Such optimistic sentiments about Winnipeg's future abounded during the first decade of the 20th century. And why not? It was the greatest boom period in the city's history. The statistics alone tell a remarkable story. In 1901, Winnipeg had a population of 42,340. This total had more than tripled to 136,035 by 1911, making the city the third largest in the Dominion. The local construction industry could not keep up with demand; in 1900 the value of building permits equalled $1.4 million, by 1912 it was more than $20 million. Property values rose to all-time highs and everyone was keen to invest in real estate. Financiers promised eight per cent returns for money spent on grand apartment blocks like the

Roslyn, built in 1909 for $205,000 at the corner of Osborne Street and Roslyn Road.

Railways and grain had put Winnipeg on the map. Reflecting this, the pace was frantic at the new Winnipeg Grain and Produce Exchange (renamed the Winnipeg Grain Exchange in 1908). A good indication of the city's status as a rising world grain centre was the amount of wheat inspected: 12.3 million bushels in 1900 versus 143 million in 1912. In 1904, the Exchange opened a futures market, making trading more sophisticated and reliable. Five years later, as a result of a bumper crop it became the largest cash wheat market in North America. In 1909, more than 188 million bushels of wheat were marketed on the Exchange floor compared to 81 million bushels in Duluth and 26.9 million in Chicago.

The city was the western headquarters of three railways, the CPR, the Grand Trunk Pacific, and Canadian Northern. And still, Winnipeg businessmen complained that there were not enough cars to meet their shipping requirements.

During these boom years, Winnipeg grew from a bustling prairie town to a city on the verge of metropolis—a leading centre for transportation, financial institutions, the grain trade, wholesale companies and cultural institutions. Its hinterland stretched as far as the Rockies. Winnipeg was dynamic, optimistic and alive with excitement. Whether it was watching the latest touring act at the majestic Walker Theatre (including the 1909 production of Ben Hur with a real chariot race), shopping at Market Square across from picturesque city hall or skating on the Assiniboine River, there was plenty to do.

It was a city of hustle and bustle where bicycles and the streetcars of the Winnipeg Electric Company were rapidly replacing horse-drawn carriages. If you were wealthy enough, you may have even owned an automobile for Sunday drives to

Located across from Winnipeg's "gingerbread" city hall, Market Square was at the hub of the city's commercial district.

the country as a member of the newly-organized Manitoba Motor League. By 1908, 20 different types of cars were for sale in the city, including Packards and Oldsmobiles which ranged in price from $500 to $6,000. Still, one of journalist James Gray's fondest boyhood memories was watching the grand departure of the horses from the Eaton's department store stables on Graham Avenue. "The Eaton wagons were assembled in a long line on the inside of the building. At the appointed moment a policeman would step into the Graham and Hargrave intersection and halt traffic in all directions. Then the big door would fly up and the first rig in line would lunge onto the street and head north."

The decision of Toronto merchant Timothy Eaton to open a store in Winnipeg in 1905 was a sign that the city was maturing. Yet from Eaton's perspective the move was a gamble. Located at the corner of Portage Avenue and Donald Street, the store was some distance away from the business and retail district on Main Street. Nevertheless, Winnipeggers were drawn to the impressive department store where the prices marked were the prices paid—no bartering allowed. Eaton's sales increased from $2.5 million during its first year of operation to more than $14 million in 1915. Within a short time, the main downtown district, led by Eaton's, had shifted westward along Portage Avenue.

At the turn of the century, optimism was in the air. "You have no idea of the enthusiasm people have here about the prospects," reported the newly arrived Methodist minister J.S. Woodsworth in a 1902 letter to a cousin in Toronto. No one was more enthusiastic about Winnipeg's prospects than its commercial elite, the small group of businessmen who ran the city as a personal fiefdom. They were ambitious, self-centred, aggressive, and fiercely protective of their interests. In fact, in their

Sir Rudyard and Lady Kipling visited Winnipeg in 1907. Kipling was pleased with the developments he saw since his first visit 15 years prior and remarked, "My heart goes out to the City of your love and your pride because I know what lies behind the mere houses in the streets one sees... I have realized here the existence of an assured manhood; the spirit of a people contented not to be other people. "

New and old transportation jockeyed for space on Winnipeg's busy streets. An electric streetcar got the better of a horse-drawn Eaton's delivery wagon on Portage Avenue, killing the horse.

The Vaudeville Era

Charlie Chaplin and Marx Brothers were among Winnipeg's stage stars

WITH THE RAPID GROWTH of North American cities like Winnipeg, there came the rise of a new social entity—the middle class. Clerks, teachers, realtors, government officials, small business operators and other members of the educated professional class became known as "white collar" workers. They worked with their brains, rather than their backs, and they earned enough money to devote considerable income to their own amusement. To address this new market, the North American entertainment industry was born.

At home, the hand-cranked gramophone became a popular diversion. Downtown, for the admission price of five cents, nickelodeon galleries entertained audiences with jerky silent movies to the accompaniment of a slam-bang piano. But live vaudeville shows were the most popular diversion. During the height of the vaudeville era, the appetite of audiences for stage entertainment was so insatiable that Winnipeg had no less than 14 live theatres.

The leading vaudeville stages in Winnipeg were the Pantages, the Orpheum and the Walker. Pantages was part of a continental chain of theatres owned and operated by a Los Angeles entrepreneur named Alexander Pantages. The Pantages dominated Market Avenue with the words "Unequalled Vaudeville" cut in stone high above its doorway. On its stage audiences could watch celebrities like heavyweight fighter Jack Dempsey, who dared members of the audience to get up on stage and go a few rounds with him. On Fort Street, the Orpheum Theatre offered competing entertainment, and several blocks to the north was the grandest of all—The Walker Theatre. Founded in 1907 by a show business couple of the same name, the Walker was a physically imposing edifice with velvet seating, ornate fixtures and soaring ceilings.

On the night of the theatre's opening, Winnipeg's elite attended in full evening dress to watch a performance of Puccini's *Madam Butterfly*. In following seasons, the Marx Brothers, Harry Houdini, Fanny Brice, Sophie Tucker and countless other big-name stars visited Winnipeg.

There is compelling evidence that Charlie Chaplin signed the contract that launched his brilliant movie career while he was staying at the Windsor Hotel on Garry Street. And there's even stronger reason to believe that Groucho Marx first laid eyes on Chaplin in Winnipeg. In a book called *The Marx Brothers Scrapbook*, Groucho states he first saw the Little Tramp perform on an August night in 1913. "I think it was in Winnipeg, in Canada, when I went for a walk down the Main Street where I came upon a nickelodeon. Chaplin was doing an act there called "A Night at the Club". I never heard an audience laugh like that. I went back to tell the boys about him. I told them, I just saw the greatest comedian in the world."

During that same visit to Winnipeg, Charlie Chaplin went fishing with his touring manager, Alf Reeves, and a Winnipegger named George Tanner. Reeves and Chaplin had placed a friendly wager with a London promoter named Fred Karno that they knew a spot in Canada where you could catch three pike in a minute. The loser had to buy dinner and wine for the entire company of comedians. Chaplin, Tanner and Reeves went up to Lockport and broke out their fishing gear. Later that same day, they sent a wire to London: "KARNO. YOU LOSE."

This postcard of the third St. Boniface Cathedral was produced in 1908, the same year St. Boniface was incorporated as a city. The strong cultural and linguistic traditions of St. Boniface continued to be reflected through the community's cathedral, hospital and college.

minds, there was no difference between Winnipeg's needs and their own.

Most of these men like James Ashdown, the "Merchant Prince", banker William Alloway, grain merchant Nicholas Bawlf, and financier Augustus Nanton had come to the city from either Ontario or England to seek their fortunes. In a frontier community like Winnipeg where there was no established upper class, they were the aristocracy. They lived in the southern part of the city in stately mansions on Wellington Crescent, where "the boulevards ran wide and spacious to the very doors of the houses", or in homes in the new area of Crescentwood west of Osborne Street.

Nanton, for example, was the director of more than 30 companies. He had arrived in Winnipeg in 1883 to set up a western office for the Toronto investment company Osler & Hammond (later Osler, Hammond & Nanton) and lived in a large home on Roslyn Road which he called 'Kilmorie'.

Throughout this period, control of the city's influential Board of Trade and of municipal government from its gingerbread City Hall on Main Street was in their hands. Indeed, the five men who served as mayor of Winnipeg during the first decade of the 20th century—John Arbuthnot

(1901-03), Thomas Sharpe (1904-06), James Ashdown (1907-08), W. Sandford Evans (1909-11), and Richard Deans Waugh (1912)—were all members of the commercial elite. They socialized together at the Manitoba and Carleton Clubs, played golf together at the exclusive St. Charles Country Club, and holidayed with their families at Victoria Beach and Lake of the Woods.

James Ashdown's story was not unusual. Born in London, England in 1844, he came to Canada when he was still a young boy. His family settled near Toronto and he apprenticed as a tinsmith. He moved for a short time to Kansas before arriving in Winnipeg in 1868. Ashdown opened a small hardware store at the corner of

James Ashdown, hardware tycoon, was one of many members of the commercial elite to serve as mayor.

Hugh John Macdonald

Manitoba's ninth premier was the son of Canada's first prime minister

ALTHOUGH HE WAS A reluctant politician, Hugh John Macdonald managed to move out of the shadow of his famous father and to leave a marked impression on the citizens of Manitoba.

Born in Kingston, Ontario in 1850 to John and Isabella Macdonald, Hugh John lived his early life without his parents. His mother died when he was seven. He was then raised by his aunts as his father was too busy with his political career to tend to him.

Hugh John attended Queen's College Prep School and the University of Toronto. His father—now prime minister of Canada—wanted him to become a lawyer, but Hugh John craved adventure. When troubles broke out in Red River in 1870, he joined the Wolseley Expedition, and got his first glimpse of Winnipeg. Returning to Ontario, he articled as a lawyer and joined his father's law firm. In 1882 he returned to Winnipeg and set up a law practice.

Although he did not share his father's deep-seated passion for politics, Hugh John reluctantly ran federally in 1891 and won his seat. He said, however, that he would not seek re-election, as he felt "a political career is not one in which I would succeed and the life of a politician is distasteful".

In 1896, Prime Minister Charles Tupper's Conservative government was under fire over the Manitoba School Question, and the PM told Hugh John that only a Macdonald could reach "the place in the public heart and confidence once held by Sir John Macdonald". Hugh John set about to win a seat, narrowly defeating Joseph Martin, the former provincial attorney general.

He lost his seat soon after when Martin argued that Hugh John's agent had violated the election rules.

Shortly thereafter, Hugh John was approached by Rodmond Roblin to rebuild the ailing provincial Conservative Party. He assumed its leadership in March, 1897 and Macdonald and the Tories won the subsequent election.

Hugh John and his party, however, were soon to clash. Prohibition had been passed, but many in the party found the legislation unpalatable, and others, such as Roblin, were vying behind the scenes to become party leader. After less than nine months as premier, Macdonald was persuaded by Tupper to leave provincial politics and run against Clifford Sifton in the 1900 federal election. Hugh John lost and promptly withdrew from active political life.

After Hugh John's son died of diabetes, the former premier sought solace in the bottle. Then in 1911, at the age of 61, his friends obtained for him an appointment as a police magistrate. In this job, Hugh John earned a reputation for being courteous and compassionate. Some claimed that he passed sentence so graciously that prisoners felt like thanking him for going to jail.

Hugh John's own health waned. He lost one leg to erysipelas in 1927, but in a short time returned to his duties as magistrate, being carried into the courtroom daily by two police officers. In 1929, he developed infection in his other leg but refused to have it amputated. The reluctant politician—and son of Canada's first prime minister—died soon after, on March 29.

Bannatyne and Main Street which he eventually transformed into a retail and wholesale empire with a chain of stores across the West. He was one of the Winnipeg's famous "nineteen millionaires" in 1910 and the director of dozens of financial institutions, including the Great-West Life Assurance Company. When he died in 1924, his estate was worth about $1.7 million, a portion of which he left to charity.

Sir Augustus Nanton was president of the Dominion Bank.

Winnipeg's monied class indulged in leisurely pursuits such as fox hunting, polo and boating. This hunting group was setting out from Charleswood.

Among the influential supporters of Ashdown and his friends was the Conservative provincial government. The Tories were led briefly by Hugh John Macdonald, the son of Sir John A. Macdonald, and then until 1915 by the indomitable Rodmond P. Roblin. An Ontario immigrant, Roblin had settled near Carman and become a prosperous farmer. But business and politics had brought him into Winnipeg. He made a sizable fortune as one of Nicholas Bawlf's partners in the Northern Elevator Company and then turned his attention to becoming the leader of the provincial Tories. Self-assured and partisan, Roblin did not always agree with the policies advocated by the city's elite, but he definitely shared their economic vision.

Whatever the issue, the city fathers nearly always approached the numerous problems they faced from a business point of view. Often their solutions proved to be the right ones, sometimes not. They generally made the assumption that what was good for business was good for people.

Promoting Winnipeg as a destination for prospective immigrants was a full-time occupa-

Winnipeg's street railway system boomed. In 1900, less than 3.5 million passengers were carried; in 1904 the paid fares had reached 9.5 million; in 1908, 20 million and in 1913 almost 60 million.

Rich Men in a Rich Land

In an article in the *Winnipeg Telegram* on January 29, 1910 they were identified as the city's 19 millionaires. By then, every Winnipegger was familiar with their names: J.A.M. Aikins, W.F. Alloway, J.H. Ashdown, Nicholas Bawlf, Edward Brown, J.D. Cameron, D.S. Currie, E.L. Drewery, Charles Enderton, Rev. C.W. Gordon, E.F. Hutchings, W.C. Leistikow, J.D. McArthur, Roderick McKenzie, Sir Daniel McMillan, A.M. McNichol, Alex Macdonald, A.M. Nanton, and Capt. William Robinson. They were entrepreneurs, politicians and directors of financial institutions like the Great-West Life Assurance Company and the Northern Crown Bank.

They had come from Ontario and Great Britain. Like so many of their generation seeking new opportunities in the west, they had arrived in Winnipeg in the years after 1870 as the city was starting to take shape. Most were self-made men who worked hard and took advantage of the situations presented them. Within a few decades, Winnipeg's millionaires had built commerical empires in the grain trade, real estate, finance, the retail business, or in all four. They also built palatial homes along Roslyn Road, Wellington Crescent and in Crescentwood which displayed their power and wealth to the world.

This handful of successful businessmen laid the foundations of the city and played a crucial role in Winnipeg's development in the first two decades of the 20th century. Their splendid homes, many of them still standing, serve as a reminder of "the gilded age".

The home of lumberman J.D. Cameron at 65 Roslyn Road.

The opulence of Augustus Nanton's Winnipeg home "Kilmorie" was testimony to his success.

The Propaganda War for Settlers

In the early 20th century, a vigorous tug-of-war emerged between Canada and the United States over where new American settlers should take up farming.

Numerous Canadian interests—public and private—began promoting the virtues of the "last, best West" to potential American immigrants. In 1904, however, the American Immigration Association of the Northwest was organized "for the purpose of keeping moving Americans away from Canada." And several other groups sprang up preaching the benefits of farming in the United States as opposed to Western Canada.

A meeting of Canadian landowners was organized in 1904, and held, ironically, in St. Paul, Minnesota. Delegations from Winnipeg city council, the Board of Trade and the Real Estate Exchange attended. The Western Canada Immigration Association was formed, with the goal of disseminating news about Western Canada and correcting false reports about the region.

The WCIA undertook promotional activities such as running free Western tours for American newspaper correspondents. It circulated to potential immigrants a pamphlet entitled "What Famous Correspondents Say About Western Canada", as well as the magazine *Canada West.*

Disputes arose as to the effectiveness of the WCIA. The *Manitoba Free Press* labelled its work "of invaluable benefit to this country." Less respectfully, the Commissioner of Immigration at Winnipeg countered that the WCIA was "nothing less than a big real estate concern, and they are using the public money for the purpose of assisting real estate men to sell their lands at a profit."

Despite the critical reviews of the WCIA, its work continued until 1908 when it was disbanded. Whether its efforts attracted many American settlers remains open to debate. As one authority later remarked, "propaganda... was not the basic cause of the migration across the line."

tion. In 1904, the Board of Trade and city council joined together to create the Western Canadian Immigration Association in order to attract American immigrants. The new group organized tours for U.S. journalists and advertised the benefits of Winnipeg in numerous newspapers and magazines south of the border. Many of the association's members, also landowners and businessmen, profited from rising real estate prices.

Similarly in May, 1906, the same group of individuals created the Winnipeg Development and Industrial Bureau to attract new industry and manufacturing to the city. Grants from city coffers helped advertise the city's commercial potential, declaring it to be the "Chicago of the North" and the "Bull's Eye of the Dominion". These efforts paid off: the net value of all products produced in Winnipeg increased from $8.6 million in 1901 to $35.5 million by 1911.

An important part of this campaign focused on the fact that Winnipeg by 1911 had the cheapest power rates in North America. This was the result of city council's earlier dissatisfaction with the Winnipeg Electric Company's high rates. With the support of the Roblin government, the city financed the construction of a hydro-

The Ogilvie Milling Company was one of several eastern Canadian milling interests attracted to the Prairies.

electric power plant at Pointe du Bois (80 kilometres northeast of the city). Thus was born Winnipeg Hydro, not out of any socialistic tendencies on the part of the city's elite but because it made good business sense.

It had been a similar case a few years earlier, when the provincial government expropriated Bell Telephone to establish what eventually became the Manitoba Telephone System, the first such publicly-owned utility on the continent.

After power and telephones, another crucial infrastructure problem for the growing city was the question of water supply. At the turn of the century, Winnipeggers were getting their water piped in from an artesian well and from the river (it was crudely filtered). But such a system could not keep up with the demands of the city's growing population, particularly in the immigrant neighbourhoods in the North End where there were inadequate sewer hook-ups. The terrible result was the outbreak of typhoid epidemics—"Red River Fever", as it was then called—in 1904 and 1905. In a 1905 study of 32 North American cities conducted by a University of Chicago professor, Winnipeg had a typhoid death rate of 24.85 per ten thousand people; the majority of other cities examined scored well below 10 per ten thousand.

Providing proper drinking water to all members of the community would cost a great deal of money and city council was in no rush, despite urgent pleas from public health officials. Not until 1913 were plans for a $13.5 million aqueduct from Shoal Lake, Ontario finalized. It then it took another six years for the project to be completed.

In many ways, Winnipeg in the early 1900's was still a frontier town. "The Winnipeg of my boyhood," as journalist James Gray so aptly put it, "was a lusty, gutsy, bawdy frontier boom-town roaring through an unequalled economic debauch on its way to the grand-daddy of all economic hangovers." On Main Street, not far from

Tory premier was tainted by scandal

Rodmond P. Roblin

PREMIER RODMOND P. ROBLIN'S substantial contribution to Manitoba was overshadowed by his reputation for arrogance and his government's involvement in the Legislative Building scandal of 1915.

Born in 1853 to Ontario Dutch loyalists, Roblin moved to Winnipeg with his family in

1877. He was a successful businessman in Carman and Winnipeg when he became involved in provincial politics. On his second attempt, Roblin was elected to the legislature as a Liberal in 1888.

The assembly was suitably impressed with his maiden speech advocating provincial rights and objecting to a railway deal his own party had sought. Roblin resigned from the Liberal caucus after his dispute over the rail agreement could not be resolved. He sat as an independent before joining the Conservatives and eventually succeeding

Hugh John Macdonald as premier in 1900.

Roblin used his considerable energy to deal with many issues, including the introduction of workmen's compensation legislation. But he was dubbed a reactionary because of his objection to progressive issues like women's right to vote. Also, Roblin's considerable self-assurance tended to rub people the wrong way. An observer could be forgiven for thinking his speech and manner were pompous.

His distinguishing trait, however, was his unquestioning loyalty to his party colleagues. His leadership created the Roblin "machine" and played an important role in the federal "reciprocity" election of 1911. Roblin was knighted and the federal Conservative election promise to extend Manitoba's boundaries was kept.

Soon after becoming Sir Rodmond, the premier's fortunes changed. He was among several Conservative politicians implicated in a scandal that erupted when money for construction of the new Legislative Building was misappropriated. He resigned as premier and the discredited Conservative party was defeated in the next election.

Two years after his arrest on charges of defrauding the Crown, proceedings against Roblin were dropped on the grounds of ill-heath. Even though Roblin's role in the affair will always be in doubt, historian W.L. Morton has characterized him as personally honourable, but "engulfed by the underworld of politics." Roblin died in 1937 at Hot Springs, Arkansas.

Portage and Main panorama

First Government Phone Utility in North America

It was necessary to bang the receiver on a table or yell into it to get someone to pick up the other end. But Horace McDougall, manager of the Northwest Telegraph Company in Winnipeg, was proud to be the first Manitoban to own a telephone. In 1878, shortly after the Canadian patent of Bell's invention was issued, McDougall acquired the western Canada rights to the new instrument and had his home and office connected by telephone.

There were about two dozen subscribers by the time he sold his interest to the Bell Telephone Company of Canada in 1881. That same year, Bell shipped a switchboard by Red River cart so that existing pairs of phones could be connected to one another. The first telephone wires were strung from the roof tops, not poles.

The initial practice of having boys as operators was a holdover from the telegraph days. That all changed when Miss Ida Cates became the first female operator in 1882. In addition to placing calls, she happily offered callers recipes, news, and advice. Perhaps it was because of her success that in years to come only unmarried women would serve as operators.

Bell introduced service to Portage la Prairie and Brandon in 1882. Five years later the first long distance line connected Winnipeg and Selkirk.

In 1893, the Canadian Bell patent expired and almost overnight dozens of telephone companies sprang up in Manitoba. Competition escalated to the point that rival companies began cutting down each other's telephone poles. Because of the anarchy and the continuing neglect of the needs of rural citizens, the Manitoba government refused to incorporate any more telephone companies.

In 1908, the newly-created Manitoba Government Telephones paid $3.3 million to take over the operations of Bell and thereby assumed little more than half the telephone business in the province. This action created the first government owned telephone system in North America. Between 1908 and 1912 southern Manitoba towns and cities were linked together and the number of subscribers increased from 14,000 to 40,000. It would be another nine years before Manitoba Government Telephones would be renamed the Manitoba Telephone System.

These 1907 operators would see the number of telephone subscribers triple over the next five years.

the CPR station, were lively, crowded bars and smoky poolrooms patronized by the army of single men passing through the city on their way west for seasonal farm work. Besides food and drink, many of them also desired "companionship". That too was readily available, though initially a little distance away.

Before 1907, most of Winnipeg's brothels were in the vicinity of Thomas Street (now Minto Street) past Wesley College down Portage Avenue. But as more middle-class families moved into the neighbourhood, the cry arose for action. Leading the charge against the "social evil" was Frederick B. DuVal, a Presbyterian minister and an outspoken moral reformer. One evening in November, 1903, 1,500 Winnipeggers showed up at a local downtown theatre to hear DuVal and his fellow-ministers denounce the ladies, their houses of ill-repute, and the inattentive police force.

Mayor John Arbuthnot, caught in the middle of a civic election campaign pleaded ignorance. "If this is such a great evil, why have they never complained about it before?," he asked at an election meeting. "Nobody has ever come to me about it!" It was too late for Arbuthnot. He was forced to drop out of the race, making the front-runner Thomas Sharpe, an alderman and businessman, and the candidate of choice of the DuVal group. He won the election easily.

Once in office, Sharpe ordered the city's police chief, "Big John" McRae, ("he habitually wore the peak of his cap well-down over his eyes, whose colour matched the steely gray of his moustache") to clean up Thomas Street. Not surprisingly, more aggressive police action did not rid Winnipeg of prostitu-

tion; the madams and their girls merely re-located to other parts of the city.

Two years later the police commission, unsure what to do, placed the entire matter back in the hands of Chief McRae. He opted for segregation. At what must have been one of the more memorable meetings in Winnipeg history, McRae sent for Minnie Woods, "Queen of the Harlots". After lengthy negotiations, it was decided that the new "red-light" district would be on Rachel Street (after 1914 called Annabella Street) in the Point Douglas area, a few blocks north of the CPR station. Neither Chief McRae nor Miss Woods bothered to ask the working-class residents of the area what they thought of the new arrangements.

Within days, a real estate agent named John Beaman made the rounds. He had arrived in the city prior to McRae's meeting with Minnie Woods

Winnipeg businesses actively promoted sports activities for their employees. For example, in 1910 the T. Eaton Company built a ten-acre athletic ground, Eaton Park, where their employees could participate in basketball, tennis, track and field, baseball, cricket and soccer.

There was no shortage of places to purchase liquor in Winnipeg, as evidenced by this well-stocked Hudson's Bay Company store. Its rival retailer Eaton's (owned by a Methodist) did not sell alcohol or even tobacco.

and purchased most of the houses on Rachel and McFarlane Street for under $3,000 each. He then sold them to the madams for $7,000 or more. Madam Lila Anderson paid Beaman $12,000 for a duplex on McFarlane, probably six times what the house was actually worth. It was later revealed at an inquiry that Beaman had bought 22 houses and made a profit of more than $70,000. Reports suggested he was a not-so-distant relative of Chief McRae.

In any event, business was booming on Rachel Street. Most of the houses had bright porch lights (not actually red) and large address numbers. The other Point Douglas residents, however, were not happy. During the hot summer months, prostitutes and their customers were not very discreet; blinds were rarely drawn and sometimes activities took place right in the backyards. McRae tried to keep things under control, but to no avail.

"By the summer of 1910," wrote James Gray in *Red Lights on the Prairies,* "the Winnipeg red-light district had degenerated into a massive orgiastic obscenity." Gray relates one story about three men who, believing a house on Higgins Avenue was a brothel, entered, put their money on the kitchen table, and began to take their clothes off. They were mistaken. The poor woman living there (and having her breakfast) fled her home in terror.

Matters came to a head with the visit to the city of Rev. J.G. Shearer, the secretary of the national Moral and Social Reform League. In an interview published in the *Toronto Globe* headlined as SOCIAL EVIL RUNS RIOT IN WINNIPEG, Shearer denounced Winnipeg as having the "rottenest conditions of things... to be found in any city in Canada." The blame for this depravity, in the reverend's opinion, lay entirely with the police and city officials.

Embarrassed city councillors quickly appointed Justice J.A. Robson to investigate the prostitution issue. By chance, Shearer's visit coincided with beginning of a civic election campaign. The incumbent, Mayor Sanford Evans, a leading member of the elite and owner of the *Winnipeg Telegram,* was forced to defend the

> **"For here the whole stream of immigration from Europe is precipitated daily. English, Irish, Scotch, Upper Canadians, French-Canadians, Icelanders, Galicians, Hungarians, Mennonites, Doukhobors, Norwegians, Italians, all jostle one another on the wooden platform and mingle their various tongues and brogues, and the costumes of their various countries."**
>
> **A description of the Winnipeg CPR station in 1902**

In March 1904, several of the city's early auto enthusiasts organized the Winnipeg Automobile Club, forerunner of the Manitoba Motor League. The Club sponsored auto races, cross country runs and social affairs. The first race, held in 1904, ran from the Clarendon Hotel to Stonewall and back. Winner J.K. McCulloch covered the route in one hour and 40 minutes.

Ed McKeown and the "less respectable" sports of early Winnipeg

WHILE MOST RESPECTABLE Winnipeggers at the turn of the century enjoyed conventional sports such as cricket, curling or tennis, there were also many citizens intrigued by more lurid offerings such as blood sports and gambling.

The middle and upper classes would watch a decorous display of cricket, then adjourn to a club room or a hotel ballroom to drink tea. They spoke in hushed tones and enjoyed the company of "polite" ladies. At the same time, another group of lesser known Winnipeggers, especially bachelors, was taking part in dog fights, cock fights, boxing matches and big money card games. After these competitions they drank beer and the women they consorted with would not be described as "polite".

In most years between Confederation and World War I, Winnipeg contained a larger number of males than females, and a high percentage of the males were between 20 and 45 years old. This meant that a bachelor subculture existed in the city. It featured and even celebrated heavy drinking, lust, violence and disreputable sports.

Cock Fighting, Boxing & Poker

Ed McKeown, a former Ontarian, was an important member of this subculture. He came to Winnipeg in the 1880's and, with the exception of a few years around the turn of the century when he joined the Yukon Gold Rush, he lived in Winnipeg until his death, about 1916. When he first came to the city he ran a general store, but soon he was convicted of selling liquor without a licence. McKeown was variously a bouncer, a pawn broker and a manager of one of the many music halls located on Main Street between Higgins and Portage Avenues.

McKeown could be a friendly fellow in a backslapping, "let's-have-a-drink" way. He could also be ornery. He was arrested several times for taking part in barroom brawls. Once he was nearly charged with attempted murder. He had heaved a bottle at the manager of a lunch counter because he believed that he deserved quicker service.

McKeown was an important participant in and organizer of the "less respectable" sporting activities of Winnipeggers. He played a lot of dice, cards and pool. He wagered heavily on foot races and boxing matches. A boxer himself, he was one of several pugilists who called himself "the heavyweight champion of Canada". He also arranged most of the dog fights and cock fights that occurred periodically on the outskirts of the city.

The blood sports associated with McKeown and his bachelor friends certainly did not disappear after World War I. But they became much less prominent. One reason was prohibition, which was enforced throughout Manitoba from 1916 until 1923. A second reason was that, after World War I, the influence of families became more significant. Winnipeg was no longer the rough and tumble "frontier" city it had once been.

Many Winnipeggers preferred more lurid sporting activities such as poker and cock fighting to respectable sports such as curling and golf.

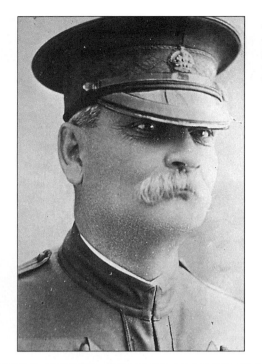

"Big John" McRae, the Winnipeg police chief who favoured controlled prostitution.

By 1912, the Winnipeg Police Department had a small but impressive motorcycle corps.

Hookers prospered in turn of the century Winnipeg

Wickedest City in the Dominion

PERHAPS IT WAS THE SO-CALLED Queen of Harlots who ignited the controversy. Perhaps it was the designation of Winnipeg as the "wickedest city in Canada". Or perhaps it was the rumoured naked women on horseback who finally forced city leaders to admit that Winnipeg's prostitution problem had gotten out of hand.

Young unattached men made up the majority of the first waves of immigration to the fledgling city; in 1911, there were 43,000 single men to 32,000 women. That same year, bars, poolrooms and brothels outnumbered churches six to one.

Prostitution became a growth industry in Winnipeg; a profession that, while illegal, was quietly condoned by the city fathers. In 1883, the brothels were isolated on Thomas Street. For a time, the whorehouses existed in relative isolation, segregated from polite society. Despite the location, they prospered, with as many as 100 women finding not-so-gainful employment. As the city grew, it encroached

upon Thomas Street and homeowners began to object to the noise and revelry. The protesters found an ally with Reverend Frederick Du Val, a fire and brimstone reformer determined to close down the brothels.

In 1903, Du Val launched a campaign that pitted him against the mayor, John Arbuthnot, and Police Chief John McRae. Both men believed segregated prostitution was an effective means of coping with an inevitable problem. The issue came to a head during that year's mayoral campaign. Arbuthnot eventually withdrew from the race, replaced in the mayor's seat by Thomas Sharpe. Prostitution continued to offend the public morality, so the police raided Thomas Street, forcing the prostitutes to other locations. Chief McRae eventually decided that another segregated location would make his job easier. After consultation with madam Minnie Woods, also known as the Queen of Harlots, an area in Point Douglas was selected.

Women quickly bought up the

houses in the area, usually at vastly inflated prices. By July, 1909 two streets in the area had been turned into brothel districts. The neighbourhood became a popular destination for a Sunday stroll, with gawkers staring at the women and their wares. Business boomed. Protests began, and reached the ears of Reverend J.G. Shearer, national secretary of the Temperance and Moral Reform Council. In an interview with the *Toronto Globe* he claimed of Winnipeg: "They have the rottenest condition of things in Winnipeg in connection with the question of social vice to be found in any city in Canada."

A Royal Commission was promptly appointed to investigate and to clear the city's good name. Prostitutes, police and politicians testified. One man claimed to have seen women riding naked on horseback through the area. Police enforcement became a reality and the district slowly began to shrivel. Minnie Woods, however, had a 30-year run as a madam in the city.

city's policies while his challenger, E.D. Martin, a leading moral reformer, attempted to exploit the issue. Yet when the votes were counted, Evans was re-elected by a vote of 7,250 to 5,660. Winnipeg's "good name" had been saved. Of course, many of the disgruntled (and poor) Point Douglas residents could not vote since they did not meet the rather stiff electoral property qualifications.

Almost a month later, Judge Robson's report more or less vindicated Winnipeg city council and Chief McRae. In the judge's view, Winnipeg was certainly not "the rottenest city in the Dominion", though Robson did find that the trade in both women and liquor had gotten out of hand. There was, however, no obvious evidence of corruption between the police and prostitutes.

The way in which city hall regarded the prostitution problems of Point Douglas symbolized its general disdain for the famed North End. As the gateway to the west, Winnipeg became the gathering place for the hundreds of thousands of East European immigrants arriving in Canada. This was in large part due to the open immigration policy of Clifford Sifton, the Minister of the Interior in the Laurier government. Sifton, who doubled as the owner of the *Manitoba Free Press,* wanted to populate the Prairies with "stalwart peasants in sheep-skin coats". He didn't care which corner of the globe they came from, only that they should be prepared to work hard on their new farms.

But once they arrived in Winnipeg, many of them stayed in the city. In 1901, Jewish, Polish, Ukrainian, Russian and Chinese immigrants only accounted for 4.3 per cent of the city's population; by 1911 this figure had increased to nearly 14 per cent. The Dominion Immigration Hall, close by the CPR station, was the immigrants' first stop, a government centre which could not handle such a large number of people. Winnipeg's elite did not view the care of immigrants as its problem and federal authorities were slow to act. Consequently, unsanitary and crowded conditions were the norm at the hall.

Those who remained in Winnipeg tended to congregate among people who spoke the same language and practised the same customs. Thus during the first decade of the century, the city was

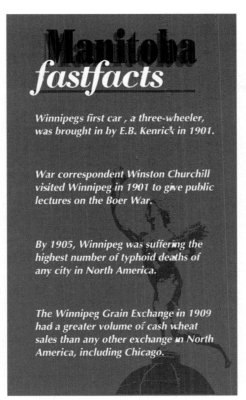

Manitoba fastfacts

Winnipegs first car , a three-wheeler, was brought in by E.B. Kenrick in 1901.

War correspondent Winston Churchill visited Winnipeg in 1901 to give public lectures on the Boer War.

By 1905, Winnipeg was suffering the highest number of typhoid deaths of any city in North America.

The Winnipeg Grain Exchange in 1909 had a greater volume of cash wheat sales than any other exchange in North America, including Chicago.

transformed into "a series of self-contained enclaves". English, Scottish, and Irish immigrants, most of whom worked for the railways, settled near the rail yards and shops in the Weston area and in Fort Rouge; while Scandinavians resided not far from the downtown around Sargent Avenue and Sherbrook Street.

It was, however, the East Europeans—Jews, Ukrainians and Poles—who were most visible. They congregated into the North End, living in overcrowded and poorly constructed tenement houses, cut off from the rest of the city by the massive CPR rail yards (street car service from the North End to the downtown via a subway at Higgins Avenue and Main Street did not commence until 1908). Although many of the British working-class also lived in the North End, the area around Selkirk Avenue—"The Foreign Quarter" or "New Jerusalem", as it was often called—was a world set apart; a world of different smells, food, and culture. Selkirk Avenue emerged as the main business district, a smaller version of New York's Lower East Side where Jewish mer-

Many ethnic groups established their own cultural and political organizations upon becoming established in Winnipeg. For example, the Chinese community organized the Chee Kung Tong (Chinese Freemasons), the Kuomintong (Chinese National League) and the Winnipeg Chinese Masonic Lodge. The Kuomintong worked towards the improvement of social conditions and tried to protect its members "against the wiles of gambling, opium smoking and other vices."

Winnipeg has had professional fire fighters since 1882. Before the advent of motorized equipment in 1913, they relied on horses to take them to all too frequent calls.

"New Jerusalem" or the "Foreign Quarter" was home to thousands of recent immigrants. Less than half their homes were connected to the city's water or sewer systems.

> **"A more congenial place for the breeding of the typhoid germ cannot well be imagined. Should this mass of filth be polluted by the stools or urine of a typhoid patient, a conveyance of the infection to the closely crowded houses, only a few feet away, must be considered as a certainty... it was aptly compared... to that which must have obtained in an European Village of the Middle Ages."**
>
> **A 1904 Board of Health report**

chants sold their goods, often on credit, as they had in the old country.

Fleeing persecution and poverty, these immigrants sought a better life for themselves and their children. The first years in Winnipeg, however, were difficult. Forced to accept unskilled low-paying jobs as construction workers or labourers for the railways, they had little choice but to live in slum housing. Adding to their discomfort were unpaved streets, an inadequate sewage system and a shortage of potable water.

In 1906, a group of ladies from the Winnipeg Ministerial Association visited a Jewish home in "New Jerusalem" and filed the following report: "Forty-five families inhabited a very small space, living in a manner that was to say the least disgraceful. Diseases of all kinds were common... It was just the spot for a plague to begin and sweep over the city, and it was a providence that such had not occurred." City health inspec-

tors discovered similar deplorable living arrangements. "A house of ten rooms was found occupied by five families," noted one inspector in 1913, "Three of the families had only one room each... There was one water closet, one sink, a bath, and a wash basin."

A few caring Winnipeggers, appalled by what they found in the North End, did something about it. Margaret Scott established a mission house in 1904 to help the destitute with food, shelter and clothing. The All People's Mission, a Methodist house started by Dollie McGuire in 1889, also reached many needy people, especially after Rev. J.S. Woodsworth was appointed its head in 1907.

Woodsworth, born in Ontario but raised in Manitoba, had witnessed the terrible conditions in the slums of London, England and was imbued thereafter with a "Christian humanitarianism". As a leader of the social gospel movement, his main objective was to establish the "Kingdom of God" on earth. He wasn't about to stand idly by while immigrant children went hungry. "God pity us," he said in 1909. "We call this a Christian land. We are complacent and self-satisfied and within a few blocks of us hundreds are enduring the most shocking misery." Soon Woodsworth and his family lived at one of the North End mission homes, setting up language classes, summer camps, job training, and assistance for young mothers.

Like many of his contemporaries, however, Woodsworth believed that the proper course for the immigrant was assimilation as a British, English-speaking Protestant. In one of his books, *Strangers Within Our Gates*, he categorized immigrant groups in Winnipeg according to their potential for successful assimilation. Hence, immigrants from Britain and Northern Europe were regarded as most desirable, while those from the east and south were, as he observed, of a "distinctly lower grade". Asian immigrants or "Orientals", in his opinion, were beyond hope.

Prejudice, discrimination and anti-Semitism were, in fact, quite common in Winnipeg during this era and for many years after. Clubs and neighbourhoods were restricted. The commercial elite tolerated immigrants—they employed them and conducted business with them—but socializing with them was out of the question. It is notable that at the Winnipeg Grain Exchange, Charles Goldstein (a broker

All People's Mission ran two kindergartens, including this one at a Maple Street church.

Crime was evident amongst all age groups in Winnipeg. Here are two youths arrested for murder and their captors.

83

European Jews helped define Winnipeg's North End
New Jerusalem

JOSEPH WILDER WAS ONLY EIGHT years old when he made the journey to Winnipeg from the town of Ploesti in Rumania. Accompanied by his parents and siblings, he travelled first to Bucharest, then to Rotterdam in Holland, and finally by ship to New York. After a long train ride via Montreal, he arrived in Winnipeg in 1904.

"Our first sight was of a mass of people behind a fence, straining to see the newly arrived immigrants," he remembered many years later. "Father walked to a vacant space and we followed. Mother, steadfast throughout the entire trip, gave way to tears. Father, hands held tightly together, tears running down his beard, recited a prayer, giving thanks to the Lord of the Universe, 'who has kept us in life, and has preserved us, and enabled us to reach this moment.'"

The Wilders, like so many Jewish immigrants fleeing persecution in Eastern Europe and Russia, found the new life they were searching for in the North End of Winnipeg. There was already a small Jewish population— about 1,100 people in 1901—which increased dramatically to 9,000 by 1911. By 1931, Jews were the second largest non-British ethnic group in the city.

A few established Anglo- and German-Jewish families had immigrated before the turn of the century and tended to live in the more upscale neighbourhoods in the south end of the city. But the vast majority of later arrivals resided around Selkirk Avenue in the North End. Here they transplanted the world of the *shtetl*—the small Russian villages where they had been born—to the streets of North End Winnipeg. It was their "New Jerusalem", the place where they could open their shops, ensure the education of their children, and practise their religion in relative peace.

To outsiders, they were all "Hebrews"; in fact, they were representative of all classes and ideological orientations. Many were fervently religious, other less so. There were Zionists, socialists, and liberals among them. Each particular segment organized their own groups and institutions: mutual aid societies, schools, and political associations. By 1914, the North End had as rich and diverse a Jewish culture as anywhere in North America.

Overseeing much of the community life was Rabbi Israel Kahanovitch who was brought to the city in 1907 from the United States where he had immigrated a year earlier. A pious man, Kahanovitch became the Chief Rabbi of Western Canada and the city's most prominent Jewish leader for the next 30 years. Most notably, he was instrumental in establishing the Talmud Torah or Winnipeg Hebrew School in 1907 in a building on the corner of Dufferin Avenue and Aikins Street. Five years later, a larger school was built a few blocks north at Flora Avenue and Charles Street which became an important educational and social center for the community.

For Jews of all walks of life, but especially those from the growing working-class, Yiddish, the German-Hebrew dialect of the masses, played an important part in the North End. It was the language of commerce, politics, literature, and at several schools, education. Along with two English language Jewish newspapers, there was a Yiddish press and the famous Queen Theatre on Selkirk Avenue where Yiddish plays—including the Jewish *Hamlet*—were performed to sold-out audiences.

North End shoppers were drawn to locations such as this farmer's market.

The stereotype Jewish pedlar or rag picker was the exception rather than the rule in Winnipeg. Though some Jews did peddle rags and bottles, many more established successful businesses and entered a wide variety of professions. A 1912 feature article in the *Manitoba Free Press* expressed surprise at the large number

Leopold Meltzer, centre, in front of his Selkirk Avenue furniture store, circa 1902.

of Jewish lawyers, druggists, doctors and architects in the community.

The city's vibrant garment industry boasted both Jewish owners and workers. Indeed, following the failed Russian Revolution of 1905 and a new influx of working-class immigrants, a strong labour movement developed in the community. During the General Strike of 1919, there were Jews on both sides of the confrontation.

By the 1920's, Winnipeg Jews had established themselves and generally lived comfortable lives. Some of the more prosperous members of the community were moving further north into new middle-class neighbourhoods. Still, anti-Semitism was prevalent in Winnipeg. Though other East European immigrants liked dealing with Jewish merchants because they were allowed to buy goods on credit, old world animosities would sometimes surface. And among Winnipeg's British majority, Jews were especially not welcome. In 1928, the University of Manitoba medical school instituted a quota system for Jews and other minorities; social clubs and property at Manitoba beaches were restricted well into the 1950's.

Despite the hardships and the discrimination, most of the Jews of Winnipeg's North End succeeded in their new home. In his 1909 book *Strangers Within Our Gates*, J.S. Woodsworth marvelled at the power of Jews to survive against all odds. Politicians like John Blumberg, Joe Zuken, and A.A. Heaps (a Member of Parliament) contributed much to the life of the city. Many writers and artists went on to great success. Others, like Joseph Wilder who went on to become a pharmacist, a writer and a Canadian army veteran, left a lasting legacy for their families and community.

The Evil Eye shop was owned by L. Abremovich. The name was derived from an old Jewish belief that some people could harm others with an evil glance, and the name may have been chosen as an attempt to ward off bad luck.

Margaret Scott Nursing Mission

Although Winnipeg in the early 1900's was touted as the "Chicago of the North" and the "Gateway to the West", it was not immune to poverty and suffering. For humanitarian reasons and sometimes to assuage guilty Christian consciences, a series of private agencies tried to exorcise some of the more obvious evils. One such charity was the Margaret Scott Nursing Mission.

From 1898 to 1904, Margaret Scott undertook private charitable work, taking food and clothing to destitute individuals she encountered while attending police court. She was also concerned about their health, although she was not a nurse. Scott made the health conditions of the needy known to the Winnipeg Health Department and to local doctors.

In 1904 those inspired by Scott's work called a meeting that attracted dozens of concerned Winnipeggers. They created an interdenominational mission (named after Margaret Scott) to provide nursing care to the needy, to give them training in proper hygiene and to "raise their moral tone to all that is highest and best".

The mission's religious overtones did not interfere with its charitable work. Bedside nursing was undertaken, with the number of visits rising from 7,000 in 1905 to 28,830 by 1913. Scott was also instrumental in having "district nursing" added to the nurses' training program at the Winnipeg General Hospital. The hospital provided nursing trainees to the mission and the curriculum change soon supplied the city with trained district nurses.

The effects of the waves of immigration were felt in Manitoba classrooms. One Winnipeg teacher found herself faced in 1905 with a class of 56 children, ranging in age from six to 14. Often recent immigrants were placed in the lower grades until they had acquired enough language skills to move on.

employed by the Bruce McBean Company) was the first Jew to be admitted as a member in 1907.

Typical of the majority's Anglo-Saxon attitude was this reaction of Manitoba journalist George Chipman: "The morality of the immigrant from continental Europe is thrown into sharp relief in the courts of justice," he wrote in a 1909 *Canadian Magazine* article. "They have not the Canadian regard for life, liberty and sanitary surroundings, and have to be regulated accordingly." His description of a Galician wedding noted that such social occasions are "a calamity... These weddings too often mean a carouse ending in a fight and frequently murder."

Chipman, Woodsworth, and other community leaders like *Manitoba Free Press* editor John Wesley Dafoe hoped that the so-called immigrant

problem could be solved by the schools where the "Canadianizing" process could be successfully completed. But there were some major obstacles. In the North End, there were not enough schools nor was there as yet a compulsory school law. It was estimated that in 1911, about 10,000 North End children between the ages of 6 to 16 were not enrolled in schools.

For teachers and educators like W.J. Sisler, daily life in North End classrooms at Strathcona (where Sisler was principal) and King Edward schools was extremely demanding. Their pupils with strange, foreign names did not speak English and parents insisted on preserving old world customs. "Imagine a young teacher facing fifty or more pupils who couldn't understand her... [and] each other!" reflected one former North End educator. "There might be twenty different languages spoken in the class." In many cases, such as with Jewish immigrants, private evening (and then day) Hebrew schools were established, making the kind of assimilation Chipman and Woodsworth had in mind difficult.

Even worse, in their view, was the fact that the Manitoba Public School Act, following the Laurier-Greenway compromise of 1897, permitted

Charming Vista, Assiniboine Park, Winnipeg, Man.

bilingual schools if enough parents requested them. This provision was intended to placate French-Catholic Manitobans and Catholic Quebec (after the public education system had been

The St. Andrew's Locks, which eased access from the Red River into Lake Winnipeg, opened May 4, 1910. Many wanted to use the water-way to exploit passenger and freight traffic, as well as the area's natural resources. However, by the time the locks opened, roads and railways made the project redundant.

Assiniboine Park

Residents of a booming Winnipeg needed "breathing places", spots to get away from the hustle and bustle of a fast-growing city, if only for a few hours. And so was born one of the city's most popular outdoor recreational facilities—Assiniboine Park.

The need for a "large suburban or outside park, as a means of enjoyment and recreation" was recognized by the Winnipeg Public Parks Board as early as 1893. However, it was not until 1904 that 283 acres of forest and prairie along the south side of the Assiniboine River west of Winnipeg were purchased for the creation of Assiniboine Park. The acquisition of native animals also began, with a zoo added to the park's north-west section.

The English Landscape Style design of Frederick G. Todd, a Montreal architect, was approved by the Parks Board in 1905. A flurry of activity followed, as roadways, path systems, sports facilities, buildings and landscaping were completed by 1914. An emphasis was placed on the importance of horticulture and flower gardens, and 1,972 shrubs and 1,920 perennials were planted in the Formal Garden.

Another popular feature of the park was the Pavilion, designed by Winnipeg architect J.D. Atchison, and completed in 1908 at a cost of $19,000. The Pavilion quickly became the heart of the social life of the park, as well as for many social functions of the city.

But it was not just the city's socialites who benefited by the presence of the park. As the century progressed and the working week was reduced, Assiniboine Park became a place of refuge for all city residents, regardless of class or ethnicity—a peaceful enclave in an otherwise sometimes harsh urban centre.

Three Winnipeg dailies battled each other for scoops and readers

Newspaper Row

The Telegram Building at 244 McDermot Avenue housed one of three daily newspapers on that block vying for the public's readership. The others were the *Manitoba Free Press* and the *Winnipeg Tribune.*

THREE BRASH DAILIES, ALL ON THE same avenue, clawed at each other for newspaper supremacy during Winnipeg's boom-time at the dawn of the century.

The city's population increased nearly ten-fold in the decades on either side of 1900. By 1904, new construction in Winnipeg outstripped even New York City. The rowdiest, fastest-growing city west of Chicago was filled with drifters, drunks and con-artists, many in the boiled shirts of successful businessmen and grain speculators. Winnipeggers were hungry for news and the press barons of "newspaper row" on McDermot Avenue were hungry for a share of their advertising dollars.

The Tory-blue *Winnipeg Telegram* and anti-CPR *Winnipeg Tribune* sniped at each other but reserved their big guns for the hated Liberal paper and "journalistic thug"—the *Manitoba Free Press*. The *Free Press* (renamed *Winnipeg Free Press* in 1931) was owned by Liberal Clifford Sifton, edited by John Wesley Dafoe, and had the biggest circulation in the community.

The three dailies situated themselves within spitting distance of each other on McDermot Avenue's newspaper row, and all followed in the American newspaper tradition of fighting to

An interior view of the busy newsroom of the *Winnipeg Telegram.* The paper was owned and edited by Winnipeg mayor W. Sanford Evans.

The two-storey Winnipeg Public Library opened on October 11, 1905. The original cost was $100,000, of which three-fourths was met by a grant from the Carnegie Foundation.

changed in 1890), but waves of new Eastern European immigrants complicated the issue.

At least that's what John W. Dafoe thought. In a series of articles in 1907, the *Free Press* editor exposed that "some thirteen different languages were being used in the provincial schools as languages of instruction". Several years later, in the *Winnipeg Tribune,* a Ukrainian teachers' association was declared to be "subversive and destruc-

tive of Canadian citizenship and nationality". This issue was not resolved until 1916 when the new Liberal government of T.C. Norris passed a compulsory attendance act and made English the only language of instruction.

Living and working alongside the "foreigners" were many skilled British tradesmen, who had

be first with local exclusives or "scoops". The world of the newspaperman in search of a scoop was a series of convulsive actions, sudden, unanticipated and disconnected. News was often what a publisher or editor decided it was, with political or personal vendettas at the base of many stories.

Each of the three dailies enjoyed its share of characters posing as "hacks". One *Tribune* writer was Chief Buffalo Child Long Lance, "as great an impostor as Grey Owl and far better looking" who was later run out of Calgary for threatening to blow up the mayor with a home-made bomb. The *Telegram* featured Kentucky-born Col. Garnet Clay Porter, as hard a drinker and as skilful a poker player as he was writer and editor.

In the summer of 1907, the three papers joined to protest the monopoly of Canadian Pacific Telegraphs which sold wire stories (mostly U.S. news and not much from the rest of Canada) and founded their own system of national and international correspondents under the Western Associated Press, forerunner of the Canadian Press.

Winnipeg's "newspaper row" disappeared when, one by one, the newspapers either folded or moved on to larger premises elsewhere in the downtown.

Winnipeg's garment industry produced clothing on both a mass market and a made-to-order basis.

also left the old country in search of a better life. Their earlier working experiences in industrial England had taught them to be wary of management. Along with their other baggage, they brought with them a devotion to the principles of trade unionism and labour politics. They organized trade councils, dabbled in socialism and Marxist philosophy, and published newspapers like *The Voice* that rallied supporters. Indeed, these years in the early part of the 20th century witnessed the slow but steady emergence of a working-class consciousness from Winnipeg labourers of all enthnic backgrounds, later so evident during the 1919 General Strike.

In no sense were the city's first labour leaders radical, however. Arthur Puttee, a printer and one of the founders of *The Voice,* saw himself more like a British Labourite than a Marxist; he wanted to change the system from within, not destroy it. In 1900, Puttee won a federal by-election in North Winnipeg to become the first labour member of the House of Commons. He won the seat again later in the year during the general

Tumultuous strikes were not uncommon in Winnipeg. Winnipeg Electric Street Railway Company workers struck violently in March, 1906 over the right to unionization. At one point, Mayor Thomas Sharpe called in the militia to quell a crowd of 12,000 demonstrators.

The Canadian National Railway's Fort Garry Hotel opened December 10, 1913, one of a series of luxury hotels operated by the company across Canada. Here workers are finishing the roof's copper sheathing.

The city's commercial class did not want to hear about unions, collective bargaining, or a "living wage". Earlier generations of workers had accepted their miserable fate, but by the turn of the century matters were changing. Starting in 1900, Winnipeg's growing working-class began demanding better wages, conditions, and respect—and they

The skyscraper was introduced to the Prairies in 1904 with the construction of the Union Bank at 504 Main Street. One of Winnipeg's first steel framed buildings, the 11-storey skyscraper was erected by the Shankland firm of Chicago at a cost of $350,000.

Winnipeg was an important banking centre during the early 1900's. For example, two city businessmen established a private bank (Alloway and Champion) in 1905, which became the largest private banking business ever known in Canada. It sold out to the Canadian Imperial Bank of Commerce in 1911.

election, but was defeated in 1904 when divisions in his own party undermined his political aspirations.

Labour laws in Winnipeg, like the rest of North America, were archaic. Often adults were forced to work 12 hours a day, six days a week for little pay. Even in 1913, children were still allowed to work 72 hours a week. For businessmen, labour was a commodity to be exploited to its fullest potential as a way to maximize profits.

backed up these demands with strikes if necessary.

Local tailors struck for 16 weeks in 1900 and railway workers followed in 1901 and 1902. Labour generally lost these early confrontations, though there were signs of a developing working-class solidarity. In 1900, at a lacrosse game at Fort Garry Park, union printer J. Sheppard refused to tend goal if his teammate Joseph Armstrong, a tailor who was "scabbing", was allowed to play.

The most serious and violent strike of the

decade occurred in 1906. The powerful owners and managers of the Winnipeg Electric Street Railway Company had never recognized their employees' right to a union and were determined to weed out the association's leaders. After several union leaders were dismissed for allegedly "insulting" company officials, negotiations between the two sides broke down. The men walked off their jobs on March 29 and within days the company made a tense situation worse by employing private police shipped in from the United States.

After public demonstrations (both in support of and against the strikers) got out of hand, Mayor Thomas Sharpe called in the militia from the Fort Osborne barracks. On March 30, as crowds on Main Street gathered, the mayor read the riot act and the soldiers arrived with bayonets at the ready and a loaded Lewis machine gun. The crowd quickly dispersed. The strike ended about a week later, with many of the workers' demands— including better wages and a ten-hour work day—having been met, except one: recognition of their union.

This volatile strike set the tone for the rest of the year. Less than a month later, machinists, moulders, and blacksmiths at the Vulcan Ironworks walked off their jobs and management took a very tough line. The company went to court to prevent the strikers from picketing near the plant and hired as many strikebreakers as they could find. The strike was broken in a matter of weeks, the union crushed.

As historian David Bercuson observed, Winnipeg labour leaders learned several important lessons from the events of 1906. Not only did they learn that management was going to fight to the bitter end to maintain the status quo, they also realized that "local government would almost automatically make common cause with business in a showdown with organized labour". With the city's glorious future at stake, the commercial class was not about to stand by while labour destroyed Winnipeg's economic potential. "This did not mean," noted Bercuson, "that a concerted campaign against trade unions was about to be launched, only that if labour challenged any of the essential components of the municipal-industrial relationship, it would draw upon itself the wrath of both."

There was one other group in Winnipeg, like labour, which was beginning to question its role in society, though it did so more quietly. Since the early 1890's, upper- and middle-class Canadian women had become much more visible. Though it would take another decade or so for real success, such Winnipeg women as E. Cora Hind, the dynamic agricultural editor of the *Manitoba Free Press* (and the only woman allowed on the floor of the Grain Exchange until World War II), journalists Catherine Simpson-Hays and Francis Marion Beynon, and Nellie McClung were already making their mark. As a sign of things to come, McClung, a teacher and writer, who had immigrated to Manitoba with her family from Ontario in 1880, founded the Winnipeg Political Equality League in 1912. This would be the organization that would lead the successful fight for the vote finally achieved in 1916.

Winnipeg in 1912 was a city with tremendous promise. It was the most important urban center in the West from which a vast hinterland was controlled and dominated by railways, grain merchants and industrialists. Since 1900, population growth had been as astounding as the construction boom. All roads did indeed lead to Winnipeg, as Chicago reporter William E. Curtis suggested. The boosterism and promotion, so much a part of the civic politics in Winnipeg for more than a decade, seemed to have succeeded brilliantly.

Or had it? In the years before World War I, Winnipeg, to quote historian Alan Artibise, "was very much a city divided; divided into areas of work and residence, rich and poor, Anglo-Saxon and foreigner". These divisions were also the legacy of the commercial elite's singular and narrow vision. As the real estate market collapsed in 1913 and the economy faltered, the citizens of Winnipeg were about to face some of their greatest challenges. It remained to be seen whether they could unite and confront this adversity together. ❦

Winnipeg's streetcars did not operate on Sundays until 1906, out of respect for the Sabbath. During the debate over allowing Sunday streetcars, the Manitoba Free Press opined that Sunday service "had become a humanitarian necessity in this city of magnificent distances..."

> "The only people who count are the English. Their fathers got all the best jobs. They're the only ones nobody ever calls foreigners. Nobody ever makes fun of their names or calls them bologny-eaters, or laughs at the way they dress or talk. Nobody, cause when you're English it's the same as bein' Canadian."

An Hungarian immigrant character in John Martyn's *Under the Ribs of Death*

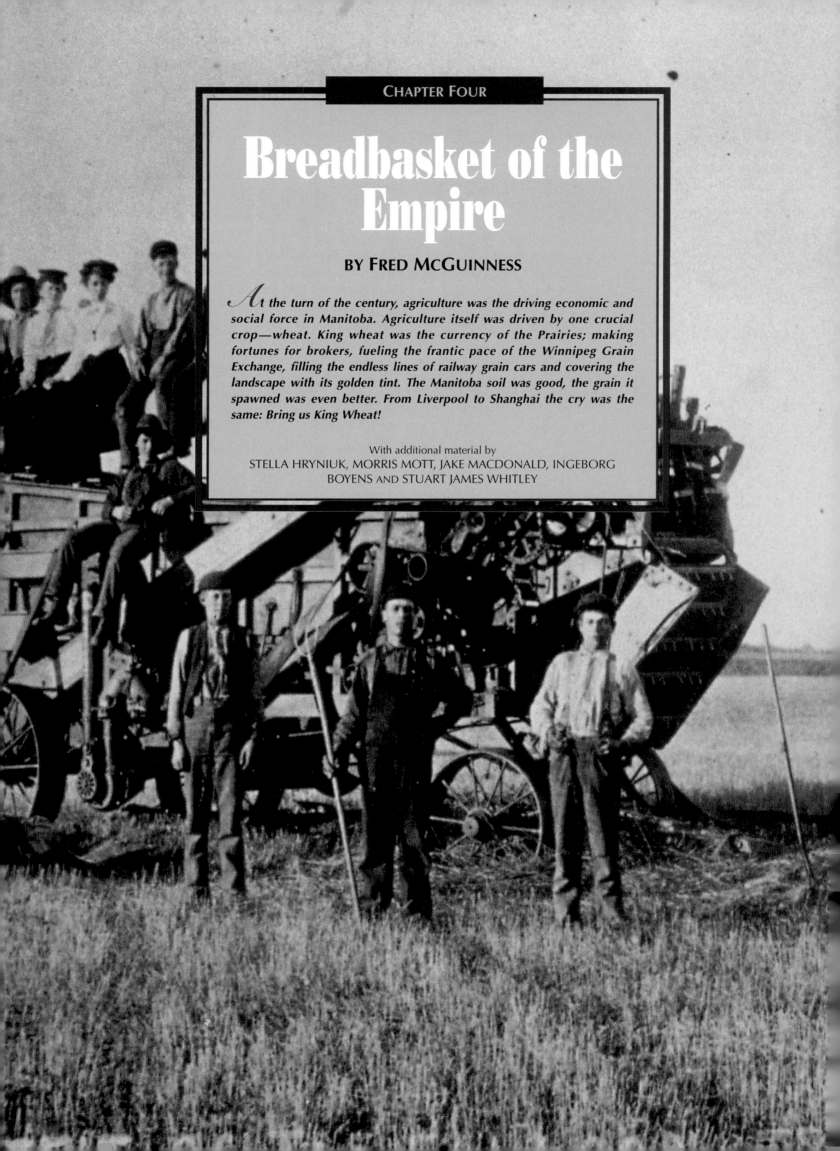

CHAPTER FOUR

Breadbasket of the Empire

BY FRED McGUINNESS

*A*t the turn of the century, agriculture was the driving economic and social force in Manitoba. Agriculture itself was driven by one crucial crop—wheat. King wheat was the currency of the Prairies; making fortunes for brokers, fueling the frantic pace of the Winnipeg Grain Exchange, filling the endless lines of railway grain cars and covering the landscape with its golden tint. The Manitoba soil was good, the grain it spawned was even better. From Liverpool to Shanghai the cry was the same: Bring us King Wheat!

With additional material by
STELLA HRYNIUK, MORRIS MOTT, JAKE MACDONALD, INGEBORG
BOYENS AND STUART JAMES WHITLEY

**Field
Irrigation, by
Charles W. Simpson**

King wheat and the rise
of rural Manitoba

Breadbasket of the Empire

When Manitoba welcomed the 20th century, its population stood at 255,000. The great bulk of this number was English-speaking and felt a strong allegiance to Great Britain or what was known then simply as "The Old Country". The three significant minority groups were the French, the Icelanders, and the Mennonites. The next wave of mainly Eastern European immigration, vigorously encouraged by Brandon MP and Interior Minister Clifford Sifton, was just beginning to be felt.

The majority of Manitobans, whether British or not, made their living from agriculture. As an industry, and also as an accepted way of life, farming was paramount. Coincidentally, the weather at the turn of the century was co-operative. Each new crop report was more promising. In the first year of the new century, 2,011,835 acres were sown to grain and they yielded 50,502,085 bushels.

The most important crop was wheat. The immensity of the Canadian (and Manitoban) debt to "king wheat" cannot be measured. Those golden kernels turned an agricultural frontier into a prosperous society; they fed so many millions around the globe that the Prairies became known as the "Breadbasket of the Empire". They made it possible for the Manitoba economy to shift quickly and painlessly from the fur trade to agriculture.

Wheat established its own literature, its own myths and fables. When John Macoun, Canada's most eminent field naturalist of that period, toured the agricultural frontier, he wrote a book detailing some of the crops being grown by the pioneers: turnips and carrots weighing 25 pounds, cabbages weighing 49 pounds, and wheat yielding 55 bushels to the acre. Those vegetable measures may have been fanciful, but there were indeed years in which wheat "hit 55" and the resulting prosperity was felt in every home.

Macoun was not the only one to boast of the agricultural potential in early Manitoba. Would-be settlers in the western United States were encouraged to migrate northward by hyperbolic land agents who claimed: "You can leave home after Easter, sow your wheat and take in the harvest and come home with your pockets full of money in time for Thanksgiving."

Wheat was more than just the backbone of the Manitoba economy; it set the rules of commerce. Insurance companies like Wawanesa Mutual scheduled premium payments for the first day of November, on the grounds that the harvest cash would be fresh in farmers' pockets by that time. Farm children were sometimes named Garnet and Marquis in honor of the type of grain that helped to lift the homestead mortgage. A new standard of measure was established when the railway companies designed a boxcar that would hold exactly 1,000 bushels. Even the governments of the day scheduled their elections for the convenience of the producers.

For farm families, the big news of each year was wheat news, stories which told of the work of plant scientists who were busy breeding and cross-breeding species—cultivars, they called them—of wheat that would resist rust, would have strong stems to withstand the unceasing prairie winds, and still be tall enough for efficient harvesting. The characteristics of each new registered species became a major topic of conversation.

Those farm families which had settled in the cooler climes of the mid-west of the province, the Russell-Roblin area, were benefited by the continuing results of agricultural research. Charles Saunders, later to be elevated to the rank of Dominion Cerealist, crossed Hard Red Calcutta wheat with Red Fife, resulting in a new variety called Markham. Markham was not a success because it did not produce uniform offspring, but kernels of Markham were further selected and became Marquis. To the farmer in northern climates this was good news indeed; Marquis could be harvested two weeks earlier than Red Fife.

However, all the buoyant talk of "55 bushels per acre" served only to gloss over many of the problems faced by farmers and their families. They had to contend with scorching heat in summer and mind-numbing cold in winter in homes that were poorly insulated, or perhaps not insulated at all. They had to face grasshoppers that blew in on the west wind and ate everything in sight, even the laundry on the lines.

They had to face, as well, the domination of those powerful eastern interests which still controlled the West's economy. The Canadian Pacific Railway, habitually hated for high freight rates, was a favourite target of farmers. The major banks were also viewed as having little sympathy for farmers whose incomes were subject to the vagaries of climate. Equally vilified, at times, were the Winnipeg grain barons who lived in mansions on Wellington Crescent while farm families were just emerging from a decade in sod huts and tarpaper shacks.

Still, despite these inequities, wheat was

The Padrone Cigar Company, a somewhat uncommon Manitoba industry, manufactured cigars in Portage la Prairie from 1906 to 1915.

By 1920, almost half the world's export wheat was supplied by Prairie farmers.

Rural Canada's most famous woman

E. Cora Hind

BOOTS, BRITCHES, BUCKSKIN: it was a most unusual outfit for a "lady" in the early 1900's. But by most accounts, E. Cora Hind was a most unusual lady. She was a full participant in what was then a man's business—agriculture and journalism. Cora Hind was the *Manitoba Free Press's* agricultural editor, the first woman in North America to attain such a status.

She was 21 when she made the move from Ontario to Winnipeg in 1882 in search of opportunity. Cora knew she had to earn a living but she was loath to take on a "woman's" career. Instead, she dreamed of becoming a journalist. But *Manitoba Free Press* editor W.F. Luxton made it clear to her newspapers were no place for a woman.

Rebuffed at the paper, Cora had to find some way of supporting herself. With the stubborn determination that was her defining characteristic, she rented one of the new typewriting machines and taught herself how to type. She set herself up as the first freelance typist in the West.

Her typing and stenography service proved to be a stepping stone into the world of agriculture. Many of her clients were key players in the farm community. She translated that new knowledge into freelance writing.

In 1898, eastern experts predicted the western harvest would be a disaster because of an early frost. John Bayne Maclean, a prominent publishing figure, asked Cora to do her own survey of the western crop. She took the assignment seriously, setting off in horse and buggy to all corners of the Prairies. Cora forecast a merely average crop. And sure enough, when the harvest came in, it was average, not disastrous.

Her prediction impressed the new editor of the *Free Press*, John Wesley Dafoe. In 1901, he hired her as the paper's agricultural editor—20 years after she first applied. Cora continued doing crop predictions each year. Cora Hind was right so often, markets would rise and fall depending on what she predicted. The *London Morning Post* expressed the amazement that was generally felt: "It would be strange enough to us if a man of great experience could soberly and accurately forecast the crop... but that this facul-

ty would be centred in a woman—this for some reason seems extraordinary."

Her work extended far beyond the annual forecasts. She became a regular in the stockyards and show rings of the West, dressed in her mannish but practical costume. She was a tireless promoter of farming and the West, often acting more as a participant than an observer. Through her enthusiasm and tireless work, she was accepted in the male-dominated environment.

Her contributions were formally acknowledged in an honorary degree from the University of Manitoba in 1935. The *Free Press* awarded her a trip around the world, which she used to send back reports on farming in foreign lands. At the age of 82, Cora Hind finally submitted to a reluctant retirement. She died of a stroke on October 6, 1942. Obituaries in the *London Times* and the *New York Times* remembered her as "Canada's most famous woman".

king on the Prairies, and there were ready markets in far-off places. In 1900, British farmers could only supply enough wheat for the United Kingdom for two months out of every 12. The docks of Hull, London, and Liverpool were busy year-round unloading boatloads of wheat from India, Russia, and the United States. However, the bread-eating habits in Europe went through a marked change in the late 1800's. Heavy rye and whole-wheat loaves had given way to those made from dough as white as snow that was also high in protein. For this purpose, nothing could match the wheat from Canada which soon became the grain of choice for European appetites.

Those successive—and successful—turn-of-the-century crops which transformed the Prairies into the Empire's breadbasket were grown by a varied assemblage of individuals from every corner of the globe. Many were from southern Ontario where the sons of that province's pioneers now sought more land to break. In general, it was Ontarians who settled Manitoba south of the CPR's mainline. There were more lands to be opened up farther north, and in the first decade of the century 200,000 new Manitobans arrived. Half of them were from Eastern Europe. The two largest groups were 12,000 Poles and 40,000 Ukrainians, who were generally described as "Galicians", since many came from the province of Galicia. A small number of them opened up bush land in the southeast part of the province, but the greater number settled near Lake Winnipeg in the Interlake, and around Dauphin Lake. Some who chose not to become homesteaders joined the urban labour force in Winnipeg, Brandon, and Portage la Prairie.

Stories of settlement by Ukrainian farmers range from the heroic to the heart-rending. In one case a group who had made no arrangements for immigration agent assistance began walking from Winnipeg to their homesteads in the Dauphin district. During this journey they were stricken by an outbreak of scarlet fever and 42 of their children died. The marker which stands near their mass grave, not far from Patterson Lakes, is mute testimony to this tragedy.

What attracted many of these persons was an aggressive advertising campaign conducted by the federal Department of the Interior. On November 7, 1900, Interior Minister Cifford Sifton was elected for the second time in the Brandon constituency. He was quick to remember his friends, with the result that Brandon's early influence on the Interior Department was profound. Sifton drafted T. Mayne Daly, Brandon's first mayor, to be the head of the department's legal branch. He brought in James Smart, Brandon's second mayor, to be his deputy minister. He asked Will White, the publisher of the *Brandon Daily Sun,* to be in charge of his department's operations in the U.S..

Manitoba *fastfacts*

One of the largest fish caught in Manitoba was a five metre sturgeon pulled out of the Roseau River by the Waddell family in 1903. They killed it with an ax.

The prairie crocus, or "gosling plant", was adopted as Manitoba's floral emblem in 1906.

By 1910, Ukrainians outnumbered Icelanders in the Gimli area.

Famed poet Robert W. Service worked at the Bank of Commerce in Swan River.

Sturgeon as tall as trees were taken from Manitoba rivers.

97

Sifton's biographers are loud in their praise of the results. By dint of full-page advertisements in British and American newspapers, supported by millions of pamphlets printed in a dozen different languages, Sifton extolled the promise of Canada West. In the first decade of the new century, Canada's population increased from five to seven million, with most of the addition being western farm immigrants.

Among Sifton's imports in that period were 168,000 who came directly from the United States. To social historians, these became the "vanishing Americans" because in future years their numbers were never recorded separately in any census statistics. Census-takers in those days recorded numbers by racial extraction rather than country of origin, so these Americans were assimilated under such categories as Irish, Scottish, German, and so on.

In 1903, in the annual report of the Superintendent of Immigration, a listing was provided of the results of departmental advertising. In part this report reads: "...all told, we had to deal with 114,124 requests for information by mail, in addi-

First settlers had to overcome poor land and discrimination
Ukrainians

BEFORE WORLD WAR I, UKRAINIANS came to Canada from Galicia and Bukovyna, provinces in the Austrian Empire. Large-scale migration to Manitoba began in 1896, following a trip to Canada by Dr. Osyo Oleskiv, an agronomist from Galicia. Oleskiv's two booklets about agricultural opportunities in Canada encouraged prospective settlers to investigate Manitoba rather than Brazil. He particularly noted the Dauphin Lake area as suitable for settlement by Ukrainians.

The first Ukrainian settlement in Manitoba got its start in July, 1896 when 27 families took homesteads in the Stuartburn area south of Winnipeg. The next month, another nucleus for a Ukrainian settlement was set up in Dauphin on the banks of the Drifting River—today the site of annual celebrations connected with Cana-

da's National Ukrainian Festival. Small groups of Ukrainians settled in other parts of Manitoba.

In the next few years, these hubs of settlement grew as chain migration brought in families and friends of the first settlers. By 1901 there was a total of 11,000 Ukrainian settlers in Manitoba—5,000 in the Dauphin area, 3,000 in Stuartburn and another 3,000 in the other areas. Over the next decade, these numbers almost tripled to 31,053.

For the most part, Ukrainians in the Austrian Empire were agriculturalists. They were hard-working peasant farmers at home, but they were hampered by a shortage of available land on which to expand and prosper. Land was the big attraction for them in Canada. Unfortunately, they found that the quantity of land in Manitoba

was not matched in quality. Only the Dauphin and Shoal Lake colonies were on fertile soil. In other parts of the province, good land had long since been taken up by earlier settlers. Ukrainian immigrants had to be satisfied with rocky, forested or otherwise marginal soils.

The first five years or so of the settlers' lives in Manitoba were usually difficult. Most settlers had little or no capital. Although farming remained their main occupation, Ukrainian families sent out their men to work on railway construction, in the mines and lumber camps, or to seek seasonal employment as farm labourers. Women and children would continue to clear land and tend animals, gather and sell wire grass, seneca roots, berries, honey and milk products—all to help the family unit

Dauphin quickly became a centre for Ukrainian settlement.

tion to many personal inquiries.... We shipped to our agents in the United States and Great Britain 575 cases, containing 637,578 pamphlets, etc., for distribution, our total output of literature being thus 1,313,909 separate copies or pieces."

The European newcomers had a major effect on Manitoba's population.

Fears began to arise that "Sifton's pets" would devel-

Land agents were often the first to greet new homesteaders.

in Manitoba

get established.

While the bulk of the immigrants were family groups, in the years 1906-1914, more than half were young single men seeking work as urban or migrant labourers. As Ukrainians moved into Manitoba's towns and into

Winnipeg, some took the risk of setting up small businesses such as general stores.

Very few of the Ukrainian immigrants before 1914 had any professional training. The exception were teachers, many of whom became central figures in the rural areas as promoters of Ukrainian cultural life. Manitoba's school inspectors noted

Ukrainian women baked bread in the "peech", an outdoor oven they built themselves.

the eagerness of Ukrainian parents to send their children to school (at a time when there was no compulsory education in the province) and their willingness to tax themselves in order to provide the needed schools and teachers. The schools were run on the bilingual principle until 1916, when T.C. Norris's Liberal government (worried about the explosion of Ukrainian and Polish schools) abolished bilingual education.

The great majority of settlers were members of the Ukrainian Catholic Church. There were few priests of this denomination in Canada. The clergy of other churches proselytized settlers, especially the Russian Orthodox, Roman Catholic, Methodist and

Presbyterian. It was not until 1912 that a Ukrainian Catholic bishop, Nykyta Budka, was named for Canada. He made Winnipeg the centre of his enormous diocese. The religious lives of most Ukrainians in Canada were given greater stability as the bishop built strong foundations for the Church. But this stability was sorely tried during the war years, for quite a number of Ukrainians resented what they termed Bishop Budka's authoritarianism, and in 1918 the breakaway group founded the Ukrainian Orthodox Church of Canada. Also during the war years, 1,000 Manitoba Ukrainians were interned as enemy aliens in prison camps.

Gradually, a visible Ukrainian community took shape. In their homeland, the village church with its resident priest had been the focal point for cultural events, though late in the nineteenth century village reading clubs also became significant. Ukrainians in Manitoba hoped to recreate their communities on this pattern. But they were hampered by the lack of clergy who could establish the institutions to which they were accustomed. Soon after arrival, settlers built small wooden churches, using volunteer labour. A community centre called a "national home" or *prosvita* (literally "enlightenment") was also established. With places to meet, choral music, drama and other Ukrainian-language activities took place, as the settlers recreated the rich cultural life of their European homeland.

op unbridgeable chasms between themselves and the British majority. Certainly, the legislative conditions of the time might be said to favour such divisions; minorities were entitled to have their children taught in their own language; there were no requirements for compulsory school attendance.

One difficulty faced by the Eastern Europeans was that most of them came as individuals, not as organized groups, as was the case with the Mennonites and Icelanders. Individual families lacked federal or provincial subsidization. For these under-capitalized hopefuls, to break new land and establish a working homestead called for all of the resourcefulness of their peasant ancestry.

Life on the agricultural frontier presented the newcomers with great hardships. Many survived—barely—in a one-room shack. Many knew only a subsistence diet of flour, potatoes, and oatmeal, which they supplemented with store-bought extras when they sold part of a meagre first crop, or had "worked out" for a neighbour.

The CPR's transcontinental line cut across lower Manitoba in as straight a line as the surveyors could devise, consistent with high ground and the avoidance of bogs and valleys. Before branch lines, it was commonplace for grain farmers to spend up to three days on the trail, delivering their grain in sacks to an elevator on the mainline.

Railways and farm settlement were inseparable. In many cases, entire villages relocated from their original sites to one that would be served by rail. In 1886, when a branch line of CPR was extended into southwestern Manitoba, the residents of Deloraine decided to relocate. They moved their homes and commercial buildings from the banks of a coulee overlooking the Boundary Commission Trail to the new site beside the right-of-way. Only a marker bearing the name of "Old Deloraine" marks the earlier site.

As new railways sprang up, each had its own so-called immigration department, which encouraged settlers

Black homesteaders discouraged in Manitoba

Racism at the Border

AS FEDERAL MINISTERS OF THE Interior, Clifford Sifton and his successor, Frank Oliver, were responsible for the settlement of the West. Both men felt that an immigrant's desirability was based on his willingness to "go on the land". Unofficially, there was another factor. The applicant had to be white.

As actively as Sifton and Oliver courted white American farmers, they discouraged black Americans. Canadian agents in the U.S. went so far as to publicize the rigorous medical examinations at the border, the threat of prejudice and the harsh northern winters. Blacks who approached agents were firmly rebuffed. Some, who travelled to Canada indepen-

> **"It is to be hoped that the fertile lands of the West will be left to be cultivated by whites only."**
>
> **A Winnipeg immigration agent**

dently, were able to cross the border. According to the 1921 census, Manitoba's "Negro" population rose from 61 in 1901 to 209 in 1911.

Expeditions of Creek Negroes from Oklahoma—former slaves of Creek Indians, and free-born offspring of Creek/Negro unions—settled on homesteads in Saskatchewan and Alberta. Manitobans were concerned that subsequent groups might want to settle in this province. Will White, founder of the *Brandon Weekly Sun,* condemned what he saw as the innately inferior character of the Creek-Negro. One of his arguments for rejecting blacks was that it was in their best interests: their system couldn't tolerate the demands of emigrating, he said, and being sepa-

rated from familiar surroundings would make them unhappy.

In 1906, and again in 1910, Oliver revised the Immigration Act so that it would be possible to "prohibit the landing of immigrants belonging to any race deemed unsuitable to the climate and requirements of Canada". He admitted in the House of Commons that the new law could be applied more or less stringently depending on who the immigrant was.

Even so, the revised Act didn't give immigration officials all the power they had hoped. When a party of American blacks en route for Alberta arrived at the Emerson border crossing in 1911, immigration officials said they "found themselves unable to stop a single member of the party. All had plenty of money, were in perfect health and apparently in good moral standing. They talked freely and stated they feared neither cold nor privation, and that all they were seeking was free land and a chance to make homes for their families".

Rumours that black settlers were heading north in large numbers sparked a racist panic throughout the West. The Winnipeg Board of Trade suggested that a head tax be imposed on Negro immigrants. Newspapers began to emphasize crimes involving blacks. The articles played on fears of social unrest, violence and sexual attacks on white women.

William Duncan Scott, a Winnipeg immigration agent, stated: "At no time has the immigration of this race been encouraged by the government... It is to be hoped that climatic conditions will prove unsatisfactory to these new settlers, and that the fertile lands of the West will be left to be cultivated by whites only."

Billy Beal

Most homesteaders in the Big Woody District near Swan River fit Clifford Sifton's ideal. They were hardy farm families who cultivated the land, built a community and planned for future generations.

William (Billy) Beal, on the other hand, was exactly the sort of immigrant the federal Minister of the Interior didn't want. Black, urban, single and a terrible farmer, he definitely would have been considered "undesirable".

Beal never wanted to homestead. A First-Class Steam Engineer, he arrived in the Swan River Valley from Minneapolis about 1907, and worked in a saw-mill. At first he was overwhelmed by the isolated, heavily forested terrain, but after a couple of years he decided he would like to stay, and applied for a homestead. In 1911, the same year J. Bruce Walker, Dominion Commissioner for Immigration in Winnipeg vowed to stop immigration of Negroes, Beal became a Canadian citizen.

Far from inciting social unrest, or being an economic liability as many Manitobans expected Negro settlers would be, Billy shared his diverse knowledge and skills to enrich his community. He was involved in the development of the Big Woody School Division, and served as its secretary-treasurer for many years. He shared his own books with students, and started a school library. He was a founding member of a literary society that sponsored debates and presented plays. In conversations with him, his neighbors learned about religion, history, philosophy and astronomy. He built a telescope, fitting lenses into lengths of stovepipe. He was skilled in carpentry, electrical work and photography.

The one thing he didn't do was farm. In his photographs, however, he recorded the pioneer family life he didn't live, a legacy as lasting as the fertile fields of his neighbours. Billy Beal died in The Pas in 1968 at the age of 94.

to locate homesteads along its lines. For the rail companies, a settling family was a source of income; at the outset they needed their household effects delivered to their home quarter-section, but once they were established, they were customers for as long as their land could produce grain, poultry, or livestock for distant markets.

The most successful competitor to the CPR was the Canadian Northern Railway, which began as a small branch line and later spanned the West. Sir Donald Mann and Sir William Mackenzie were the founders of Canadian Northern. In 1896, they built a line from Gladstone to Dauphin, and later extended it northward to Winnipegosis,

thus opening up the mid-west of the province to settlement, notably to Ukrainians who favoured the parkland country which reminded them of the

Some Jews who emigrated to Manitoba took up farming, particularly in the Interlake settlement of Bender Hamlet (1903). The colony failed as the land was ill-suited to farming. More successful were those Jews who established themselves as dairy farmers in West Kildonan, and who supplied much of Winnipeg's milk.

wooded landscape of their homeland.

Never men to rest on their accomplishments, the Mackenzie-Mann team two years later built north to Swan River, before extending the line west to Prince Albert. In 1902 they built an exten-sion to Grandview, and in later years they built to Gypsumville, Amaranth, and Grand Beach.

Mackenzie and Mann were gamblers; what they were gambling on was the prospect of new strains of wheat that would mature in territories

The Wreck of the S.S. Princess

Singing was heard as the ship slipped under Lake Winnipeg's raging waves

IN THE RECORDED HISTORY of navigation on Manitoba waterways, there have been many sinkings, burnings and wrecks. But the most famous shipwreck was the loss of the steamer *Princess* on Lake Winnipeg on August 26, 1906. Six people, including Captain John Hawes, perished that day.

The *Princess* was a beautiful ship, with 26 well-appointed state-rooms. She left Warren's Landing (on Lake Winnipeg) bound for Selkirk, a voyage of over 400 kilometres. On board was a crew of ten, 11 passengers and a full cargo of fish. The weather was not rough initially, but the wind shifted to the south-east, and soon began to blow very hard. Three hours after passing George's Island, the winds exceeded gale force, and the vessel began labouring in heavy seas. At 9:30 in the evening, the *Princess* took on water, and even though all hands turned out to the pumps, the water continued to gain.

According to survivors, the Captain seemed strangely immobilized. He wouldn't speak, and only after the mate pressed him did he agree to come about and run for the lee of George's Island. But by 3 a.m., with the wind and water tearing at the stricken ship, the engines failed, and the *Princess* was swept broadside.

Still no order was given to abandon ship. Passengers were terrified. At the inquest, the vessel's final moments were described by the survivors: "About 4:15, the steamer gave a great lurch and towering waves 25 feet high struck her, breaking her almost in two, and the smoke-stack went down through the bottom of the hull... a deckhand making for the boats went down through the hole and was never seen again. The passengers and crew struggled to reach the lifeboats. Mrs. Joe Swindon had two small children. She threw one into the yawl boat which was afloat on the deck... Mr.

Sinclair freed the falls with an axe. The strain broke the *Princess* entirely in two, and she settled aft, going down at the stern."

As the 14 survivors pulled away in the yawl, a woman and her baby were sighted in the water and pulled to safety. The night had given way to a brooding grey dawn and the breakers threw themselves violently against what was left of the *Princess*. In the wind-driven cauldron of spray, foam and noise, the thin notes of singing voices could be heard from the sinking ship. Clinging to the ruined deckhouse, the Captain, Stewardess Flora McDonald and Cook Toba Johansson were singing "Nearer My God To Thee."

It was impossible for the small lifeboat to put back into the wind, and the *Princess* soon disappeared from view forever. It was this tragedy, more than all others, that gave Lake Winnipeg its fierce and treacherous reputation.

where the number of frost-free days frequently stopped short of 100. To these entrepreneurs, Marquis wheat was a blessing.

But they did not wait for fortune to smile upon them. One of their superintendents was to write in his memoirs, "Service was our motto: we had more stopping places to the ten miles I think than any railway in the world. Only a few of them were on the

Ice cut from rivers and lakes was stored in a homesteader's ice house, and provided cold storage during the summer months.

timetable. Over most of the route where settlement was beginning we put down and took up passengers and way-freight to suit our pleasure."

When they weren't building new lines, Mackenzie and Mann were acquiring them from other builders. From Northern Pacific they were to secure lines which ran Winnipeg to Emerson, Morris to Brandon, Winnipeg to Portage la Prairie, Hartney Junction to Hartney, and they built or purchased other lines from Carman Junction to Carman, Beaver to Gladstone, Muir to Neepawa, Portage la Prairie to Delta, and Oakland to Beaver.

Before the turn of the century, the Grand Trunk Pacific had existed only in eastern Canada, but in 1903 it announced its intention to expand into a transcontinental service. That year they began to build west from Winnipeg. As their construction was under way, Canadian Northern matched them, side-by-side. By the time their rails

Summer Afternoon, The Prairie, 1921, by L.L. FitzGerald. He was the only Manitoba member of the Group of Seven.

reached the Pacific Ocean, Canada had more miles of (clearly uneconomical) railway per person than any other nation in the world.

What happened after a pioneer family was dropped off the train on the bald, featureless prairie, carrying little more than tools, grain seed and hope? In a typical case, the settlers would be shown to their homestead by a land agent who worked for a settlement company or one of the railways. Once the surveyor's markers had been located, the agent rode off, leaving the family to their own devices.

About them was nothing but a sea of grass. The sky stretched to a limitless horizon. Due to regular prairie fires, there were no trees, save for those knotted cottonwoods which grew along the banks of streams. For the fortunate few who had some river frontage, water was not a problem, but this was not the case with the majority, who had to immediately dig a well.

Most settlers brought with them the makings of their first residence, the fabled tar-paper shack. With lumber, and some sash-and-door fixtures, they at least could fashion a square box and get in out of the elements. They covered the raw wood with a layer of tarpaper against drafts.

Even before the house was built, settlers had to fashion a rudimentary enclosure for the horses and cattle. They needed to prepare their tools for the breaking of the sod and the planting of the all-important first crop. They also had to learn the location of the nearest town because there they hoped to find schools and churches, stores for

More affluent settlers could afford an ox cart to travel to their farms, while poorer homesteaders often walked to their new homes.

supplies, and a rail line for the shipment of farm produce to far-off markets.

If these settlers happened to be near a place where two trails crossed, or where a rail line was scheduled to be built, there was a chance that a town might develop. Early surveyors of the rail line rights-of-way knew that they needed a town, or at least a scheduled stop, every 16 kilometres, that being a reasonable distance for the delivery of grain by team and wagon.

Manitoba, by the turn of the century, had a network of towns destined to become regional centres: Portage la Prairie, Dauphin, Steinbach,

Morden, Pilot Mound, Souris, Boissevain, Virden, Russell, Neepawa, Selkirk, Stonewall and Swan River among them. At the same time, literally hundreds of small communities developed across the south as settlement advanced and the rail lines were extended. While some of the towns originated mainly in the dreams of urban developers, most owed their existence to the location of a grain elevator. With that distinctive structure dominating the skyline, other trappings of commerce and society were certain to follow.

Once the railway depot was established and the grain elevator built, a store, a restaurant, and a hotel soon followed. With this as the commercial core, a school, a couple of churches and a post office were certain to be next. For the average family, a town was nearly complete when it had a drygoods store for the ladies and a blacksmith where the man of the house could take his ploughshares for sharpening. The town had really arrived when it acquired a Chinese cafe, the proprietor of which had been brought to Canada to work on the CPR.

The early style of town planning was simplicity itself; all the early commercial establishments faced the rail line, and the thoroughfare on which they were located was called either Main Street or Railway Street.

There was no magical formula by which farm towns acquired their names. If not already named by a passing railway baron, someone had to take the initiative to contact the postal service and make enquiries about how they were to receive their letters and parcels. They would be told that it was their responsibility to develop a distinctive name and have it registered; this registration was expedited if the chosen name was not in use in that province, and preferably in no other provinces.

The story of these names is the story of early Manitoba civilization. French settlers brought names from home: Aubigny, Beausejour, Dauphin, and Fannystelle. The Icelanders favored Arbakka, Arborg and Gimli. Scots chose Argyle, Carberry, Dundee and Dunottar. The Ukrainians liked Berlo and Ukraina; the Irish preferred Boyne and Clandeboye; the Belgians imported Bruxelles. A flurry of headlines during the Boer War led to anomalous South African names like Mafeking and Durban.

Settlers took town names from plants, like Broomhill. The local floral cover on their hard-won acres caused some families to name their localities Amaranth, Clematis and Crocus. The animal kingdom was the source of many names: Badger, Beaver, Bison, Buffalo, Deer, Elk and Ermine. Even animal parts were honoured in Antler and Elkhorn.

If You Are Willing to Work Hard, Come to Manitoba

Letter sent by immigration agent and farmer Almon James Cotton to Henry Galarueas, a prospective settler from Lewis County, New York. When Cotton moved to Manitoba from Ontario in 1888, he became a tenant farmer in the Treherne area, but he later acquired extensive land holdings in the Swan River Valley. Cotton acted as an unpaid agent for the Department of Immigration, carrying on correspondence with prospective homesteaders. A booster by nature, his letters reflected his enthusiasm for the Canadian West, and in particular Manitoba.

...I am glad you are still inclined to settle in the West because I think you will do better. I have been here since 1888 and have had the experience. [I] came here poor and have made a good honest living, raised a good healthy family.... We have 19 quarter sections of land in the valley and over 800 acres under cultivation. But [we] are only working 400 ourselves, having the rest rented out.

I want people to understand what the West has done for me and it is ready to do the same for them. I don't think there is any country under the sun can offer such encouraging inducements to intending settlers, in the way of free homesteads, cheap land, good water, timber, firewood and building material, good soil, quality of grain, average yield, growth of stock and healthy climate. I am stating facts that I have had from experience. When I go east in Ontario and Quebec and in the States and see farmers that are using up the best part of their lives renting land and making nothing but a bare living, and working hard to do that and a time coming when age will not allow them to work as hard and still no bank account to help them out. This increased worry added on shortens their life.

Now by coming to the West perhaps you will have to put up with hardship in the beginning and many inconveniences and very likely meet many discouragements at the beginning. But a little backbone and sand with sleeves rolled up will soon chase that away and before you are aware of it you will find yourselves comfortable and on the way to prosperity. I will guarantee that if you come up here and take up a homestead and buy a quarter of railway land and work and manage as hard as you do now on a rented farm that you will soon have a comfortable house of your own.

A popular rural diversion was the box social. Ladies brought box lunches which were auctioned off to the men at a midnight supper, and the men would dine with the lady who had put up the lunch. Proceeds raised went to pay for the fiddler and the coffee.

Farming on the Prairies was a race against the weather. There was a cycle to early farming practices, and each element in that cycle was critical if there was to be a true Thanksgiving at the end of the growing season.

Long before winter had released its grip, farmers were cleaning grain in their fanning mills in preparation for spring seeding. This process was assurance that their seed would be free of weeds and other impurities. The cleaned seed then was treated with formaldehyde which made it resistant to most forms of smut.

In the spring, the fields were harrowed to break up the clods, and then seeded by horse-drawn drill-seeders which poured a continuing stream of kernels into the furrows. Those seeds later were covered in a second passing of the harrows. Some farmers favoured a third harrowing when time and their other chores permitted. To the serious producer, every drop of moisture was critical, and

repeated harrowing broke up the surface lumps and "sealed the cracks" which permitted that precious moisture to escape.

In some seasons, allowing for the vagaries of rain, and the painfully slow work with the horses, seeding might take up to two months. In those pre-chemical days, farmers were in an unceasing battle with noxious weeds. The early promotional literature of the Department of Agriculture advised them to have a broom with them at all times in order that they could sweep their implement clean of seeds of all types when they were leaving a field. Without this precaution, the pamphlet warned, weed seeds would be transferred from one field to another.

Some farmers, more notably the purists, could be seen in their fields in June and July hand-picking weeds, or non-conforming grain plants. In the early years of the new century, many farmers were complaining that they didn't want a government weed

Cover of Dutch emigration booklet on Manitoba which, somewhat surprisingly, advertised salmon fishing.

Alonzo Fowler Kempton

Not all Manitoba entrepreneurs lived in Winnipeg

WAWANESA'S Alonzo Fowler Kempton created Canada's biggest mutual insurance company, but he also found time to invent a new wagon seat and market a best-selling hemorrhoid cure.

Kempton came to Manitoba from Nova Scotia with his parents in 1881. From the beginning he never enjoyed manual work, preferring instead to use his brain. A smooth talker, the young Kempton left school and turned his abilities to sales. He set out across the Manitoba prairie in a horse and buggy to sell household goods to new immigrants and, later, insurance to farmers.

Kempton's biggest sales job was convincing the stolid farmers of Wawanesa to join him in forming the new Wawanesa Mutual Insurance Company. At this time, Eastern stock companies controlled the insurance business. Their rates were high and

Alzono Fowler Kempton, centre front, always had the biggest car in town.

they didn't understand the special challenges pioneers faced. Kempton figured he had the answer—a farmers' insurance co-operative. While the new business started slowly, it soon became successful across the country. By 1910, it was the largest fire mutual in Canada, employing scores of people in Wawanesa.

A man of large appetites, Kempton had the biggest house, the newest car and the fanciest suits of anyone in the village. He hired a Chinese

cook/chauffeur and brought in expensive foods from around the world. Kempton was also notorious for using profanity freely, both in the office and on the street. On one memorable occasion Kempton bumped into a cross-eyed neighbour while walking along the sidewalk. "I sure wish you'd watch where you're going," yelled the man. "God damn it," Kempton shouted back, "I wish you'd go where you're looking."

Kempton was a natural entrepreneur. His other ventures included a stock insurance company, the Wawanesa Wagon Seat Company (manufacturing a more comfortable seat for wagon boxes) and the Canada Hone Company (which made leather razor strops and a 'magnetized' razor paste). The indefatigable Kempton also manufactured and marketed a best-selling hemorrhoid cure.

The Bard of Carberry

ERNEST THOMPSON SETON was a world famous artist and nature writer who published more than 40 books, delivered more than 3,000 public lectures and achieved great personal wealth from his writing. Seton was a world traveller with roots in many places, but his favourite place was Carberry, Manitoba—the place where he said he spent his "golden days".

Seton grew up in the shadow of an abusive father. After an unhappy childhood in Toronto he moved west to his brother's farm in Carberry. There, at the age of 22, his creative life began. In and around Carberry he rambled the prairies and sandhills with a sharpened pencil and sketchbook, recording images of the wildlife around him. He also began writing stories, and these fanciful depictions of Manitoba's deer, jackrabbits and foxes later became the perennial best-seller *Wild Animals I Have Known.* With that book, Seton pioneered a literary genre that later served as a model for Walt Disney's *Bambi.* Before he left for fame and fortune in the United States, the Manitoba government awarded Seton the office of Provincial Naturalist in 1892.

As an artist Seton was a scrupulous realist who studied animal anatomy and devoted a great deal of attention to scientific accuracy. Before drawing a Brewer's blackbird, for example, he carefully examined and

Seton's works were noted for their incredible attention to detail.

counted the bird's feathers, all 4,915 of them.

As an author, however, he was a romantic who humanized his animal heroes. In Seton's stories, a bighorn sheep flings himself off a cliff to deny a hunter his trophy. A wolf dies of a broken heart after his mate is killed by trappers. And a magnificent old bear commits suicide to escape the indignity of growing old. At their core, Seton's stories are morality tales celebrating the simple virtues of duty, sacrifice and fair play. Not accidentally, these virtues also form the basic philosophy of the Boy Scouts of America—an organization which Seton co-founded when he later moved to the United States.

After several years of living in New York City, where he married a socialite and associated with people like Buffalo Bill Cody and Theodore Roosevelt, Seton felt the urge to return to the wilds. But by now, the plough had conquered southern Manitoba so he moved to the wild hill country of New Mexico. There, powerful buffalo wolves still ranged the grasslands, pursued by ranchers and their bounty hunters. Some of these wolves were near-mythic outlaws, and they had a special hold on Seton's imagination. He believed he was descended from the man who trapped the last wolf in the British Isles, and he himself incorporated a wolf's paw print into his signature.

A lifelong feminist, Seton idealized women. His proper name by birth was "Ernest Thompson". As a way of disowning his father and honoring his mother, he adopted "Ernest Thompson Seton" as his pen name. Seton died in 1946, and many of his Manitoba-based sketches, paintings and manuscripts can be seen at a museum established in his honor at Cimarron, New Mexico.

inspector "on my farm" as if that new breed of public servant were an enemy, rather than an important farm educator.

The quietude of the growing season came to an abrupt end when there was a nip in the early-morning breeze, and the crops were turning gold in colour. Harvest time brought an abrupt change of pace to rural life. In the towns, even those persons who had only a limited knowledge of farm production wanted daily bulletins from the harvest gangs; after all, if enough of that grain was of good quality, and fetched a good price, the economy of the town was secure for another year.

There was a rigid sequence of connected events which culminated in the harvest. At the proper stage of maturity, after the kernels were hardened but before shattering occurred, the grain was cut with a binder. This machine, pulled by three or four horses, cut the grain and tied it into sheaves which were dropped on the ground. The sheaves were then stooked, which meant they were stood on end with six or eight other sheaves in order to dry.

Then came the excitement. Threshing crews of 20 to 40 men, mostly neighbours, descended on

More than 100,000 impoverished British children were sent to new homes in Canada. Many worked as indentured servants on farms such as this one at Russell.

the harvest to pick up the sheaves and extract the grain. The early threshing machines were powered by large steam engines which moved from farm to farm at a breathtaking pace of two miles per hour. As they belched smoke down the roadways, they pulled a caboose. This was a crew shack on wheels, about eight feet wide and twice that length, fitted out with three bunks on each wall.

At dawn each working day the engineer fired up his power plant. It transferred power to the separator by means of an endless belt. The next crew to report for duty were the teamsters, who drove their teams and racks out to the fields to pick up the sheaves. They were helped by field pitchers. The sheaves were hauled back to the threshing site and fed into a separator by spike pitchers using pitch forks.

The separator separated the grain from the straw. The straw was blown into a pile to be used for fuel for the steam engine and for livestock feed and bedding. The threshed kernels were elevated up a spout where a weighing device calculated the yield in pecks. Every half-bushel caused the mechanism to trip, and the grain then flowed down into a wagon. Each wagon load was delivered to the farmyard where it was shovelled into the granary to await shipment to the rail head.

Farm women, thoroughly accustomed to provid-

Rural health facilities were often lacking. When a travelling photographer was stricken with smallpox while staying at the King Edward Hotel in Gilbert Plains in 1906, horrified citizenry called the police. Constable Robert Logan and Dr. William Morrison carted the sick man in a sleigh to a building known as the pest house. There he was given medical attention until he recovered.

Mobile threshing crews would roam the province at harvest time.

ing three large meals a day for a busy family, now had to feed ten or a dozen additional workers who wanted not only those three meals, but also lunches in between. The boys and girls of the family were kept busy delivering snacks and honey pails filled with drinking water to the work crews. It was customary for homemakers to help each other out as the "outfit" went from farm to farm, and in many cases pots and roasting pans and cups and saucers moved from farm to farm with the harvest crew. For everyone involved in this annual burst of energy, the work day began at 6 a.m. and continued until the sun went down.

Every wife in a pioneer family was living proof of that old adage, "Man may work from sun to sun, but woman's work is never done". The farmer's wife was certain of only one thing; there were too many chores, and too few hours. The keeper of the home was expected to keep the girls at their appointed duties inside the residence, and to supervise the boys whose chores were generally in the yard or the outbuildings.

Depending upon the time of the year, the demands on her time usually revolved around the preparation of food. If she wasn't preparing it for immediate consumption, she was preserving it for future use. While her husband was away in the fields working with horses and harrows, the wife was farming on a restricted basis right beside the back door. She was the family gardener who was expected to plant and maintain a garden of sufficient size that it would supply the household with fresh greens for summer treats and root vegetables for the rest of the year.

The farm wife was also the keeper of the poultry flock. She ran the butter churn. She cleaned clothes often with soap she made herself.

Empire Day celebrations at Langruth School

She canned fruit and vegetables. She baked on a daily basis. Pioneer records tell the story of these remarkable women working over outdoor coal-and-wood stoves making breads and pies and full-course meals for the harvest gang. For so-called pin money, money she could call her own, she was often allowed to keep the proceeds of the sale of the eggs and cream. And she did all these things in the absence of refrigeration, running water, or indoor plumbing.

An important element to the harvest rush was the phenomenon known as the "harvest excursion". So great was the need of manpower, and so important was that harvest to the economy of the Prairies, that men were imported on special trains from around the country for this back-breaking chore.

Early annual reports of the Manitoba Department of Agriculture described the annual Harvest Excursions as the "greatest movement of labouring men ever witnessed in the Dominion." When this source of workers was introduced by the railways in 1890, a scant 2,175 tickets were sold to individuals who wanted casual labour. The year following, the number had jumped to 3,000; in 1899 it was 11,004; by 1912 it had swollen to 26,500.

At the outset, the fare charged on harvest excursion trains was half the regular rate. As the volume of this annual traffic increased the rates varied, some of them as low as $10 for the round-trip. The workers, in general, came from the Maritimes, Quebec, or Ontario. There was a double inducement for them to make the trip; the wages they would receive, up to $5 a day, were more than double the going

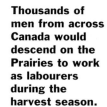

Thousands of men from across Canada would descend on the Prairies to work as labourers during the harvest season.

Timothy Eaton revolutionized the retail business with the promise of "goods satisfactory or money refunded". After the turn of the century, almost half of every retail dollar in Manitoba was collected by Eaton's. But it was the Eaton's catalogue that most affected the buying habits of rural citizens. Consumers could obtain everything from a seven-room house ($999.77) to mail-order bacon (17¢ a pound. Equally invaluable when finished, the catalogue became dual-purpose outhouse reading material.

Home Remedies

Prairie pioneers often faced illness or accident on the farm. Doctors were few and difficult to reach; money was scarce and medical supplies not readily available. There were a few commercial stand-bys, such as Wonder Oil and Alpenkrauter, but usually home remedies were used. The following are some of these cures:

Severe Infections

Fresh, warm cow manure: place between two cloths and apply to infection.

Carbunkle Boil

Onion, meat and bread: chew, then mixed with sour cream. Place mixture in cotton bag, bury for seven days, then apply to boil. This draws out the tendrils of the pus.

Jaundice

Garlic: wear string of garlic around neck.

Weak and Tired Back

Bear fat: rub in.

Burns and Scalds

Aloe Verce (healing plant; also known as Zipplefee): apply the slimy substance found inside the slender leaves.
Raw egg: apply to prevent blisters.
Salt: apply generously.

Skunk fat: apply—also good for festering sores that will not heal.

Earache

Fried onion: place on cloth and apply to ear.
Cigarette smoke: blow into affected ear.

Chest Colds and Coughing

Dry mustard, flour and hot water: mix, apply paste between two cloths to chest and back.
Camphor ointment: rub on chest—gives off heat which opens up any congestion.
Woolen stocking: wrap unwashed, used stocking around throat for the night.

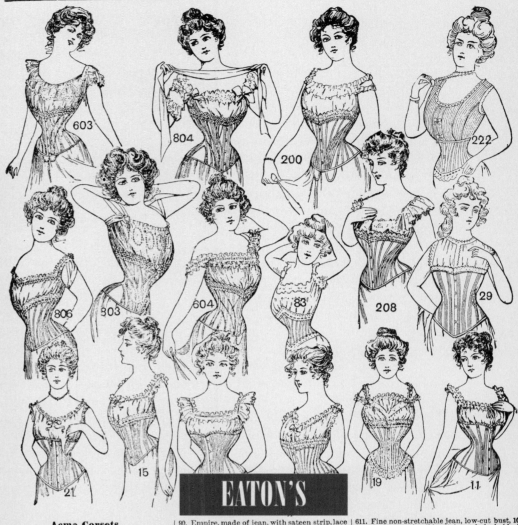

EATON'S

Acme Corsets.
11. Jean throughout, lace-trimmed, medium length, 2 side steels, white and drab, 18 to 30 ......28c
13. Jean with sateen strips, boned bust, medium length, embroidery, white and drab, 18 to 30, 35c
15. Coutil, with sateen strips, straight front, boned bust, lace and baby ribbon, white and drab, 18 to 30...........................50c
19. Sateen, single strips, filled with fine tempered steel wire, lace top and bottom, short hip, white, drab and black, 18 to 30 ....75c
21. Nursing, coutil, steel wire filling, embroidery trimmed, white and drab, 18 to 30 ...75c
29. Misses' corset, coutil, 2 side steels, lace edging, white and drab, 19 to 26...........35c
31. Misses' coutil, sateen stripping, 2 side steels, embroidery trimming, white and drab, 19 to 26 ....50c
35. Ladies' fine sateen, single strip, medium length, filled with fine wire, lace and baby ribbon, white and drab 18 to 30 ......1.00
74. Straight front, coutil with sateen strips, lace and baby ribbon, steel wire filling, white, drab and black, 18 to 30 ....75c
83. Empire, fine sateen, single strip, lace and baby ribbon, white, drab and black, 18 to 24 ....75c

90. Empire, made of jean, with sateen strip, lace and baby ribbon, white and drab, 18 to 24..50c
91. Straight front, English coutil throughout, filled with fine steel wire, single strips, baby ribbon and lace at top, finished with tab for hose supporter, white and drab, 18 to 30..1.00

B. & C. Corsets.
200. Straight front, heavy jean, drab, white or black, girdled and lace-trimmed, 18 to 30, 1.00
201. Same, steel boned, tan jean 1.00
207. Same, featherbone-filled, drab only ...1.00
208. Straight front, "hip-spring," non-stretchable jean, steel-boned, white or drab 1.00
211. Straight front, "hip-spring," in fine coutil, white or drab 1.25
202. Straight front, jean, sateen strips, drab only, 18 to 30 ....75c
204. Straight front, drab only, 18 to 26........50c
215. Straight front, short girdle, drab jean, 18 to 26 ....50c
Kabo Bust Perfector, drab and white jean or summer net, 18 to 26 ....1.00

Kabo Corsets.
605. Short length, 10-inch clasp with 5 hooks, 3 lower hooks in close relation, white batiste, 18 to 30.......................1.25
603. Same as 605, only medium length 1.25

611. Fine non-stretchable jean, low-cut bust, 10-inch clasp, satin ribbon trimmed, drab, black and white, 18 to 30...........1.25
604. Fine, low bust, sateen, 10-inch clasp, good long skirt, white, drab and black, 18 to 30..1.75
608. 11½-inch clasp, long skirt, non-stretchable jean, handsomely trimmed, black, white and drab, 18 to 30 ....1.25
806. Medium length, trimmed with broad lace and silk embroidered. French coutil, white, drab and black, 18 to 26.... ....2.25
804. Drab and white French coutil, black, in English sateen, medium length, low dip bust, 10-inch clasp, lace-trimmed and embroidered at gores, 18 to 26...........................2.75
803. Medium length, coutil of extreme fineness, buttonholed by hand, flossed and trimmed handsomely low cut, white and drab only, 18 to 26.......................3.75
805. Medium length, diamond sateen, low-cut bust, lace-trimmed, embroidered and buttonhole stitched at gores, four-hook clasp, black only, 18 to 30...........................4.00
811. Long skirt, finest French coutil, in white drab, diamond sateen in black, satin ribbon trimmed and flossed, gores buttonhole stitched, for stout figures, 18 to 30 ....5.00

111

rate for labourers in their home locations. As well there was the intriguing prospect of becoming members of the "New Society", perhaps even signing up for a homestead and making that giant leap from labourer to member of the landed class.

The railway official who labelled the trains "excursions" was using that word loosely. The men travelled in uncomfortable colonist cars, 56 to a car. They were seated in fours, two facing two. At night, the seats made into a double bed, while two other travellers could sleep in the overhead bunk.

The harvest trains held the lowest priority and it was common for them to spend hours on a siding waiting for profit-making freight trains to pass. The men flooded out of the cars at each stop in search of food. Seven-day trips from the Maritimes to Winnipeg were common. The literature of the period reports on families who lived alongside the mainline keeping their children close to home when they knew a farm excursion train was due. The workers engaged in fights, in drunken brawls, and occasional high-jinks. When the station agent at Cochrane, Ontario, attempted to remonstrate with the rambunctious workers they took umbrage and nailed him into a packing crate.

Exhibitions allowed farmers to show off their work

The

PROUD FARMERS WANTED TO PUT the best of their production on display and they wanted it judged against a known standard. To meet this need, Manitoba developed a province-wide network of agricultural fairs and exhibitions for judging purposes.

The rapid expansion of rail lines across western Manitoba, all of them serving Brandon, enabled that community to assume the role of Manitoba's agricultural capital. Also assisting in this achievement was Brandon's success with its early fairs and exhibitions. Beginning in 1897, Brandon became the home of Manitoba's major agricultural judging fair. In that year a new stable, grandstand, and half-mile racetrack were completed.

There was a solid commercial ring to these early events. Railways wanted more settlers growing more shippable wheat, so they introduced excursion rates to passengers who wanted to visit the fair. The boxcars necessary to move the livestock from distant towns to judging rings were supplied at a rock-bottom charge.

In this period, when there were no farm newspapers and no glossy brochures, the rural fairs had an educational purpose. They became the established means for manufacturers to introduce their new ploughs, harrows, and binders. A popular annual display featured C. Braithwaite, provincial weed inspector, who hosted a display of more than 90 noxious weeds. He was kept busy answering questions of farmers who wanted to learn more about how to destroy these hated enemies.

While the Brandon fair soon became the leading event of its type in Manitoba, it alone did not suffice to satisfy local boosters. If the provincial economy was based on agriculture, then surely a second agricultural fair, concentrating on livestock, was needed. A group of businessmen, politicians and farm representatives convened in Brandon in 1906 to organize the province's first full-scale Winter Fair, which was held two years later.

These leaders thought on the grand scale. They scheduled the first provincial Spring Stallion show, a

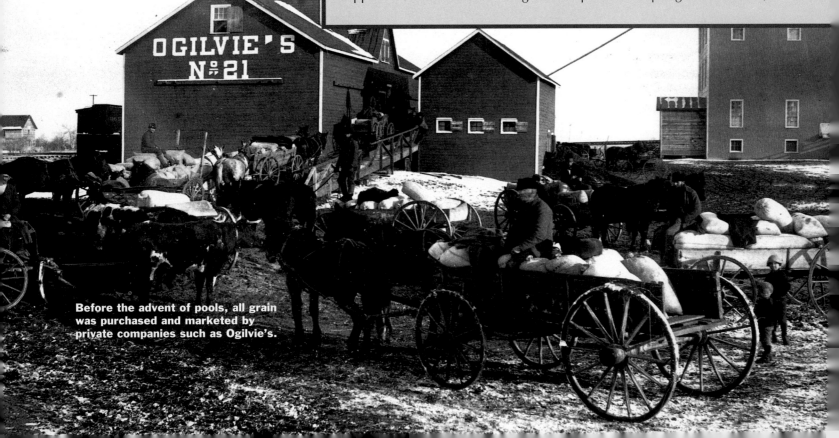

Before the advent of pools, all grain was purchased and marketed by private companies such as Ogilvie's.

Brandon Agricultural Fairs

The Brandon summer and winter fairs attracted thousands of visitors. In addition to livestock and horticultural displays, the fairs showcased farm technology. The moose and sulky was more a curiosity than a practical idea.

Seed Grain Fair, a School of Stock Judging, a Poultry Show, and during fair week they also scheduled the annual meetings of the Cattle Breeders' Association, the Horse Breeders' Association, the Sheep and Swine Breeders' Association, the Canadian Seed Growers' Association, and the Grain Growers' Association.

The first Winter Fair was received enthusiastically. In an editorial, the *Brandon Sun* said, "It is worth more to Brandon than half a dozen spasmodic, pin-head publicity campaigns." The fair is still held every winter in Brandon.

It was the opinion of Prime Minister Sir Wilfrid Laurier that, "Agriculture is not only a work of the hands. It is an art which should take a foremost rank in the curriculum. It is the finest of all studies and sciences."

For Manitoba farmers, this comforting philosophy was reassurance that they indeed were engaged in a holy calling and fulfilling a vital function for society. After all, the prime minister had acknowledged that they were more than mere tillers of the soil; they were experts in husbandry, biology, plant science, even in the field of commerce.

While many Manitoba pioneers had farmed in their homelands, thousands of others were not so fortunate. These were the persons who took up homesteads because of the excitement of the times, or perhaps to fulfil the dream of owning "a place of our own". Trained farmers were required if the soil, the greatest of all natural resources, was to be protected for future generations.

The government recognized this problem and set about to rectify it. In 1903, the Legislature created an Agricultural College. Three years later the first class of 84 registered at the new site west of Winnipeg. W.J. Black was principal and professor of animal husbandry; W.J. Rutherford was professor of agriculture and W.J. Carson was professor of dairy science. Other lecturers taught veterinary science, horticulture, English, mathematics and mechanics.

Farmers also gained access to new farming techniques through Dominion Experimental farms, such as the one at Brandon, which freely shared their research findings. Women were not left out of this educational process. Home economics

Portage la Prairie was thriving when it became a city in 1907. It had six banks, six hotels, and it was the only place in Canada where mainlines of three transcontinental railway systems intersected—the Grand Trunk Pacific, the Canadian Northern and the Canadian Pacific.

classes began at the Agricultural College in 1909, but not until 1918 were the first six women awarded degrees.

Manitoba farmers were pioneers in introducing quality cattle to Western Canada. The first pure-bred livestock came to Manitoba in 1868 when Portage la Prairie area settler Kenneth McKenzie secured a Shorthorn bull calf. McKenzie's son Adam purchased Shorthorn cattle from Minnesota, and Walter Lynch of Westbourne imported similar stock from Ontario.

Another fan of Shorthorns was John Barron. Barron, an Ontario emigrant, established the Fairview Stock Farm on the Carberry Plains in 1878, and four years later he bought and imported a registered Shorthorn heifer. He continued his practice of importing Ontario heifers, and quickly became one of the province's leading purebred breeders.

Other pioneer cattle producers were Robert Hall, of Griswold, who was the first in the West to breed Aberdeen Angus, and the Sharmans, of Souris, who were the first to produce purebred Herefords.

One Manitoba cattle man was recognized across Canada by his initials J.D.—James Duncan McGregor, of Rapid City. There he established the Glencarnock line of Aberdeen Angus on which he built his reputation as a breeder of championship livestock.

McGregor took several entries to the prestigious 1912 International Livestock Show at Chicago. He won ribbons for grand champion bull and reserve grand champion cow, first prize for a two-year-old and also the coveted grand championship for steers. In 1913, he again won the supreme championship, marking important victories for Western Canadian beef on the international stage.

The rise of wheat and cattle marked a turning point in prairie agriculture. The decline of subsistence farming gave way to an agriculture industry that exerted considerable influence in many fields. Manitoba farmers realized there was strength in unity and formed a number of organizations—political and otherwise—to further their particular interests.

For example, the Western Stock Growers' Association worked towards improvements for livestock producers, such as better branding regulations and the suppression of cattle rustling. Grain farmers joined organizations including The Grange, the Manitoba and North-West Farmers'

Union, the Farmers' Alliance and the Patrons of Industry to lobby for reduced tariffs, improved transportation services and government grading of grain.

Grain growers in particular were concerned about protecting their interests from those of big business—the financial institutions, railways, elevator and milling companies. Producer-distributor conflicts became increasingly common. Grain growers believed their crops were subjected to improper grading, excessive dockage, short weighing and excessively high storage and transportation costs. They especially resented railway

Cattle for the Klondike

 When John Howey, a Bradwardine farmer, and his cousin William Burchell, a butcher from Brandon, learned that miners at the Yukon gold rush would pay a dollar a pound for beef that was bringing three cents a pound in Manitoba, they reached an historic conclusion: they would supply that market.

Twice in four years at the turn of the century, Howey and Burchell made the incredible trek from Brandon to Dawson City. On both trips they left Brandon in May, with parties of nine herdsmen and large herds of cattle. They travelled to Vancouver by train, and then north by ocean-going vessel to Skagway.

That was the easy part. From Skagway they had to drive the cattle over 800 kilometres of forest, bog, and tundra. They then had to move the animals over the last 150 kilometres by barge to the gold fields. While the herdsmen worked a full month building a fleet of barges, the cattle were fattening themselves up in the ample pastures of the mountain passes.

It took six months for these trips, but both Howey and Burchell came home with profits. They had been to the gold rush, and they had struck it rich. But no, there was no digging involved.

policies that encouraged grain elevator monopolies.

The *Winnipeg Daily Tribune* argued in 1897 that a combine made up of "practically all the grain dealers, big millers and grain syndicates" was trying to drive the price of wheat down by six cents per bushel and was pressuring the banks "to

Not all Manitoba farmers concentrated on growing wheat, as evidenced by the many herds of prize-winning purebred cattle.

shut down on small traders and drive them out of business". The *Tribune* railed: "It will not do to leave our farmers in the hands of the Philistines any longer."

Under pressure from both grain producers and distributors, the federal government appointed the Royal Commission on the Shipment and Transportation of Grain in Manitoba and the North-West Territories. The Manitoba Grain Act—described as "a veritable agrarian Magna Charta"—was passed in 1900.

The Manitoba Grain Act protected the farmers' right to set up flat warehouses from which to load grain directly into rail cars, bypassing elevators. It provided for a grain inspector and for specific procedures for weighing, cleaning and storing grain. And, it ostensibly made improvements to the distribution of grain cars. However, as D.J. Hall has pointed out, the Act "provided nothing more than the grain interests and the CPR were

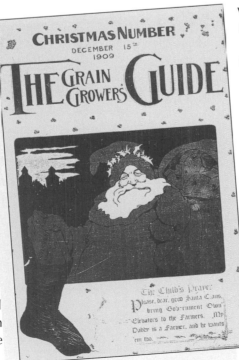

willing to concede".

Manitoba farmers continued to exert pressure on several fronts. In 1906, the Grain Growers' Grain Company was organized and later secured a seat on the Winnipeg Grain Exchange. That same year, they successfully lobbied the province for the creation of North America's first government-owned telephone system—Manitoba Government Telephones—which was desired to improve rural communications services.

The farm lobby tackled the elevator monopoly as well. Rodmond Roblin's Conservative government was persuaded to enter the grain elevator business, and between 1909 and 1912, 170 elevators were built or acquired as a public utility. Heavy losses later forced the province to lease the elevators to the Grain

Many farmers, unhappy with the domination of private elevator companies, formed their own associations.

115

Curling and Baseball Dominated Rural Sports

Disgraced 1919
Black Sox played
for Virden

RURAL LIFE OFTEN SEEMED all work: forking manure, weeding the garden, gathering eggs and hauling grain. But there was time for recreation and the favourite activities were curling in the winter and baseball in the summer.

A combination skating and curling rink was constructed in nearly every town. Skating and especially hockey attracted the young and the robust. Curling attracted nearly everyone old enough to lift a rock. This was especially the case after 1900, as more women tried the game.

Meanwhile, usually on the grounds used for a summer fair or next to the one-room school house, a ball park was established. From the time spring seeding was completed until fall harvest was begun, base-

In Manitoba, baseball and softball were played by locals on a field full of gopher holes

ball and softball were played almost every evening.

In the bigger towns, baseball was played on a nice, level field in front of a big crowd. On these occasions, the teams were staffed by highly skilled, even imported, professional players. A famous example of this was the Virden semi-pro team of the 1920's.

The winning team at the Russell Bonspiel in 1913: R. Young, skip, A. Simpson, 2nd, D. Tisseman, 1st, and Reverend G.R. Tench, 3rd

The Virden owner brought in two of the most notorious players in baseball history—Oscar "Happy" Felsch and Charles "Swede" Risberg. Felsch and Risberg were key members of the infamous Chicago Black Sox team that threw the 1919 World Series to the Cincinnati Reds. Banned from the major leagues, some Black Sox ended up playing for small-town Canadian teams.

Felsch was a bubbly player who entertained the crowds and could throw the ball to home plate from the deepest part of the outfield. Risberg, on the other hand, was a loner and a drinker who never got over the shame of his expulsion from the big leagues.

More frequently in Manitoba, however, baseball and softball were played by locals on a field full of gopher holes. Most of the participants could not hit or throw or catch very well, and they played with ragged gloves and the same shoes they used when they worked in the fields.

What made curling and baseball so popular? For one thing, they were slow-moving team games. Throughout the English-speaking world the team games were highly valued because they encouraged admirable qualities like determination, co-ordination, capacity to think quickly and willingness to work with others. Second, although baseball and curling rewarded skill and endurance, one did not have to be highly co-ordinated or conditioned in order to enjoy them.

Finally, unlike soccer or lacrosse or hockey, curling and baseball were one-play-at-a-time games, which meant that every few seconds there was time for players and spectators to talk about the crops, to finish telling a joke, to check on the children playing nearby, to reflect upon the significance of the pitch just thrown or the shot just played. And those brief seconds were no doubt a welcome reprieve in an otherwise busy rural existence.

Growers' Grain Company (which later became United Grain Growers).

By 1910, the landscape of rural Manitoba had changed considerably. Log shanties and sod buildings were being replaced by spacious farm homes and hip-roofed red barns. Some rural communities and farms enjoyed improved communications as telephone coverage reached across the province.

Railways and road systems threaded across the province, making once distant communities accessible and expanding trading areas. Towns large and small offered a wider variety of services. Fields once trod by oxen and horse-drawn farm equipment, reverberated under the weight of steam-powered threshers and the first combustion engine tractors.

In the years just before the outbreak of World War I, farmers made up the majority of Manitoba's population. They helped feed the country, the Empire and the world. The humble sodbuster, only a few years removed from the tar shack and the hand-held plough, was now the main engine of the province's economy. The years ahead would prove challenging, but Prairie farm families—whether from Parry Sound or Krakow—had proved they could overcome the greatest adversities and still prosper. ❦

> **"No one is in a better position to assert that motors and their chauffeurs are cordially disliked... No longer will we have denied to our wives and daughters the freedom of the king's highway. I sincerely trust the bill you are bringing down before the house will cover the situation, and that we will have protection from those crazy men's cars."**
>
> **A Brandon constituent complains to his MLA about the rising number of automobiles on the roads**

Church reflecting on the Boyne River at Carman

The automobile was not warmly greeted in some Mennonite communities. The Blumenort area Kleine Gemeinde church excommunicated two of its members for owning cars.

CHAPTER FIVE

Growing Pains

BY TERENCE MOORE

As steady immigration fueled growth across the Prairies, Manitoba matured into a full-fledged partner in Confederation. The province's boundaries were extended to Hudson Bay in 1912, its population swelled to 450,000 and its importance as a gateway to the west was beyond dispute. Growing pains, however, were evident. Disparity between rich and poor caused social and labour unrest. The ruling Conservatives stood accused of corrupt politics. Women were insisting on the right to vote. And on the horizon lurked the threat of war—a war so terrible in its effects that the best of a generation would be lost forever.

With additional material by
J. EDGAR REA, DAVID BERCUSON, JIM NAYLOR, JAKE MACDONALD,
MARGARET SWEATMAN, DAVID ROBERTS AND LLOYD FRIDFINNSON

Frank Simon's watercolor of the interior of the proposed Manitoba Legislature, circa 1912

The Great War and its bloody aftermath **Growing Pains**

I n July, 1913, construction crews started digging the foundations for Manitoba's new Legislative Building on the site of the old Fort Osborne Barracks on Broadway. Manitoba had outgrown its 1884 Legislative Building, which stood beside Government House on the west side of Kennedy Street. With a dozen years of explosive growth behind it and seemingly boundless prospects ahead, Manitoba was ready for a magnificent new architectural showpiece.

But Manitoba was also ready for a new government and a new style of public life. The serious work of turning a booming but still frontier society into an industrial state was at hand. Ironically, the

ambitious, corrupt men who authorized the Legislative Building would not survive politically to occupy it, nor oversee the new society the building foreshadowed.

Sir Rodmond P. Roblin, Conservative premier of Manitoba since 1900, was his usual confident, bombastic self a few months later on January 28, 1914 when a delegation from the Political Equality League came to tell him why he should allow women to vote. Reform organizations had been demanding votes for women in Manitoba for 20 years and Roblin, secure in the leadership of a powerful political machine, had been refusing. He did not know that the political ground was already shifting beneath his feet.

Women's franchise was one of many changes Roblin was resisting. He was also refusing growing pressure for compulsory schooling in English, the prohibition of alcohol and the creation of a system of petitions and referendums (called direct legislation) to allow the public to make laws over the heads of the elected legislature.

Roblin met the delegation at the Kennedy Street Legislative Building. Novelist Nellie McClung told him women would help remove corruption from politics. He replied that talk of corruption in government was only the imagination of a wicked and vile mind. "I have been in politics for many years and I do not know of anything corrupt," Roblin said, drawing laughter from the spectators. "If you know that politics is corrupt, why do you want to interfere with it?" he asked. As the delegation filed out, Mrs. McClung told the premier: "I believe we'll get you yet, Sir Rodmond."

Get him they did, the very next evening. Before a full house at the Walker Theatre, Mrs. McClung played the part of a female premier refusing voting rights to a delegation of men. Her performance was a devastating lampoon of Roblin's style and reasoning:

"If, without exercising the vote, such splendid specimens of manhood can be produced, such a system of affairs should not be interfered with. Any system of civilization that can produce such splendid specimens... is good enough for me, and if it is good enough for me it is good enough for anybody. Another trouble is that if men start to vote they will vote too much. Politics unsettles men, and unsettled men mean unsettled bills—broken furniture, broken vows, divorce.

It has been charged that politics is corrupt. I don't know how this report got out, but I do most emphatically deny it.... I have been in politics for a long time and I never knew of any corruption or division of public money among the members of the house, and you may be sure that if anything of that kind had

SUFFRAGETTES WHO HAVE NEVER BEEN KISSED

"Get the thing done and let them howl."

Suffragette Nellie McClung

"...nice women don't want the vote."

Premier Rodmond P. Roblin

been going on I should have been in on it."

The audience loved it. The show was repeated the following night at the Bijou Theatre and later went on tour outside Winnipeg. The ticket sales solved the PEL's financial problem. McClung's wit punctured Roblin's air of invincibility. After 15 years of Conservative rule, Manitoba was in a mood for change.

Organizations had been arguing for women's suffrage in Manitoba since the early 1890's but aroused little interest in the general public. The campaign heated up with formation of the Political Equality League in early 1912. When League President Dr. Mary Crawford led the delegation to see Premier Roblin in 1914, she brought representatives of the Icelandic Women's Suffrage Association, the Women's Christian Temperance Union, the Trades and Labour Council, the Canadian Women's Press Club and the Young Women's Christian Association. The small, determined group of journalists and political activists had now found wider support.

The Arlington Bridge, erected across the CPR yards in 1911, was originally built to span the Nile River in Egypt. The Egyptians failed to take delivery, and the city of Winnipeg purchased it at an auction in England from the Cleveland Bridge and Iron Works. It was then shipped, in pieces, to Winnipeg.

A child's funeral in 1914

Novelist helped Manitoba women become the first in Canada to vote
Nellie McClung

HUMOUR AND social action were the two constants in Nellie McClung's life. Prohibition and women's suffrage were her two life-long missions. This duality sprang from the contrasting attitudes of her stern Calvinist Scottish mother and her easy-going Irish father. Nellie preferred her father's philosophy, and would later sum up her feelings this way: "I have a sort of [religion], but I'm afraid it's not up to much. I pray, Lord, keep me from being mean and stingy.... Let me see something to laugh at, at least once a day, and give everyone else as much as you do me."

Nellie Moonie was born in Ontario in 1873 and moved west when her family decided to homestead in Manitou. Her life was typical of the frugal pioneer experience, where each rug or each curtain in a kitchen window was a measured achievement. From the beginning, Nellie was a fighter, pressing for a chance at a higher education, already rebelling against the custom that kept women at home.

She graduated from Winnipeg Normal School and taught in Treherne and in Manitou. It was in Manitou that she married Wes McClung, a local druggist. On this subject, McClung was typically independent minded: "I knew I could be happy with Wes. We did not always agree but he was a fair fighter, and I knew I would rather fight with him than agree with anyone else." She wanted desperately to be a writer, but she was afraid that marriage would force her into a stunted domestic sphere. Wes McClung assured his new wife that she needn't devote her whole life to him.

McClung soon joined the Women's Christian Temperance Union. The WCTU advocated many kinds of reform, including women's suffrage. Later, when she saw for the first time an intoxicated woman, Nellie admitted that her understanding of sobriety had been naive.

The woman came from "one of Winnipeg's best-known families" and "her lapse from sobriety rather upset my theory that people drink to relieve the monotony of a drab life".

She began to write when she was first married: children's literature, short stories, and in 1908, her first novel, *Sowing Seeds in Danny,* which became a Canadian best seller. Writing gave her some financial independence and it strengthened her confidence. In 1911, when she and Wes and their four children moved to Winnipeg, she had a blossoming career.

This marked the most dynamic period of her life—from her entry into the social and political life of Winnipeg until the momentous occasion in 1916 when women in Manitoba finally won the right to vote.

After joining the Political Equality League in 1914, McClung gave one of the most famous theatrical performances in Manitoba history. The PEL

> **"Mike!—old friend Mike! Dead these many years! Your bones lie buried under the fertile soil of the Souris Valley, but your soul goes marching on! Mike, old friend, I see you again—both feet in the trough!"**
>
> **Nellie McClung compares Premier Roblin to an old ox at her family farm**

Women's suffrage movements were tied in with Manitoba's numerous temperance organizations. One of the most powerful of these, the Manitoba Social and Moral Reform Council, established in 1907, representing temperance groups, the Winnipeg Trades and Labour Council, the Manitoba Grain Growers' Association and a wide range of Christian denominations, urged the government to close the saloons that were the major liquor outlets and sources of disorder.

Premier Roblin and the ruling Conservatives refused to "banish the bar" though the social costs of widespread alcoholism were evident in the brawling drunkenness of Winnipeg's Main Street saloon strip. The Manitoba Direct Legislation League, meanwhile, had aroused growing interest in the system, devised by progressive thinkers in the United States, of petitions to initiate laws, referendums to approve them and mid-term votes to dismiss elected officials. The league collected

staged a mock women's parliament at the Walker Theatre, a parliament in a fantasy world where women would listen to a request for suffrage from a delegation of downtrodden men.

In a brilliant impersonation of the premier, Sir Rodmond Roblin, Nellie McClung complimented the men on their appearance. "If men were all so intelligent as these representatives of the downtrodden sex seem to be it might not do any harm to give them the vote. But all men are not intelligent... There is no use giving men votes. They wouldn't use them. They would let them spoil and go to waste. Then again, some men would vote too much."

A few months later, an election was called, and the Liberals chose to back suffrage and prohibition, issues that won the support of the PEL, especially McClung. The Liberal Party had McClung follow Sir Rodmond around the province presenting her sharp satire of his views on temperance and suffrage. The Conservatives argued that the Liberals (and the PEL) would give the franchise to "ignorant" foreign women. Nellie argued that all women must be enfranchised.

The Conservatives won the election, but not long after Roblin was forced to resign when the Legislative Building scandal erupted. Another election was called and this time the Liberals were elected. On January 28, 1916, the women of Manitoba became the first in Canada with the right to vote in provincial elections and to hold office.

10,000 signatures in 1913 on a petition to the government. Roblin replied that he supported the British system of responsible government.

The election of Robert Borden's Conservative government in Ottawa in 1911 brought Roblin a quick success in his long effort to expand the province northward. Since 1881, Manitoba's northern boundary had lain near the 53rd parallel. Swan River and the Porcupine Hills lay in Manitoba, The Pas was outside, and the north basin of Lake Winnipeg was half in and half out. Borden and Roblin agreed in November, 1911, on terms for the addition to Manitoba of the Canadian Shield country all the way up to the Hudson Bay coast and the 60th parallel. Parliament approved the transfer in March, 1912, but retained control of the natural resources, as it did throughout the western provinces.

As a result, Manitoba more than tripled in size. Its area of 190,966 square kilometres increased to 650,037 square kilometres. Boundary extension brought into Manitoba the timber of the boreal forest, the furs and fish of the forests and lakes, the minerals of the shield and the power of the Nelson River. The province acquired the Hudson Bay coast, which had been a shipping route to Europe since the start of the fur trade. A rail line across the muskeg to the bay was already under construction. Though grain remained Manitoba's mainstay, new northern prospects beckoned.

Boundary extension added a few thousand persons, mainly Cree, to the Manitoba population, which at the 1911 census totalled 455,614. The population had grown steadily—from 255,211 in

Getting clean in early Manitoba often entailed a trip to a public bath. The City of Winnipeg opened the Pritchard Avenue Public Baths on May 6, 1912. Three years later, the Cornish Park Baths were opened. Both had plunge baths, as well as 32 shower baths each.

Shadow on the Southern Horizon

At the very moment Winnipeg was establishing itself as the Canadian equivalent to Chicago—a transportation and distribution centre for the entire West—the city was being undermined by American engineers digging a canal through the jungles and swamps of Central America.

The proposed canal, linking the Atlantic and Pacific oceans at Panama, would shave 8,000 kilometres off the ocean journey from the Pacific to the ports of Europe. This had been the dream of many adventurers, including Vasco Nunez Balboa, who first raised the possibility in 1517.

But the Americans brought the dream to reality and, in 1914, the *S.S. Ancon* was the first ship to sail through the canal. The canal cost the United States $380 million and, almost overnight, made the nondescript lumber town of Vancouver a rival to Winnipeg as a grain shipping terminal.

Because of the canal and the levelling of ocean and rail freight rates, other prairie cities—Regina, Calgary and Edmonton—began to assume larger roles as wholesale hubs. But while Winnipeg lost some of its influence, it did not lose all. Many of the businesses west of Winnipeg were branch plants of Winnipeg firms, and so while the Manitoba capital lost some rail traffic because of the Panama Canal, the grain barons and wholesalers in the city managed to retain financial control of much of the western agricultural marketplace.

1901—by settlement of immigrant farmers on the homesteads and by recruitment of workers for Winnipeg's developing industries.

Since Manitoba school law technically allowed the use of any classroom language and did not require school attendance, education authorities feared that many of the children of East European immigrants were not learning English. By the Education Department's estimate in February, 1913, 64,126 children were attending English schools in the province while 12,437 were attending French, German, Ukrainian and Polish language schools that were said to be bilingual though the quality of English-language teaching varied widely. As in other Canadian provinces at the time, many children did not attend school at all.

Loans from British and Central Canadian investors had financed the years of economic boom during settlement and breaking of the prairie. Farms were mortgaged on optimistic valuations. Implement dealers sold their machines on credit. Railway companies sold bonds in Britain to finance construction. The 1913 and 1914 drought in the Palliser Triangle of southern Alberta and southwest Saskatchewan, however, reminded lenders that profits on Prairie investments depended on good grain-growing weather and good wheat prices. The investors became edgy. The

Canadian Farm Implements magazine urged implement dealers in June, 1913, to "get in your accounts" and as the implement dealers shortened credit lines, other lenders followed suit. Suddenly, the speculative boom was over and the Manitoba economy fell into recession. The value of building permits issued in Winnipeg, which had exceeded $20 million in 1912, dropped to $18 million in 1913 and $12 million in 1914. Wages for grain harvesters, which averaged $3.13 a day in 1912 and 1913, dropped to $2.55 a day in 1914.

News of a gold discovery at Rice Lake, east of Lake Winnipeg, produced a flurry of prospecting in the summer of 1913 and led to the creation of mines and a townsite at Bissett, but its effect on the Manitoba economy was slight. Manitoba had boomed for about 20 years on borrowed money whose lenders hoped for indefinite growth in the grain economy. That growth was nearing its limits, since the best land was already settled and in production. The economic tide, fueled on massive immigration, was slowly turning against Manitoba and the Canadian West.

The political tide, at the same time, was turning against Rodmond Roblin and his Conservative government. As the 1914 election approached, he refused to budge on votes for women, prohibition of alcohol, direct legislation or compulsory education in English.

The Path of Progress, by Reinhold Gundlach, 1913

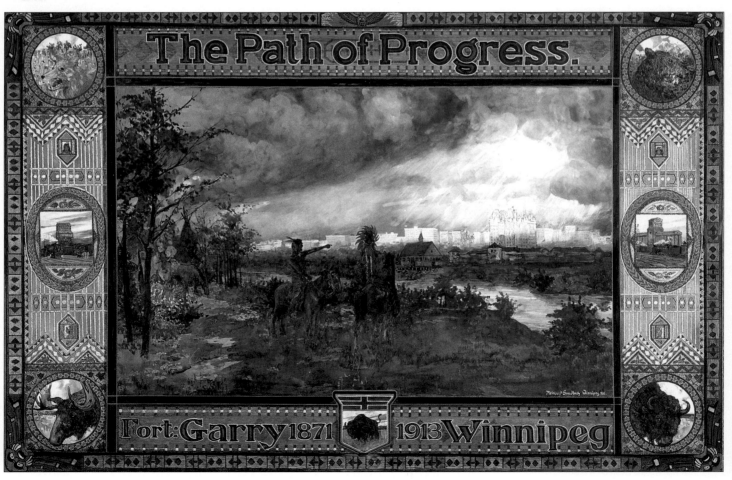

Winnipeg the Pooh

The famous British children's book character Winnie the Pooh derived its name from an unlikely source—the city of Winnipeg.

Winnipeg veterinarian Harry Colebourn was a militia officer with the Fort Garry Horse, and in 1914 he signed up for war duty. While en route overseas, Colebourn acquired a black bear cub. His diary recorded the purchase: "On train all day Aug. 24. Bought (Winnie) Cub Bear at White River. Amt. paid $20.00." The orphaned bear cub was dubbed Winnie after Winnipeg.

The bear accompanied Colebourn overseas. Colebourn was assigned to the Second Canadian Infantry Brigade at Salisbury Plain, where Winnie kept the soldiers company. When Colebourn was sent to the French battlefields, Winnie was left in the care of the London Zoo.

The playful, friendly bear cub was a hit with zoo visitors, particularly Christopher Robin Milne, son of writer A.A. Milne. The boy adored Winnie, and the senior Milne noted his son's affection for the bear. In 1926, he wrote Winnie-the-Pooh, the story of a young boy and a bear. This and the other Winnie the Pooh stories became children's classics.

Colebourn continued to visit Winnie, hoping to retrieve her when the war ended. However, he left her at the zoo when he saw the impression she made on London's residents. He returned to Winnipeg and resumed his veterinary practice.

Winnie died in 1934. Obituaries for the cherished bruin ran in the London newspapers. However, the bear's memory lives on in the hearts of anyone who has visited the "Hundred Acres Wood".

In the contract for the new Legislative Building, Roblin had taken on a project that was too complex and expensive for his government's ethical standards and administrative methods. Even while he was telling Nellie McClung and the Political Equality League that he was not corrupt, he and his colleagues were instructing contractor Thomas Kelly to submit grossly inflated bills for the work and kick the excess back to Dr. R.M. Simpson, the chief fund-raiser for the Manitoba Conservative party. In the simple management methods of that trusting time it was easily done, but when Manitobans sniffed the political winds in 1913 and 1914, they smelled corruption. The *Emerson Journal* wrote in March, 1914:

"Three weeks ago the Roblin government kindly donated or inflicted on us a party of surveyors and this week they sent a party of twelve telephone men. The telephone service has been on the hummer here for at least two years that we know of and it's as if the powers that be have just found out about it. Elections are undoubtedly coming off soon if present indications mean anything."

In this climate of growing impatience with Roblin, Manitobans voted on July 10, 1914. The Liberals under T.C. Norris entered the election advocating women's franchise, a prohibition referendum, compulsory education in English and direct legislation. They enjoyed the formal backing of Baptist ministers, the Methodist and Presbyterian conferences, the Social Service council, the Orange lodges, the Political Equality League, the *Manitoba Free Press,* the *Winnipeg Tribune* and the *Grain Growers' Guide.* Nellie McClung and other Political Equality League speakers appeared at Liberal election meetings across the province. Against this rising tide of reform sentiment, the Conservatives

He may have been Manitoba's most progressive premier
T.C. Norris

I F HE IS REMEMBERED AT ALL, TOBIAS CRAWFORD Norris is usually recalled as the low-profile premier who played such a negligible role in the settling of the 1919 Winnipeg General Strike. Most historians agree, however, that Norris was a significant political figure who placed Manitoba at the forefront of progressive government in Canada.

Born in Brampton, Ontario, in 1861, Norris came to Manitoba as a homesteader. He took up auctioneering as a profession and was well known across western Canada. Elected to the Manitoba legislature in 1896, he became Liberal leader in 1910.

Frustrated by Tory premier Rodmond P. Roblin's 15-year grip on power, Norris hoped to broaden Liberal support by courting special interest groups. Foremost among those to back him in the election of 1914 were advocates of women's suffrage and the temperance movement. When the votes were counted, however, Roblin was returned as premier with a slim majority.

A few months later, Norris took a short cut to the premier's office when Roblin was forced to resign after being implicated in the Legislative Building scandal. Norris called an election almost immediately and ran his campaign on the same progressive platform of the previous year.

This time the Liberals won in a rout—taking 42 of a possible 49 seats. In spite of wartime constraints, Norris honoured the promises made to his special interest group supporters. The result was legislation that pioneered the social service state in Canada: minimum-wage guidelines; compulsory school attendance; a public nursing system; rural farm credit; prohibition; and a mother's allowance.

Most significantly, Manitoba became in 1916 the first legislature to grant women the vote and the right to hold provincial office. As well, a remodelled Elections Act was introduced to thwart corruption at the polls, and a civil service commission was created to fill government jobs on the basis of merit. Norris also tried to pass legislation for direct government through the Initiative and Referendum Act. This action was ruled unconstitutional by the Supreme Court.

The undoing of Norris came at the hands of the increasingly powerful labour and farm movements. The Winnipeg General Strike divided the city politically and Norris' views reflected neither side of the debate. Meanwhile, in rural areas, farmers were uncomfortable with the Liberals' social legislation and free-spending ways.

The election of 1920 turned into a populist protest vote against career politicians. It left Nor-

T.C. Norris instigated proceedings that eventually brought down the Roblin government.

ris with a minority government ruling over a raucous and fragmented legislature. A quick no-confidence vote led to a July, 1922, election. The Liberals won a mere seven seats, and Norris —one of the province's most activist premiers— soon faded from the political limelight. The man who made Manitoba "the centre of reform activity in Canada" died in Toronto in 1936.

applied the campaign fund they had filled through systematic fraud in the Legislative Building construction. The popular vote, 71,616 for Conservative candidates, 62,798 for the Liberals and 15,654 for Independents, produced a legislature of 25 Conservatives and 21 Liberals. Roblin and his government were, for the time being, back in office.

The election was scarcely completed when Manitobans' attention was drawn to Europe, where a Serbian terrorist's bullet had led Austria-Hungary and Germany to go to war against Serbia, Russia, France and Belgium. Britain declared war on Germany on August 4, 1914, in defence of Belgium and France and to prevent Germany from controlling continental Europe.

The 40,000 signatures on a petition presented to the T.C. Norris government demanding women's suffrage were the most ever presented to a Canadian legislature.

Canada joined Britain in declaring war almost immediately. Britain was the ancestral home of the majority of Canada's people, the source of its institutions, of its dominant language and of much of the capital that had built the country since the fur trade days. It was the main market for the wheat Manitoba farmers grew and, for many Manitobans, the home of the religions they practised and the ideas they honoured. Germany was challenging the British Empire. Manitoba, an outpost of that empire, knew its duty.

Within weeks, Manitoba men were crowding the recruiting halls and giving generously to public subscriptions to aid the war effort. Those who enlisted in 1914 expected a quick and glorious victory. Instead they were thrown into a long, cruel, indecisive conflict that bloodied fields in France and Belgium. Manitoba's death toll averaged one out of 60 persons, the highest in the Dominion. The war dragged on for years, devastating Canada's population of young men.

In Manitoba, the Conservatives' return to power was short-lived. Roblin at first refused a commission of inquiry into evidence the Liberals presented showing large-scale corruption in the Legislative Building construction contracts, but when he sought to prorogue the assembly on April 1, 1915, Lieutenant-Governor Douglas Cameron told him he must either allow an inquiry or resign. As it turned out, he did both: the evidence publicly presented to the T.G. Mathers inquiry showed that the premier and his associates were up to their eyeballs in fraud, looting the public treasury they were elected to administer. Roblin resigned on May 12 and Norris's new Liberal government was sworn in the following day.

The Norris government promptly called an election and, on August 6, 1915, was swept into power. The Conservatives had chosen a new leader, Sir James Aikins, and endorsed women's suffrage, direct legislation and prohibition, but to no avail. They were reduced to five seats in the 49-seat assembly, four of them from French districts worried about the Liberals' school policy. Two Labour candidates, R.A. Rigg and F.J. Dixon, were elected from Winnipeg's North and Centre districts. Norris's Liberals elected 42, an overwhelming majority and ample authority to start implementing their ambitious program of reforms.

Norris and his government produced an avalanche of legislation reflecting the intellectual and political ferment of the time. He invited the temperance organizations to write the Manitoba Temperance Act which was approved at a men-only plebiscite on March 13, 1916, with 50,484 voting for and 26,052 against. Many Manitobans had believed for years that easy access to alcohol was wrecking lives and families. They had already voted heavily in favour of temperance at plebiscites in 1892 and 1898. The temperance act was proclaimed in 1916 and took effect on June 1. All sales of liquor were banned, except by druggists on a doctor's prescription. The mayor of Winnipeg reported three months later that crime and public drunkenness had markedly declined. Druggists, meanwhile, prospered.

Norris's Initiative and Referendum Act of 1916 introduced the theory of direct legislation, which allowed voters to suggest their own laws. The act was later judged unconstitutional and was never used.

The Norris government quickly honoured its promise to give women the right to vote and to

Camp Hughes (formerly Sewell), west of Carberry, was the site of military training facilities during World War I. Some 30,000 soldiers were trained at the site, which included amenities such as a hospital, two theatres, two banks, a barber shop and two cafes. Eighteen battalions were sent directly overseas from the camp.

hold public office. On December 23, 1915, a delegation of 60 men and women brought Premier Norris suffrage petitions with more than 40,000 signatures. The premier introduced a women's suffrage bill on January 10, 1916. Third reading was given January 27 before crowded galleries and in an atmosphere of celebration. Manitoba women became the first in Canada with provincial suffrage. A further act of 1917 made women eligible for all municipal offices if they had the property qualifications.

Also at the 1916 session, the Liberals overturned the 1897 provision in the School Act allowing bilingual teaching. Ukrainian and Polish schools had multiplied under the shelter of the 1897 compromise, which had been designed to accommodate French Catholics and German Mennonites. Education Minister R.S. Thornton concluded that bilingual education must be abolished. French-speaking members of the legislature, both Liberal and Conservative, strenuously objected, but Thornton said: "We are building for the

Socialist leader believed some immigrants made better Canadians than others

J.S. Woodsworth

JAMES SHAVER WOODSWORTH IS BEST remembered as a reform-minded clergyman who made an outstanding contribution to the early social democratic movement. His writings, however, reveal a complex figure, torn in his religious convictions and uneasy with the ethnicity of the immigrants to whom he ministered.

Woodsworth moved with his family from Ontario to Brandon in 1885. In 1896, he followed in his father's footsteps and was ordained as a Methodist minister. The young Woodsworth had spent the previous year studying in England, where he came to question the literal interpretation of the Bible. He also embraced the institutions of the British, while feeling some disdain for the English people, many of whom he found to be "vulgar".

Woodsworth returned to Canada with increasing doubt about his church's emphasis on personal salvation. He felt his work should address the abject living conditions of the poor. In 1907, Woodsworth attempted to resign from the ministry but he was persuaded instead to become superintendent of the All Peoples' Mission in Winnipeg. In this capacity, Woodsworth felt he could pursue social justice and the establishment of a Kingdom of God in the "here and now".

Two years later, Woodsworth wrote *Strangers Within Our Gates*. It addressed the topical question of immigration and its impact on the emerging Canadian way of life. Woodsworth argued that an immigrant's success in Canada depended upon complete assimilation. He concluded that people from Britain, Germany, Scandinavia and America would make the best citizens. The absence of democratic traditions among eastern and southern Europeans made them unsuitable. Orientals and blacks were even less desirable because they

were, in his view, unable to assimilate. Incongruously, Woodsworth also admonished Anglo-Canadians for their arrogant attitude toward immigrants.

By the outbreak of the World War I, Woodsworth's mission work and written musings on race were overshadowed by his involvement in the labour movement. He became a well-known and controversial supporter of trade unions. When the editors of the *Western Labor News* were arrested for speaking out in favour of the Winnipeg General Strike, Woodsworth took over the newspaper until he too was briefly jailed.

Even though Woodsworth had little to do with the General Strike, he became identified as one of its leaders. On the strength of labour support, Woodsworth ran for the Manitoba Independent Labour Party and was elected to Parliament in 1921 for Winnipeg North Centre. That riding returned him to Ottawa in every subsequent election until his death in 1942. Staunchly anti-Marxist and anti-Communist, Woodsworth's political platform most closely resembled that of the British Labour Party. In 1933, he helped form (and became the first leader of) the Co-operative Commonwealth Federation (CCF), the precursor of today's New Democratic Party.

Canada of tomorrow and our common school is one of the most important factors in the work. In this Dominion we are building up, under the British flag, a new nationality. We come from many lands and cast in our lot, and from these various factors there must evolve a new nationality which shall be simply Canadian and British."

The act banning bilingual schools was passed on March 10, 1916. A week later the legislature passed a School Attendance Act, which required all children between six and 14 years of age living near a school to attend a public school or a private one that met provincial standards. Bilingual teaching in fact continued unofficially where it was already practised, but its spread was curbed.

A year later, the Liberal government turned its attention to the University of Manitoba. By the University Act of 1917, the government took over from the church colleges the power to appoint the board of governors of the university. The annual grant to the university was increased, but the new buildings it needed were not provided.

While the Norris government was decisive and energetic in stamping out liquor trade and

minority languages and in advancing women's rights and direct legislation, the Liberals made only modest gestures in support of the workers of Winnipeg's growing industries. The Roblin government's Workmen's Compensation Act was amended. The Factories Act and the Building Trades Protection Act were amended. The Bureau of Labour was given additional duties and a Fair Wage Board was set up. The Shops Regulation Act was amended to free children for school attendance. None of these gestures responded to the growing feeling in trade union circles that workers and their unions deserved far more recognition

Trench at right was used in Winnipeg as a recruiting device. The model trench didn't compare to the reality, below, of trench warfare overseas.

A Soldier's Letters Home

Harry Orde was born in Brandon in 1898. He moved to Winnipeg and graduated from Kelvin High School. Orde enlisted with the 90th Winnipeg Rifles ("Little Black Devils") in February, 1916. He was sent to France in May, 1917 and killed in action on August 15, 1917.

France, July 31, 1917

Dear Mother & Dad,

I received your letter of July 7th and also one from Dorothy of July 5th. I was very glad to hear Dorothy was able to walk around again and I hope a few swims at Minaki will fix her up again. I wouldn't mind a swim down there myself right now but I guess I will have to wallop a few more Fritzies before I can get one. I had a few swims in a big tank and it was certainly fine but I am still as lousy as ever which is the best way to be as you can occupy yourself catching big fat ones. I am out resting at present but expect to go into the line again shortly which never worries me till I get there and it is "no bon" (as the French say) at times but the only thing to do is grin and bear it. I think we have Fritz licked to a frazzle & it is only a question of time until he quits. I have had a few narrow escapes but "a miss is as good as a mile".

If the Frenchmen in Quebec start anything they ought to turn a few machine guns on them and that would quiet them down "tout suite".

If you catch a big "lunge" at Minaki be sure and land him and have a few steaks off him for me. I could eat anything now from moccasins to fishworms and believe me I will never turn down bacon again. I sure missed a lot when I wouldn't eat it for a long time. If it weren't for cigarettes rum and bacon all the soldiers out here would be dead long ago and I have never seen a man turn down a rum issue yet. (We only get it when it is cold and wet in the summer but I understand that it is issued every day in the winter.)

If you send me a dollar bill every little while it would help some as we are only allowed to draw a franc a day out here and a franc is only about 18 cents. You can buy quite a bit of stuff to eat in the canteens out here and it is nice to have candies cigarettes chocolate etc. to take into the line with you. Well I guess I will have to close now. Lots of love to everybody.

Your loving son,
Harry

P.S. I will get Dorothy some kind of a souvenir but not what she asked for.

Gun in full recoil after being fired on the fields of Cambrai, France

France, Aug. 11, 1917

Dear Mother,

I received your letter of July 19th and also one from Dorothy and one from Jean.

I also got the parcel with the cake olives cigarettes in it and it came at a pretty good time as I got it the night I came out of the line. I was out of cigarettes and feeling pretty fagged out and it was certainly fine opening that parcel and having a good feed out of it.

Dad's parcel from Eatons also came along today and it certainly has some swell grub in it. Believe me, the troops will live high for a few days anyway. We are out resting now for a few days and we are having pretty good weather.

I suppose the Colonel [his grandfather] is having as much trouble as ever with the motor-boats. He ought to sell the bunch & buy one good boat as those blooming things never were any good.

I guess I will close now but I will write another letter in a couple of days and I might have a little more news to write about.

D'Arcy [his cousin] was pretty lucky getting wounded & going to England but I guess he had a pretty narrow escape.

Love to everybody.

Your loving son,
Harry

Note: This was Harry's last letter.

and power than governments and the owners of industry were willing to grant them. This feeling was encouraged by the 1917 Bolshevik revolution in Russia.

The Norris government also established a civil service commission to recruit by competitive examination, offered government-guaranteed mortgages to farmers and government support for rural credit societies, protected widows' claims on their husband's estates and established the provincial electric power utility.

Its legislation added up to a sweeping reform of the morals, the laws and the political system of the province. Apart from women's suffrage and prohibition, most of the changes made little daily difference in the lives of the farmers and workers of the province. But within the limited scope of typical government action in those years, the Norris reforms quickly took Manitoba from its era of noisy frontier boom to a new era of ordered civility.

The war on Germany's western front, meanwhile, had turned into a series of attacks and counter-attacks against strong defensive positions in a line of trenches snaking across Belgium and France. Machine guns cut infantrymen down by the tens of thousands and artillery shells reduced them to fragments. With the methodically prepared capture of Vimy Ridge in April, 1917 by the Canadian Corps, Britain and her allies began the series of successes that concluded with Germany's defeat. By the end of the war, the achievements of Canadian troops had helped turn

Pine Street in Winnipeg's west end was renamed Valour Road to honour the extraordinary fact that three men from one block—Corporal Leo Clarke, Sergeant-Major Frederick Hall and Lieutenant Robert Shankland—won the Victoria Cross in World War I.

Red Cross train used to transport the wounded waits beside a Canadian field dressing station at Camiens.

Faced with 60 German Fokkers, "Lone Wolf" Billy Barker decided to attack

IN A WAR THAT PRODUCED MORE THAN ITS share of heroes, one man stands out for his audacity and fearlessness—Dauphin's William (Billy) Barker. His fame was such that one British commander later commented: "Of all the fliers of two world wars, none was greater than Billy Barker."

Enlisting in Winnipeg in 1914, Barker

One of Billy Barker's many victims

began the war as an infantryman. At Ypres, he was part of the Canadian Mounted Rifles who courageously stood their ground as the German army unleashed wave after wave of poison gas. Barker survived, but the experience strengthened his resolve to try to escape the muddy frontline trenches. His dream, as with so many other soldiers, was to take to the air and fly with the aces of the Royal Flying Corps.

In 1915, Barker achieved a transfer to the RFC. Starting out as a gunner, he soon

Canada from a province of the British Empire into an independent power in world affairs.

Many Manitobans were singled out as examples of the great courage that gave their country a new international status. During a Canadian attempt to break through the German line and advance to the French town of Cambrai on November 20, 1917, for instance, Harcus Strachan of Winnipeg's Fort Garry Horse cavalry regiment led a mounted squadron on a daring raid

Dauphin's Ace of Aces

passed his flight test and got his pilot wings. Barker proved himself to be a natural pilot and a deadly shot. He acquired a reputation as a "lone wolf", often flying sorties by himself—searching the skies for German planes. Barker flew on the French and Italian fronts and survived without serious injury until 1918 (an amazing feat in itself). In that time, he shot down 46 enemy aircraft.

Barker's greatest exploit, however, occurred in the last month of the war. Ordered home, the much-decorated ace filled the tanks of his Sopwith Snipe and took off for England on the morning of October 26. Flying north towards the Channel, he noticed a German observation plane flying below him. Unable to resist one last kill, Barker pounced on the two-seater and split it open with a long burst from his machine guns.

Just as he pulled from his dive, Barker heard the chatter of another gun and felt a bullet tear through his right thigh. Banking hard left, he turned the Snipe to discover the entire Jagdgeschwader 3—60 Fokker D VII's—arranged in the sky around him. Judging escape to be impossible, Barker decided to make his last flight a memorable one—he attacked.

Charging the Fokker that had wounded him, Barker let loose a fury of bullets that sent the surprised German down in flames. He then turned on a second fighter, latched onto its tail and shattered it with two bursts.

The German pilots quickly regrouped. Using their huge numerical advantage, they began to attack Barker from all sides. Within a few minutes, despite his twists and turns, Barker's plane was shredded. More than 300 bullets tore through the Snipe, one of them piercing the Canadian ace's left leg.

At this point, Barker passed out. His plane spun towards the ground, out of control. After a few moments, however, he revived and saw a Fokker following him. Enraged, Barker attacked again and, a few seconds later, another German was dead.

His plane destroyed and his cockpit awash in blood, Barker tried to land next to the British trenches. Hitting the ground at a high speed, the Snipe plowed through the mud and somersaulted onto its back. British Tommies pulled a blood-soaked Barker from the wreckage, certain that he was dead. Amazingly, even though both legs were almost severed, the young Manitoba pilot survived—and went on to be awarded the Victoria Cross at Buckingham Palace.

An artillery colonel who witnessed the display said later that Barker's incredible display of courage had a profound impact on the Allied troops: "The hoarse shout, or rather prolonged roar, which greeted the triumph [of Barker] and which echoed across the battle front, was never matched."

---

behind the German lines in which they destroyed an artillery battery, inflicted well over 100 casualties, cut telephone cables and took about 100 prisoners. The ground gained that day was soon lost to German counterattacks, but Strachan's achievement earned him a Victoria Cross, the British Empire's highest military decoration.

Christopher Patrick John O'Kelly quit St. John's College to enlist in 1916. He led a company of infantry in storming three German pillboxes near Ypres during the Flanders campaign of January, 1918. He himself took the middle pillbox. His company sent 12 machine guns and 75 prisoners back from the captured pillboxes, advanced to German trenches 200 yards farther on, took a further 30 prisoners and defended their position against counterattacks in the night. This action earned him a VC.

Two Manitobans earned VCs in the August, 1918, Battle of Amiens. Robert Spall had come to Winnipeg at age two in 1892 with his parents from Suffolk, England, and quit an office job to enlist in August, 1915. His platoon of the Princess Patricia's Canadian Light Infantry, advancing toward Amiens, was caught by a German counterattack. While his comrades retreated to safety, he

Nurses and babies at the Grace Hospital, 1914

single-handedly held the German troops off with a Lewis gun until he was shot and killed. Raphael Zengel, a child of Swedish parents born in Minnesota, was working on a farm near Virden when war started. During the Canadian advance toward Amiens, he rushed ahead of his platoon to attack the German machine gun that was stopping their advance, killed the officer and the operator and scattered the rest of the crew. Hit by a shell fragment, he was left for dead but revived and rejoined his platoon.

Alan McLeod, of Stonewall, won his VC in the air. Flying a FK 8 bomber, he and his observer were attacked by a squadron of Fokker triplanes on March 27, 1918. The observer, Arthur Ham-

The Winnipeg

Manitoba's first mega-project was an engineering marvel

IN THE SPRING OF 1912, WINNIPEG was preparing for another boom period. In one important respect, however, the city was still a backwoods town: foul-tasting well water dribbled from every faucet. In the grand hotels along Main Street, the toilets and ornate claw-footed bathtubs were disfigured by rusty stains. Typhoid epidemics struck with alarming regularity. Unpleasant to behold and dangerous to drink, Winnipeg's water was the single greatest impediment to its progress.

For decades "watermen" on ox carts hauled untreated water from the Red and Assiniboine Rivers and delivered it by barrel around the city. The city then switched to artesian wells, which produced unreliable—and sometimes dangerously polluted—drinking water. In the early 1900's a series of typhoid epidemics killed hundreds of citizens and by 1912 it was obvious that Canada's third largest city needed a fresh and reliable supply of water.

In September of that same year, American engineer Charles Slichter strongly condemned the current system. Slichter said the city had three options. It could drill new water wells north of the city, a cheap but unreliable water source. As a second option,

the city could build a pipeline to the Winnipeg River—a marginally better alternative. But in describing the city's third option, Slichter became uncharacteristically excited. He used words like "daring" and "visionary". He told officials he had recently visited a fabulous source of water, a lake of "clean Laurentian granite" which had "collected together a body of water of exceptional softness and purity". The name of the source was Shoal Lake.

City council examined Slichter's report and rejected it emphatically as too expensive. But the citizens of Winnipeg had their own ideas. According to an editorial in the *Manitoba Free Press,* Winnipeggers were looking to the future. They wanted "water of good quality and lots of it". More importantly, they were willing to pay for it.

The following year, new mayor Thomas R. Deacon won the mayoral

campaign and soon after submitted a water plebiscite to voters. The expensive Shoal Lake plan won by a landslide. Now planners had to figure out how to get the water to the city.

Just as the ancient Romans built aqueducts to transport water over long distances to Rome, Professor Slichter recommended that Winnipeg build an aqueduct to Shoal Lake. In Italy or other temperate

mond, managed to shoot down two fighters but the Germans attacked vigorously and soon both men were wounded. The bomber caught fire, forcing McLeod out of the cockpit and onto the lower left wing. He somehow guided the plane to a controlled crash landing in No Man's Land. McLeod then, although wounded five times, pulled his observer out of the burning wreck. Hit again by machine gun fire from the German trenches, he managed to drag Hammond to safety. (Ironically, after surviving this encounter, McLeod died in Winnipeg during the flu epidemic of 1918-19.)

The thousands of Manitobans who enlisted were supported by tens of thousands more who gave money or volunteer effort to support the war. Augustus M. Nanton, a lender of Scottish capital to Prairie farmers and developers for the firm of Osler, Hammond & Nanton, donated $1,000 a month to the Canadian Patriotic Fund, of which he was the Manitoba chairman. He also led the Manitoba committee for the 1917 Victory Loan campaign and opened his Winnipeg house, Kilmorie, to entertain recruits in training. Working parties of volunteer women gathered at Kilmorie to knit clothing for the men in the trenches. In 1918, the Nantons' summer home at Kenora served as a convalescent hospital for wounded veterans.

Aqueduct

climates, builders could get away with open-air aqueducts that were really just a canal. But in Canada, cold winters meant that an aqueduct would have to be buried below the frost line. To complicate matters, the aqueduct would have to cross some 110 kilometres of muskeg, forest and rivers. Fortunately, Shoal Lake's elevation was 100 metres higher than Winnipeg, so simple gravity would move the water to the city.

On May 15, 1915, work on the aqueduct began. In cross-section, the aqueduct was a dome-shaped concrete shell mounted on a concrete floor, or "invert". The sections of pipe were poured into concrete forms and coupled together with copper expansion joints to allow for changes in temperature.

At the Seine and Red Rivers, tunnels were drilled down into bedrock 25 metres below the riverbed and lined with precast sections of concrete pipe three metres in diameter. Builders had to contend with endless problems: muskeg "soup" that flowed into the ditch as quickly as they excavated, soft sections of Red River gumbo that caused the heavy pipe to sag and crack, and even forest fires that burned off the aqueduct's insulating blanket of earth.

On April 6, 1919, several million gallons of fresh clean water gushed into the new aqueduct and began flowing towards Winnipeg. After four years and $17 million the project was complete. The aqueduct is still in use.

Manitoba's 15,000 Mennonites stood apart from the war effort, the flag-waving and the nationalism that the war aroused, for they were religious pacifists wishing only to be left in peace in their two settlements, one around Steinbach, the other around Winkler. They had come to Manitoba in the 1870's because the federal government promised them exemption from military service and freedom to practise their religion and maintain their schools. They were left in peace through the war, but in the fall of 1918 the Manitoba government began prosecuting Mennonite parents who refused to send their children to school. Mennonite schools were teaching English in addition to German, but the government insisted on assimilation through the public schools.

Mennonites did not object when the federal government's Wartime Elections Act denied them a vote in the 1917 election. They were worried, however, when a June, 1919, federal order-in-council forbade further Mennonite immigration because of their refusal to assimilate and to accept military service. Leaders of some Mennonite congregations began negotiations with the Quebec government and with the governments of Mexico and Paraguay in search of a safer haven.

More difficult was the position of Manitoba's Ukrainians, who were the dominant ethnic group in the rural municipalities of Ethelbert, Stuartburn, Dauphin and Rossburn and were steadily increasing in Winnipeg's North End. Theodore Stefanyk in 1911 was elected as Winnipeg's first Ukrainian

Examples of wartime propaganda used to boost morale for both troops and civilians back home

alderman. Taras Ferley won Gimli for the provincial Liberals in the 1915 general election, the first Ukrainian in the legislature.

Ukrainians' origins in Austria-Hungary, which was allied with Germany, raised suspicion among British Manitobans. A 1914 pastoral letter from Winnipeg Bishop Nykyta Budka, urging Ukrainians to return home for service in the Austro-Hungarian army, was taken as evidence of disloyalty. Canada interned a thousand Manitoba Ukrainians, along with many Germans, as enemy aliens at an internment camp on the grounds of the Brandon Winter Fair. Naturalization of Ukrainians was suspended by Parliament in 1919.

Icelanders, who had first settled on the west shore of Lake Winnipeg in 1875, willingly sent their children to English-language public schools and enthusiastically assimilated to the dominant British culture. When war came, Manitoba Icelanders enlisted in the army, navy and air force. At the same time, the women of the Jon Sigurdson chapter of the International Order Daughters of the Empire played their part in sending parcels overseas and supporting soldiers' families at home.

Winnipeg's Jewish community had grown to 9,000 in 1911 and had produced a first Jewish alderman, Moses Finkelstein, elected in 1905, and the first Jewish member of a Canadian legislature, S. Hart Green, elected in 1910. Jews encountered barriers to the assimilation many of them sought. The *Israelite Press* of Winnipeg wrote in 1914: "We don't want to separate ourselves from others, but this is only possible when we gain full recognition like others." Winnipeg Jews were extremely diverse in economic condition and in political views and they reacted in different ways to the European war and assimilative pressure.

The war's first effect on Manitoba farmers was a new credit crunch added to the effects of the recession of 1913 and 1914. Lenders in Britain, fearful for their European investments as soon as war broke out, pressed

Bloody Jack Krafchenko was the most infamous of the country robbers

Harvesting

A S THE "BREADBASKET OF THE empire", the Canadian prairies hit their height of prosperity in the early 1900's. Every August, as harvest season commenced and threshing crews roamed the country, great sacks of money for equipment and wages were shipped to small Manitoba towns. Locked in the vaults of banks in villages like Emerson and Plum Coulee these whopping piles of cash proved tempting to big-city bank robbers, who soon learned that a drive in the country could prove worthwhile. So problematic were these rural heists that cops began calling autumn on the Prairies "robbery season".

Rural banks were soft targets. Local police constables were usually part-time employees without communication equipment or even cars. On more than one occasion the boom of an exploding safe woke up the entire town. But few townspeople were willing to confront professional robbers armed with explosives and Thompson machine guns. More than one constable—jumping up at the sound of the blast—was ordered back into bed by his wife. In any case, there wasn't much sympathy for the victims, the butt of all farm humour, the banks. In one robbery just after World War I, a group of combat-seasoned war veterans cruised into Winkler at midnight, climbed a pole, cut the telegraph wires, captured the bank manager, tied him up, (making sure that his gag and bindings were comfortable) then blew the safe to pieces. They made off with an "undisclosed sum of money" and the bank's promissory notes, thereby reducing the Winkler community debt to zero.

Perhaps the most infamous rural bank robber was John Larry Krafchenko, or as he named himself,

"Bloody Jack". Born in 1881, of Ukrainian parents in Rumania, Jack Krafchenko grew up in Plum Coulee, Manitoba, where he became known as a boisterous teenager with a bevy of girlfriends and a contempt for the police.

After numerous minor scrapes with the law, Krafchenko migrated briefly to Australia, returning a couple of years later as a professional wrestler. He toured the United States under the name of "Australian Tommy Ryan". Tiring of ring life Krafchenko then travelled as an evangelical lecturer, specializing in the evils of liquor. Between lectures he passed numerous bad cheques which led eventually to his arrest in Regina. En route to an 18-month prison term in Prince Albert Peniten-

Money During 'Robbery Season'

tiary he demonstrated another skill— escaping police custody. He jumped out the train window, but was quickly recaptured.

Soon after, he escaped from the

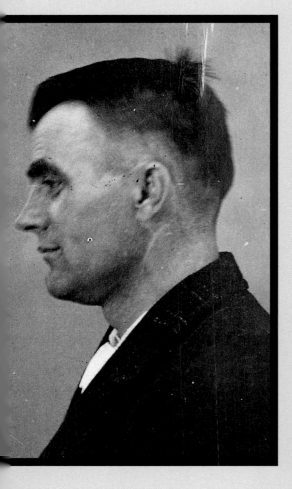

penitentiary and from that point he was no longer satisfied with petty crimes. With guns and disguises he robbed banks across Canada and the United States, then travelled to Europe and blazed a trail across England, Germany and Italy. Always, he demonstrated his trademark flair. In a Milan bank he locked up the manager, then joined the crowd outside to watch the police try to cut the man out of the vault.

In 1905, he returned to Canada and moved back to Plum Coulee with a new bride. He couldn't resist the occasional bank robbery though, and his

first target was a bank near Winkler. Although never arrested for that crime, he was high on the wanted list. In 1908, a pal of Krafchenko's went on trial in Winnipeg for shooting a man to death at the CPR yards on Higgins Avenue. Krafchenko showed up as a surprise witness, destroying the Crown's case by testifying that the pistol supposedly used as a murder weapon belonged to him. The Crown lost their case but charged Krafchenko with bank robbery, and he finally ended up in Stony Mountain. After doing three years Krafchenko returned to Winnipeg where he somehow convinced the Winnipeg police to hire him as a robbery consultant. Chief Donald MacPherson agreed to pay Krafchenko a consulting fee. Bloody Jack thanked him, and promptly disappeared with the money.

Krafchenko never had much respect for the law, but he showed incredible chutzpah by proceeding to rob $4,700 from the bank in Plum Coulee, his home town. Although Krafchenko was disguised, the manager recognized him and pursued him with a gun. Krafchenko fired one shot and killed the manager, and by doing so crossed the line that eventually led to his own death. Winnipeg police turned the city upside down, looking for the so-called Ukrainian Robin Hood, who was now rumoured to be utilizing any number of bizarre disguises—passing himself off as a doctor, a college professor, even a woman. Schoolboys avidly pursued any odd-looking character, fascinated by the outlaw's fearsome reputation and simultaneously rooting for his escape. Finally he was ferreted out of a College Avenue rooming house by a squad of police and hauled off to jail.

Authorities weren't taking any chances with Krafchenko. Instead of incarcerating him at the Vaughan Street jail, they made a special lock-

up in the Rupert Street courthouse. But on a bitterly cold January night in 1914 a jailhouse constable named William Flower felt something nudge him in the ribs. He turned around and saw that it was a .32 Colt automatic, held in the steady fist of his prisoner— Bloody Jack Krafchenko. "I'm going to leave here and I'll kill anyone who tries to stop me," said Krafchenko. "Go into the closet and don't call for help for ten minutes."

Krafchenko scrambled out the fourth-storey window and began climbing down by rope. But the rope snapped and he fell 25 feet to the sidewalk. Badly injured and lightly dressed, he limped northward through the icy darkness, heading for the North End where sympathetic friends would give him shelter. In the Burris Building, at 686 Toronto Street, he recuperated for several days, concocting a plan to mail himself out of the country in a piano crate.

On the morning of January 18, 1914, the door burst open and police stormed into his hideout. The injured bank robber gave up without a fight. His well-attended trial took place in March and Krafchenko was found guilty of murder. He was then locked up, very securely, at the Vaughan Street jail. It was a warm and lush summer that year, and from Krafchenko's jail cell he could hear the chirrup of robins and the knock of hammers from the courtyard of the jail. Early in the morning of July 9, the infamous Bloody Jack Krafchenko walked onto the wooden gallows and, at a signal from the executioner, dropped through the trap door into history. ∎

Farmers were exempted from military service during the war, as they provided what was considered an essential service.

from foreclosure, Prime Minister Robert Borden told him in February, 1915, that such action "will diminish and perhaps dry up the stream of capital which has been continually running from the United Kingdom to Western Canada for the purposes of development". But the stream was already dry.

Nature solved the problem. Good weather produced a spectacular wheat crop in 1915 and put an end to the recession. Wartime scarcity drove wheat prices up in 1916 and 1917 so that, even with smaller crops, the Prairie region was awash with cash. Many farm families who had relied on a horse and buggy bought a Model T Ford or a Chevrolet 490, which allowed them to go to town more often for community meetings and cultural events. In Winnipeg, proud new owners of cars started impromptu taxi services, cruising the main arteries along the street car lines at rush hour

mortgage companies for payment of their loans to Prairie farmers. Mortgage-holders and implement dealers called in their loans, threatening Manitoba farmers with repossession of land or machinery. When Premier Roblin attempted to protect mortgaged farmers

taking passengers at five cents a ride. The Winnipeg Electric Street Railway Company persuaded city council to put these private operators out of business in April, 1918, in return for improved street car service. The company started its first gasoline-powered bus route on Westminster Avenue the same year.

Signs of prosperity were everywhere. Farmland that sold at $13.55 an acre in 1915 was fetching $21.53 an acre in 1917. Daily wages for farm labourers, which had averaged $2.55 in the 1914 recession year, rose steadily to $2.60 a day in 1915 and $2.75 in 1916. These rates, far exceeding farm wages in Ontario, Quebec and the Maritime provinces, drew tens of thousands of workers through Winnipeg to the grain-growing districts on the railways' harvest excursion trains each August. Grain farmers needed these labourers at harvest time for the backbreaking work of standing the sheaves of cut grain up in stooks for final ripening in preparation for the highly skilled threshing crews whose steam-powered equipment separated kernels from straw. As the war drew more and more workers into military service and into the war production industries of eastern Canada, farmers found fewer and fewer harvesters available. Harvest labourers' pay shot up to averages of $4.00 a day in 1917, $4.55 in 1918 and $4.69 in 1919. Women and children joined the harvest excursions in 1917.

Gasoline-powered tractors were available but they were expensive and unreliable. Manitoba farmers in the war years continued to use horses for most of their farm work. The provincial telephone service was spreading across the province, allowing farm families to keep in touch with their neighbours and call for help in emergencies. Radio also caught on after the first Winnipeg radio station opened in 1910, keeping farm families abreast of the news.

Rising prices caused hardship for working families. Rail unions in Brandon in 1917 demanded city council action to curb prices for the coal and wood used in home heating and cooking. The Brandon Trades and Labour Council, inactive through the recession years, started a Labour Representation League to run council candidates demanding a municipal fuel depot, a public library and other progressive reforms. The 1917 Bolshevik Revolution in Russia deeply affected A.E. Smith, minister since 1913 at Brandon's First Methodist Church and delegate to the labour council from the Brandon Ministerial Association,

Soldiers beside train on return to Winnipeg from war duty

who later wrote: "The shock of the Russian Revolution was powerful enough to be felt even in Brandon.... I was aroused. I began to seek information. I sent away for a number of books dealing with communism. I got the Manifesto. I remember the first time I read it through. It was like a revelation of a new world into which I felt I must enter and to which I seemed to belong."

In the spring of 1918, Brandon's Labour Representation League was broadened into a branch

of the Dominion Labour Party demanding, among other things, the transformation of capitalist property into social property with production for use instead of for profit.

Discontent was also growing among Winnipeg workers. The Journeymen Tailors' Union, moribund since 1913, was surprised by the success of its organizing drive in the early months of 1917. Encouraged by swelling numbers, the union approached 19 tailoring firms in the spring of 1918 demanding a 15 per cent increase in piecework rates and a 10 per cent raise in hourly rates. When the employers hesitated, the union struck April 1, 1918. All but three of the shops had accepted the union's terms by April 15.

Four years of slaughter finally ended in Europe on November 11, 1918, with the surrender of Germany. At two o'clock Monday morning, Novem-

Rural Manitoba workers participated in a number of sympathy strikes during the Winnipeg General Strike. For example, telephone operators struck in Portage la Prairie, Souris, Carman, Minnedosa, Neepawa and Virden, while firemen and coal trimmers struck in Brandon.

The Winnipeg General

A S THE GREAT WAR DREW TO A
close, Winnipeg workers became increasingly militant. The cost
of living had risen dramatically, with
no increase in real wages. The stock
of affordable housing was diminish-
ing. And Winnipeg employers seemed
unconcerned with the complaints of
labour. Hence wartime appeals to pa-
triotism had little impact on a scepti-
cal labour leadership now further
aroused by charges of business profiteering.

More radical workers were also
becoming alienated from the Canadian Labour Congress, traditionally
dominated by the comparatively conservative craft unions. When westerners failed to persuade the national
body to move towards industrial
unionism, they held their own Western Labour Conference in Calgary in
March, 1919.

The largest delegation came
from Winnipeg and gave enthusiastic
support to a resolution endorsing "the
principle of Proletarian Dictatorship
as being absolute and efficient for the
transformation of capitalist private
property to communal wealth". R.B.
Russell and Dick Johns, of Winnipeg,
were among those who took the lead
in creating the One Big Union, the
practical expression of industrial
unionism. It was an attempt to gather
all workers, skilled and unskilled, into
one union; to mobilize the entire economic strength of the working class
and direct it to working class objec-
tives. And its weapon would be the
general strike.

Such rhetoric was certain to
raise exaggerated fears. In the spring
of 1919, North Americans caught up
in the "Red Scare" and alarmed by a
general strike in Seattle were easily
persuaded that the Bolshevik revolution had been packaged for export.
This was the background for Winnipeg's anxious spring.

**Returned soldiers divided into pro- and
anti-strike factions. This group, made up
largely of officers, marched on June 4th
in support of the Committee of 1,000.**

On May 1, the construction
trades went out for more money. They
were followed the next day by the
metal workers who struck for the
same reason and, in addition, for the
controversial claim to be represented
by a metal trades council, an umbrella group that the employers had rejected as bargaining agent. Almost
immediately, both groups sought the
support of the Winnipeg Trades and
Labour Council which polled all 70
affiliated locals on the question of a
general sympathetic strike and received overwhelming endorsement
from Winnipeg's 12,000 unionized
workers. At 11 a.m., May 15, workers
from all sectors shut the city down.
Even essential services such as hospi-
tals and fire protection were curtailed,
although the police, who had also
voted to strike, remained on duty at
the request of the Strike Committee.

The complete withdrawal of
labour put the community on the
edge of chaos. This was precisely
what gave a general strike its force
and effectiveness. But workers had
families as well, and everyone in the

Strike of 1919

community required essential services. The Strike Committee was thus obliged to authorize the resumption of milk, bread and ice deliveries, water pressure and hospital services. But this begged the question: who was running the city, the Strike Committee or the elected government?

The response of the business and professional class was to create the Committee of 1,000 (Citizens' Committee) whose primary aim was to restore services. This meant, of course, they were on a collision course with the Strike Committee.

The latter's heady rhetoric of the first days of the strike soon dissipated and they proclaimed daily that the strike had been called to protect collective bargaining and a living wage. The Citizens' Committee felt no such restraint and branded the general strike an alien tactic and set about to associate non-British Winnipeggers

with the general work stoppage, a difficult task since every strike leader had been born in Britain except

> ## "Canada did not give her sons and die in order that the old rag of anarchy might float over the country."
>
> *Weekly Manitoba Liberal* (Portage la Prairie) editorial on the Winnipeg General Strike

George Armstrong, who hailed from Ontario. This charge by the Citizens' Committee left a bitter legacy in multi-ethnic Winnipeg.

The strike lasted six weeks. There was little violence, largely because the strike leaders urged their supporters to stay off the streets and out of trouble, fearing intervention by the military. But the final outcome would be determined not in Winnipeg. The federal government could not allow the strategy of the general strike to succeed in Winnipeg. Otherwise, the workers would effectively take over administration of the city.

On June 21st, Bloody Saturday, strikers rioted, overturning a street car. Shortly after, mounted police fired into the crowd, killing two strikers.

This was the fundamental reason that the federal authorities ordered the arrest of the strike leaders and the mobilization of the military. Events came to a head on June 21 when Mounties charged their horses into rioting workers (who were protesting the arrest of labour leaders). Two strikers were killed in the resulting melee. The general strike collapsed soon afterward, although its effects reverberated for decades.

Anti-strike activists called "specials" replaced the fired police force. On June 10th, specials mounted on borrowed milk horses charged assembled strikers at Portage and Main.

Viewpoint One:
Was the General Strike a Success for Labour?

The Winnipeg General Strike has suffered an odd fate at the hands of its historians. One of the most dramatic events in Canadian history has been tamed and a massive social crisis drained of historical significance. Dismissing as alarmist the employers' and government's fears of "revolution", these historians have gone to the opposite extreme. They view the event as a straightforward industrial dispute.

This approach fails to answer all sorts of questions. Most of the strikers in Winnipeg belonged to no union. What did they hope to gain by walking off their jobs? Middle-class residents in the city's south end guarded their houses with rifles. What were they afraid of? The strike is obviously a lot more interesting, and significant, than a simple labour dispute.

Participants in 1919 spoke and acted as if they knew that the shape of the world was up for grabs. The slaughter, profiteering and assaults on civil liberties associated with World War I had undermined the credibility of the world's leaders. Swept up in a crisis of authority evident in the insurrections, revolutions and mass strikes that swept Europe and North America from 1917 to 1920, Winnipeg workers were demanding a more just post-war social order than the one being imposed upon them. For the 30,000 strikers and their opponents this was, if not a revolution, certainly a revolt against the old order of things.

It was specifically a labour revolt. Almost everywhere workers organized sympathetic strikes, broader unions and new labour parties. Earlier in 1919, the federal government had recognized this by establishing a Royal Commission to tour the country in a search for safe outlets for workers' anger. What they heard from labour witnesses was the same kind of idealism that led thousands to endure the loss of wages and often the permanent loss of their jobs. One of the most remarkable features of the labour revolt was the thousands of women and immigrants drawn into unions. While ethnic and gender hierarchies were hardly abolished, this new solidarity did prove strong enough in Winnipeg to withstand a venomous campaign against "aliens" by the anti-strike forces.

Was the strike a failure? By placing the blame on the unions' strategy rather than on the inequality of power between workers and their bosses, right-wing historians turn the event into a morality tale warning of the dangers of radicalism. They also accuse the strike leaders of leading Winnipeg workers into a blind alley, but the incessant demands for just such a confrontation from the ranks of labour is perhaps the best measure of the depth of the revolt. Union leaders ignored it at their peril; more than a few were deposed.

Of course, the strike was broken and the workers' demands were ignored. But the unprecedented class consciousness and solidarity was a harbinger of future gains. The election of three strike leaders to the Manitoba Legislature was evidence of this. On the other hand, Immigration Act amendments, increased security measures, and a renewed campaign to propagate the social values of the Citizens' Committee were less promising consequences of the confrontation. As with any such epic battle, the terrain of social conflict was reshaped.

—James Naylor is a professor of history at Brandon University.

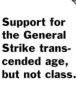

Support for the General Strike transcended age, but not class.

Viewpoint Two:
Or Was It, as Many Argue, an Epic Failure?

William Varley took the measure of the Winnipeg General Strike less than three weeks after it ended in 1919. Varley was a former member of the Winnipeg Street Railway Employees union who had been hired by the American Federation of Labor to help reorganize the union movement in that city after the strike. In Varley's opinion: "There never was in history a strike in which the workers answered the call so spontaneously, and there never was a strike in which the workers were so badly trimmed."

Few people can dispute the short-term results of the strike. The city of Winnipeg was virtually occupied by the police and the militia. The leaders of the Winnipeg labour movement were in jail. The aims of the original strikers in the metal and building trades were not achieved. The working class of Winnipeg was exhausted after six weeks of strike and had neither the will nor the strength to resist their employers' demands for wage cuts. In essence, the starch had been taken out of them.

The real question is, what did the strike accomplish not in the months, but in the decades that followed? Was this short-term defeat in reality a long-term victory? Many of the strike's supporters have long proclaimed that it was. They view the strike as a watershed in Canadian labour history, one that eventually led to the rise of the industrial union movement in Canada, the founding of the CCF/NDP and the building of the Canadian welfare state. Is any of this correct?

The claim that the strike was a triumph in the long-term is based substantially on the political activities of the Winnipeg labour movement after the strike and especially on the victory of Independent Labour Party candidate J.S. Woodsworth in the riding of North Winnipeg in the 1921 federal election. Woodsworth went on to help found the Cooperative Commonwealth Federation, forerunner to the NDP. The CCF and the NDP, it is claimed, have given Canada its modern welfare state, including our medicare system.

The federal government called out the militia, armed with mounted machine guns, to quell angry demonstrators.

In fact, this view of events is extremely simplistic. First, the election of Woodsworth (or anyone else, for that matter) was not an aim of the strike. Second, the Winnipeg labour movement had been increasing its participation in civic, provincial and federal politics since the turn of the century. The strike did not push the workers into politics; they were already in it. Third, far more is claimed for the CCF/NDP and the "founding" of the Canadian welfare state than the facts will support. Liberal prime minister William Lyon Mackenzie King was the father of the Canadian welfare state, initiated during World War II. Finally, the strike was not a struggle for industrial unionism; it was simply not an issue at the time. Therefore, to link the strike to the rise of industrial unionism in Canada in the early 1940's is to connect two unconnected events.

The Winnipeg General Strike has assumed mythic proportions to the Canadian labour movement. The leaders are looked upon as martyrs whose cause triumphed in the end. That makes for a good fairy tale; it is not good history.

—David J. Bercuson is a professor of history and Dean, Faculty of Graduate Studies, at the University of Calgary.

Everyone from police officers to these *Free Press* newspaper carriers wore masks to avoid being infected with the deadly Spanish Influenza.

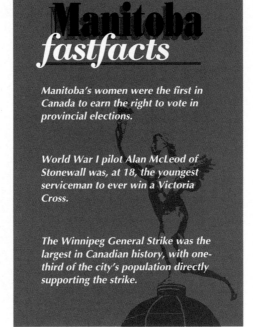

Manitoba
fastfacts

Manitoba's women were the first in Canada to earn the right to vote in provincial elections.

World War I pilot Alan McLeod of Stonewall was, at 18, the youngest serviceman to ever win a Victoria Cross.

The Winnipeg General Strike was the largest in Canadian history, with one-third of the city's population directly supporting the strike.

To lessen their risk of acquiring the flu during the deadly 1918 outbreak, Clanwilliam area farmers wore masks soaked with oil of eucalyptus when delivering grain. Trains were also forbidden to stop in Clanwilliam for fear of spreading the virus to local residents.

ber 11, Winnipeggers who heard the joyous news from France were already starting to gather on Portage Avenue to blow whistles and ring bells. All day long the crowd grew and the noise of celebration increased. Shops closed. Bands played hymns of thanksgiving. The people poured out their relief, their joy, their pride.

Amid the joy, however, returning soldiers had already brought the Spanish influenza virus to Manitoba. Two returned men who had arrived home sick died of the flu on October 3, 1918, and new cases were reported on October 12. The epidemic raged all winter throughout Canada and the United States, infecting one of every six Canadians. Three of the four doctors in Carman were stricken, leaving Dr. A.E. McGavin as the only medical man able to help the many flu patients within 60 kilometres of Carman. Dr. McGavin was meticulous about sterile procedures, wearing a gown and mask when he saw flu patients, disinfecting his clothing and instruments afterwards. His wife and children remained healthy. With the coming of spring, the epidemic abated.

As the euphoria of war's end subsided, long-smoldering domestic conflicts flared. Hostility had been growing between patriotic war veterans and the anti-war labour leaders at home. The Fort

Garry Horse cavalry regiment arrived back in Winnipeg at the Canadian Pacific Railway station on Higgins Avenue in May, 1919, and marched along Main Street and Portage Avenue to the Minto Armoury for final payment and demobilization.

To their astonishment, the returning soldiers found the streets lined with jeering, hooting civilians. They quickly learned that the city was in the midst of a general strike, that public services were in chaos and that returning soldiers were regarded by some strikers as class enemies. A group of the Garrys formed a posse, borrowed milk-wagon horses and patrolled the streets after the Winnipeg police were fired. Other returned men paraded in support of the strike.

The city-wide unrest culminated on the 21st of June. Thousands of strikers marched on city hall to protest the arrest of labour leaders. A street car operated by strike breakers was stopped, seized and set on fire. At that point, Mounties on horseback charged the crowd, firing their weapons directly into unruly strikers. Two men were killed and several others injured. "Specials" or vigilante policemen, armed with homemade clubs, then waded into the crowd, beating anyone with reach.

The protesters fled and it soon became clear that the general strike had been crushed. By June 25, the handful of strike leaders not in police custody voted to abandon the strike. Services soon returned to normal but resentment between the commercial and working classes continued for many years.

Meanwhile, the establishment moved quickly to punish the strike leaders. R.B. Russell was prosecuted first, for seditious conspiracy (plotting against the government), in November, 1919. He was convicted before an unsympathetic judge, Justice Metcalfe, who seems to have taken his guilt for granted. Russell was sentenced to two years imprisonment.

In a trial which lasted from January to April, in 1920, the remaining leaders (R.E. Bray, George Armstrong, R.J. Johns, A.A. Heaps, John Queen, W.A. Pritchard, W. Ivens) were all tried together for seditious conspiracy. All were convicted save Heaps, and imprisoned. The editors of the paper which was supportive of the strike, the *Western Labor News* (J.S. Woodsworth and Fred Dixon), were prosecuted for seditious libel before Justice Galt. Dixon was acquitted, and charges against Woodsworth were never proceeded with, in spite of the "Red Scare" that seems to have had pervasive influence with a large segment of Winnipeg's community at the time.

Pritchard and Dixon defended themselves. Though neither was legally trained, Pritchard was so eloquent that the courtroom was packed with curious lawyers when he gave his closing address to the jury. Dixon's speech was brilliant by any standard. The central core of both men's argument lay in this passage from Dixon's presentation: "The imprisonment of those who hold unpopular opinions is the negation of democracy. While these men are in jail, not one of us is really free. It was their turn yesterday. It may be ours tomorrow."

The Dominion Government was vigorous in support of measures to suppress the strike, which some have suggested had to do with the failing fortunes of the federal government, which did not wish to appear soft on "Bolsheviks" or other threats to public order. The prosecutions were federally funded. Amendments to the Immigration Act were rushed through, providing for more severe penalties, and pursuant to its provisions, four "undesirable aliens" were deported.

Subsequent legal analysis of the cases tends

Strike leaders at Stony Mountain, circa 1920. Back row, l–r: R.E. Bray, George Armstrong, John Queen, R.B. Russell, R.J. Johns, W.A. Pritchard. Front row, l–r: W.A. Ivens, A.A. Heaps.

"I wouldn't advise any man to go out there. His life is in danger if these women find out that he is at work, or had been working during the strike."

Winnipeg police detective commenting on angry women strike sympathizers in Weston and Brooklands

to be critical of the entire affair. From about the turn of the century, there was a powerful intolerance against new immigrants, especially those from eastern Europe. The presence of such people was viewed, in particular by the monied class, as a threat to the social order and "purity of our homes". Many members of the legal community seemed to have been caught in the popular prejudices and fears of the time, to the discredit of the justice system.

Work on the Legislative Building had continued through the war. By late 1919, the central dome was ready to receive the statue Manitobans dubbed Golden Boy, Paris sculptor Georges Gardet's gilded bronze image of youth and hope, based on Giovanni da Bologna's 16th-century statue of Mercury.

The Manitoba that greeted the completed building was greatly changed from the province that started the project. Since the launching of the design competition in November, 1911, the province had tripled its size, advanced women and schools, suppressed liquor, dealt with political corruption and thrown its wealth and its people into a European war. Grain growers had shown their enormous capacity to enrich the province. Unions and the urban middle class had tested their economic muscle against each other, with unions (for the time being) the decisive losers. Ethnic minorities had been told to learn English but had nonetheless managed, with increasing numbers and stubborn pride, to affirm their distinct identities.

In November, the five-metre Golden Boy figure was hoisted to its lofty perch high above the Assiniboine River, high above the tumult of busy Winnipeg, facing north to a new unexploited frontier, where Manitoba saw its future. ✺

In 1919, during Prince Edward's Royal Visit to Winnipeg, the delicate young prince shook so many of his subject's hands he was forced to go to Tuxedo Military Hospital to treat his injured royal appendage. While there doctors warned him to beware of the "Western Canadian grip".

CHAPTER SIX

Dream of Expansion

BY JIM MOCHORUK

For many years after the decline of the fur trade, Manitobans were preoccupied with the southern half of the province—with its fertile soil and expansive space for settlers. By the turn of the century, however, business realized that resources other than fur—lumber, hydro-electricity and minerals—were available in the north. Soon prospectors, promoters, miners and lumbermen were added to the large native population of the region. Some struck it rich, many others returned south in defeat. The hardiest souls stayed on and contributed to the colourful flavour of Manitoba's north country.

With additional material by
JAKE MACDONALD, CHRISTOPHER DAFOE AND GREGG SHILLIDAY

The Last Dog Train Leaving Lower Fort Garry, 1909, by Charles Comfort

Dream of Expansion

Rediscovering the riches of the north

Although most Manitobans know little about the northern portion of their province, the region has played a crucial role both in Manitoba's history and in the history of the entire West. It was through the north that Europeans explorers like Henry Hudson first landed on the shores of western Canada early in the 1600's. And it was this northern approach to the Canadian interior that—through the fur trade—helped determine the course of western Canada's history for the next 200 years.

From 1670, when the English Crown granted the Hudson's Bay Company its charter to the entire drainage basin of Hudson Bay, until well into the 19th century, all of what was then referred to as Rupert's Land was the fiefdom of the "Company of Adventurers". However, for a century after the HBC received its charter the company did precious little to explore its vast domain. Rather, HBC officials were content to have their traders perch in their northern bayside "factories" and wait for the aboriginal peoples of the region to bring furs to them. These furs were then sent to England on HBC vessels—a perfect monopoly conducted with a minimum of fuss and expense.

Other Europeans soon arrived, however. The French wreaked havoc on the Company's bayside posts on and off until 1713, when the Treaty of Utrecht finally left the northern approach to the Canadian interior firmly in HBC hands. Undaunted by this diplomatic exclusion, La Vérendrye and his sons penetrated Rupert's Land by a southern, overland route from New France. Then, shortly after the English conquest of New France in 1760, independent Montreal-based traders (who eventually formed the North West Company) did the same.

This later invasion of Rupert's Land led to large-scale inland trading by whites and, in 1774, forced the HBC to set up its own inland posts. The competition between rival traders often had disastrous consequences for the aboriginal population because of the introduction of diseases and liquor.

A division between the north and south developed during the 19th century as a result of four major factors: the establishment of the HBC's agricultural colony at Red River in 1812; the merger of the HBC and the North West Company in 1821; the mid-century decline in the European demand for beaver pelts; and finally, the development of east-west railway transportation.

By the mid 1800's, the north had ceased to be the economic heart of what would become Manitoba and was becoming an economic backwater, notable for its declining fur trade and its increasingly impoverished natives. Because of this, British and Canadian politicians tended to ignore the north while they determined the fate of the agriculturally useful portion of southern Rupert's Land between 1857 and 1870. Only the HBC, a few white missionaries and the aboriginal peoples of the north seemed to care what would happen to the region during that crucial 13 year period when Canadians clamoured for the annexation of Rupert's Land, which was formally transferred to Canadian control in 1870.

The official indifference to the once allimportant north continued long after the new Dominion of Canada replaced the HBC as the formal governing power of the region. To begin with, the north was lumped into the vast jurisdiction known as the North West Territories and was thereby cut off from the West's one major population centre, the Red River settlement. Then, in 1876, the north was constitutionally dumped into the even less significant jurisdiction of Keewatin.

In both instances the area that was to become northern Manitoba was theoretically governed by the lieutenant-governor of Manitoba but in reality was left under the effective control of the HBC officers and some missionaries, who acted as unpaid

Gathering at Norway House, circa 1880

proxies for a Canadian government that knew little, and cared even less about, its new northern possessions.

Between 1870 and 1900, businessmen were the first to develop an interest in the potential of Keewatin. The region's usefulness as part of a water transportation route to the fertile lands of the West, as a source of wood products, as a fishery and as a source of valuable minerals, slowly became apparent.

The HBC led the way. Having surrendered its charter rights over Rupert's Land in 1869-70 in exchange for £300,000 and 1/20 of all the arable land of western Canada, the Company was in the process of recreating itself as a new type of enterprise. Instead of focusing solely upon fur trading—over which it no longer had a legal monopoly—the HBC decided to combine this traditional economic activity in the north with retailing operations, transportation services and land sales in the southern

The Ojibway chief Nah-Wee-Kee-Sic-Quak-Yash, also known as Jacob Berens, sat for this 1909 portrait by Marion Nelson Hooker. Berens's grandfather came from the Lake Superior region to the west side of Lake Winnipeg where Berens River was named in the family's honour. Jacob Berens served as chief for four decades.

parts of the Canadian west.

Central to all aspects of the HBC's new economic plan was the development of a transportation system linking both north and south with the western interior. Thus, during the mid-1870's, specialized lake steamboats were purchased for use on Lake Winnipeg and a tramway was constructed at Grand Rapids on the northwestern corner of the Lake (in order to pass freight around the rapids which separated Lake Winnipeg from the Saskatchewan River).

Although a costly investment, the HBC saw several advantages to creating such a system. First, it would increase the profitability of the northern fur trade by drastically reducing the labour costs of the old system of York boat, canoe and cart brigade. Second, the HBC expected that the value of its western lands would rise more rapidly as a result of this investment, for it was assumed an all-steam transportation route for settlers (and eventually for their produce) from Selkirk to Edmonton would attract many settlers. Beyond this, such settlers would eventually provide revenue-generating freight and passenger traffic while simultaneously acting as a market for the

Logging operations sprang up to supply lumber for growing southern communities.

Warren's Landing on the northern tip of Lake Winnipeg was one of several hamlets supplying Manitoba's commercial fishing industry.

Hudson's Bay Company shifted its focus from northern posts to southern cities

IN 1870, THE HUDSON'S BAY Company's chartered territory in the West—most of old Rupert's Land—was transferred to the government of the newly-created Dominion of Canada in return for a modest cash settlement and a healthy portion of land in the Prairie's fertile belt. In the years that followed, the Company would move from its old staple of fur-trading to land dealing, settlement, and in what would eventually become its most important activity, shop-keeping.

The fur trade remained significant in the north and HBC steamers and canoe brigades continued to ply the rivers, serving the distant posts above Lake Winnipeg. As newcomers poured into the West, however, the prospects for expanded retail trade became apparent. Indeed, by the last half of the 19th century the importance of York Factory was in steep decline. As the railways arrived and the Prairies opened up to settlement, the focus of Company administration shifted south to Winnipeg.

In Winnipeg, stores within Upper Fort Garry had long served the community, but as the young city grew, the Company moved with the times. During the early part of the decade the fort was gradually dismantled, leaving only the north gate, which still stands as a memorial to the old Red River settlement.

The demand for general merchandise prompted the Company to establish "Saleshops" in major settlements across the West, the finest being the great department store opened on Winnipeg's South Main Street in 1881, near the Main Street-York Avenue intersection.

The store, which also contained wholesale offices and fur storage, was three storeys high and a block long, had elevators and has been described

Fur Trader to Retailer

Interior of Hudson's Bay Company trading post at Churchill, July, 1919

as "Ali Baba's cave". Winnipeg had not seen anything like it before. The store sold all the basic necessities of life such as pots and pans, washboards, trousers and shirts, hats and coats and all the everyday foods. One could get farm supplies and even pictures to decorate the walls of a sod house out in the Brandon Hills.

One early 20th-century shopper, Ruth Harvey (daughter of impresario and theatre-owner C.P. Walker), recalled childhood visits to the "Big Store" at Christmas in her memoir *Curtain Time*. Of particular interest was the exotic foods department that provided sophisticated Winnipeggers with "small jars of bloater paste, pink shrimp, lobster, anchovy, ham and

turkey. Russian caviar that did not look nice and tasted just as bad... sardines invisible in flat tins, but lying there, I knew, silvery in pools of amber oil. And pate de fois gras in shallow, yellow-glazed pots, each with a lid and a thin layer of creamy fat beneath it to protect the velvet pate." All this in a town that had once been the centre of the pemmican trade.

By the turn of the century, Baymen began to realize that if the future lay in department stores, old fur traders would have to stand aside and bring in experts. By 1912 plans had been laid for new, modern department

stores on the European and American models, with the flagship store to be built on part of the Company's large land reserve in Winnipeg. War intervened, however, and it was not until the 1920's that the seven-acre site on Portage Avenue and Memorial Boulevard was cleared for the creation of the department store that opened for business in 1926.

In northern Manitoba, the HBC establishments continued to be, in many cases, the chief contact with the outside world, with Baymen serving in almost every capacity from postmaster to amateur physician. The Company brought radio communication to northern communities and aircraft chartered by the HBC revolutionized transport in the north. HBC ships brought supplies and people to remote communities.

Still officially controlled and directed from London, the Hudson's Bay Company, in practice, was for many years a Winnipeg-based operation, with activities in the vast Canadian hinterland directed from its headquarters on Main Street.

On Northern Patrol

RCMP officers such as Inspector E.A. Pelletier patrolled vast areas of the north and then filed comprehensive reports. More than policemen, Mounties were expected to dispense justice, explore new country and oversee the welfare of the native population. This is Pelletier's report on a winter patrol from Norway House to Sandy Lake and back.

The Commanding Officer, Depot Division, Regina.   Norway House, March 18, 1908

Sir: I have the honour to report that according to instructions received from you I proceeded on a patrol to Sandy Lake, leaving Norway House on February 19, and returning on March 16, having been 27 days on the journey [at] a distance of about 600 miles with dogs.

I left Norway House on the date mentioned above, accompanied by the following: Constable Cashman driving one team of dogs, Special Constable W.T. Towers as guide, "Indian," ex-prisoner Angus Rae, "Indian," of Red Deer Lake near Sandy Lake, Mr. Donald Flett, a Hudson's Bay Company man as interpreter, with his train of dogs. Myself driving one train of dogs.

Angus Rae came as far as Sandy Lake where I left him with sufficient provisions to reach his home about two days distance. We were obliged to carry him on the sleigh most of the way as he completely played out, before the first day was over, his feet got bruised and he got in very bad shape. On his account we were delayed considerably as in those places where riding on the sleighs was impossible we had to wait for him, as he could not go faster than a slow walk; however, he proved useful from Island Lake to Sandy Lake where he acted as guide....

While at Oxford I heard three complaints, two of which were settled there and then, amicably, and one of which I could not attend to as the party was away on his hunting ground...The first was a case of housebreaking with no intent to steal, but to borrow. The defendant claiming that the informer had given him permission to go into his house and use his stores while he was away hunting. This happened the winter of 1906-7. A compensation was given by the defendant and both were satisfied.

Second complaint was about a man from Island Lake who was keeping from its mother a child of his later brother's. The mother wanted the child back. After making enquiries I found that she was a good worker and able to provide for the child, and when at Island Lake I told the chief to make that Indian "Adam Harper" No. 1, return the said child to its mother as soon as possible. Adam No. 1 was away on his hunting grounds a couple of days from Island Lake.

Third complaint, was about an Indian beating his wife. I could not see the Indian as he was away to his traps, but I left word that if I heard any more of this about him, "he would feel very sorry for it." This expression is about the only one which can convey the meaning intended. This Indian I heard is very much addicted to beating his wife.

From Norway House we go down the Nelson for about 14 miles, until near Sea Falls, then cut across into a big swamp which drains into Lake Nelson, known as "Lake Winnipegosis" by the Indians. A large lake of about 30 miles and of good width. From the lower end of this lake we follow the water course into Oxford Lake making such portages as are required to avoid bad places and rapids.

The general appearance of the country seems unfit for agriculture, mostly muskegs and sandy soils with small jack pines, very few poplar or birch bluffs are met, in few places it is solid rock, and at others the ground is covered with boulders. There are patches of timber but none of any commercial value.

Interior of Cree
trapper Albert
Monias' camp

The Inuit would travel
to Churchill to trade and
collect supplies.

HBC's expanded re-
tail sales division.

Even as this grandiose business plan was
being implemented by the HBC, a number of
smaller-scale entrepreneurs were also turning their
attention northwards. For example, no longer con-
strained by the HBC's monopoly over the fur trade,
numerous independent traders began setting up
shop in the north. Stobart, Eden and Company,
I.G. Baker and Company, Carscaden, Peck and
Company, and later, Revillon Freres added a keen
edge of competition to the fur trade of the post-
1870 era.

Meanwhile, timbermen such as Walkley and
Burrows, Brown and Rutherford, Smith and Pratt,
Captain William Robinson and many others, real-
izing the great profits to be made by supplying a
wood-starved Winnipeg with lumber, set up cutting operations on the shores of Lakes Winnipeg
and Manitoba.

From modest begin-
nings, commercial fishing on the big
lakes increased dramatically in the 1880's with the
arrival of the transcontinental railway. Concerns
such as Reid and Clarke, Hugh Armstrong (on
Lake Manitoba) and William Robinson quickly
transformed the fishing industry of the middle
north from a local, consumption-based business to
a rich U.S.-export-based industry.

Finally, there was the beginning of a mining
industry along the northern frontier. The
discovery of gold in the Rat Portage (Kenora) area
in 1880-81 had touched off
a minor gold rush which
spilled over into the Winnipeg River/Whiteshell districts and from there onto
the shoreline and islands of
Lake Winnipeg in the early
1880's. This search for precious metals was soon
expanded into a hunt for any
mineral of value, which led
to attempts to mine iron ore
on Black Island in Lake Winnipeg between 1884 and
1905.

As it happened, these
early attempts at gold and
iron mining came to naught.
But more prosaic mining
and quarrying operations did
succeed. For example, lime-
stone was being quarried at

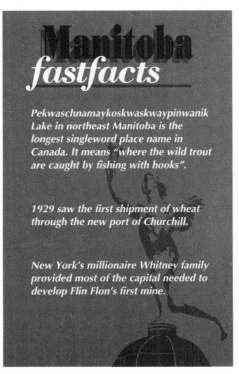

Manitoba fastfacts

*Pekwaschnamaykoskwaskwaypinwanik
Lake in northeast Manitoba is the
longest singleword place name in
Canada. It means "where the wild trout
are caught by fishing with hooks".*

*1929 saw the first shipment of wheat
through the new port of Churchill.*

*New York's millionaire Whitney family
provided most of the capital needed to
develop Flin Flon's first mine.*

Ojibway gave up prime land for scrub

The Great Land Robbery

THE LOWER RED RIVER area, from the Assiniboine to the marshes of Lake Winnipeg, is among the richest land in Manitoba. A band of Ojibway (Saulteaux) once owned much of that land— 48,000 acres of prime real estate known as the St. Peter's Reserve. But in 1907 the Ojibways were persuaded to part with their possession, amidst circumstances so questionable that the St. Peter's "land transfer" has become known as one of the great swindles in Manitoba history.

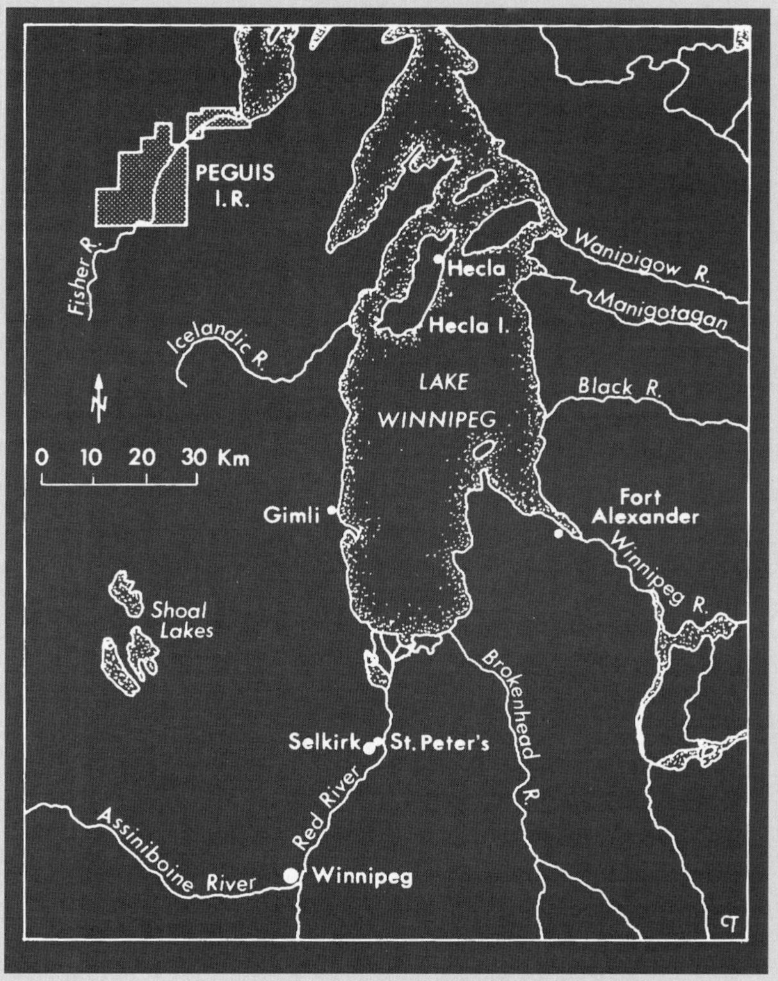

It began on a rainy day in 1907, when a well-educated Ojibway named William Asham attended a meeting at a small schoolhouse on the St. Peter's Reserve. It seemed that representatives of the Dominion government, accompanied by businessmen from Selkirk, were proposing to buy the reserve for $5,000 plus another piece of land farther north.

Asham believed the offer was outrageous. But he was astounded to learn that the chief and council were in favour of the deal. Upon investigating, he discovered that band leaders had been bought off. In a letter to Ottawa, Asham complained that: "The Chief would receive 180 acres of land and each Councillor 120, and each Indian would receive only 16 acres. I immediately demanded the reason why the Chief and Councillors should receive more land than the ordinary Indian. Mr. Pedley (from the Dept. of

[MAP: Lake Winnipeg region showing PEGUIS I.R., Fisher R., Hecla, Hecla I., Icelandic R., Wanipigow R., Manigotagan, LAKE WINNIPEG, Black R., Fort Alexander, Winnipeg R., Gimli, Shoal Lakes, Brokenhead R., Selkirk, St. Peter's, Red River, Assiniboine River, Winnipeg. Scale 0 10 20 30 Km]

Indian Affairs) replied that they were getting the extra land for their recognition."

Asham knew that most of the Indians could not understand the terms of the deal, so he tried to translate the proceedings. The crowd was so big that many people couldn't fit into the schoolhouse. Asham relayed minutes of the proceedings out the window. On the second day, he was approached by a Member of Parliament named S.J. Jackson, who offered him a package equal to the one given the Chief and Councillors. Asham said, "I declared that had I agreed, I would have felt that I would be accepting a bribe to desert my friends."

Finally, the matter came to a vote. Mr. Pedley of Indian Affairs displayed a fat satchel stuffed with $5,000. Reverend John Semmons, an Indian agent and land speculator, announced the options to the assembled natives: "All you that want $90 go to this side. The others go to the opposite side."

Asham protested the wording of the vote, saying that Semmons should have said: "You who want to surrender the reserve go to one side." But the vote proceeded, with Asham counting votes on the "nay" side. When he was done, he moved to the "yea" side, but officials stopped him, saying that those votes had already been counted. Asham was taken aback. "I did not know who counted the other side, and they claimed they had a majority of seven. I was astonished to hear this, and sized up the two sides and satisfied myself that there was a larger number standing on my side."

But his protests were overruled. For a couple of dollars per acre, the land "deal" went through. Despite shouting matches in Parliament and accusations of fraud through 53 pages of Hansard, the Ojibways were soon herded onto steamships and transported to their new home—an expanse of stony, desolate poplar scrub named Peguis, after the great Indian leader who founded the St. Peter's Reserve and provided so much help to the first Red River settlers.

Steep Rock (Lake Manitoba) by 1899 and gypsum was being quarried and milled into powder near present-day Gypsumville as early as 1900. And, after three decades of failed attempts to locate a sizable gold deposit, a gold vein was discovered in the winter of 1910-11 in what would become known as the San Antonio/Bissett region.

At the outset, natives were crucial to the success of all these activities, as they provided a local source of low-cost labour for the owners of lumber-camps and fishing companies and acted as both guides and casual labourers for prospectors. However, after the collapse of the Manitoba railway and real estate boom in 1883, the cost of white labour in Keewatin fell and many natives were forced out of the employment picture.

New industries also had a negative impact on traditional northern resources. The commercial fishing companies, for example, took ever increasing amounts of fish to supply their export market, and in the process decimated stocks in the inshore fisheries of the big lakes—fisheries which provided sustenance to many native communities. For their part, timbermen tended to cut trees regardless of reserve boundaries—thereby robbing many bands of one of their few valuable resources—and then employed such careless clean-up practices that entire districts were threatened with forest fires. Thus, instead of receiving benefits from the development of their homeland, most native northerners found that they were being excluded from employment and, simultaneously, were seeing their traditional economic base diminished by the activities of white businesses.

The only agency which could have helped northerners to cope with these problems was the Canadian government. Unfortunately, succeeding administrations were interested only in opening up the north to developers. For example, Treaty Number 5, which had been concluded in 1875-76 between Lieutenant-Governor Morris and the various native bands of the Lake Winnipeg, Norway House, Grand Rapids and The Pas areas, was undertaken not so much to aid the natives as to open up the district for whites.

The Dominion's parsimony and its cavalier attitude towards the north was per-

Indian residential school in a fire at Norway House

haps most obvious in four vital areas: native policy; the administration of justice; the provision of education services; and general governance.

In the first case, the government consistently refused to extend the terms of Treaty 5 to natives who lived north of the original treaty area, even though conditions for many of these people were horrendous. For example, those Cree and Inuit living closest to Hudson Bay were in dire straits, for the animal and fish stocks of that region were badly depleted. From the late 1880's onwards the lieutenant-governor of Keewatin, the detachments of Mounties who made occasional patrols into the region and several leading missionaries all brought the plight of these natives to the attention of the Dominion government.

Unfortunately, neither the entreaties of natives nor the recommendations of officials such as Lieutenant-Governor John Christian Schultz were of any avail. If promoters, developers and white settlers saw no value in the lands beyond the 1876 limits of Treaty 5, the Dominion saw no point in going to the expense of paying for the surrender of aboriginal title. Thus, not until the construction of a railway to Hudson Bay became a distinct possibility in 1907-08 did the Dominion finally consent to treaty adhesions for these

Even two centuries after the arrival of the voyageurs, portaging was still an essential part of northern transportation.

Many northern forest fires were started by unscrupulous prospectors who set fires to burn off the overburden to see what minerals were available in the rock beneath.

northern natives.

In much the same way, police services were also withheld from the north simply because the Dominion refused to spend the necessary funds. The only exception was occasioned by liquor smuggling activities from Manitoba into the NWT, via Keewatin, in the late 1880's. By the mid-1890's it was obvious to NWMP Superintendent John Cotton, local Indian Agent Joseph Reader and HBC Chief Factor McFarlane that a more substantial police force was required in this district, particularly at The Pas and Grand Rapids during the summer. But Ottawa consistently refused to sanction the necessary expenditure.

It was only the American infringement of Canadian sovereignty in Hudson Bay—occasioned by the whaling and trading activities of New Englanders in the late 1890's—and the northward progress of the Canadian Northern Railway which finally convinced Sir Wilfrid Laurier's government to fund year-round police detachments at strategic spots in the north.

Then there was the matter of education. As Ebenezer McColl, the Chief Inspector of the vast Manitoba Indian Superintendency, often pointed out to his superiors in Ottawa, the schools on the reserves of Treaty 5 were staffed by under-paid and under-qualified teachers. Indeed, with annual salaries for teachers at Indian day schools set at a maximum of $300 well into the 20th century (as compared to the $620 paid to teachers in the NWT during the 1890's) it is surprising that any teachers could be recruited at all.

Finally, complicating all of these matters, was the Dominion's general indifference to the governance of the north. And, while this indifference had been quite remarkable from 1870 to 1900, it became almost staggering between 1900 and 1911. For example, in the process of defining the physical limits of the proposed province of Saskatchewan, the Dominion not only ignored several existing boundaries but also the sentiments of many of the people most directly affected by the proposed boundaries. Instead of assigning Saskatchewan an eastern boundary that followed the outlines of the old provisional districts of Saskatchewan and Athabaska, Ottawa opted for a continuation of the slightly westward sloping border between the province of Manitoba and the district of Assiniboia, in the south.

As soon as word of Saskatchewan's proposed boundary was received in the north, the electors of the district around The Pas sent off a petition to the Prime Minister, pleading that their area should be included in the province of Saskatchewan. Laurier was not about to allow a handful of northerners to alter his plans. Thus, the Autonomy Bills of 1905 were pushed through Parliament without any changes being made to the eastern boundary of Saskatchewan.

At this point, because Ottawa was uncertain about the ultimate fate of the lands lying north of Manitoba's boundary, temporary arrangements had to be made for the governance of the north.

Mounted Police's prisoner cells in Churchill

"There ain't no law of God nor man that goes north of 53 degrees."

Northern Manitoba proverb

The RNWMP arriving at York Factory with treaty payments in 1914

As a result, a new political entity was created under the terms of the North West Territories Amendment Act of 1905. This cobbled together all the areas left over from the creation of Saskatchewan and Alberta plus all of Keewatin and all districts not included in any province (excluding Yukon, which was given special status because of the gold that had been discovered there a few years earlier).

From the outset, the reformed North West Territories was a travesty of organization and administration. It was a vast area, virtually ungovernable because of its size. To make matters worse, this sprawling jurisdiction was to be ruled by one official and an appointed council of four advisors. However, the Dominion never bothered to appoint a commissioner or council, leaving all administrative matters in the hands of the elderly comptroller of the Royal North-West Mounted Police, Lieutenant-Colonel Frederick White.

White, second-in-command of the Mounties, was confronted with the near impossible task of administering an area which included all of present-day northern Quebec, northern Ontario, northern Manitoba and the far north from his

The True Story of Iron Will

The Campbells of northern Manitoba were a legendary clan of Métis dog-racers, trappers and woodsmen. In 1917, husky-musher Albert Campbell won the famous Winnipeg-to-St. Paul dog-sled race, which started with a flurry of cheers and excitement in front of the *Manitoba Free Press* building. In 1993, the Walt Disney Corporation immortalized the race in a movie called *Iron Will*. Unfortunately, the film makers changed a few important facts of Campbell's life.

In the film version, the hero and winner of the race is an American. "Iron Will" Stoneman races against an assortment of Swedes, Canadians and other villains. But in real life it was Albert Campbell and a team of mushers from The Pas who won the marathon race and the only American in the competition was Fred Hartman, a 26-year-old Bostonian who was accused of cheating and lost the race by four hours.

Albert Campbell seems to have been a good sport and a generous man. For example, when Hartman's lead dog was mauled to death, Campbell loaned him a replacement. To return the favour, Hartman tried to get a jump on his Canadian opponent by sneaking off in the middle of the night. Evidence also suggests that Hartman and his dogs intentionally veered off course and hopped aboard a freight train for a part of the race.

Despite Hartman's double-dealing, Albert Campbell and his team from The Pas displayed their own brand of iron will and eventually mushed to victory in St. Paul. Even though Hartman lost by more than four hours, he insisted on claiming victory and went on to promote his self-styled exploits on the vaudeville circuit.

As the real hero, Albert Campbell returned to The Pas with $2,000 in prize money and one of the carnival queens as his bride.

More famous than the Winnipeg to St. Paul dog sled race was The Pas' "Great International Non-Stop Dog Derby". The leading musher of the north was Emil St. Goddard and his team of racing hounds.

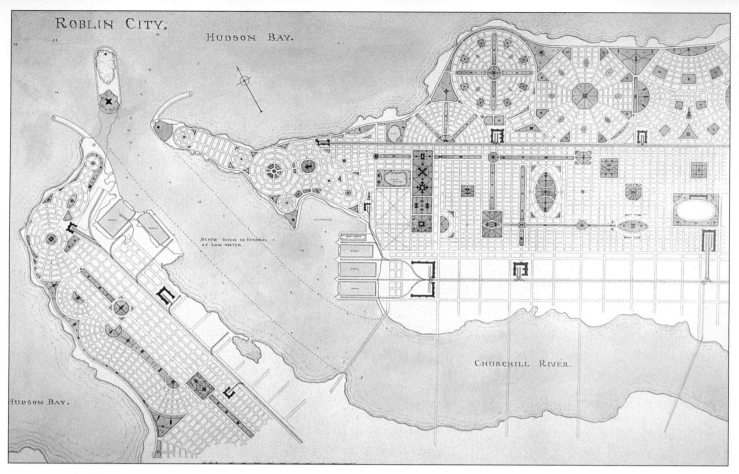

ROBLIN CITY.   HUDSON BAY.

HUDSON BAY.

CHURCHILL RIVER.

Roblin City, 1912, by Winnipeg architect William Bruce. This ambitious plan for a city of 500,000 at present-day Churchill features baroque radial and circular streets.

office in Ottawa—supported by the princely appropriation of $5,000 per annum. He had considerable aid in administering his fiefdom by virtue of the recently established detachments of Mounties between Hudson Bay and the Manitoba border. These offi- cers, already under White's authority as comptroller of the RNWMP, became his proxies in ruling this vast territory.

In a sense, this made the new NWT a police state. In fairness to the Mounties, they were not imposing a draconian order upon the north. Indeed, there is much evidence which suggests

Grading Fischer Street in The Pas, 1912. Note the tall tree, centre right, trimmed as a lobstick or direction finder.

that the police were a positive force. For example, in 1907 at the Churchill detachment, Superintendent Moodie frustrated the plans of the HBC to increase its profit margin by one-third—at the expense of the native trappers—by threatening to trade with the natives himself if the Company followed through on its plans. Beyond this, when the pace of northern development picked up in 1908 because of the initiation of the Hudson Bay Railway, the police detachment at The Pas became the unofficial protector of workers against the worst excesses of railway sub-contractors and lumber camp operators. Living up to their reputation for fairness, the regime of the Mounties was, on balance, a decent one.

The year 1912 was a pivotal year in the history of the north, for it was then that Manitoba formally took possession of all those territories which constitute its present area. The province's assumption of authority had a series of beneficial results.

Manitoba did not, however, take an interest in the north out of simple altruism.

To cope with muskeg and uneven terrain, corduroy roads provided an uncomfortable but effective road surface.

The administration of Premier Rodmond P. Roblin wanted control over what promised to be the major frontier of economic development of the early 20th century.

The construction of the Canadian Northern Railway—which both Manitoba and Ottawa subsidized quite heavily—had been central to the process of increasing the value of the north. It had pushed the agricultural and stockraising frontier all the way from Dauphin to Swan River by the turn of the century. Extensions of this line to Winnipegosis (1897) and Mafeking (1903) had also made possible the development of commercial fishing on northern Lake Winnipegosis.

The completion of the Hudson Bay Junction to The Pas extension in 1907-08 opened up the fur trade frontier for smaller traders who had been excluded because they could not afford their own transportation lines into the north. More importantly, though, this extension also heralded the building of the long awaited Hudson Bay Railway, which promised western farmers a shorter route, through Churchill, to international markets.

What had been a declining fur trade region was being transformed into a dynamic multi-resource frontier. And because this railway expansion happened to coincide with the development of new mining and lumbering technologies, the "New North" promised to become increasingly valuable to the provincial economy. Small wonder then that Manitoba's political leaders had been willing to take on the costly responsibilities of governing this area in 1912.

The economic potential of the north was manifested almost immediately. The fur trade underwent a renaissance. Small-scale traders, using the new railway to The Pas, revolutionized the trade with their cash-and-carry approach. No longer tied to the HBC's debt/barter trade system, new money was injected into the northern economy.

Then there was the lumber industry. By 1913, the Finger Lumber Company at The Pas was established as Manitoba's largest logging and milling operation; an operation which boasted a milling capacity of one million board feet per day, a summer workforce of 400 and a winter logging workforce of 1,000. There were also sizable lumber camp and milling operations such as

Andy Taylor, a prospector, was once lost in the Burntwood River country for 46 days. Taylor had an axe, but soon lost it. This left him with only a penknife with which to fend for himself. He survived by eating bugs and frogs and burying himself in the ground in the evenings to stay warm.

159

The Hudson Bay

BEING WELL AWARE OF THE HISTORIC fur trade route that had linked Manitoba to Europe's markets via Hudson Bay, it was hardly surprising that many in the West wanted a rail line that could ship grain via this "short route". Even before the CPR reached Winnipeg, Manitobans were already advocating the building of just such a railway.

In April, 1880, two companies received federal charters for northern rail projects: the Winnipeg and Hudson Bay Railway and Steamship Company (Lake Winnipeg to Port Nelson) and the Nelson Valley Railway and Transportation Company (Winnipeg to Churchill). Both were serious undertakings. The Nelson Valley Company backers included Senator Thomas Ryan, Alexander Murray of the Canada Shipping Company, Alfred Brown of the Bank of Montreal and Peter Redpath of Redpath Sugar. The other company had a less impressive Board, but men like John Christian Schultz, Hugh Sutherland and William Bannerman were not without influence in western business circles.

Unfortunately, even after these two rival projects amalgamated in 1883 (under Hugh Sutherland's leadership) the lack of investor interest in Britain and Prime Minister John A. Macdonald's manipulations prevented

Laying track near Churchill in the winter of 1929, Mile 510

the amalgamated company from proceeding. Thus, not long after Manitoba's government guaranteed a bond issue in 1885, which allowed 65 kilometres of construction, Macdonald effectively shut the project down (and destroyed the political career of Premier John Norquay) by engineering a financial crisis concerning the bond issue.

Premier Thomas Greenway, the Liberal who was catapulted into power by Norquay's sudden fall from political grace, made some attempts to get this project back on track but, in 1889, he reduced Manitoba's financial support for the HBR so that he could channel more aid to shorter

lines running to the U.S. border.

Donald Mann took over Sutherland's charter in 1895 and used it to build a series of northerly running rail lines between 1896 and 1908. None of these lines, which Mann built with his partner William Mackenzie, duplicated Sutherland's original scheme but the Canadian Northern Railway did prove instrumental in opening up the middle north.

Prime Minister Wilfrid Laurier was opposed to the project. However, when Laurier and the Liberals were forced to call an election in 1911, the government miraculously produced a contract for the first 300-kilometre section of the railway.

Railway

After the election, the new Conservative minister of railways, Frank Cochrane, immediately suspended all work on the line. Westerners and Liberal MP's protested this violation of an election promise, an outcry which lasted until January, 1912, when Cochrane's pleas for time to determine the best port site were overruled by his own caucus. Despite the minister's misgivings, work was resumed on the line to avert a major political disaster for the new government.

Cochrane's caution had been well advised as there was still considerable debate over whether the HBR should go to Port Nelson or Churchill. In the end, Nelson was chosen simply because it was closer. As matters turned out, Port Nelson had a terrible harbour and had to be abandoned after $6 million had been pumped into it. Indeed, after spending $14 million building the railway as far as Kettle Rapids and clearing the line up to Port Nelson, the whole project was abandoned from 1918 to 1926.

When construction finally resumed in 1926—as a result of Prime Minister Mackenzie King's desire to win western support—Churchill was chosen to replace Port Nelson. After an innovative series of building campaigns, including laying track on frozen muskeg before preparing a gravel roadbed, the HBR was completed in 1929 and the Port of Churchill was declared open in 1931. It had taken more than 50 years and $60 million to realize Hugh Sutherland's 1880 vision and, as most Manitobans know, the debate over the value of this railway and port site has never ended.

> **"I looked sideways into the bush and to my surprise, there was a big polar bear staring at me about 25 feet away. I could feel the hair standing on end on my head. Automatically, I started running as fast as I could... I'm sure a jackrabbit couldn't outrun me that time."**
>
> **Construction worker on the Hudson Bay Railway**

Driving the last spike on the line from The Pas to Flin Flon, a branch of the Hudson Bay Railway, 1928

After spending $6 million on Port Nelson, including this bridge, the site was abandoned in favour of Churchill.

the Red Deer Lumber Company at Barrows and the Mutchenbackers mill at Mafeking—to say nothing of the hordes of tie-cutting and portable saw-milling operations between Swan River and The Pas.

But the considerable impact of these enterprises paled in comparison to that of the Hudson Bay Railway. In 1912-13, construction on this project commenced with the upgrading of the CNR line that ran into The Pas. As the temporary "end

The art of mine development by any means possible
Jack Hammell

WHEN WORD OF A NEW, AND very promising, optioning arrangement for a Flin Flon ore-body was released in March 1920, the north was plunged into a frenzy. It was soon known that two shafts were to be sunk, two mining plants purchased, thousands of tons of mining and food supplies purchased and extensive hauling work to be commenced immediately. In fact, everything had to be in place at Flin Flon before the April thaw.

Jack Hammell, who was put in charge of purchasing and transporting all the supplies, was well aware that he was about to "boom" the north. He was happy to do so, but he would brook no profiteering from the northern business community. Therefore, he assembled all of The Pas' storekeepers and assured them that he would purchase all supplies from them rather than buying them wholesale in Winnipeg, but he warned them not to mark up prices beyond ten per cent if they hoped to retain this business.

Hammell then turned his attention to the companies from whom he wished to purchase used mining equipment. In the case of the Mandy Mining Company at Schist Lake, there was no problem in purchasing their mining outfit, for they had already ceased operations. However, because two shafts were to be sunk, Hammell needed another mining outfit. He turned to the owners of the defunct Beaver Lake Gold Mining Company and offered to purchase their equipment for $10,000. The directors, knowing of Hammell's need for a

speedy transaction held out for $15,000. Hammell refused, but the Prince Albert businessmen who owned the mine were confident that he would be obliged to meet their price.

When spring break-up was almost upon them, they finally realized that Hammell was not going to budge and they accepted his offer. As soon as Hammell took their receipt, he explained he had already moved the outfit from Beaver Lake to Flin Flon and, as of the day of its purchase, it had been operating for two weeks. This, of course, constituted theft, but, armed with his receipt, Hammell could have cared less. He felt that his actions had been justified both by his need and by Beaver Lake's attempts to "hold him up".

It was also necessary to convince the provincial government to aid the developers in building a railway to Flin Flon. Hammell persuaded Provincial Treasurer Edward Brown to use his influence with the government to push for such aid. Then, after the 1920 election where Brown and the Norris government had been returned to power with a shaky mandate, Hammell arranged to invite the entire provincial assembly to journey north. He wanted to convince a ma-

jority of MLA's, regardless of party affiliation, of the value of the Flin Flon mine. In effect, Hammell was again hedging his bets—something that he did better than almost any other mine promoter of the era. His methods may not have been ethical, but they certainly were effective.

Prospector Tom Creighton, in white shirt, pointing to original ore discovery in Flin Flon

Tractor trains such as this one travelling from Port Nelson to Churchill hauled tons of supplies each winter.

With the HBR under construction, the biggest problem of hard rock mining— the transportation of equipment and ore—was resolved. Hence, 1913 and 1914 witnessed a major claim-staking rush in the region surrounding The Pas and all along the proposed rail line. This burst of prospecting activity resulted in iron and gold discoveries made at Wekusko (Herb) Lake, marble at Elbow Lake and copper at Wintering Lake. Most significant, however, was the news that the prospecting party of Tom Creighton, Dan Milligan, and the Mosher and Dion brothers was moving from their gold claims in Saskatchewan to the great Flin Flon copper/zinc deposits. As a result of this activity, there were many in The Pas who believed that large mines and perhaps even smelters would soon be functioning nearby, giving yet another boost to the region.

Even the occasional setbacks seemed to have a silver lining. For example, when the tremendous disadvantages of Port Nelson as a HBR harbour became apparent in 1914, no one had the political courage to abandon the site for the much better port

of steel", The Pas boomed as the warehousing, service and employment centre for the railway's general contractor, J.D. McArthur. However, places such as Norway House and Whisky Jack Portage also became important centres. Winter roads had to be built and construction camps had to be established along the proposed rail line. Meanwhile, McArthur's Hudson Bay Construction Company kept several hundred men working in the northern bush throughout that winter, preparing the 200,000 railway ties needed for summer track-laying.

Still, it was The Pas that became the economic success story of the north. As the centre for railway construction, lumbering, fur trading, fish handling and prospecting, The Pas became a mecca for anyone who had a service to offer a swelling population. Because of this, real estate values went through the roof. Town lots which had been selling for $50 to $250 in 1910 sold for as much as $7,000 in 1912. Then, when the government announced that The Pas would be the southern terminal of the HBR, the real estate market surged again. Indeed, in the ten-day period following this announcement, one real estate company sold $100,000 worth of building lots.

The editor of the local newspaper, the *Hudson Bay Herald,* predicted in 1913 that the north's wealth of natural resources and The Pas' geographic position would soon make The Pas into "one of the biggest cities on the North American continent, comparable only to such cities as Winnipeg, Minneapolis, Chicago, St. Louis and other such big geographical and commercial centres".

Immigrant labourers did much of the work on the Hudson Bay Railway. Under the direction of Claude Johnson, a CNR engineer, some 3,000 Swedes, Russians, Belgians and Finns laid 483 kilometres of track between 1924 and 1929.

Railway handcars provided a primitive form of passenger service.

Mine "salting" and the destruction of a community

The Bingo Scandal

ONE OF THE MORE NOTORIOUS mining swindles occurred after gold was discovered at Herb Lake. The so-called Bingo claims were purchased in 1919 from the original prospectors by a Winnipeg-based syndicate of mine promoters headed by a card-sharp and hustler named Joseph Myers. Myers, who hailed originally from New Zealand, began his swindle immediately. After arranging to purchase the claims for $10,000 he turned to his Winnipeg backers and tried to collect $20,000, which he represented as the purchase price.

His backers, including the prominent Winnipeg lawyer H.R. Drummond-Hay, were taken in, and formed Bingo Mines Limited in December, 1919. Shortly thereafter Myers headed to England to secure the funds needed to undertake shaft sinking.

The ore that was mined in 1920 was found to have gold values of only $1 per ton—hardly a viable grade for a commercial mining operation. Undaunted by these reports, Myers hired new assayers, "salted" their results by giving them hand-picked ore samples and, armed with their far more positive assessments, headed back to England in search of more capital. Once there, a new company, Bingo Gold Mines Limited, was formed early in 1922.

Soon, Herb Lake was booming. The population grew from 40 during the war to 450 by 1924. Sadly, this community which had come to life so quickly was destined to die even more swiftly. Discrepancies between Myers' figures on the value of Bingo's ore and those produced by independent assayers (sent by suspicious company offi-

cials) led the company's secretary, H.R. Drummond-Hay, to abandon his friendship with Myers and file charges against him late in 1924.

Myers, who was once again in England raising funds, was arrested on fraud charges and brought to Winnipeg to stand trial early in 1925. The evidence brought against Myers was telling but, on a technicality, he was acquitted. To investors, however, it was clear that Bingo had been "salted" by an unscrupulous promoter.

The Bingo mine had been tarnished in the only court that really mattered; the court of financial opinion. Investors and developers began withdrawing their support from virtually every Herb Lake property, leaving the once-booming camp but a thinly populated settlement of trappers and fishermen by 1926.

---

site of Churchill. Instead, the decision was made in Ottawa to pump even more money into Port Nelson: the mainland wharf complex was to be dismantled, an artificial island was to be constructed in the middle of the Nelson River, a shipping channel was to be dredged around the island, wharf and grain-handling facilities were to be built on this island and a railway bridge was to be built to the mainland. When it was finally admitted that Port Nelson was totally useless as a deep-water port, it was simply abandoned in favour of the Churchill site which, in the late 1920's, became a major construction site itself—once again creating hundreds of jobs in the north.

The outbreak of war also helped the economy. Indeed, in one area, World War I led to a mini-boom. Copper was needed for millions of bullets and shells and therefore the metal's price rose dramatically. From under 20 cents per pound before the war to almost 40 cents per pound by its end, lowly copper skyrocketed in value. It became both profitable and patriotic to develop copper deposits in northern Manitoba.

The first major copper find occurred in the winter of 1914-15 when Tom Creighton and his party came across the Flin Flon ore body. Soon

after, a staking frenzy broke out in the surrounding region. Of course, many of these new claims were speculative and of little value, but Sydney Reynolds and Fred Jackson, working at nearby Schist Lake, hit paydirt in October of 1915 when they discovered the high-grade copper deposit that would become famous as the Mandy Mine.

The north was now abuzz with mining news and mining men. Engineers, promoters and outright crooks were drawn to The Pas—the home of the mine recorder's office. Northerners and mine company executives alike hung on every word of men like Jack Hammell, the energetic promoter of the Flin Flon discovery. Meanwhile, the Tonopah Mining Company of Nevada purchased the Schist Lake claims from Fred Jackson (who cut his partner out of the deal by simply registering the claims in his own name).

The boom and bust cycle of the northern economy manifested itself in late 1915. Employment and expenditure levels on the HBR declined as the result of a wartime shortage of building materials. As well, The Pas—which was at the heart of the boom—was losing some of its most vital economic players. The reason for this was that the HBR had progressed so far northwards that the Hudson Bay Construction Company and its various sub-contractors were moving their bases of operation out of The Pas to Pikwitonie (Mile 214) for the spring building campaign of 1916.

A temporary halt to northern development resulted when shortages of track and other materials needed for the war effort ended construction on the railway and Port Nelson projects in 1917. Indeed, having reached Mile 332 at Kettle Rapids late in 1916, not another mile of track would be laid until the latter half of the 1920's.

Manitoba's Commissioner of Northern Manitoba tried to put a brave face upon matters, and his report for 1919-20 spoke glowingly of how the HBR and its fortnightly Muskeg Special train service to Mile 214 was helping fishermen, trappers, prospectors and mining companies to develop the north. However, his own figures on resource development told another story: in 1918-19 mining, lumbering, fishing, agriculture and trapping in the north produced only $3,457,733 worth of goods.

All in all, it was hard to see how the $20 million invested by the Dominion government in transportation infrastructure had paid any real dividends. But there were those who, far from suggesting financial retrenchment in the north, were arguing that the only way to really ensure development was to spend even more public money in the region. Provincial bureaucrats like Commissioner Campbell and his successor, Professor R.C. Wallace, were unabashed northern boosters who had faith that good times would soon return.

There was good economic news in March, 1920, when Jack Hammell convinced the Mining Corporation of Canada and William Boyd Thompson to take out a new option on the Flin Flon ore-body, an option which called for the expenditure of at least $200,000 in development work. Now everyone in Manitoba seemed to be enthralled with the north once again. Premier T.C. Norris' Liberal administration began negotiating with Hammell, Thompson and the newly formed Canadian National Railways for a rail line to Flin Flon. Meanwhile, deals were being struck between the developers at Flin Flon and the federal government concerning royalty exemptions. In every conceivable way the businessmen were being given what they wanted and, by March of 1921, the development of a vast mine and smelter complex at Flin Flon seemed a sure thing.

Lost Stakes Cost Native Prospectors

 When Duncan Twohearts discovered gold at Rice Lake in the winter of 1910-11, he did more than just discover Manitoba's most important gold mine. He also began a tradition of natives making many of the significant mineral discoveries in Manitoba.

There had, of course, been natives working as guides and paddlemen for prospectors before this. There were, as well, many Indians who acted as independent prospectors—a development which had worried the Department of the Interior sufficiently to seek a legal opinion concerning whether or not treaty Indians even had the right to make mineral claims.

One such individual was Phillip Sherlett (or Shellett), a Cree hunter and sometime prospector. He had been examining mineral occurrences along his trap-line in the Kissing (Cold) Lake area since 1913 and formally staked several copper claims after Jacob Cook's (yet another native prospector) Copper Lake discovery.

Bob Jowsey, an experienced mine promoter from Ontario, heard of Sherlett's claims and made plans to examine them. Jowsey never made it to Cold Lake because his party deserted him en route (probably to go and stake their own claims) and Jowsey was forced to return to The Pas. Years later, however, Jowsey, J.P. Gordon and a number of other mining men would be instrumental in bringing these claims into production as the Sherritt-Gordon mine.

Unfortunately for Sherlett, a registration foul-up allowed two American prospectors to re-stake his claims. These men, Carl Sherritt and Dick Madole, had been prospecting and trapping in the Cold Lake area since the early 1920's and, according to some sources, took great pleasure in "jumping" Sherlett's lapsed claims because the Indian had reported them for trapping with poisoned bait. As a result of all this, Sherlett never made a penny from his discovery.

While it is obvious how important men like Twohearts, Collins, Sherlett, Cook and other native prospectors were in Manitoba's mining history, their role has been played down—just as they were passed over by white prospectors and mining companies when it came time to pay them for their services.

Unfortunately, nothing is inevitable until it happens, as was proven yet again at Flin Flon. The recession that had commenced in 1920 was beginning to take a toll both on credit supply and copper prices. Then, on March 21, 1921—just ten days before the option on the Flin Flon property was to be officially taken up—ten of America's largest copper companies suspended all opera-

Flying Into Unknown Territory

Manitoba's first bush pilots braved near-impossible conditions

Western Canada Airways
plane unloading supplies at a
lakeside outpost

The first commercial flight to northern Manitoba occurred in October, 1920. Winnipeg pilot Hector Dougall and mechanic Frank Ellis were asked by a fur buyer to fly him home to The Pas. The startled crew discussed the feasibility of such a flight and decided, in the spirit that later defined the bush pilot, that they would try.

Taking off in a three-seater Avro biplane, the men flew along the eastern slope of Riding and Duck Mountains, landing at Dauphin to refuel. Continuing north, they ran into bad weather and had to land to the west of The Pas—at Hudson Bay Junction in Saskatchewan. There were no roads, no cars and therefore no gasoline at this remote settlement. The owner of the local Chinese cafe offered the adventurers eight gallons of lighting fuel. Thus supplied, the men took off and later landed in The Pas to a large crowd of enthusiastic onlookers. The era of the bush pilot had begun.

Over the next few years, dozens of daring young men (mainly World War I veterans) took to the northern skies in search of adventure and for-

O F ALL THE DARING MEN AND women who opened the north to development, none is more celebrated than the bush pilot. Quintessentially Canadian, the bush pilot overcame horrendous weather, finicky aircraft and fantastic distances to deliver people and equipment to the new frontier.

In post World War I Manitoba, the commercial use of aircraft was initially limited to barnstorming exhibitions at local fairs and the occasional passenger flight. Railways and roads provided plenty of transportation options for business.

In the newly developing north, however, transportation still depended on the York boats and canoe brigades of the voyageur era. Moving equipment from Winnipeg to a new mine site could take weeks. An airplane, on the other hand, could move people and supplies in a matter of hours.

The Canadian Air Force was the first to survey remote northern locations for mining companies.

tune. Flying Fokkers, Fairchilds and Junkers, pilots like Wop May, Roy Brown, Fred Stevenson, Doc Oaks and Punch Dickins soon became as famous as movie stars. They risked their lives and planes to fly equipment to remote mines, to ferry survey teams for the Hudson Bay Railway and, all too often, to search for lost trappers and prospectors.

Roy Brown, flying out of Cranberry Portage for James A. Richardson's Western Canada Airways, provided a dramatic example of the effectiveness of the bush plane. In 1927, he encountered a trio of depressed prospectors at Lac La Ronge. They had discovered a "glowing red mound" of copper somewhere to the north of Flin Flon. Unfortunately, while waiting for assay returns to confirm ore quality, word leaked out about the bonanza. A group of rival prospectors had headed out four days earlier with a team of expert Indian guides.

Brown agreed to help the men try to find their stake. Flying northward, it soon became clear the prospectors couldn't recognize landmarks from the air. Lost and almost out of fuel, Brown saw a lake where he remembered the Air Force had stored some gasoline.

After refueling, they set out once more. Below them, the Manitoba north stretched out in an endless canvas of muskeg, rock and water. Finally, eyes straining into the distance, one of the men saw a shining red mound. As the prospectors shouted excitedly, Brown looked down on the lake below and saw two canoes with men digging their paddles furiously in the water. Brown pushed the throttle down and managed to land his party well ahead of their rivals. The copper claim was later sold for $150,000.

By 1930, bush pilots had become an integral part of northern development. As famed World War I ace Billy Bishop put it, without these daring young men, "...the opening of the rich Canadian North was impossible. Then the bush flier came along and wrought a miracle".

Western Canada Airways

A handshake between a bush pilot and a powerful Winnipeg grain baron became the basis for Canada's first commercial airline—a venture that eventually evolved into today's Canadian Airlines International.

When rough-and-ready bush pilot H.A. "Doc" Oaks showed up in 1926 at James A. Richardson's Winnipeg office, the grain millionaire was impressed by Oaks' intelligence and practical expertise with aircraft. A decorated Royal Flying Corps hero, Oaks had already become one of Canada's first "bush pilots". He convinced Richardson that, with a mining boom in the North, bush flying was on the verge of being extremely profitable.

James Richardson, at right, with Ben Smith, J.G. McDiarmid, and Mitchell Hepburn

Until then, much of the North had been an impenetrable wilderness, accessible only by dog team or canoe. But World War I brought rapid advances in the development of aircraft, and rugged new planes like the Fokker Universal were showing up in northern skies. Oaks told Richardson he needed money and Richardson announced he was looking for innovative business opportunities. With a handshake, the two men agreed to start Canada's first commercial airline.

Oaks travelled to New Jersey where he purchased a new Fokker Universal. He then flew the little open-cockpit plane through bitterly cold weather to Sioux Lookout, Ontario. Oaks immediately put the plane to work, delivering passengers and mail. This single-engine machine was officially registered as G-CAFU and named "The City of Winnipeg".

Western Canada Airways quickly began acquiring other planes, and to fly them, Oaks hired the best pilots in Canada—Fred Stevenson, Roy Brown and Punch Dickins. These pilots were adventurers at heart. For example, Dickins became the first commercial pilot to cross the Arctic Circle.

Meanwhile, Richardson landed a federal contract to move mail between Winnipeg and Calgary. As in the North, his aviators suffered through the growing pains associated with a fledgling industry. For example, aircraft were equipped with only the most rudimentary navigational tools, especially for night flying. To assist pilots, the federal government installed navigational beacons every ten miles, and a powerful revolving searchlight every hundred miles. From the air, the beacons formed a chain of light leading across the darkened Prairies, and WCA pilots could see the piercing flash of the searchlight from miles away.

In 1930, WCA formed, along with the two national railways, a venture called Canadian Airways. With that move, Richardson's company became Canada's first national airline. Later, the CPR bought Canadian Airways and created Canadian Pacific Airlines. Thus, Doc Oaks' rickety open-cockpit bush plane operation eventually grew into one of the most respected airlines in the world. CPA, now known as Canadian Airlines International.

Bush plane at San Antonio mine in Bissett

tions in the face of disastrously low copper prices. All plans for developing Flin Flon were put on hold.

The price of fur dropped drastically in 1920, making that industry both unprofitable and unstable for the next few years. For their part, fish prices held steady until 1921 but then they too fell precipitously and remained low until well into the latter half of the decade. Finally, because of the depression of the early '20's, the demand for northern lumber declined. Employment levels dropped dramatically as lumber companies cut back on production.

Rev. Emile Desormeaux, who served as a missionary in the Pukatawagan area from 1926 to 1978, spent his early years travelling 4,000 kilometres each winter by dog sled and another 4,000 kilometres each summer by canoe to reach his parishoners.

The sole bright spot in the north during the early '20's turned out to be gold mining. At Herb Lake development work between 1921 and 1923 brought the Rex claims into production while the infamous Bingo property also underwent development. And because of the seeming success of these ventures, a whole host of lesser claims were being developed throughout the north.

Despite the damaging revelations concerning Bingo and its promoter, Joseph Myers, 1925 proved to be a year of revival for the north. Steadily rising copper prices on the world market plus a breakthrough in mineral separation techniques induced the Whitney family of New York to take out an option on the Flin Flon property in the fall of 1925. Meanwhile, Phillip Sherlett's copper find at Kissing (Cold) Lake was optioned by its new owners to J.P. Gordon that same summer. These two developments would finally set in motion the process of mine-making at both sites.

In the Central Manitoba mining district, mat-

ters also began looking up after 1925. The increasing availability of investment capital played a key role in finally developing the Kitchner claims, which became the nucleus of Central Manitoba Mines Limited in 1927; a gold mine that would remain in production for more than a decade. Shortly thereafter, Former Mountie E.A. Pelletier's San Antonio gold discovery of 1910 was finally developed, a mine which would continue in operation for 40 years and help to keep Bissett a viable community for that entire period.

Pine Falls was quickly becoming one of the major pulp and paper suppliers of the West.

Nor was mining the only resource industry to flourish. Entrepreneur J.D. McArthur succeeded in putting together the Manitoba Pulp and Paper Company in 1925. This resulted in mills and a company town being built at Pine Falls by 1927 in order to take advantage of the vast stands of timber that had been granted to this company. Meanwhile, after a lengthy hiatus, hydro-electric development along the Winnipeg River also picked up during this period as major additions were made to the Great Falls power plant and massive new power plants were under construction at Slave Falls and Seven Sisters in the later '20's.

Even the older resource industries were booming. The fishing industry regained most of the ground it had lost during the early '20's as prices began to rise. The value of fish caught roughly doubled between 1924 and 1927 while employment levels in the industry rose from 2,800 to 4,000. The fur trade also revived as fur prices climbed and by 1929-30 over 7,000 trappers were once again employed in this once decimated industry. And, needless to say, with the overall buoyancy of the economy, the timber industry also experienced its own boom.

The real stars of this period were the new resource industries and the railway. The development of Flin Flon by the Whitneys (they eventually formed the Hudson Bay Mining and Smelting Company), which began in earnest in 1927, led to a large capital investment and the creation of a town with an initial population of 5,000. The development of the Sherritt-Gordon Mines at Cold Lake in the same period called for the building of another short line and the establishment of another new mining town at Sherridon. When these figures are added to the monies spent developing hydro-electric sites on the Winnipeg River, the mills and town at Pine Falls, the gold mines in the Central Manitoba mining district, something in the neighbourhood of $70 million worth of private investment capital found its way to the resource frontier between 1925 and 1930.

With this amount of private capital invested in the resource frontier, it was almost inevitable that millions more worth of public monies would also have to be invested. The provincial government and the CNR, for example, collaborated with private developers to construct short lines to company towns at Flin Flon, Sherridon and Pine Falls. Meanwhile, mining roads had to be built throughout the Central Manitoba mining district by the province in order to serve the mines and towns in that area. And local governments at Flin Flon, The Pas, Lac du Bonnet and a host of other resource communities also had to invest heavily in infrastructure.

In 1926, bending to western Canadian pressure, work on the HBR was renewed by the Dominion government. The $40 million investment required to rehabilitate the existing line from The Pas to Mile 322, to lay new track to Churchill (rather than Port Nelson) and to construct a town site, harbour and grain handling facilities, provided thousands of short-term construction jobs and gave birth to a series of new railway towns such as Gillam, Wabowden and Thicket Portage.

By the close of the 1920's, the north was, once again, the hotbed of the provincial economy. Nine major new towns were created and employment opportunities abounded (one source estimates that over 35,000 seasonal jobs were created along the frontier between 1925 and 1930).

Not everyone stayed in the north. Like all frontiers, it attracted its share of fast-buck artists, con-men and prostitutes. But many others came to love both the beauty and the economic potential of the north. As mines opened, railways expanded and daredevil bush pilots pushed ever northward, no one could blame northerners for looking ahead with anticipation of even better things to come. ✎

Aircraft were used to detect and suppress forest fires beginning in the early 1920's. The federal government still controlled the province's natural resources, so flying was done by the Canadian Air Force.

CHAPTER SEVEN

Charting a New Course

BY WILLIAM NEVILLE

The Roaring Twenties in Manitoba was a time of renewal and expectation. World War I left an entire generation disillusioned with pre-conflict institutions. New political and farm movements sprang up, with a decidedly populist outlook. At the same time, a certain rebelliousness animated the decade. Illegal profits could be made from booze-running to the United States. Young flappers seemed determined to shock the older generation with their short dresses and wild parties. After four years of horrendous war, the people of Manitoba wanted change, and they were prepared to go to great lengths to get it.

With additional material by
MARGARET SWEATMAN, JAKE MACDONALD, ALLAN LEVINE AND
LLOYD FRIDFINNSON

The Elks Jazz Band in concert, 1922

Charting a New Course

Renewal and expectation animate the Roaring Twenties

The Great War proved a watershed for Canada and for Manitoba. So vast were its repercussions on the imaginations of those who lived through it that there was a sense, at war's end, of a world transformed. Much of pre-war society had been swept away, but there was also great uncertainty as to what would take its place. Expectations were high that the sacrifices of war would be redeemed by a new world—better, safer and more just than the old. Such hopes were not to be realized easily in the decade that followed, and at its conclusion, like a bookend, lay a watershed of another kind.

The decade that began in 1919 marked the end of an epoch in Canada, especially in its politics. Before the war, political life was dominated by two parties whose strength was rooted firmly in the populous, powerful provinces of central Canada. The Great War and its aftermath shattered that two-party system; if Liberal and Conservative parties continued to be parties of government, their shared monopoly was ended. For those who believed there were no important differences between Grits and Tories, their national cohabitation after 1917 offered proof, if proof were needed. Intertwined with the challenge to the old parties, was a challenge to central Canada by a West that had finally decided to use the political system as an expression of its grievances.

Within Manitoba, the decade saw two major challenges to the established political order: one from labour and the other from farmers. The first came from labour. The General Strike in Winnipeg had been pivotal, attempting as it had to alter the balance of economic power within the city. That challenge, although strongly felt, was defeated.

Deeply divisive when it occurred, the strike acquired a kind of mythological significance whose enduring effects may have been determined less by actual events than by the way the working and business classes perceived and portrayed the motives of the other. The result was a major cleavage in municipal politics, and one with remarkable endurance.

This was immediately evident in the resolve of the Citizen's Committee of One Thousand and its successors, that labour should not win at the ballot box what it had failed to achieve by the strike. To paraphrase historian J. Edgar Rea, having shattered labour's economic power, their next objective was to extinguish its political potential.

In the fall of 1919, the Citizens' Committee metamorphosed into the Citizens' League, for the purposes of contesting the November civic elections in which half the 14 council seats and the office of mayor were at stake. Simultaneously, under the auspices of the Dominion Labour Party, an organization and platform were put together to support a slate of Labour candidates.

The campaign observed something less than the Queensbury rules. The Labour candidates, already on the defensive in the post-strike climate, were painted by their opponents as Reds, revolutionaries and fanatics. Labour was further disadvantaged by the greater financial resources of their opponents and by the prevailing electoral laws which carried a property qualification, and which, for aldermanic elections, allowed property owners to vote in as many wards as the owner had property. Given these circumstances, the result was close; the Citizens won the mayoralty and elected four aldermen to Labour's three—all in the North End—but the new council, with seven carry-overs from the previous election, was evenly split. Mayor Charles F. Gray, engraved in memory as the man who during the strike actually read the Riot Act from the steps of City Hall, had the deciding vote.

The result was far too close for the Citizens' leaders. This was clear both from their private correspondence and from their subsequent actions: by the election of 1920, they had the legislature approve a new electoral system for Winnipeg. Three six-member wards were created and the single transferable ballot was introduced. Now the bulk of working class voters were lumped into a single area—Ward Three. The property qualifications, including those allowing plural voting, were retained. These changes, coupled with rifts in the ranks of Labour, proved very helpful for the commercial elite: in 1920 the Citizens elected 12 aldermen and Labour six.

The strike was less explicitly an issue in 1920 (and hardly at all thereafter), but the elections of 1919 and 1920 revealed a cleavage between the North End and the south, and between those who sought a more active civic role in social policy and those who emphasized services to property. In 1922, when the city elected its first Labour

The Winnipeg Falcons, 1920 Olympic and world junior hockey champions

nipeg Falcons. World's Ice Hockey Champs. VII Olympiade 192

mayor, S.J. Farmer, it became clear that the strengths of the two sides might ebb and flow; but in that election, and in most that followed, the protagonists were usually clear. Winnipeg's politics—then and thereafter—had largely polarized along lines defined by perceived class and ideological differences.

Mike Swistun, an Olha area farmer, was billed "The Strongest Man in the World" when he toured with the Ringling Brothers Barnum & Bailey Circus in 1923. Swistun was so powerful that he could bend iron bars with his teeth or hold two automobiles at a standstill with his muscular arms.

Labour's failed challenge was to the powers of the city of Winnipeg; the farmers' far more successful one was to the established political order of the province as a whole. And if labour's failed challenge produced sharp and distinct cleavages in municipal government, the farmers' highly successful challenge had an almost opposite effect: it virtually killed party government by treating the province like an overgrown municipal council.

The provincial government of Liberal T.C. (Toby) Norris had come to office in 1915. It was an activist government: it brought in temperance legislation and enfranchised women; it also introduced minimum wage, a public health nursing system, compulsory education and many other measures. These measures had a cost—the government ran up deficits in three of its first five years. In depressed times the deficits made the Liberals vulnerable. What made them more vulnerable was the simmering discontent in the agricultural community.

Western, and more especially agrarian, grievances had been largely set aside in the interests of the war effort. During the war, moreover,

Winnipeg's social elite gathered regularly at the Manitoba Club.

the national government had established machinery for the orderly marketing of grain as a means of ensuring price stability. The post-war economic recession saw a dramatic decline in the prices paid for grain, without any corresponding drop in the cost of its production; with the war over, however, the national Union government announced its intention to maintain protective tariffs and the "free" market.

Persuaded that a return to normalcy meant returning to policies designed for the commercial interests of central Canada, farmers talked increasingly about direct political action. The 1919 Ontario election, in which the United Farmers won an unexpected victory, was powerful evidence of the potency of angry farmers, and was a spur to further action.

In the Manitoba election campaign of 1920, Premier Norris and his government campaigned on their record; the United Farmers of Manitoba, possessing neither a leader, a common platform, nor a province-wide organization, ran essentially an anti-party campaign which argued that the old parties possessed neither the will nor the integrity to serve farmers' interests.

The Revolution of Radio

Suddenly, Manitoba was linked to the world

Twenty years after Guglielmo Marconi directed the first radio signal across the Atlantic, Manitoba was the site of a number of firsts in Canadian broadcasting. In April, 1922, the *Manitoba Free Press* put Canada's first commercial station, CJCG, on the air. In March, 1923, Canadians heard their first church broadcast from the Fort Rouge Methodist Church. And in 1923, Manitoba launched CKY, the country's first government-run radio station.

In the early 1920's, radio receivers were still relatively rare in the living rooms of the country. It wasn't until 1925 that an electric-powered receiver was developed. The "Rogers Batteryless" was a mantel-top model, available for $250—the loudspeaker was an extra $45. Many people still cobbled together their own battery-powered tube radios from kits available through the Eaton's catalogue.

The *Free Press*'s radio effort was a feeble one by today's standards. The station's transmitter had a rating of only ten watts. At Winnipeg's other major daily, the *Winnipeg Tribune,* staffers called it the "Carlton Street peanut whistle". In the spirit of the newspaper wars, the *Tribune* launched its own radio arm—with a 500-watt signal.

By 1923, the broadcast arms of the two newspapers had established a weekly pattern, but with limited hours. There were noon-hour news, grain, stock market, and sports reports; a two-hour evening program of local musical talent; and church music programs on Sundays. Most Manitobans turned up their noses at local radio, staying tuned to the stronger signals from the United States, many of which could be heard in Winnipeg by the most basic single tube receiver.

It was not a concern about Canadian culture that prompted the Manitoba government to step into broadcasting. The motivation was entirely economic. The Manitoba Telephone System was afraid radio might be used for sending and receiving messages, bypassing the publicly funded telephone service. The *Free Press* and the *Tribune* announced they would relinquish the field of broadcasting to MTS. They were probably eager to, as stringent early prohibitions on advertising limited revenues.

A cowboy group prepares for a broadcast at CJGX.

The Manitoba Telephone System's CKY went on the air in March, 1923, with a welcoming address from Premier John Bracken. CKY set up its own round of news and sports reports and hours of live music from the Roseland Dance Gardens on Portage Avenue. The station's most inventive and popular program was "University Hour", a series of lectures by university professors on such topics as "The Elements of Human Nature" and "Modern Ideas of Electricity".

CKY managed financially because it received half of Manitoba's share of the $1 fee charged by the federal government to every Canadian who owned a radio receiver. In 1926, the station netted about $9,000 from its share of the licence fee; by 1930, that income topped $18,000. Ottawa also allowed Manitoba to veto any other radio licences in the province. But there were few complaints about the monopoly from listeners; most were apparently happy that local stations were not hogging the dial, blocking access to the U.S. signals.

In the late 1920's, pressure from the business community against the monopoly began to grow. James Richardson and Sons issued a direct challenge to CKY by setting up a powerful transmitter on the Saskatchewan side of the Manitoba border. Ottawa itself was also becoming unhappy that Manitoba claimed jurisdiction over broadcasting. So in 1932, the federal government cancelled the unique licence fee split and one year later granted the Richardson firm approval to relocate to Winnipeg. The experiment in a government radio monopoly had come to a close.

CKY was finally purchased by the CBC in 1949 and renamed CBW. The call letters CKY were later picked up and are still used by a privately-owned Winnipeg station.

The Legislative Assembly which convened after the election was altogether remarkable: it was, to begin with, the first to assemble in the magnificent new Legislative Building. This building, which had brought down an earlier government, proved both handsome and elegant, and was probably the finest such structure in the land.

The new legislature also included its first woman MLA, Edith Rogers of Winnipeg. However, the most significant change lay in the shattering of the Norris administration and, indeed, of certain traditional assumptions about the nature of parliamentary government.

The Liberals, though the largest group in the

The Grain

A toe-to-toe battle between Winnipeg's wealthy grain men and western farmers

Fortunes were made and lost daily at the booming Winnipeg Grain Exchange.

7435-3
FOOTE

WHEN WHEAT WAS KING ON THE Prairies in the early years of this century, its princes were the grain merchants of Winnipeg and its palace was the Winnipeg Grain Exchange. Organized in the 19th century, the Exchange dealt primarily in agricultural commodities, particularly wheat. It was Canada's entry point into the world grain trade, connecting the Prairies with the trading centres of Chicago and Liverpool.

Winnipeg's grain men prospered magnificently: dealers like Nicholas Bawlf, Charles Bell, George Galt and James A. Richardson were leading members of the city's commercial and social elite. They created an efficient, competitive and lucrative empire selling the wheat of Prairie farmers to Europe. But the farmers themselves were

convinced that the "speculators" in the Exchange, manipulating the futures market to their own advantage, were siphoning off far too much of the profit in wheat.

World War I changed the Canadian wheat business profoundly. With supplies from Argentina and Australia cut off, Britain and its Allies became dependent on North American wheat. Prices escalated rapidly. Alarmed by the rapid increase, Britain closed the private grain trade and became the sole European purchaser. With only one power in the field, the Canadian government had little choice but to act in concert with the United States and close the open market. A Board of Grain Supervisors was appointed to sell the wheat crops during the war and through negotiations with Britain

and America a uniform price was set that delighted farmers on both sides of the border.

When the war ended, the United States and Europe reestablished the free market. Winnipeg grain dealers impatiently urged the Canadian government to do the same, but the first Canadian Wheat Board was created as a temporary expedient to handle the 1919 crop and then expired. In the summer of 1920, the Winnipeg Grain Exchange was back in business. At the same time, a short but very severe recession drove wheat prices down. The farmers made an obvious if not necessarily accurate connection. They clamoured for the return of government marketing through a new wheat board, but the Canadian government had no wish to return to the grain business.

Early in the 1920's, western farmers decided to take on the Grain Exchange themselves through the technique of pooling. The campaign for the pools was led by Aaron Sapiro, an American lawyer who spread the gospel of pooling through the Prairies like an evangelist. He debated the urbane Robert Magill, Secretary of the Grain Exchange, in the winter of 1924 at a sold-out meeting in Saskatoon while 2,000 disappointed supporters milled around outside. A Regina radio station broadcast the event across the wheat belt. Sapiro's message was simple and clear; he urged the wheat farmers to sell their grain themselves, since the "Winnipeg Grain Exchange is becoming the most conspicuous foe

House, had lost their majority and, as became clear, their compass. The UFM, with 12 members, were the second largest group in the House; but they declined to assume the role of Official Opposition. Their MLAs didn't hold with conventional views of government or the parliamentary system: they saw themselves not as a party, but essentially as a group of delegates reflecting the interests of their constituents. They wished to be free to support or oppose legislation, as they saw it, on its merits. Indeed, when the new Legislature assembled, one of the UFM Members proposed that the executive—the Cabinet—be drawn from all groups in the House, in proportion to their elected

Exchange vs the Pools

of real marketing in the world".

To be viable, a pool had to sign up at least half the producers in a geographic area. A producer contracted to deliver his grain to the pool for a specified period, usually five years. The pool paid him an initial price (which it borrowed from the banks), based on its forecast of world prices for the forthcoming year. This was followed by an interim payment about seeding time and then a final payment when the business for the year was concluded. The final price was the average price received over the year less the cost of running the operation. Pool producers would receive the same price for the same grade over the entire crop year. This was the theory, and the promise of Sapiro and the pool enthusiasts.

By 1924, Manitoba, Saskatchewan and Alberta had organized wheat pools and they combined to create a Central Selling Agency with offices overseas. Within three years they were handling half the Prairie wheat crop which made up 40 per cent of the world export total. The Grain Exchange tried to hold back the tide. They bought a Yorkton radio station to combat the pools' organ, the *Western Producer,* and preached free enterprise along with the daily quotations. The mid-1920's were fat years with stable prices and markets expanding quickly enough to drive the price of an Exchange seat from $9,000 to $25,000. The pools and the traders flourished.

All pool grain was unhedged as they virtuously avoided the futures market. Hence in the autumn of 1929, when the price of wheat fell below their initial payment, the pools were devastated. They tried to hold back wheat in what J.W. Dafoe of the *Free Press* called "the biggest game of stud poker the world ever witnessed". But with only 20 per cent of the export trade the pools could not control the price. Their small reserve funds were wiped out and eventually the federal government had to save them.

The pools ultimately survived and have continued to perform valuable services for their members. The Grain Exchange also weathered the Great Depression. Consolidation, partially provoked by the pools, resulted in powerful and competitive corporations which continue to play an important role in world commodity trade.

HOMEWOOD
CO-OP ELEVATOR
ASSOCIATION
POOL № 78
"SERVICE AT COST"

The rise of pools and co-operatives marked Manitoba farmers' desire to control their own economic future.

Portage la Prairie's Prime Minister

Arthur Meighen was Manitoba's first and only PM

A RATHER PATRICIAN FIGURE of great intellectual and oratorical gifts, Arthur Meighen was able, conscientious and principled. To many, however, he lacked the common touch necessary for political success in a democratic age.

Born in 1874, Meighen—like most Manitoba politicians of his era—was a native of Ontario. He settled in Portage la Prairie, opened a law practice and was elected to Parliament in 1908. There he was gradually recognized as one of the most brilliant minds and effective debaters in Canadian parliamentary history. In 1913, Sir Robert Borden appointed Meighen to the cabinet and to a succession of portfolios, including solicitor general, minister of the interior and minister of mines. The workhorse of the government, Meighen was involved with the reorganization of the railways, the introduction of closure, the introduction of conscription and the Wartime Elections Act; all were highly controversial.

When Borden retired in 1920, Meighen was the obvious, though by no means unanimous, choice as successor, in part because of the controversial baggage he carried with him. Nonetheless, he became prime minister—the only Manitoban to hold the office—in July 1920. His tenure was brief; he was badly defeated at the polls late in 1921.

Arthur Meighen, left, and Reeve E.H. Muir of the RM of Portage la Prairie

In the 1925 election Meighen's Conservatives emerged as the largest party in the House, but without a majority. The Liberal government of Mackenzie King carried on, supported by the Progressives until the so-called "King-Byng" consitutional crisis of 1926. Then, facing a censure motion in the Commons, King asked the governor-general, Lord Byng, to dissolve Parliament. Byng declined, King resigned, and Meighen was invited to form a government. This new government was soon defeated in the Commons and, in the general election that followed, Meighen's party lost ground. Meighen relinquished the premiership for a second and final time, and the Tory leadership soon thereafter.

Meighen served as Tory leader in the Senate in the 1930's and in 1942 briefly resumed the leadership of his party; but, attempting to return to the Commons, he was defeated in a by-election, after which he retired from politics. He died in 1960.

While in public life and in retirement, Arthur Meighen was in great demand as a public speaker. In the 1930's he delivered a speech on Shakespeare —"The Greatest Englishman"—without notes, even though the speech required quoting hundreds of lines from Shakespeare's plays and poetry.

members. This proposal was defeated only on the deciding vote of the Speaker; it was, nonetheless, a significant foreshadowing of their future attitudes towards the operation of parliamentary government.

Shorn of its majority, and buffeted by the recession, the Norris government seemed unable to control the legislative agenda; given this and given the UFM's radical approach to governance, the party system in the legislature gradually dissolved. Defeated on a confidence motion, the premier submitted his resignation, only to be rebuffed by Sir James Aikins, the lieutenant-governor, who insisted that his ministers carry on until the session had been concluded. That done, the House was dissolved and a further election called for July, 1922.

Between the Manitoba provincial elections of 1920 and 1922, a federal election had intervened. That election reduced the Conservative Party to third place, and removed from office Arthur Meighen of Portage la Prairie, the only Manitoban ever to serve as prime minister. The Tories were routed by the combination of a revived Liberal Party under Mackenzie King and a sweep of western Canada (and all of Manitoba outside Winnipeg) by the Progressives—the federal cousins of the United Farmers.

To some degree, therefore, the results of the 1922 provincial election were preordained. The UFM won a narrow majority with 28 of the 55 seats, but the opposition was hopelessly fractured: eight Independents, seven Liberals, six Conservatives and six Labour. The orthodox parties had been battered by a party that didn't believe in parties. More unusual still was the fact that the new government was leaderless: who was to be premier? The newly elected UFM Members caucused and canvassed a number of possibilities, even including the outgoing Liberal premier, Toby Norris. In the end, however, their unanimous—and unlikely—choice was John Bracken, principal of the Agricultural College,

A number of co-operatives and pools set up information tents at the Brandon fair in 1928. Note the sign which charts the steady growth of prairie pools.

The Women's Institute

Rural women often lived in isolation. They longed for the company of other women and for information to improve their lives. Into this void stepped the Women's Institute.

The idea of creating a Women's Institute in Manitoba arose after Mrs. F. Mackenzie visited Ontario. There she learned of the Women's Institute, a group formed by women who realized they needed access to information in their role as homemakers.

Mackenzie shared her findings with women in Morris. Manitoba's first Women's Institute was formed there in August, 1910, with 36 members. The WI's objective was "to provide educational opportunities that will enable rural women to develop their skills and then use those skills to improve their homes and to advance the interests of the community at all levels..."

By 1919, some 118 chapters of the popular organization were operating. The WI, whose motto is "For Home and Country," was initially dedicated to the improvement of homemaking, but its role soon evolved. For example, in the 1920's, it sponsored public health education classes and was the first provincial organization to work with the Cancer Institute in promoting cancer control programs. During the Depression, the WI provided educational programs on mental health care and classes on how to economize.

The WI also made a physical impact on rural communities. It helped developed more than 100 rural libraries. As well, it ran a number of women's rest rooms, places where rural women and children could rest and refresh themselves while visiting towns.

The Women's Institute continues its activities and has become one of Manitoba's most durable institutions.

Gathering of members of the Manitoba Women's Institute at the Legislative Building

A New Kind of Prairie

Manitoba's first literary all-stars were Ernest Thompson Seton and Reverend C.W. Gordon. Seton wrote wildlife stories while Gordon (under the pseudonym Ralph Connor) produced adventure novels that sold millions of copies around the world.

Both Seton and Gordon were essentially 19th-century romantics whose characters triumphed through their commitment to honour, optimism and courage. But after the Great War, Gertrude Stein's "lost generation" no longer believed in the fundamental goodness of the world. American expatriates like Hemingway and Fitzgerald created a new amoral style of writing. In Canada, authors like F.P. Grove, Martha Ostenso and Douglas Durkin built literary reputations based on the same unflinching treatment of the darker side of life. During the 1920's, most of Canada's leading writers were Manitobans. ❧

FELIX GREVE WAS A YOUNG GERMAN writer who suffered a number of financial failures and, in 1908, wound up serving a prison term for fraud. A year later, Greve disappeared from Germany and turned up in Winkler, Manitoba, where he landed a job as a schoolteacher under a new identity—Frederick Philip Grove.

Despite his embarrassing past, Grove was a decent man who worked hard during the daytime as a school principal and wrote obsessively in the evening, compiling a mountain of unpublished stories. From Winkler he moved on to Virden and then to Gladstone, where he first began achieving success as a writer. On weekends he climbed on his horse and rode from Gladstone to Falmouth, where he lived with his wife and daughter. Riding through the winter landscape, Grove discovered a pristine beauty that connected with something deep in his soul. His startling ability to recreate this landscape in fiction caught the attention of a Toronto publisher. And upon being "discovered" Grove sent McClelland & Stewart his collected works—a huge bundle of ink-stained stories embodying 30 years of unpublished writing.

Grove eventually produced a dozen books, in which he created stark portrayals of small town life. But his efforts weren't always appreciated.

Community leaders attacked books like *Settlers of the Marsh* for their sexual explicitness and alleged immorality. And although Grove eventually won the Governor-General's Award for Literature, his life tended towards tragedy. In photos, loneliness and overwork are written in the lines of his face. Grove received critical praise for his books but the loss of his pretty little daughter May—who died at the age of 11 from a simple appendix operation—broke Grove's heart and haunted him for the rest of his life.

Frederick Philip Grove

BORN, LIKE ERNEST HEMINGWAY, IN the first year of the new century, Martha Ostenso was an attractive 22-year-old by the time she arrived at the University of Manitoba in the early 1920's. Although young, she had already published newspaper stories and worked as a schoolteacher in rural Manitoba before enrolling in the university's creative writing program.

Her teacher was an experienced middle-aged novelist named Douglas Durkin. Cynical, weathered, and very married, Durkin was nevertheless a talented man who posed an irresistible temptation to the young Ostenso. During the school year, they became closely involved, and when Durkin temporarily left his family and moved to New York to take a teaching position at Columbia, Ostenso followed.

In Manhattan, Ostenso and Durkin forged their remarkable partnership, both as lovers and literary co-conspirators. In 1924, the Dodd Mead publishing company announced a nation-wide contest for a best first novel. Durkin was working on a promising manuscript, but as a published author he was ineligible. Ostenso qualified, however. With Durkin's collaboration, she redrafted her creative writing class novel about working as a schoolteacher in Hayland, Manitoba and submitted it to Dodd Mead. The Roaring Twenties was a decade of volcanic artistic activity in the United States and Dodd Mead received more than a thousand entries. But when New York newspapers announced the prize it was, unbelievably enough, *Wild Geese*, by a young Manitoba woman named Martha Ostenso.

Like many of the best novels of the 1920's, *Wild Geese* was a vivid and sensual exploration of the natural world, with the sort of crisp and erotic lyricism that few modern novels have been able to improve upon. The story

~~Lit~~ature

Martha Ostenso

...inest
...the rest of
...hey continued to collaborate, co-
...that earned them 30 or 40 thousand
...ar in royalties alone. During the
...as an enormous amount of money,
... able to keep a variety of luxury
...oats and homes in Beverly Hills,
... the lake country of Minnesota.
...ambling stone cottage in Brainerd,
...ey lived every writer's fantasy exis-
...g until noon, going for a swim, hav-
...ch and then tapping at their
...ough the afternoon. At five, they
...had cocktails with a never-ending
...seguests, who included friends like
...s Fairbanks, John Barrymore and
... This often continued on into an
...nfoolery and wild behaviour that
...ed until daybreak. By the late
...elf-indulgent lifestyle had begun to
...rk and their writing began to read
...lywood fiction. Ostenso eventually
... the life of a full-blown alcoholic,
...e died of cirrhosis of the liver.
...g F. Scott Fitzgerald to Martha's
...nly five more years.

and a man sufficiently reluctant that he agreed only upon the third request.

Bracken's reluctance stemmed from a considerable lack of interest in politics: he had never sought nor held public office and had not even voted in the election. He was a respected agronomist who understood the problems facing the farming community. Beyond that, he shared their general view of government: that it ought to be a matter of administration—sound, careful, prudent administration—and not a matter of ideology or partisanship. Like them, he had little interest in parties and party government; his approach was to seek the most expert opinions available and to proceed on the basis of the widest possible agreement. It was an approach, apparently, with some appeal: the reluctant politician was to serve in the office longer than any other Manitoba premier.

Like any new government, Bracken's faced inherited problems. A major one was education, on which the government appointed a Royal Commission in 1923. Its report was damning. The commission concluded that excessive adherence to the principle of local control (an article of faith for the UFM) often resulted in school districts too

A domestic science class involving students from Winnipeg's King Edward and William Whyte schools

181

small and too poor to provide adequate public schooling; ten per cent, indeed, were insolvent and closed, and their children's prospects bleak. The report recommended special educational grants for the poorest districts, larger schools and a minimum income for teachers. A further report strongly criticized the province's inadequate support of its university and Agricultural College and recommended their amalgamation. The government proceeded with the amalgamation in 1925 but reduced university funding; it did little with the education recommendations even when prosperity returned in the mid '20's. Economy was its watchword; education was not.

Burglarized safe at Assiniboine Park in May, 1929

From the outset, the government rejected the spending excesses of the Norris regime and emphasized, instead, prudent administration and fiscal conservatism. It reduced expenditures and introduced a provincial income tax as a means of addressing the deficits it had inherited. It was able, within two years, to declare a surplus—partly the result of its management, but partly a result of general economic recovery and an infusion of revenue from liquor sales. However, even with the return of prosperity, the government remained parsimonious: not only did it reduce its expenditures, it sometimes proved unwilling to spend even what the legislature had approved.

This was true not only in education, where expenditures declined even as the school population grew, but in welfare and in health: one of its first acts was to reduce allowances for widows and deserted mothers. The government was unmoved by official reports which recorded higher disease and mortality rates amongst the immigrant populations—these people were not the middle-class on whose support the government depended.

> ## "The cure is ten times worse than the disease."
>
> **Letter to the editor,
> *Winnipeg Evening
> Tribune*, on the
> problems associated
> with prohibition**

The philosophy was pay-as-you-go: any notion that long-term public investment in education or health—or, indeed, in encouraging economic activity— might reap long-term dividends, had no place in the philosophy of the government. With all the creativity and dynamism of a sleepy parish council, the legislature ensured solvency at the price of progressive legislation.

Legislatures and cabinets during the 1920's were dominated by rural members, predominantly British in origin, amongst whom there was considerable similarity of outlook and values. It was true that a number of Win-

Prohibition had little impact on thirsty Manitobans

BEFORE PROHIBITION, LIQUOR AND beer were not hard to come by in Manitoba; you only had to find the nearest hotel bar. In Winnipeg especially, that was not difficult.

Along the Main Street strip from the CPR station at Higgins Avenue down past Portage Avenue, nearly every other place of business was a hotel, complete with a smoke-filled saloon and an adjacent pool hall. Floors were covered in sawdust and the stale odor of tobacco juice hung in the air from the over-flowing spittoons. Beer sold for a nickel a glass and whisky for ten cents a shot. One establishment claimed to have the longest bar—one city block—in all of Canada.

Inevitably, where there was liquor there was drunkenness, disorderly behavior, broken families and crime. During one of Winnipeg's periodic boom periods, the police arrested more than 2,000 people for alcohol-related offenses. As D.B. Murray, the city's chief of police put it at the time, "many hotels are resorts for thieves and blackguards and are hotbeds for drunkenness. They would better be described as cesspools operating under the guise of hotels".

Combating the evils of drink were an army of preachers, housewives, doctors, politicians and other citizens determined to rid the province of booze. Temperance groups were organized as early as 1883 and cries for outright prohibition were heard a few years later. At the forefront were the Women's Christian Temperance Union and the Banish-the-Bar movement. Its members held rallies and lobbied the various levels of government in what was one of the earliest examples of interest group politics in Canadian history.

Even though plebiscites indicated that a majority of Manitobans favoured prohibition, governments

ng on the Booze

act. Not until World
election of Liberal re-
Norris did prohibition be-
ty, at least for a brief
most prominent group op-
he bartenders' union
ht American lawyer Clar-
into Winnipeg to speak
ibition on the grounds
attack on freedom.
he provincial government
the flow of booze at
tels, it could not control
m other provinces since
deral responsibility. Nor,
antly, could it curb peo-

St. Boniface police chief Joe Gagnon's term, more than 40 illegal bars and brothels flourished while police concentrated on other activities.

If there was a way to sell liquor in Manitoba—and the prohibition legislation had plenty of loopholes in it—inventive businessmen like the Bronfmans found a way. The Bronfmans (in Yiddish literally "whisky-man") had immigrated to Canada from Russia in 1889, eventually set-

A still located in the attic of a Boyd Avenue home. Many such illicit operations sprang up to quench the public's thirst during prohibition.

Sam Bronfman, then only 21, was placed in charge, the beginning of his long and successful career as whisky tycoon.

In 1917, the Bronfmans set up a lucrative liquor mail-order shop in Kenora and for the next few years reaped a sizable profit selling booze back to Manitobans. When the federal government placed more restrictions on their mail-order operation, the Bronfmans created the Canada Drug Pure Company to store and sell liquor for "medicinal" purposes. It did a booming business in drugstores across the Prairies.

Liquor suppliers also found a ready and available market south of the border. During America's prohibition era, from 1919 to 1933, thousands of gallons of booze were discreetly carried over the border, destined for the gangster-controlled bars of Chicago and New York.

Until the Canadian government clamped down on some of this export activity in 1922, rum-runners raced through border towns in Manitoba and Saskatchewan in large sedans (whisky-sixes) equipped with powerful six-cylinder motors to evade the Manitoba Provincial Police and customs officers. Suppliers like the Bronfmans, who were doing nothing illegal according to Canadian law, could not keep up with demand.

Support for prohibition in Manitoba was short-lived. Ordinary citizens were turned into criminals every time they sipped an illegal beer. Moderates soon demanded a legislative compromise. This led to the repeal of prohibition in 1922 and the creation of a government liquor monopoly. The monopoly was accompanied by a whole array of bureaucratic regulations, including a cumbersome permit system and men-only beer parlours—anachronisms that lasted well into the 1960's.

egal stills proliferated,
near beer" bottles were
real stuff and bootleg-
openly in Winnipeg
in St. Boniface). During

tling in Winnipeg's North End. After having some success in the hotel business in Emerson and Yorkton, they purchased the Bell Hotel on Main Street in 1912 for $200,000. Young

The Walker Theatre featured
everything from Sarah
Bernhardt to mind readers

The Golden Age of

IT IS SAID THAT MANITOBA THEATRE "was cradled in the sentry box and nurtured on pipeclay". The first theatre company was the Ontario Rifles Musical and Dramatic Association. Sent out with Wolseley's expedition in 1870 to put down the Riel rebellion, the Ontario Rifles took on the responsibility of entertaining as well as protecting the settlement.

The soldiers opened the Theatre

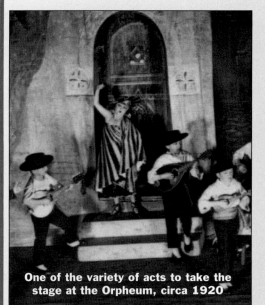

One of the variety of acts to take the stage at the Orpheum, circa 1920

Royal, spent approximately $1,000 on a stage and curtains and scenery, and found enough chairs and benches for 200 people. A box seat cost two shillings. The first performance was "a new sensational burlesque, in three acts, never before played on any stage" called *The Child of Circumstances, or The Long-Lost Father*. The *dramatis personae* were Robinson Porpero, "monarch of all he surveys"; Caliban Friday, "a faithful follower of Porpero"; and Grace Whatshername, "a child of circumstances". Both male and female parts were played by men of the regiment. When the regiment was moved, the theatre shut down.

A theatre would be recommended for its safety as much as the quality of its fare. The second Theatre Royal was advertised as fireproof because the building had a mud floor. The City Hall Theatre had to close after seven years of popular entertainment because the walls were bulging so badly they could no longer be propped up. It was replaced in 1883 with the 1,300-seat Princess Opera House. Fire was a constant problem: the Princess

burned down in 1892, the Grand in 1897 and the Winnipeg Theatre in 1926.

The best theatre in Winnipeg, and one of the best anywhere, was the Walker. Corliss Power Walker was an American stage manager who left Fargo for Winnipeg in 1897. He leased the Bijou Opera House on Notre Dame and Adelaide adding to the circuit of theatres for which he booked touring American companies. He opened a lavish new theatre—the Walker—on February 18, 1907. The souvenir program described it as "ultra-modern, ultra-luxurious, ultra-safe". The sightlines were excellent, the Edwardian decor boasted recessed lights, ornamental plaster work on the proscenium and crimson plush seats. There were workshops for electricians, carpenters, and property people. A special animal room downstairs could house lions, tigers, and camels.

The Walker hosted most of the great tours coming from

nipeg businessmen endorsed the UFM, and continued to support it, but opposition to the new income tax was strongest in Winnipeg where many saw it as an enforced urban subsidy of rural Manitoba by a government of farmers. Winnipeg became the centre of political opposition to the government, and the locale of many of the social problems the government wished to ignore; in these years the gulf between city and country widened.

Fudging the traditional role of ministers and

Well-known individuals such as Arthur Conan Doyle and MacKenzie King made their way to Hamilton House on Henderson Highway to attend seances. Hamilton House belonged to Thomas Glendenning Hamilton, a prominent Winnipeg doctor. In this photo, "spirits" have manifested themselves in the form of ectoplasm emanating from a medium. The spirits were probably photos placed on gauze and then re-photographed to appear as apparitions.

eatre

England. *Ben Hur* was
a special orchestra, 200
people and 12 horses in a
. This was the period of
ouring in Western Cana-
ssible by the expansion of
The Walker survived until
e touring period, only oc-
aving to resort to films or
ts staple productions were
, musical comedies, min-
ballets, mind readers, lec-
olitical meetings.
at touring era lasted from
ly 1907 until 1925. Win-
ces could see the Marx
y Langtry, Fred and Adele
Phyllis Neilson-Terry (who
merset Maugham's *The
nise*, a play set on a Man-
arah Bernhardt appeared
1913 at the age of 69
ne leg). Ethel Barrymore
Atkins's *Declasse;* Mrs.
bell appeared in *The
Tanqueray, Hedda Gabler,
rious Mrs. Ebbsmith.*
ere also local companies
usicals and comic opera,

The Mikado, staged by the Virden Operatic Society. Virden was home to one of the best equipped opera houses in western Canada, which opened in 1912 in the Virden Municipal Auditorium.

as well as Ukrainian and Yiddish the-atre companies. Stock companies such as the Community Players pro-duced plays written and performed by Canadians. But stock companies were noted generally for their short lives, large repertoire and low quality.

The first vaudeville theatre, the Dominion, opened on December 12, 1904, with a bill featuring "a high

leaping clown and his clever dog Fox". Later, the Orpheum and the Pantages offered big-name acts like Charlie Chaplin, W.C. Fields, Harry Houdini, Jack Benny, Eddie Cantor and others.

By the end of the 1920's, the talkies were taking over the theatres, leaving few suitable facilities for stage performers. The great Walker Theatre, which cost $330,000 to build in 1907, was sold in 1936 for back taxes. Then, like most Prairie theatres, it surren-dered to Hollywood and was convert-ed into a movie house, the Odeon.

---

ines between parties was consistent
ulist approach. Open votes were
s led to UFM members rejecting a
bill approved by Bracken—without
party discipline. This tendency
ensus produced a style of govern-
itoba quite unlike any other in the
since consensus was likely to be
rrower the issue, consensus became
doing little.

ober a regime, there was no little
act that one of the biggest issues
alcohol. Outlawing bars in 1916,
luction of prohibition in 1920, had
utopian society. People now slaked
h homebrew and bootleg liquor; a
nitobans reputedly grew rich on the
um-running and, as W.L. Morton
integrity of the police and the

respect for law were seriously threatened. Prohibi-tion was in danger of creating a greater evil than the booze it sought to prohibit.

The aptly named Moderation League suc-cessfully pushed for a plebiscite on a proposal to allow government sale of liquor; this was approved by a vote of 108,000 to 69,000, lead-ing the Legislature, in 1924, to pass the Govern-ment Liquor Control Act. The sale of liquor was thus made lawful; it was not made pleasant—with petty regulations and liquor stores which were singularly uninviting. Later, Bracken was to observe that he had come a long way from being the Worthy Patriarch of the Sons of Temperance at age 6, to being Chief Bartender of Manitoba at 40. In 1928, a new Liquor Control Act legal-ized the public sale of beer; the effect overall was to provide a more temperate approach to temper-ance, while simultaneously providing substan-

Manitoba Chief Justice T.J. Mathers, an advo-cate of prohibition, confided to his diary that his own liquor cellar contained, "5 gallons Scotch, 1 case Sparkling Burgundy, 1 case Saturne (sic), 1/2 case Sparkling Mouselle, 2 bottles brandy, (and) two bottles sherry."

tial—and welcome—assistance to the treasury.

Despite a more liberal approach to liquor, the prevailing mood of the establishment was highly conservative when it came to what they judged as the pressing moral issues of the day. In the roaring twenties, the era of the flapper and the Charleston, not everyone was amused. A movie censorship board was established with sweeping powers—though probably insufficient for at least one rural MLA who saw illegitimacy being fostered by fast times and the movies. The lengths of flappers' skirts proved to be a contentious issue, and reports of "sexual orgies" on beach-bound trains filled with Winnipeg's young middle class outraged respectable opinion.

A common form of entertainment in rural communities in the 1920's was the Chautauqua, described by contemporary journalists as "a great social, moral and educational movement". The event was named after Lake Chautauqua in New York State, where Sunday school teachers were taught. The Canadian Chautauqua movement was formed in 1916 by J.M. Erickson of Calgary, and various companies were soon travelling the rails to Canadian communities. A typical show featured educational skits, lectures, magicians, acro-

During prohibition, doctors were allowed to write prescriptions for alcohol for "medicinal purposes". In August 1920, one doctor-pharmacist team combined to write and fill 5,800 such prescriptions.

bats, clowns and comedians. Admission was $2 per week for adults, $1 per week for children or 50 cents per show. Prominent speakers such as Arctic explorer Wilhjalmar Stefansson and British suffragette Emaline Pankhurst travelled through Manitoba with different Chautauqua companies. The movement died out in the 1930's due to the Depression and the rise of movies and radio.

Horse-racing—and betting—became hugely popular around the province. The legislature, after arduous debate, authorized parimutuel betting on horses—thus assisting the emergence of highly successful tracks in Polo Park and Whittier Park. Meanwhile, the natural beauty of Assiniboine Park was proving an attraction for Winnipeggers, and within it, the Pavilion became a centre for the socially smart.

Society and social behaviour were also experiencing change driven by technology. The 1920's saw the beginnings of the radio era, the herald of a new popular culture. The latest trends—not to say the latest fads—in music, comedy and drama were almost instantly communicated and recognizable in both town and country.

No less important were changes driven by the automobile. In the 1920's the family car came into its own, and begat a whole series of changes—from the rituals of courtship to the rela-

Manitoba Farmstead, by W. J. Phillips

een town and
led to improved
n facilitated the
ottage and resort
es Winnipeg and
nd in the White-
ages great and
l those desperate
anitoba's short
routed in areas
accessible. The
—facilitated by
e's takeover of
nk highways as
esponsibility—
ablish tourism,
merican tourism,
rtant industry.
ted easier travel
mmunities, from
ge, from town to
Winnipeg which saw reinforced its
antial commercial and cultural domi-
s provincial hinterland.
gh Winnipeg was now falling behind
rates enjoyed by Toronto, Montreal
ver, its industrial base continued to
e needle trades of north Winnipeg,
and the packing plants of St.
Boniface were but two industries
that grew to significance in this
period. In 1928, for the first time,
the value of agricultural production was exceeded by that of
industrial production, though the
latter certainly encompassed
many industries engaged in processing agricultural products.

Within agriculture itself,
diversification was also the pattern. More attention went to cattle, sheep and hogs, to dairy
farming, market gardering, even
to the production of honey. In
grain production, wheat was no
longer king: in 1928, Manitoba
produced more than 50 million
bushels each of wheat, oats and
barley. Indeed, to some degree,
change was king: not only was
agriculture diversifying, but its
methods were also changing:
gasoline displaced steam, and
the tractor replaced the horse.

Other broad social devel-
opments were more problematic. This was particularly true in

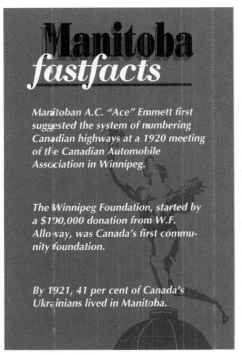

the complex relationships
between Manitoba's ethnic
minorities and the politically
and socially dominant British
majority. There was some
easing of ancient quarrels. In
the legislature, the election of
a French-speaking MLA to the
Speakership, and the later
elevation of another to the
cabinet, involved some coming together. But it would be
a long time before Ukrainians
and other ethnic minorities
entered the political mainstream.

Before the Great War,
the position of the ethnic
minorities was unquestion-
ably one of political and
social inferiority; but with the
war, their position worsened: they became objects
of deep suspicion and sustained hostility. Three
events had been critical: the war itself, conducted
against the German and Austro-Hungarian
empires, whence many of Manitoba's immigrants
had come, gave rise to questions about the newcomers' loyalties. Then, the Russian revolution
exposed immigrants to suspicions and charges
that they served not just foreign powers, but an
alien and revolutionary ideology. In such a climate the General Strike in 1919 lent itself to being
characterized as the handiwork of aliens, with
Slavs and Jews becoming particular targets. To
those whose interests were served by such tactics,
it had mattered little that virtually all of the strike
leaders were British or Canadian born: as Stephen
Leacock observed, a half-truth is like a half-brick,
and carries better in an argument.

Immigration in the 1920's did not assume its
pre-war proportions, but it was nonetheless significant. Although some British immigrants were
amongst the newcomers, many were eastern Europeans who had been uprooted by the war, by the
collapse of the old empires, and by the revolution
and civil war in Russia. They brought new perspectives and experiences to the existing communities and enriched Manitoba's social fabric.

The environment, however, remained not
altogether welcoming: in 1924, a leading member
of the Winnipeg establishment, Sir Augustus Nanton, spoke darkly of "the teaching we hear of that
is going on behind closed doors. This should be
done away with. We welcome all good citizens
from foreign lands but if they do not believe in the
Christian religion, nor intend to keep our laws,
they should be asked without delay to return from

187

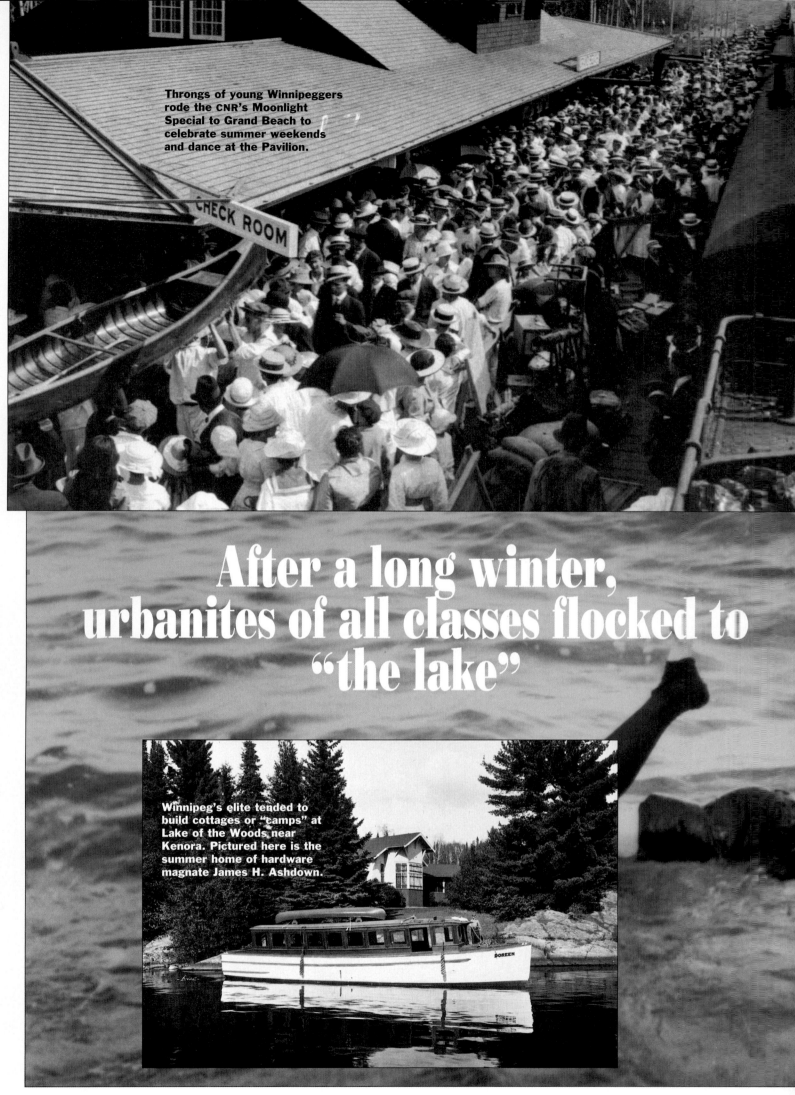

Throngs of young Winnipeggers rode the CNR's Moonlight Special to Grand Beach to celebrate summer weekends and dance at the Pavilion.

After a long winter, urbanites of all classes flocked to "the lake"

Winnipeg's elite tended to build cottages or "camps" at Lake of the Woods near Kenora. Pictured here is the summer home of hardware magnate James H. Ashdown.

TOURIST PARK
WINNIPEG BEACH.

"Gorilla Man" Nelson

Killer Earle Nelson had city in stranglehold of fear

Earle Nelson under arrest. Within 48 hours of his arrival in Winnipeg, he had strangled two people and sent city residents into a panic.

ON FRIDAY, JUNE 30, 1928, William Patterson returned home from work to find his children at a neighbour's and no of sign his pregnant wife, Emily. Searching the house he noticed the family savings of $60 was gone, as was his best suit. Then he caught sight of something under the bed. It was the naked body of his wife. She had been bludgeoned, strangled and raped.

Unbeknownst to anyone, the previous day 14-year-old Lola Cowan had also been strangled and raped before being placed under a bed at a Smith Street rooming house. Her body would not be discovered until the following Sunday.

News of the murders set off the greatest manhunt and mass hysteria the Prairies ever witnessed. Both women were victims of Earle Nelson, an escaped American mental patient whom authorities had failed to connect with a succession of stranglings across the U.S.. He arrived in Winnipeg the day before killing Cowan. Winnipeg's most famous serial killer impressed the Smith Street rooming house landlady with his religious conviction and desire for a quiet place to meditate.

For nearly a week, city newspapers carried banner headlines about a brutal killer they dubbed the "gorilla man". Prairie residents were gripped by fear as vague descriptions of the strangler circulated. Children ran to and from school. Repair and delivery men took time off because housewives refused to open their doors. More than 1,000 transients were taken in for questioning before Nelson's capture.

In the meantime, Nelson had made his way to Saskatchewan and was heading back into Manitoba. He had been spotted and reported to the police twice near Boissevair. Soon after, the provincial police in Killarney arrested Nelson without a struggle as he walked the rails near the town.

Nelson was to be held in Killarney until the authorities from Winnipeg arrived. Foreseeing a long night ahead, the constable assigned to watch Nelson slipped out to get tobacco for his pipe. While unattended, Nelson used a file to pick the double padlocks and make his escape. The brief calm that came with capture vanished as the manhunt was on once again.

Slipping in and out of the outbuildings of Killarney, Nelson made his way to the train station. Just before sunrise he once again set out along the tracks. A frantic housewife reported sighting Nelson and the police raced after him. Because the excited woman got her directions confused, the police ended up surrounding a bush area east of town while the killer walked west. Hearing the whistle of an approaching locomotive, Nelson prepared to jump what he thought was a freight train. In fact, it was a train specially commissioned to bring men to aid in the hunt for Nelson. The cargo of constables saw Nelson and quickly made the arrest.

On a cold January day seven months later, the psychotic killer who may have committed 20 cold-blooded murders, drew his last breath at the end of the hangman's noose.

came". Compared to some oth-
's warning was not the worst or
ting. Its import was nonetheless
part of the community—includ-
ho were clearly and unashamedly
—were there on sufferance only.
ulting pressures to assimilate were
ny non-English names were angli-
e years. The experiences of these
ders of many ethnic communities
rstanding that they could not
heir relative isolation, still less on
protect their interests. One conse-
a burgeoning of political activity
nic communities, particularly
nks of the mainstream political

dual, and often painful, integration
minorities into the mainstream
sented a significant reorientation
. Other changes were also taking
significantly, the limits of agricul-
nt in Manitoba had been reached
overrun. The breakdown in the
was directly related to the settle-
rginal and sub-marginal lands.
could be made barely profitable
vere good and prices were high,
onary or even more normal times,
frequently forced off the land,
oned communities in their wake.

r that the era of new agricultural
as finally at an end, it was also
orthern Manitoba offered new
s. Premier Bracken showed an
in northern development, believ-
rovince's well-being was tied to
on of the economy: fishing,
g and the development of hydro-
er were seen as providing that
Precambrian Shield represented
barrier to exploitation of northern
did the continuing control by Ottawa
e's natural resources. Technological
ually assisted with the first hurdle
political negotiations resolved the
end of the decade. In the mean-
of copper, zinc and gold proceeded;
ame into use for prospecting, aerial
ansport, leading to the development
al flights into remote areas of the

the provincial government agreed
he costs of a rail line to a Flin Flon
ther into northeastern Manitoba. In

Guilt by Association

A design contest held in 1925 for a monument to victims of World War I was won by Emmanuel Hahn, a prominent Toronto sculptor. His war memorials had already appeared in several eastern Canadian cities. Hahn's design was lauded for its "great dignity and picturesque effect".

Protests arose, however, when it was learned that Hahn (although a long-time Canadian citizen) was born in Germany. Several groups, including returned soldiers' associations, the Winnipeg Board of Trade and the Travellers' Association, claimed Hahn's work would be an insult to the war dead.

A heated memorial committee meeting in 1926 agreed to award Hahn the prize money, but to hold a second contest open only to "Canadian citizens born in Canada, elsewhere in the British Empire, or in any of the late allied countries". Appeals for fair play were lost amid cries that all Germans were murderers.

The second contest's winner was Canadian-born sculptress Elizabeth Wyn Wood. Her entry was hailed by the judges as "remarkable for its originality". However, it was soon discovered that Wood was Hahn's wife. The committee unceremoniously rejected her design.

English-born designer and Winnipeg resident Gilbert Parfitt was finally selected to design the cenotaph. It was unveiled on November 7, 1928 amid considerably less controversy. Parfitt later became Manitoba's provincial architect while both Wood and Hahn enjoyed prominence in the larger Canadian arts community.

the same year, Mackenzie King's precarious minority government suddenly saw the merits of building the Hudson Bay Railway to Churchill, an enterprise to which the Progressives in Parliament and the prairie provincial governments had been long committed. The construction of this line, in the minds of its advocates, would provide the West with its own ocean port, and increased control over the movement of grain.

By the mid-1920's, John Bracken's dominance of his government and, substantially, of the province's politics was increasingly clear. He was a solid, stolid figure, not given to humour, passion, drama or flamboyance. One observer, writing in

Frogs were so plentiful in the Dominion City area from 1926 to 1928 that an Illinois company set up a buying station and processing plant. Frogs from the area, as well as Stuartburn, Tolstoi, Gardenton and Vita, were canned and shipped all over the world.

the *Free Press*, commented: "He comes of Irish Presbyterian stock... who neither make jokes nor feel comfortable when they encounter wit. Incessant and laborious campaigns with the dry minutiae of provincial business have not exasperated his imagination, because he is not imaginative..."

It did not seem to hurt him. As his biographer John Kendle has pointed out, Bracken's "man-

they did not move or stir..." It was, nonetheless, a style in its own right and one that proved to have considerable appeal. As the 1920's progressed, and the United Farmers began to withdraw from active politics, the constant and cohesive element in the government was Bracken himself and "Brackenism" became increasingly the term used to describe the style, content and tone of Manitoba's government.

Bracken's appeal, unlikely as it seemed, affected his political opponents. Within the provincial Liberal party—and amongst important Liberals in Ottawa like the prime minister—there was a growing feeling that the United Farmers and the Liberals had more uniting than dividing them; that if they remained divided each was threatened by a reviving Tory party; and that the Liberals had a better chance of absorbing the UFM than they had of defeating them. Crass (and powerful) as this last consideration was, it wasn't enough to bring about "fusion" of the parties the first time the idea was canvassed.

The result was that in the next election, in 1927, the voters faced substantially the same cast and array as they had in 1922. The Brackenites campaigned on their record and promised more of the same for this they won the support of a large part of the Anglo-Saxon farm

KKK Vowed to Clean Up Booze Cans and Bordellos

"Ku Klux Klan Plans to Clean Up Winnipeg" shouted the headline in the October 17, 1928 *Manitoba Free Press,* announcing the arrival of the notorious KKK in Manitoba.

The Klan, infamous for their attacks on blacks in the American South had, ironically, become a voice for moral reform on the Prairies. Prohibition and sober public behaviour had wilted under the onslaught of a rowdy post-war generation. Into this void stepped the KKK, vowing to clean up the booze cans and bordellos of the Roaring Twenties.

The Manitoba KKK's chief organizer was D.C. Grant of Moose Jaw. His first meeting was infiltrated by a *Free Press* reporter, who reported Grant's inflammatory statements: "We strive for racial purity... Vice, wantonness, graft and corruption walk hand in hand in this city and the Ku Klux Klan is going to abolish this."

Grant first set about attacking Catholics in St. Boniface. However, his catcalls about the "petticoat" wearing priests of St. Boniface College were safely made from Norwood. Monseigneur Jubinville called Grant a coward and warned him to stay out of St. Boniface.

Grant was a poor organizer and paranoid. He feared his recruitment meetings would be infiltrated by Catholics, Jews or the police. Those wishing to attend meetings had to provide letters of reference and the $13 admission fee up front before being admitted.

Under the cover of the Protestant Orange Lodge, the KKK flourished briefly in some parts of rural Manitoba (even burning crosses on Brandon's North Hill). But the Klan never really took hold in this province. Conversely, recruitment meetings in Saskatchewan drew huge crowds. A June, 1927 meeting in Moose Jaw attracted more than 7,000 potential Klansmen from across Saskatchewan, including 400 who had been hauled in by a special train from Regina.

Manitobans' interest in the KKK waned quickly. Klansman Grant retreated to Saskatchewan, where in 1935 he became the CCF organizer for Tommy Douglas in the Weyburn constituency.

ner was always considered and authoritative and his style more like that of a university professor than one normally associated with a politician... His speeches were dry and fact-laden... they were nearly always logical and carefully structured but

vote, the rural ethnic vote and the French Canadian vote. The UFM won two of Winnipeg's ten seats and 27 of the 45 rural constituencies; overall, they had one seat more than in the previous House and, though not the sweep Bracken had

Scottish tenant farmers were among the many immigrants still making their way to Manitoba in the 1920's.

WE'RE SAILING WEST, WE'RE SAILING WEST, TO PRAIRIE LANDS SUNKISSED AND BLEST— THE CROFTER'S TRAIL TO HAPPINESS.

...as nonetheless, a win. The Liberals, ...divided and distracted, simply held ...bour, suffering from the general ...ich dampened urban unrest, lost ... the Conservatives gained signifi- ... the beneficiaries, apparently, of ...ntent five years of Brackenism had

...ving year, the United Farmers for- ...v from direct political action; and ...vernment donned the name "Pro- ... making formal an identification ...een made by everyone else. This ...ed at a time of increasing rap- ...tween the federal Liberals and the ...ssives. In Manitoba, the drift to ... relations was thus sanctified by ...aw arrangements of their federal ...by the fact that all the signs— ...1927 Manitoba election itself

—were that when Liberals and Progressives fought, Tories danced.

The year 1927 marked the 60th anniversary of the Canadian Confederation. The occasion prompted some reflection on the nature of the Canadian federation. In Manitoba there was certainly a sense of grievance—a feeling that many

Ukrainian wedding at Oakburn. At such celebrations, the meal was served indoors, and dancing took place outdoors to music provided by violin and dulcimer players.

Manitoba's longest-serving premier disliked politics

John Bracken

THREE DAYS AFTER THE UNITED
Farmers of Manitoba upset the Liberals to win the 1922 provincial election, John Bracken, principal of the Manitoba Agricultural College, was awoken by a midnight telephone call. The representative of the leader-less UFM, asked Bracken if he was interested in becoming the next premier of Manitoba. Bracken, who hadn't voted in the election and had only moved to Manitoba in 1920, reluctantly agreed to consider the idea.

Bracken was being asked to enter politics at a time when public opinion had turned against politicians. The electorate wanted radical change after revelations of Tory corruption in the construction of the Legislative Building and charges of extravagant spending directed at the subsequent Liberal government. The Manitoba Grain Growers Association adopted a "Farmer's Platform" and created the United Farmers of Manitoba. The UFM was a reaction against political parties and had no wish to become one itself. Elected members were expected only to serve their constituents.

In 1920, the UFM elected 12 members to sit across the house from the minority Liberal government. In 1922, the UFM won 24 seats and formed the government. There was only one problem; they had been represented in the house for two years and had run two election campaigns without the benefit of a leader. After reviewing a short list of candidates Bracken was the unanimous choice of the UFM caucus.

Bracken considered himself unsuited for the job. He twice declined the offer before being finally persuaded to accept the premiership. In his maiden speech to the House as premier he said: "We are not here to play politics or to represent a single class, but to get down to the serious business of giving this province an efficient government, and in that task we will welcome all the co-operation offered to us from the opposition side of the House."

So began the free-vote era of "Brackenism" that would extend beyond his retirement in 1943, through the premierships of S.S. Garson and Douglas Campbell. This phenome-

non, which has been called asocial government, introduced few new programs. Fiscally conservative the Bracken philosophy was to administer programs inherited from earlier governments and to remain doctrinally flexible. So flexible, in fact, that after the UFM withdrew from politics in 1927, Bracken became a Progressive, and then in 1932, a Liberal-Progressive after an alliance with Liberals.

Bracken's first concern was to balance the provincial budget. Education, health and even the Mother's Allowance experienced cutbacks. On the revenue side, Bracken introduced a provincial income tax. Particularly popular among the rural constituents who elected the UFM, the tax legislation alleviated the heavy burden of the land tax. Another popular and profitable, change was the creation of the Manitoba Liquor Commission when prohibition was abandoned.

The booming economy of the second half of the 1920's put the province in a favourable position to nurture mining interests the North. The North grew in importance throughout Bracken's premiership. This was underlined

so-called national policies like the protective tariff benefited central Canada at the West's expense—but it was also clear that there was a growing sense of national pride.

This was doubtless reinforced by an awareness that Manitoba would not, after all, realize the dreams of an earlier era. The sea, via Panama, now offered a transportation alternative to the rails, via Winnipeg; and Vancouver now surpassed Winnipeg in size and growth. Other centres on the Prairies were serving their own hinterlands, thus challenging Winnipeg's dominance as the major commercial centre of the region. Clearly, Manitoba was not to become a province whose population and

...n successfully negotiated
...control over natural re-
...province in 1930. This
...marked Manitoba's ac-
...Confederation as an
...under the same terms as
...ovinces.
...he Depression, Bracken
...monstrated his commit-
...rmer and the West. He
...usly for the removal of
...at favoured manufactur-
...Canada at the expense
...racken also successfully
...a for relief assistance.
...left the Premier's office
...he accepted the nation-
...f the newly named Pro-
...rvatives. His vocal
...he wartime policies of
...g's Liberals had once
...e attention of a party in
...r.
...ng the traditional role
...adoption of a non-
...oproach, he dominated
...ics longer than anyone

Woolworth's fire in Winnipeg, May 27, 1929. Here firemen came to the aid of a fallen comrade.

riches rivalled those of Ontario; it was increasingly doubtful, indeed, that it could preserve even regional pre-eminence.

These realities were becoming apparent even before the market crash of 1929 and its attendant calamities. Realism suggested that Manitoba was likely to develop as a province of middling size and middling wealth. With that understanding, however, came an appreciation of the critical role the national government might play in ensuring equality amongst the provinces. Manitoba began the decade as part of the regional challenge to the national government; it ended the decade, prophetically, advocating a strong federation as the surest instrument of regional accommodation. ✳

CHAPTER EIGHT

The Lost Decade

BY DON BAILEY

Perhaps no decade in the 20th century began so inauspiciously—or ended so forebodingly—as the 1930's. In Manitoba, the Great Depression took an enormous economic toll on people of all backgrounds. But added to the financial chaos of the Depression were the effects of a catastrophic eight-year drought. Homes and farms were lost. Jobs disappeared. Soup kitchens and relief lines became an unwelcome fact of life. There were many stories of courage and determination, some of them recorded here. But it was, for most Manitobans, a decade to forget—the Lost Decade of the 1930's.

With additional material by
MAUREEN COUSINS, BYRON REMPEL, AND GREGG SHILLIDAY

Grain Elevator at La Salle,
by W.J. Phillips, 1931

The Lost Decade

**Drought and depression
humble the land**

In 1929, Canada suffered a series of crippling blows to its economy. Wheat, the nation's most lucrative export, was unable to penetrate a glutted world market. Despite frantic efforts, much of the 1928 bumper crop could not be sold. As well, sales of metals, pulp and paper and other products plummeted to disastrous levels. The engine of over-production that had fuelled the economies of North America and most of Europe since World War I was now running out of steam.

As the year progressed, huge inventories of stockpiled foodstuffs and manufactured merchandise were dumped on the world market. The value of these goods tumbled to their lowest levels since the beginning of the century. On October 4, 1929, a frightened New York Exchange unloaded grossly overvalued stocks at basement prices. This panic grew and spread to the Toronto market. Losses of $200 million were recorded in one day. Canadian investors, desperate to salvage their evaporating assets, conducted a frenzied liquidation sale of the country's future. On both Wall Street and Bay Street, many high-rollers were too late. Traumatized, some of these financiers jumped to their deaths from their office windows. Others put bullets into their brains.

The impact of the global stock market crash was soon felt in Manitoba. For years, Manitoba farmers had been expanding their acreage, wageing ever higher stakes in their annual bets against crop disease and the weather. At the same time, they took on larger debt loads to secure land and to buy equipment. In the affluent 1920's credit was easy to obtain but when wheat prices fell, the day of reckoning arrived in the form of foreclsures and eviction notices from the formerly friendly banks.

Despite collapsing prices in late 1929, the farmers' representatives on the boards of local wheat pools attempted to fight back by flexing their muscles in world markets. They argued that united action among pool members to hold back their crop would cause the price of wheat to rise. After all, Canada was one of the largest exporters of wheat in the world. So the pools held back on sales. The beginning of a new crop year in August, 1930, saw the pool directors steadfast in their optimism. They were so committed to this strategy that even though wheat prices continued to decline, the directors promised farmers an initial payment of one dollar per bushel. Another stunning drop in world commodity prices late in 1930 made a mockery of these calculations. The pools were

ankruptcy.

ter, a second blow was struck against ers. The rains stopped. They didn't summer, not even for a year. Unbe-ly any moisture was recorded in the elt of the West (especially southern) for nearly eight years.

drought year was followed by freez-with little snowfall. This resulted, the in a scorched earth effect. The il blew away in high winds almost vas ploughed. Russian thistle thrived conditions and polluted any other aged to take root. Remaining vege-voured by hordes of grasshoppers. of insects would swarm in gigantic ng thick brown, sticky juice over their path. These conditions pre-

A long hot summer led to a devastating fire in Cranberry Portage in 1929. Women and family possessions were piled into canoes and anchored in the lake until the fire passed.

vailed in much of the southern Prairies until 1937.

As one farmer later told author Barry Broadfoot, the great plains' fertile topsoil slowly but surely blew away: "We had this loose sub-soil that had no holding power. Then we had the winds. I've seen them blow for two weeks at a time. Clouds of dust, which was our earth and our

Maintaining a good water supply was a problem for Altona during the Dirty Thirties. Town wells were locked up overnight so rural residents would not steal the water and attempts were made to prevent area farmers from hauling water out of the town ponds.

Windmill near Vidir

livelihood, would blow for scores of miles, and airplane pilots had to fly higher to get over them. Millions of acres blowing away."

As the Depression deepened and spread around the globe, eastern manufacturers called for increased protection against the dumping of foreign products in Canada. The federal government responded with stiff tariffs. In the words of Prime Minister R.B. Bennett, Canada would "blast her way into the markets of the world". It was a bold policy, but Prairie farmers—despite receiving a fixed minimum price for wheat—felt they were Bennett's cannon fodder.

This was not as true for resource industries in

Dafoe of the Free Press

Under the editorship of John W. Dafoe, the *Free Press* became the voice of Western Canada.

IN 1901, THE *MANITOBA FREE PRESS* promoted a 35-year-old firebrand to its editorial chair. John Wesley Dafoe—a "strong, rugged, large man with plenty of dark red hair"—accepted the invitation from Clifford Sifton, the paper's new publisher and the most important Liberal on the Prairies. It was to be a partnership that would turn the *Free Press* into the voice of Western Canada.

Dafoe wrote scathing editorials and directed the paper's decidedly Liberal politics for the next 40 years, doling out advice and admonishment to Wilfrid Laurier, Robert Borden, Vincent Massey and Mackenzie King—all of whom, if not valuing his advice, respected his insight and convictions.

Dafoe, who described his profession as "one of those who essay to hurl the bolts of Jove", never stinted on thunderbolts. To attract a readership, Dafoe said, a newspaper "must have politics, convictions, loyalties, principles—in short, it must have personality".

Personality it had. Dafoe's high-pitched, rasping voice rang through the offices of the *Free Press*, alternately rallying behind the Liberals as the only hope for the farmers of Western Canada, and then dashing the party against the wall for failing to support conscription in World War I.

Sifton and Dafoe clashed on some issues (Sifton scornfully mocked the idea of a newspaper presenting both sides of an issue) but their disputes never hindered the paper's quality. Both men agreed wholeheartedly on the *Free Press*'s two main tasks: to instruct the West in the virtues of Liberalism; and to inform the rest of Canada of the interests and desires of the West.

By 1917, those interests had expanded to an international scope and Prime Minister Robert Borden praised Dafoe as "far above the class which our Western newspapers command". It was this respect that earned Dafoe the invitation to the Paris peace conference in 1919, where he began extolling the League of Nations, the only answer he saw to world peace. He also advised Mackenzie King at the Imperial Conference of the British Empire in 1923.

For his loyalties he was offered cabinet and diplomatic posts, which he promptly turned down. When asked to represent the Liberal party in 1926, Dafoe claimed: "When I were, I am a candidate for Parliament I shall first give up the editorship of the *Free Press;* and, as upon the whole I think I would sooner be the editor of the *Free Press* than Prime Minister of Canada I don't think I am likely to be a candidate." In 1944, Dafoe died at the age of 78. He had spent an unprecedented—and still unmatched—43 years at the helm of the *Free Press.*

hada. Newsprint, wood pulp,
metals, and hydro-electric
all protected by a stable
he United States. The west-
remained tied to traditional
the United Kingdom and
se were customers who had
on Canadian wheat to pro-
wn crops. No industry suf-
uch as agriculture in the
he Depression, and none
o slowly. As economist A.E.
mmented: "Western agricul-
e whole brunt of both fluc-
ort income and the rigid
Canadian economy."
sult was that the national

this loose sub-

had no holding

hen we had the

ve seen them

two weeks at a

uds of dust,

as our earth and

hood... millions

blowing away."

description of the dustbowl
the Prairies

The $2 Million Man

Reeling from the economic effects of the Great Depression, Manitobans were shocked to learn in 1932 that a pillar of the community had embezzled more than $2 million from the University of Manitoba and the Anglican Church.

John A. Machray was the nephew of an esteemed Anglican archbishop. He was senior partner in both a law firm and an investment counselling business which handled the U of M's trust funds. Machray was the university's bursar, financial agent and chairman of its board of governors. Machray was also Chancellor of the Diocese of Rupert's Land of the Church of England and Chancellor of St. John's College. At his fingertips were the trust funds, endowments and investments for all these institutions.

For more than 25 years, Machray systematically milked the accounts that had been entrusted to him. Working with accountant R.H. Shanks, he switched assets back and forth to hide his embezzlements from auditors.

In August 1932, shocked Manitobans learned that Machray had lost the majority of the university's endowments, some $971,086. As well, he stole roughly $800,000 of Anglican Church funds, including one particularly nasty act—raiding the clergymen's widows and orphans fund. Moreover, the greedy Machray stole another $300,000 in private funds entrusted to him for safe-keeping.

A royal commission investigated. It discovered that misappropriation of these funds had begun as early as 1903. Successive provincial governments, the university and Machray's law firm were chastised for giving so much power to one individual without making him answer for it.

The university reorganized its operations to incorporate greater accountability. To make up for the losses, salaries were cut and students' tuition fees were hiked. Some staff were laid off or worked reduced hours. Machray was sentenced to seven years and died in prison about a year later.

ose employed in manufacturing, ser-
es and other better-insulated occupa-
uring the first couple of years of the
hary producers like Manitoba farmers
per cent of their income.

ing back on those harrowing times, it
acle that the rural population did not
se onto an eastbound train. But it
membered that the early 1930's was
ntradictions. Rural life had improved
ver the first decades of the century.
of the country had been somewhat
by the arrival of the telephone.
specially, could find relief from chil-
ores in telephone chats with the
he wagon was replaced by the car
the building of new roads. Visits
hbours became common. For those
ford it, the magic of radio beamed
actions as the *Amos 'n' Andy* show.
networks broadcast a dozen soap
These serials, scorned by critics as

"washday weepers" were listened to like a telephone party-line on which real people discussed their problems. The difficulties of Papa David or Rose or Claudia were often critically appraised at a quilting bee or a church social.

Some aspects of rural life were improving but, at the same time, young people demonstrated a growing restlessness. This agitation was enhanced by the rise of the urban mass media. Radio, movies and magazines fed the fantasies of rural young people that a better life awaited them somewhere else.

As 1930 unfolded, it became clear that the world's free-market system was staggering. Even in the face of this economic calamity, however, Manitobans showed they were a stubborn and proud people. So it was that the population rallied together on June 15 to celebrate the Diamond Jubilee of the province's entrance into Confederation.

Night-time on Portage Avenue, c. 1931, with the street decorated for Christmas

Although times were tough during the Depression, some communities fared better than others. In Portage la Prairie, crops and gardens still flourished, and shipments of food were sent to those living in the "dustbowl" areas.

The provincial flag was flown proudly in the smallest hamlets and the biggest cities. Thousands of citizens gathered at the Legislative Building to pay tribute to those determined pioneers who had built a diverse and thriving society in the middle of the continent. Families wearing their best clothes arrived with box lunches. Blankets were spread on the rolling lawns. Children played baseball while the adults listened to the Queen's Own Cameron Highlanders' pipe band play marching tunes.

The buoyancy of spirit exhibited by these crowds stemmed from a belief that Manitoba was strong, and that it was an integral part of the difficult but noble experiment called Canada. If economic hard times continued, people would pull together—just like their pioneer forebears. So when the Royal Winnipeg Rifles fired a 21-gun salute across the Assiniboine River, and the night skies sparkled with exploding fireworks, hope was nurtured in the hearts of many.

This optimistic view was based on decades of growth. No one seemed to notice that the 30-year construction boom in Winnipeg had already ended. No one seemed to realize that the seeds of decline for Winnipeg had been planted long before the stock market crash. For almost a century, the city had been a thriving trading and business centre. It served as a toll-gate on the only practical route through to the rest of Western Canada. A million settlers had passed

Whittier and Polo Parks attracted horses, gamblers and the unemployed

THE FIRST TIME THAT MORRIS PLANK, long-time Winnipeg horseman and retired vice-chairperson of the Manitoba Racing Commission, went to the races was in 1937. He was 13 years old. "My dad took me. It was at the new Whittier Park in St. Boniface, quite a city trip from where we lived in the North End. Three different trolleys until we arrived at the Bay and then one more that got us over the Provencher bridge. It cost a buck to get in but kids were free. One of the funny things I remember was seeing these row boats out on the Red River looking like they were going to sink, each one weighed down with five or six guys. They were setting out from the Higgins train yard so I thought it was maybe a picnic sponsored by the railway. I asked my dad and he laughed and said no, these guys were sneaking into the track. "

The feature race that year was the Winnipeg Futurity. The better-known Eastern horse owners sent their horses in, as did some Americans. The winner received $2,500 and the minimum purse on other races was $300. The money, by today's standards, wasn't huge, but Whittier Park, along with Polo Park, had prestige. They also had gambling

Winnipeg since 1900, each of them
[...]g a few dollars with the local mer-
[...]r supplies, accommodations or enter-

[...] freight trains that brought all the con-
[...]ods and production machinery into the
[...]re broken up in Winnipeg. The con-
[...]e then distributed throughout the huge
[...]of wholesale warehouses in the centre
[...]y. From there they moved out again,
[...]small army of travelling salesmen who
[...]eir order books as far afield as the
[...]er in Alberta.

[...] wheat crop that grew in volume each
[...] result of steadily expanding plantings
[...]way to world export markets over the
[...]way system. The wheat merchants,

after claiming their commissions, oversaw the
construction of opulent mansions along the banks
of the Assiniboine River, on Roslyn Road and
Wellington Crescent.

Winnipeg's slaughterhouses rivalled those of
Toronto and St. Paul as cattle from the West, especially Alberta, moved through the city's stockyards
to world markets. All of these operations depended on the railways which employed thousands of
skilled craftsmen in three mammoth railway
shops.

In the centre of all this shipping and receiving enterprise, towering along a four-block stretch
of Main Street, was the financial heart of western
Canada. Here were the western offices of all the
chartered banks, trust companies and insurance
companies. Inside these marbled cathedrals of

Sport of Kings

[...]was betting, of course,"
[...]led. "Two dollars, just
[...]t there wasn't any regu-
[...]of the federal Depart-
[...]ulture. They were
[...]oversee the pari-mutuel
[...]you weren't cheated if
[...]vager. Nothing was auto-
[...]n people made bets at
[...]and the odds changed
[...]nners would be sent out

to the guy who worked the big odds
board. He'd get the information and
rub out the figures which were in
chalk and put in the new figures."

Gambling existed throughout
Depression-era Winnipeg. High-
rollers from Toronto and Chicago
would come in for the track, then look
for a floating crap game or a back-
room poker game. Off-track betting
usually consisted of unemployed men

making 50 cent bets with a barroom
bookie or the owner of a corner Chinese cafe. There was also a well-established wire service which allowed
Winnipeggers to gamble on American
races. It was linked to the Capone
mob out of Chicago with a dozen
local bookies controlling the action in
Winnipeg.

Moriss Kaplan remembered the
betting and the high-rollers but felt
the track itself was the real attraction.
"For the common person, I don't
know if gambling was the thing. It was
the pageantry of the track that sticks
in my mind. The stakes race my first
day there was won by Budsis who was
owned by Harry C. Hatch from Toronto. I haven't got a clue what the payout was but I still recall the smells of
the place, the fresh green grass, the
sweat of the horses, women's per-
fume, hot popcorn, steaming roast
beef sandwiches. It lifted my spirit,
made my heart beat a little faster, let
me know I was alive. In those crush-
ing days, that was the important
thing."

**Despite economic hard times, thousands
of Manitobans were drawn to race tracks
like this one at Polo Park in Winnipeg.**

"Winnipeg's Sweetheart", actress Edna Mae Durbin, was born in 1922. Renamed Deanna for stage purposes, she was, by age 14, the highest-paid actress in the world. Starring in such movies as *Three Smart Girls* and *That Certain Age*, the young actress was on the cover of every movie magazine. Durbin, however, hated celebrity, and ended up spending the rest of her life secluded in a quiet French village.

ing of the Panama Canal. The canal had enabled Vancouver to take over many of the western markets Winnipeg wholesalers had traditionally supplied. Winnipeg—gateway to the West— was gradually being reduced to a mercantile. By 1932, the once proud third city of Canada yielded its place to Vancouver.

It was the citizens of Winnipeg who first felt the sharp bite of the Depression. Thousands lost their jobs and were left idle. Hundreds of families were forced to seek relief during the winter of 1929-30. Under the terms of the British North American Act, the provinces were responsible for public welfare. They passed on their responsibility to municipal corporations. Relief costs were soon beyond the capacities of most local governments. Winnipeg had the heaviest load and continued to carry it by borrowing from the province. Rumour had it that many rural communities would pay a family's fare to Winnipeg and then sustain the family until they qualified for the city's relief rolls. This increased the resentment felt over civic authorities towards their rural cousins.

Winnipeg's per capita unemployment continued to grow until 1932 when it was the second highest in Canada. City council responded by approving a scheme for "voluntary repatriation to their native lands" of all unemployed aliens. Independent Labour Party councillors argued against the policy, saying it was "inhuman" to deport immigrants (mainly East Europeans) who had been attracted here by aggressive immigration campaigns and now could not find work. Right-wing councillors, on the other hand, voiced concerns that Winnipeg would become known as a relief haven.

The matter was turned over to the Unemployment Relief Department where the bureaucrat in charge, J.D. Fraser, devised an application form that made use of the Federal Immigration Act. It contained a provision in which anyone not a Canadian could be deported if he became a public charge. Immigration officials held a hearing for each person whom they claimed had signed an application of voluntary deportation. A lawyer could represent the so-called applicant but most had no money for this and were represen-

Portage Avenue looking west from Donald Street, 1930

commerce, armies of clerks processed the outflow and inflow of credit that fuelled the western boom.

Business, however, had problems. It was still contending with the aftermath of the 1919 General Strike and the effects of the 1914 open-

A rare photograph of an early Manitoba Provincial Police detachment. The force was disbanded during the Depression, replaced by the RCMP.

The Forgotten Force

anitoba Provincial lice served for 60 colourful years

TH LITTLE FANFARE, the Provincial Police Force ed. This uncelebrated and ten group of men—crigi-he Mounted Constabu-rovided police services s from 1870 until the ad-MP .

a in 1870 was a rowdy o militiamen battled the aftermath of the Riel nks and card-sharps River saloons. Col. Gar-s Imperial troops provid-ction, but hesitated to ved in police duties.

the government estab-unted Constabulary

, later known as the incial Police, assumed es. They supervised the prison. They also pa-ler when a Fenian raid ing the fall of 1871. A uis de Plainval—was 872. A former opera singer, de Plainval lobbied for improvements, but financial difficulties compelled him to cut his department from 24 to 16 men. A year later the "mounted" police had their horses taken away. By 1874, the force had been reduced to one man.

Over the next few years, the MPP re-established itself. The force grew dramatically during the Manitoba-Ontario boundary dispute of the 1880's. Both Manitoba and Ontario claimed Rat Portage (Kenora) as their own and maintained police detachments there. Trouble arose when the Manitoba police arrested an Ontario constable for violating Manitoba's liquor laws. Ontario authorities retaliated by arresting the entire Manitoba detachment and burning down their jail. Premier "Big John" Norquay led a force of MPP to Rat Portage, freed his men and arrested the Ontarians. Similar incidents were replayed over and over until Ontario was finally awarded control of the Kenora area.

The importance of a provincial police was driven home by the Winnipeg General Strike, when the city's police force was fired. The fear of further police strikes encouraged the provincial government in 1920 to strengthen the MPP . The force grew to 100 men, many of whom were war veterans. Detachments were set up in the province's main towns to handle serious crimes. During prohibition, however, the MPP spent most of its time chasing rum-runners and bootleggers on the back roads of southwestern Manitoba.

One of the MPP 's more celebrated exploits, and ironically a last hurrah, was the capture in 1927 of the notorious Earle Nelson. The serial killer was arrested by the MPP near Killarney after a well-publicized manhunt.

Financial restraints caused by the Depression led to the dismantling of the MPP in 1932. The province contracted to receive RCMP services and the MPP was transferred, lock, stock and barrel to the federal force.

Political Discussion, Depths of the Depression, Winnipeg, 1932, **by Cavin Atkins**

He was defeated and Richard Bedford Bennett from Calgary, corporate lawyer, bank director and mortgage company director, became the prime minister. His battle cry was: "The Conservative party is going to find work for all who are willing to work, or perish in the attempt."

Relief payments were a growing burden for Premier John Bracken's government. In 1929, a mere $70,000 was set aside by the province for unemployment relief. In 1930, the figure jumped to $1,300,000. This was under a new formula that Bracken had been instrumental in bullying the federal government into accepting. Under this scheme, each municipality was supposed to contribute one third of the cost of relief with the other two levels of government sharing the rest. By 1932, the provincial government had spent $2 million on relief—but the Depression continued to ravage the population.

In 1932, Premier Bracken arranged an alliance with the Liberals—renaming the new nonpartisan party the Liberal-Progressives. With

tation. The process intimidated the majority of people.

Soon councillors from immigrant wards in the North End were overwhelmed by angry and fearful residents suddenly placed under order of deportation. The issue became public and 1,000 people marched on the Winnipeg immigration office. They accused the federal department of participating in a conspiracy to get rid of unwanted citizens on relief and demanded an end to this practice. To this day, no one knows how many immigrants signed up and accepted "voluntary" deportation. Certainly hundreds and probably thousands were taken off the relief roles by being shipped back to Europe.

Nineteen families, including 40 children, camped in the Legislative Building in September, 1931. The squatters, who had been forced off their farms due to the drought, had not lived in Winnipeg long enough to qualify for relief. A crowd of 150 supporters blocked the entrances to the building in an attempt to prevent authorities from evicting the families.

The best effort of all levels of government could do nothing but slow down what was an almost complete breakdown in the functioning of society. Since the world had never experienced such a massive and far-ranging collapse of the free-market financial structure, there was no fall-back position. Those in power had no plan as to how to respond to the catastrophe and, worse, most of them had no inkling of how bad things were for farmers and the unemployed.

On July 28, 1930, Mackenzie King, the feisty, hypochondriac prime minister, consulted with the spirits that guided him and decided it was time for an election. During the campaign he was asked how he would respond to demands for unemployment relief from Conservative-run provinces. Carrying partisanship to new levels, he replied: "I would not give them a five-cent piece."

As the Depression deepened, many Manitobans turned to Communism in an effort to find solutions to their problems.

FOR A WORKERS & FARMERS GOVERNMENT IN CANADA

strength, he went to Ottawa and
that Prime Minister Bennett agree to
rger share of relief costs.

as a persuasive speaker and told tales
, hungry men arriving at one of the
s set up at Riding Mountain and at the
lls at Sandilands. These men had been
om their home communities of Garson,
Vita simply because they were single,
ob and the municipalities did not have
upport them.

en related how, upon arrival, each man
some underwear, a brown shirt and
s and heavy work boots. It was a uni-
ot one to be worn proudly like a man
war to fight for his country. These men
d like convicts and one of the supervi-
sergeant major, had boasted to Brack-
were his slaves. The men cut firewood
hiking paths. It was "busy-work" for
were paid 20 cents a day, not the kind
nat made them feel that they were an
important part of the
country. The food
served up was ade-
quate but the pre-
mier remarked that
he found it shameful
that decent men
were cut off from
their families.

Listening to
Bracken, Prime Min-
ister Bennett had a
problem. During his
campaign he had
spoken out against
the dole in his usual
blustering fashion.
He was also con-
scious that he had
said that relief was
no longer a local
problem but had
become "national in
importance". Now
he was faced with
the premier of Mani-
toba insisting that
the federal govern-
ment pay half the
costs of relief. He
balked and mouthed
a favourite platitude,
that the economy
was basically sound
and that the setback

> "As a result of the drought,
> grasshoppers and extreme heat,
> the citizens of this community
> find themselves faced with
> a situation unparalleled in the
> fifty years' history of this
> district. It is now a foregone
> conclusion that... no grain will
> be threshed this fall."
>
> *Deloraine Times*, **July 11, 1934**

Soup kitchens were established to feed the army of unemployed.

the country was experiencing was temporary.
More public works projects were the answer, he
insisted.

Bracken then put into words for Bennett
what a lot of Manitobans were thinking: "...It is
unthinkable that we can let our people go hungry
without the comfort of a fire or stay out of school
for lack of shoes and clothing. But this is happening and will happen in greater degree unless some
immediate relief is given."

It was decided that before more relief help
was forthcoming, Manitoba must balance its budget. If this were not done, Bennett insisted, a
financial controller "satisfactory to the Dominion
Government, would have to be appointed". This
was a low point in Manitoba history, when the
province essentially became a financial ward of
Ottawa.

It was at this time that a new political party,
the Co-operative Commonwealth Federation (CCF),
was formed. Combining the faltering western
labour and farm movements of the 1920's, the
socialist CCF was stood in counterpoint to the conservative Christian roots of the new Social Credit
party. Neither party was yet ready for power, but

207

The Anonymous Executioners

A retired farmer from the McAulay area provided this oral history. He is still disturbed by some of the incidents recorded here and preferred to remain anonymous. His story, although tragic, was by no mean unusual during the Dirty Thirties.

There was this spur track at McAulay where our farm was situated in the southwest corner of Manitoba. It ran up from the CPR's mainline and the hoboes seemed to know about our place. Three or four would show up at our door twice a week and my mom would feed them.

We had the drought pretty bad but we were better off than others because ours was a mixed farm with beef cattle, a few Jerseys, hogs and chickens. The Birdtail Creek ran through our land so we could water the stock. We always had milk, cream and butter on the table. The same with meat and eggs. Money was scarce but none of us went hungry.

In 1934, [our family] got a real taste of how bad this Depression thing was. The wheat grew in small skinny patches and my dad was forced to harvest it by hand. Me and my older brother worked alongside of him, cutting the clump of grain he grabbed in his hand with a scythe. My dad would then shake the stalks over a wooden box that my brother carried, and this would catch the dry kernels of wheat. Using this, we managed to harvest five bushels per acre. In years past the same land had yielded thirty or forty bushels.

That same summer our beef cattle began to die in the fields. There was no grass to speak of so they chewed into the earth and ate whatever roots they could find. But the dirt got in their lungs. They got the heaves and just choked to death. Nothing we could do. Dad got a neighbour to help him and they hauled two wagon loads of the healthy ones into Brandon and returned with eleven dollars. That was for about twenty cows. It was devastating to a proud man like my father. I don't know how he kept his sanity.

We kept the remaining stock alive for the next couple of years by feeding them a tobacco can full of grain each that we managed to scrape from the ground. In the spring there was thousands of minnows in the creek and my dad set up nets and hauled them home for the chickens. Between the fish and the grasshoppers they caught, the chickens got fat. No one could eat their eggs though and when my mom tried to use them in her baking the stink stayed.

In 1936, between what he owed the banks and the tax collector, my dad lost seven quarters of land that had been in his family since his great grandfather. We were left to live and farm on a half section. The spring of '37 was the worst. No leaves appeared on the trees. The only thing that grew on the ground was weeds and most of that was Russian thistle. Hoboes were piling off the freights and filling up our yard. My mom still fed them but the pickings were lean.

One day my brother was hitching up his team of Percherons. There were six of them. Big draft horses and one of them got skittish in the heat. My brother Roy gave him a tap on the leg with a curry comb to get him in line, and that animal just reared back and kicked him square in the face. We got Roy to the doctor but his head was all swelled up. The second day infection set in and he died that night. He was twenty years old.

Two days after the funeral, a couple of fellows came to the door for food. My dad said he had a little job for them first. He brought out all seventeen of our Percherons from the barn and marched them to the manure pile. He took the first horse to the top and left him there. Then he gave these two fellows a rifle and a box of shells. Shoot them all, he said. After the first shot, the other horses got nervous so I stayed with them, patting them, saying their names, trying to keep them calm. My father sat on the porch in an old rocker and he cried like a baby each time another one was led up to

shot. All the bodies toppled down to
and soon there was a circle of dead
 barn yard.
boes would not stay to eat the smoke
ches my mother had made. She put
ag and they ran from our property.
ter the carcasses had dried out in the
tink of them rotting, hardly any flies
 like the sun tanned them on the spot.
reepy to go out at night and see their
 legs straight up, pointing at the sky.
ut the horses to work the land, we
re finished. My dad and a cousin
ght hoping to find work further east.
om and I went out to the fields and
an thistle and whatever little clumps
growing. .. It was barely enough to
ock alive but they survived. But then
r from my father, who was working
Winkler which had a bumper crop.
would be returning next month with
full of hay, straw, crab apples and
molasses.
as good as his word. Several neigh-
m haul his bounty from the train
ext few days were spent storing hay
r and mixing Russian thistle and
utting box where it was ground up
was added. Both the beef and dairy
the stuff. Mom made pies and pick-
ab apples. By the time 1938 rolled
d learned to operate on a smaller
my dad was buying property again.
we did so well, he built us a brand
since that awful day at the manure
there's never been another horse on

both expressed the deep-seated anger and
resentment of western Canadian voters.

As the Depression wore on, doctors often felt
ethically bound to provide free services for
those unable to pay. In rural Manitoba, many
general practitioners were offered chickens,
jams and fire wood in return for treatment.
Similar exchanges occurred in the cities.

In the early 1930's, a prominent Winnipeg surgeon, Dr. W. Harvey Smith, estimated
his profession had provided more than $2 mil-
lion in free services to Manitoba patients. Doctors' incomes had fallen by half but still they
were required to maintain staff at their offices.
The Winnipeg Medical Society was persuaded
by a group of activists to spearhead a movement that sought "payments of minimum fees
to doctors who attend sick people who are on
city relief".

The provincial government's reaction was
to suggest a royal commission be established
to study the issue. The medical community

**Government job-creation projects led to
many new roads being built.**

Children representing 21 different nationalities, Aberdeen School, 1938

was not pleased. They put forth the argument that civic authorities allotted funds for those on relief to pay for rent, food and fuel and even clothes. Were not medical services just as important?

Finally, doctors decided to strike in order to make their point. City officials thought it was a bluff but on July 1, 1933, the medical profession of Winnipeg withheld services except in cases that were considered emergencies. City bureaucrats anticipated a backlash from patients. Instead, the far-sighted physicians formed alliances with several unemployed associations. These interest groups organized demonstrations in favour of a medical services plan to be paid for by the public purse.

At one rally, the police were sent in to disperse an angry crowd with tear gas. Over the next six months, the city proposed that a set number of doctors be put on the civic payroll to provide services to those on relief. This plan was opposed as much by the public as it was by the medical profession. Patients were disturbed that they no longer could be treated by the family doctor who had been a tower of strength during a previous illness. As well, this new proposal suggested an implicit class system where, for those that could afford it, family doctors could be kept.

Grey Owl, the celebrated conservationist who championed the Indian way of life, was at the height of his fame when he was appointed a warden of Riding Mountain National Park in 1931. In truth, he was Archibald Stansfeld Belaney, a well-born Englishman. He was discredited once the truth of his identity surfaced after his death in 1938. A generation later, recognition of the genuine contribution Archie Belaney made to the conservation movement helped rehabilitate his reputation.

ontinuing resistance from both doctors
ts prompted the city to develop a
lled the Greater Winnipeg Medical
Doctors who voluntarily signed up to
were paid a small fee for treating relief
he average payout to each
as $40 a month. This con-
s viewed as a victory not
medical profession but by
community. It was also an
irst step in the process that
lly to universal medicare.

ression deepened, Manito-
hed out a living however
. Without work many felt
ers responded to the chal-
unemployment with great
ess.

Winnipeg man, unable to
sold all his belongings for
nd hopped a freight train to
om there he walked south
small town on the Souris
he once hunted as a boy.
ecked in with the local
showed that he had money
e wanted to camp along-
r for the summer. The offi-
this was fine as long as he
self.

n found a flat area on a
river, put up his tent and
out of rocks. There was
wood and a nice spot for a
in weeks, the vegetables
ng up and the man was
eady diet of freshly-caught
the odd partridge. Later,
ated a high spot on the
river where he figured he
out a cave, complete with
was never cold that winter.
ld the heat and he rarely
kets.

f the local people thought
but most were tolerant.
s, the man stayed in his
out the bad times. In his
knew he had a good life.
olden to no one and,
people, he had plenty to

coming place to another. At night, the fires flick-
ered in the "hobo jungles" where wandering
vagrants gathered to sleep before moving on. Railway police or "bulls" initially tried to keep the
vagrants off the trains, but eventually gave up

International Peace Garden

 More than 50,000 people "choked the roads
with motor and foot traffic" to witness the
opening of the world's only peace garden on the
Manitoba-North Dakota border on July 14, 1932.

The International Peace Garden was conceived by
Dr. Henry J. Moore, an Islington, Ontario horticulturist
and graduate of London, England's famous Kew Gardens.
He envisioned a place "where the people of the two
countries could share the glories found in a lovely garden and the pleasures found in warm friendships".

Moore pitched his peace park idea to the 1929
National Association of Gardeners meeting. A committee
surveyed sites and recommended the park be located in
the Turtle Mountains area in southwest Manitoba due to
their beauty and their location near the continent's geographic centre.

The governments of North Dakota and Manitoba
donated 888 acres and 1,451 acres respectively. The
headquarters were established in North Dakota with
Manitobans also participating in the Peace Garden's
management.

Dozens of organizations in both countries worked
on the park. Efforts were made to preserve wild flowers,
and more than 50 varieties of trees and nearly 150 types
of flowers were planted to turn the facilities into an
international showpiece.

To commemorate Peace Garden promoters from
both countries, Lake Udall on the U.S. side honours W.V.
Udall, publisher of the *Boissevain Record*, while Lake
Stormon on the Canadian side honours American John A.
Stormon, for many years the Peace Garden's secretary.

A simple boundary marker sums up the park's goal:

To God in His Glory
We two nations dedicate this garden
And pledge ourselves that as long
As man shall live, we will not take up arms
Against one another.

eople were not so lucky. The freight
rawled back and forth across the
ed the unemployed from one unwel-

under the sheer weight of numbers. This army of
unemployed shifted back and forth in an endless
(and fruitless) search for work.

An army of unemployed rode the boxcars looking for work

Riding the Rails

BY 1932, CANADA BEGAN TO LOOK like a nation of hoboes. As many as 100,000 men (joined by the occasional woman) walked, hitchhiked and rode railway boxcars across the country. They represented a phenomenon never before seen: an undisciplined, ragged, hungry and often desperate army of unemployed. "We weren't heading anywhere in particular," recalled a survivor of the era, "but it was better than sitting still and watching the world fall apart."

It was illegal to ride the freights but the railway companies took a lenient view until the summer of 1932. The federal government, uncomfortable with newspaper photographs of this legion of vagrants squatting on freight trains, insisted the practice be stopped. The RCMP raided trains and threw off transients who were going west in the hope of finding harvest work. In Manitoba, this resulted in thousands of begging, homeless hoboes being dumped into small towns and farms.

The resulting outcry forced the government to rescind the ban. The task of policing the trains was left to railway "bulls". In many towns, these men soon acquired a reputation for beating up lone vagrants they caught sleeping in a boxcar. A kind of moccasin telegraph developed among the community of transients that identified good and bad towns.

These rail-riders were not traditional bums. Some were forced out of their home municipalities because they were single and unemployed. Others took to the tracks as a way to escape life that was without hope. Movement itself was an act of protest against the harshness of the times. For many the lure of jumping aboard a moving freight was a desperate snatch at freedom, adventure and even danger.

One woman from Falcon Lake rode the rails for three years. Her parents had four children and the family was on the "dole". She recounted in a later oral history that when she was 16 she cut her hair with sewing shears, right down to the scalp. Then she dressed in a pair of her father's work pants, a flannel shirt and a ratty cardigan. Three pairs of socks stopped the relief boots from sliding on her feet. She rolled up the blanket from the bed and left while it was dark.

It was a short walk down to the track where she met four men heading into Winnipeg. Two of them were smearing hog grease on the rails from a can. This slowed the train down and made grabbing hold of the ladder on a boxcar easier. Jumping a freight was fraught with peril. If the train's speed was misjudged and a person made a bad grab, they could end up under the wheels.

She learned to travel the branch lines. She rode boxcars in the summer; well-insulated refrigerator cars nicknamed "reefers", in the winter. There was no work, but there was food and companionship. Back and forth across the country she travelled with thousands of others, sleeping and eating in the hobo jungles. In Winnipeg, she contributed to the mulligan stews in the local jungle by begging bacon scraps at the butcher shops on Main Street, and taking vegetables from Point Douglas gardens.

Life on the rails could sometimes be as lonesome as a train whistle, but it was also a gypsy life that many recalled fondly in later years.

icken farmers sometimes
ricks from manure. In Flin
y wagons" were used to
age.

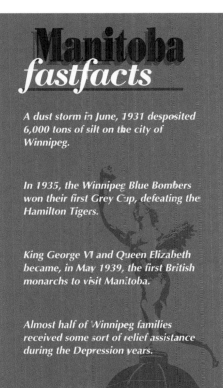

med that the Depression
r end. In 1935, Prime Min-
tt used the radio to assure
on that he understood their
ugh he had entered office
e richest men in Canada,
ed to govern through the
y-stricken period of Cana-
This changed the way he
world: "The old order has
not return. Your prosperity
rrections in the old sys-
y mind reform means government
. There can be no recovery without
competition and the open market, as
own in the old days, have lost their
system.... It means government con-
lation."

out as a dyed-blue Tory,
vented himself as a crusad-
reform. Unfortunately for
atives, most voters viewed
icky attempt to save his
and Bennett was defeated
election by Mackenzie
s. But it was Bennett who
Farmer's Credit Arrange-
at wiped out more than
in farm debts to banks and
npanies. The Prairie Farm
on Administration, an
to tackle the problem of
was created during his
ett also established the
da and paved the way for
oyment insurance and a
h scheme. His success on
was obscured by his prick-

cation became the criti-

cal dynamic in Manitoba's attempt to recover
from the Depression. Production of livestock, butter, and honey was increased. This helped allevi-
ate some of the economic hardships but did not
restore prosperity. In Winnipeg, the garment
industry grew but
not enough to ab-
sorb the mass of
unemployed labour.

The fuel of
choice to get a
family through the
cold winters was
coal. Ninety-five
per cent of the low-
grade lignite coal
that ended up in
Manitobans' stoves
came from the
Henderson and
Salter mines, locat-
ed in the southwest
corner of the prov-
ince. Known as
"Turtle Mountain
Mud" it sold for $2
a ton. The city of
Winnipeg also set

Manitoba fastfacts

A dust storm in June, 1931 desposited 6,000 tons of silt on the city of Winnipeg.

In 1935, the Winnipeg Blue Bombers won their first Grey Cup, defeating the Hamilton Tigers.

King George VI and Queen Elizabeth became, in May 1939, the first British monarchs to visit Manitoba.

Almost half of Winnipeg families received some sort of relief assistance during the Depression years.

To cope with the Depression, the Winnipeg Polish community formed a fuel co-operative which purchased and distributed among its members coal and wood supplies.

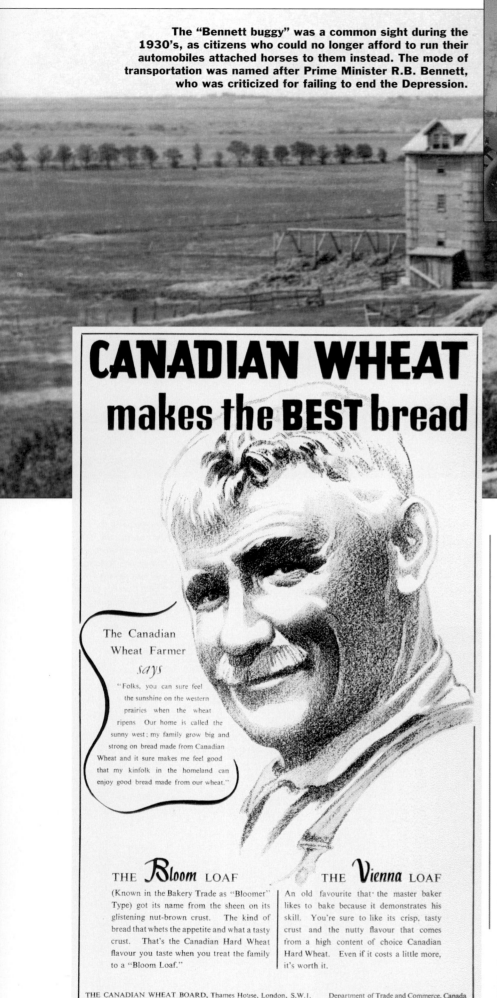

CANADIAN WHEAT
makes the BEST bread

The Canadian
Wheat Farmer
says

"Folks, you can sure feel the sunshine on the western prairies when the wheat ripens Our home is called the sunny west; my family grow big and strong on bread made from Canadian Wheat and it sure makes me feel good that my kinfolk in the homeland can enjoy good bread made from our wheat."

THE *Bloom* LOAF

(Known in the Bakery Trade as "Bloomer" Type) got its name from the sheen on its glistening nut-brown crust. The kind of bread that whets the appetite and what a tasty crust. That's the Canadian Hard Wheat flavour you taste when you treat the family to a "Bloom Loaf."

THE *Vienna* LOAF

An old favourite that the master baker likes to bake because it demonstrates his skill. You're sure to like its crisp, tasty crust and the nutty flavour that comes from a high content of choice Canadian Hard Wheat. Even if it costs a little more, it's worth it.

THE CANADIAN WHEAT BOARD, Thames House, London, S.W.1. Department of Trade and Commerce, Canada

up wood yards where people could chop and collect their own fuel.

In Mennonite communities near Steinbach people could not afford to buy coal. During the summer they spread manure on the ground and made a pile that was half a metre high. All the family members then walked on in their bare feet to pack it down. The pile was left to bake in the hot sun. Near the end of the summer the dense manure was cut into squares, each one placed on its side so it would dry out even more. Finally it was stored in a shed behind the house. During the winter, these blocks of animal waste were burned as fuel. Since the same stove was used for cooking, however, bread, meat and even potatoes had a slightly manure-smoked taste. It reminded people that they were poor.

As in all bad times, the price of gold rose. As a result, more than 50 companies were organized in Manitoba to exploit the precious metal. Many were small and did not survive, but the deposits at the San Antonio gold mine near Bissett were good. For a while, people saw this diversification

The Canadian Wheat Board was formed in 1935 to represent Canadian farmers in foreign markets. This poster appeared in British publications.

Some areas in Manitoba were not as adversely affected by the drought, as this Brandon district farm shows.

Charles A. Lindbergh and his wife Anne made a stopover in Churchill in 1931 as part of their honeymoon flight to the Orient.

rescue Manitoba economically from
f ailing King wheat.

the development of these natural
vas a positive step, it also led to
of workers. Unemployment
gh and a job was a prized
no matter how difficult the
For example, miners in Flin
retly and discussed forming
could represent their con-
e owners, but they were
vould lose their jobs if they
Instead they sent out a call
go, a Ukrainian Communist
eg.

ad been drawn into the
ement as a child when he
father's copies of radical
such as *One Big Union*
d the *Ukrainian Labour*
e time he arrived in Flin
is an experienced labour
later recalled the difficulty
g a union: "As a company
tough from the standpoint
any had undisputed sway
ffairs and, of course, the

workers and through them, the whole population.... We organized groups of five members, and
seven members, and quite a few hundred were
brought together. Because the men knew that their

215

The Incredible Pogue Carburetor

 Reports of a carburetor which ran vehicles at 200 miles to the gallon fuelled wild speculation amongst cash-strapped Manitobans during the Dirty Thirties.

Inventor Charles Nelson Pogue (originally from the Minitonas area) believed he could develop a more efficient carburetor. He reasoned that if gasoline was better vaporized by heat, more power would be generated and an engine would become more fuel efficient.

Working out of a shop in Winnipeg, Pogue toiled for months on his invention. His experiments were sponsored by W.J. Holmes, a hockey promoter. In 1928, Pogue and Holmes formed the Pogue Carburetor Co. and filed their first patent. Between 1928 and 1936, 12 patents were taken out in Canada and the United States.

During this time, newspaper stories reported that "Three Models of Device Reported Capable of Producing 200 Miles to The Gallon Stolen In Daylight From Workshop of Inventor, C.N. Pogue in Winnipeg." The missing carburetors weren't recovered, which led to rampant speculation that the big oil companies were conspiring against Pogue and his invention.

Other press reports said that Ford Motor Company tests had proven the astounding gas mileage. However, Winnipeg trials suggested the carburetor caused engines to wear prematurely. Pogue objected to the advanced publicity, wishing to perfect the carburetor first.

In the late 1930's, Pogue and his wife relocated to Montreal where they ran an oil filter business. Some claimed that Pogue sold his ideas to the oil companies and automobile manufacturers who would have been hurt by his inventions, but he consistently denied this.

Roller skating was so popular during the Depression that 600 people applied for membership in The Winnipeg Fancy Skating Club within its first few weeks of operation. The club, whose success was recognized internationally, taught waltzing and dance skating.

own security was involved they didn't talk about it. We were very careful not to be exposed by a spy sent by the company."

The result was the formation of the Mine Workers' Union of Canada. To protest wage cutbacks, the newly organized miners went on strike in June, 1934. The company, Hudson Bay Mining and Smelting Company, accused union leadership of being Communists and brought in the RCMP to break up unruly strikers. In the end, most of the miners returned to work and, a year later, wages were restored to their former level.

The political scene at mid-decade remained as uncertain as the economy. John Bracken called an election in 1936 and suffered a stinging setback. Voters resented the steady rise in taxes. So confused was the electorate that no party won a clear majority. Bracken applied his negotiating skills to bring about a coalition government. As premier again, he realized that Manitoba could not continue to carry the mounting weight of indebtedness that had resulted from the Depression. More than a third of the provincial budget was eaten up by interest charges. The only hope of relief was a readjustment of financial responsibilities among the provinces and the federal government.

The federal government was sympathetic, but the richer provinces which had fared better in the Depression did not support change. They insisted that the Prairie provinces had not managed their finances properly. The new Bank of Canada scrutinized the Manitoba situation and found that the province had done what it could to discharge its responsibilities and remain solvent. The Bank recommended that a Royal Commission be appointed to examine Dominion-provincial financial relations. The first hearing was held in Winnipeg in the fall of 1937.

It would be more than two years before the Rowell-Sirois Report would appear, but it contained recommendations that reflected Manitoba's central concerns. In essence, the report stated that a system of equalization payments processed through the federal government to the provinces was the only way to assure that a consistent way of life could be enjoyed by all Canadians. It was perhaps ironic that it had taken 60 years for Manitoba to achieve equal provincial powers and only seven more to acknowledge that financial equality among the provinces was impossible.

In 1930, when Manitoba finally obtained control of its own natural resources from the federal government, the action was perceived by some as a burden. Others saw the potential for economic diversification and thus the provincial Department of Mines and Natural Resources was established.

Government officials felt they should form partnerships with people in the community in order to conserve and develop the wealth of Manitoba's natural heritage. One the of the examples of this collaboration was the rehabilitation of the marshes of the Saskatchewan Delta. This was the natural habitat of the muskrat but their numbers had been decimated by falling water levels. Trappers from The Pas and surrounding areas had been reduced from simple poverty to destitution as a result of the poor catches and low prices for pelts. Working with local people, the Department of Mines and Natural Resources restored water levels by building dams.

e muskrats multiplied, an open and
on was established with quotas on the
furs that could be harvested. This sys-
successful that it was expanded to
of marshland at Delta, Netley Marsh,
Bay on Lakes
and Winnipeg.
pirit guided the
n of the regis-
ne in the east-
rthern parts of
. Now, instead
an area of all
rappers were
d to conserve

ilar approach
improve man-
f the lands,
ery, and water services. In co-opera-
cal communities, forest reserves at
ds, in the Duck and Porcupine Moun-
nd at Sandilands were created. Refor-
introduced, as was the increased use
g as a means to determine areas of
ivers and lakes were re-stocked with
nized study of water power resources
ed to guide future hydro-electric pro-

jects, although at that time both the hydro plant at
Slave Falls and the other at Seven Sisters supplied
more power than was needed.

In the southwestern drought areas, the re-
seeding of abandoned land was begun, as was the
use of drought-resistant
grasses. New methods of
tillage that preserved moisture and protected the soil
with a layer of weeds
(trash) were encouraged.
Community pastures were
established so that grain
farmers could also raise
livestock. Dams were built
to control the spring run-
off of the Prairie rivers, first
on the Souris and then the
Long River. Farmers shov-
elled out dugouts to store water in the event of
low rainfall. A farm with a good garden and some
animals might even survive low wheat prices. It
appeared that the people of Manitoba, using
courage and ingenuity, were determined to work
out a satisfactory way of life within the limits
imposed by nature.

> ## "It enabled farm people to shut themselves away from the Depression itself, from the dust, and from the wind that blew night and day..."
>
> **Author James Gray commenting on the popularity of radio**

Unemployed workers at The Pas. Job losses were common throughout all regions of Manitoba.

Drewry's beer truck, 1938. Drewry's was later bought by Molson's.

Economic recovery was slow but most people managed to find ways to cope with the daily grind of the Depression years. Because many Manitobans had more leisure time than they wanted, they sought respite in the arts and sports. During this dreary period, local festivals sprang up all over the province. Miss Gweneth Lloyd opened a school of ballet dancing (precursor to the Royal Winnipeg Ballet) in 1937 that offered recitals to initially small but appreciative audiences. Movie theatres were busy: for a nickel a person could see the World War I drama *Captured* or watch such popular actors as James Cagney and the Dead End Kids star in *Angels With Dirty Faces.* Mae West sashayed across the screen drawling lewd double entendres. This permissive behaviour caused uneasiness at the new Manitoba Film Censor Board which was charged with classifying all movies that appeared on public screens.

Dance halls did a brisk business. One such establishment was the Normandy Hall on Sherbrook Street in Winnipeg. It was run by Sid Boughton and George Evans. For 25 cents, as many as 1,000 people packed into the place and danced polkas, jigs and two-steps to the music of Andy Desjarlais and his Red River Settlers. River Park on Osborne Street drew thousands of Winnipeggers happy to forget their cares on the terrifying Big Dipper roller coaster.

Sports also flourished. The great Winnipeg Bonspiel broke up the long winter, and brought together hundreds of curlers from city and country in a game

Aristocrats and movie stars flocked to the Delta Marsh

ONE HUNDRED KILOMETRES west of Winnipeg is the great inland sea of Lake Manitoba. At the south end of the lake is a 40-kilometre long expanse of bullrush, cattail and cane grass known as the Delta Marsh. Before hydro dams and modern agriculture choked much of the life out of the Delta, it was one of the great waterfowl staging areas in North America. Each autumn, literally millions of ducks and geese poured down through the funnel shaped Delta on their southward journey.

In St. Ambroise, St. Laurent and other tiny communities along side the Delta Marsh, the last surviving clans of 19th-century Métis buffalo hunters settled. Unlike the members of other hard-pressed Métis communities, these people maintained a good standard of living by harvesting the waterfowl, fish and fur-bearers that inhabited the Marsh. In fact the Ducharmes, the Lamirances, the Lavallees and other clans developed an international reputation as outfitters and hunting guides. The Marsh, in those days, was still a legendary staging area for waterfowl. No wealthy industrialist, prince or entertainment celebrity would think of planning a shooting safari in the wilds of Manitoba without first acquiring the services of a capable Métis guide.

On an October afternoon in 1901, a flag-draped Royal Train pulled into the CPR station at Poplar Point and discharged a hunting party which included Governor-General Lord Minto, Prime Minister Wilfrid Laurier and the Duke of York (later King George V). With their guides, they embarked by canoe for an eight-kilometre paddle through the

nting Styles of the Rich
amous

n to the tent camp erect-
visit. Over the next few
yal hunters arose every
chilly darkness, paddled
marsh, and shot ducks
arved wooden decoys.
skill or regal protocol,
t-shot everyone else in
gging 82 birds in several

ood movie stars also
Manitoba's famous
ring the 1930's, many of
leading men and
serious competition
Rogers, Fred McMur-
eche, Ginger Rogers,

The Prince of Wales, later Edward VIII, visited Delta Marsh in 1919. He is shown here, standing, centre, with his hunting party and Métis guides.

Clark Gable walking along the railway tracks in Portage la Prairie. Gable was one of numerous Hollywood celebrities to hunt in the area.

Howard Hughes, Gary Cooper and other celebrities hung out and broke clay pigeons at Hollywood gun clubs. When they swapped rumours about exotic places to go hunting, the Delta Marsh of Manitoba was a name that came up again and again. Some of the glitterati found time between movies to make the trip. Robert Stack came for the geese; Mary Hemingway loved to hunt the tricky little Manitoba bluebills.

One afternoon in 1940, the girls behind the counter at Cadham's Hard-

ware in Portage la Prairie did a double-take when a bewhiskered, twinkly-eyed gent strolled up to the cash register and slapped down a box of shells. It was Rhett Butler, better known as Clark Gable, fresh from making *Gone With the Wind*. During his one-week stay at the Marsh north of Portage, he played poker with the guides and helped the kitchen girls wash the dishes. His guide Jimmy Robinson remembered the legendary Gable as "strong as a bull. He's six feet one inch tall, weighs 200 pounds, and is fast as a cat. He's an exceptionally fine duck shot".

Manitoba's Nazi Newspaper

A nationally circulated pro-Nazi newspaper, the *Deutsche Zeitung fur Canada*, was produced in Winnipeg until the eve of World War II.

The National Socialist Party in Germany wanted to spread propaganda through German newspapers in Canada. However, the six German language newspapers on the Prairies offered greatly varying degrees of support for Nazism.

The solution was to create a Nazi-controlled newspaper, the *Deutsche Zeitung fur Canada*, which was launched through the efforts of Nazi converts Heinrich Seelheim, German consul for Western Canada, and Bernhard Bott, former editor of the German language *Courier*. Financing came from the German consulate.

As Bott noted, they wanted "an entirely independent and forceful German newspaper which could act unhindered as the herald and defender of the German-Canadian movement". The weekly newspaper began operations in June 1935, offering a mix of local and international news, sports and features. Many of these items came from the German News Bureau, an agency run by the Propaganda Ministry. Each edition also contained an English-language supplement to target non-German readers. It reprinted Nazi propaganda which favourably presented the Third Reich.

The newspaper peaked in 1938 when its circulation reached 6,000. Concerns had been voiced by the Jewish community and the Canadian Communist Party, but widespread condemnation by public officials did not appear until early 1938 when Germany annexed Austria. At that point, A.A. Heaps, MP for Winnipeg North, asked the Minister of Justice to stop the spread of Nazi propaganda. He claimed that the newspaper contained "nothing but incitement to racial hatred..." J.S. Woodsworth, another Winnipeg MP, denounced the paper as anti-Semitic and anti-British.

The RCMP monitored the newspaper and, upon the outbreak of war in 1939, arrested and interned Bott, effectively ending production of *Deutsche Zeitung fur Canada*.

Citizens (below) scanning maps charting the progress of the war, October 1939. The maps were located on the exterior of the *Free Press* building on Carlton Street.

ged their skills and provided relax-
all, especially the Grey Cup champion
ers, rivalled hockey for the public's
Those who found their nurturing in
tinued to read old favourites Nellie
id Ralph Connor. The appearance of a
rederick Philip Grove, *Fruits of the*
hailed as a piece of authentic Manito-
was met with resentment by the pub-
sidered his portrayal of rural life too

ong decade of drought and Depression
ced great changes to agriculture. Farmed their production, but not by break-
id. Better tillage methods, crop rotation
e of artificial fertilizer were responsible
rops. Adaptation to regional soil conditions meant that more exotic crops like fall rye,
flax, field peas and alfalfa were now being planted
with confidence. On the Portage Plains, wheat still
cast a golden wave on the horizon while on the
lighter lands of the Assiniboine Delta, it was oats
and barley for livestock which filled the fields. The
drought had finally ended and a new, diversified
age of agriculture was on the horizon.

The drought was over, and soon—with the
coming of war—the Great Depression would also
end. For all those who lived through the Dirty
Thirties, its impact would never be forgotten. But
Manitobans wouldn't have much time to celebrate
the imminent return to prosperity—a former corporal in the German army named Adolf Hitler was
about to unleash a new, even worse devastation
upon the people of the world. ❧

Population of Manitoba by Ethnicity, 1901–1936

Origin	Census Years						
	1901	1911	1916	1921	1926	1931	1936
English	64,542	127,379	159,297	170,286	172,554	172,715	172,715
Irish	47,418	60,583	64,148	71,414	71,858	77,559	75,530
Scottish	51,365	85,948	93,652	105,034	106,766	112,326	108,912
er British	914	2,349	2,824	4,258	4,175	5,133	5,232
French	16,021	31,293	33,635	40,638	42,574	47,039	47,683
Austrian	4,901	8,454	21,193	31,035	15,772	8,858	3,414
Belgian	940	2,460	4,580	5,320	5,536	6,323	6,541
& Slovak	—	—	—	1,028	1,328	2,396	2,446
Finnish	76	1,080	373	506	624	1,013	796
German	27,265	34,979	25,862	19,444	25,535	38,078	52,450
Greek	27	317	250	257	284	295	321
ungarian	186	727	1,029	828	1,462	1,955	1,872
Italian	217	985	1,926	1,933	2,114	2,379	2,432
Jewish	1,514	10,850	16,508	16,669	15,948	19,341	18,596
Dutch	925	3,028	6,993	20,728	22,481	24,957	25,521
Polish	1,674	22,321	16,571	16,594	25,277	40,243	35,316
Romanian	98	123	292	919	1,485	2,087	1,776
Russian	3,326	7,831	15,962	14,009	14,445	11,573	6,101
Danish	—	—	1,647	3,429	2,321	3,235	2,988
Icelandic	11,924	17,644	11,923	11,043	12,848	13,450	13,898
Norwegian	—	—	3,367	4,203	4,347	5,263	5,277
Swedish	—	—	7,571	8,023	8,180	9,449	9,341
Ukrainian	3,894	31,053	45,763	44,129	63,213	73,606	86,982
Yugoslavic	—	—	57	111	196	291	339
European	223	397	835	1,309	1,783	1,478	1,120
Chinese	206	885	1,108	1,331	1,360	1,732	1,199
Japanese	5	5	30	53	41	51	58
Syrian	45	—	330	310	371	424	404
her Asiatic	3	80	57	21	57	48	35
Aboriginals	16,277	13,239	14,090	13,869	13,216	15,417	13,431
African	61	216	295	491	491	465	481
Other	1,265	7,168	1,512	896	414	683	8,189
Total	**255,211**	**461,394**	**553,860**	**610,118**	**639,056**	**700,139**	**711,216**

Building the Province

The following companies and organizations played a key role in the development of Manitoba. Their commitment to the province is continued to this day, as evidenced by their support for projects like the MANITOBA 125 history series. The story of our Heritage Patrons is an important part of the story of our province.

Compiled by
MURRAY MCNEILL

F. R. JACKES & Co.
HOUSE FURNISHINGS,
HARDWARE STOVES & TINWARE.
FAIRBANKS SCALES.
MERCHANT
TAILOR.

Province and railway shared growth and development

CP Rail System

THE "NATIONAL DREAM" of Canadian politicians in the late 1800's was for the country to become a "dominion from sea to sea". To achieve that goal, a transcontinental railway was needed.

The first Manitoba efforts began in the Red River Valley about the same time as the province was being established. Progress was slow and uncertain for a decade. Difficulties were also encountered in eastern Canada. Then, in 1881, the Canadian

Assiniboine rivers. The 72-hectare marshalling yard, in the heart of Winnipeg today, was considered to be the largest in the world early in this century. It handled all of the traffic moving in both directions between eastern and western Canada.

Vast change over more than a century is reflected in the railway itself. Even the name has evolved—the CPR is now CPRS (CP Rail System). The nature of Manitoba-based railway services have also evolved over the

nipeg is also headquarters for The Grain Team, CPRS's marketing team for Canadian grain transportation.

Weston is the main heavy repair facility in CP Rail System. Similar na-

A network of seamless rail connects grain terminals to major coastal ports.

tional services, established more recently, include a diesel shop which services a large part of the total CPRS locomotive fleet, a Transcona shop that welds standard rails into quarter-mile-long continuous welded rail for installation in main line track across the country, and one of two main equipment repair shops for CPRS in Canada.

The railway employs about 3,500 Manitobans and each year spends nearly $2 billion in Manitoba on payroll, provincial taxes, purchases and capital spending. This is in addition to indirect spending generated by business done with Manitoba-based suppliers.

CPRS maintains and operates a 2,047-kilometre network of rail lines to serve its Manitoba customers. This provides customers with seamless rail links to terminals and major coastal ports in Canada, the United States and Mexico. ❧

Mail being sorted inside an early CPR mail car

Pacific Railway Company was formed, took hold of the stumbling project, and completed the transcontinental line in five years. Since that time, both the province and the railway have contributed much to each other's growth and development.

In 1881, construction of the railway was supervised from offices in Winnipeg. In subsequent years, many facilities needed by the railway operation, both nationally and locally, were located near the forks of the Red and

years, but servicing operations across the nation have always been included.

That reality was emphasized anew in 1994 when the railway began consolidating customer service for all of its Canadian operations in a new centre in Winnipeg. When consolidation is complete (scheduled for the fall of 1995) the 24-hour operation will employ more than 200 people—many of whom will have been transferred from points across the country. Win-

CP Rail System

Canada's largest earner of foreign exchange

The Canadian Wheat Board

[TH]E DUST AND THE DROUGHT
[of the] 1930's, along with a trend
[to co]-operation in agriculture,
[brought] life into the Canadian
[Wheat Boa]rd (CWB) in 1935.

[The] 1930's brought depression
[and low w]heat prices to the Prairies.
[The gover]nment attempted to assist
[Canadi]an farmers first by working
[with the] existing open market sys-
[tem, fin]ally through the establish-
[ment of] CWB.

[Origin]ally, the Canadian Wheat
[Act] called for the creation of a
[pooled] marketing board. Farmers
[were as]sured of a guaranteed ini-
[tial paymen]t per tonne of grain deliv-
[ered. The] futures market would be

Threshing in Manitoba, c. 1940

voluntary agency and farmers were
more inclined to deliver on higher
prices offered by the private trade. Canadian grain commitments to the Allied cause were put in jeopardy and
grain prices in the Canadian market
were skyrocketing, resulting in higher
food prices. The urgency of the situation resulted in the closing of the fu-

tures market in 1943, making the CWB
the sole marketer of wheat.

During the late 1940's, a movement began to include coarse grains
under CWB jurisdiction. Wartime price
controls over these grains had been
removed and Western interests
stressed their preference for a system
in which all grains would be handled
on the same basis as wheat. After
much debate, parts of the Act were
extended to include oats and
barley for the 1949–50 crop
year.

CWB

[oper]ate. Initially, however, the
[CWB was m]arketing only wheat; those
[parts of] the bill that provided for
[oats and b]arley were to apply only
[to their for]mation.

[In this] situation, the CWB be-
[came a resi]dual receiver of wheat.
[When] market prices
[were higher] than the CWB's ini-
[tial payme]nt, it received no
[grain. Whe]n prices fell below
[the initial pa]yment, as they did
[for a good] portion of the
[1930's, farm]ers delivered large
[amounts to] the CWB thereby
[causing a lo]ss of revenue for
[the federal g]overnment.

[When W]orld War II came
[Canadia]n grain production
[soared.] This caused in-
[creased exp]ort demand and
[higher pr]ices on the Ameri-
[can and Cana]dian grain futures
[market. The] CWB was still a

**Food products made with Canadian
wheat. Canadian wheat and barley are
exported to over 70 countries.**

There have been many
changes to the world grain
business in the 60-year history
of the CWB. Today, Western
Canada's grain industry is
widely viewed as one of the
most dynamic in the world.
The CWB, as the sole seller of
all Prairie wheat and barley, is
one of the largest exporting
companies in Canada. It sells
to over 70 countries worldwide
and is Canada's largest earner
of foreign exchange. ✿

A yearning for independence led to the rise of the credit union movement

Manitoba's Credit Unions

FOUR MEN FROM ST. VITAL deserve a place on the honour roll of Manitoba business pioneers: David Harriman, Fred Everett, Walter Thomson and Leonard Shaumloffel. They founded the credit union movement in Manitoba.

Evolution of Credit Union Movement Trademarks

The original "Little Man Under the Umbrella" was created by famed newspaper artist Joe Stern in 1923, at the request of Roy Bergengren, credit union pioneer. The mark was copyrighted in 1936.

During World War II, the "Little Man" appeared in the centre of the letter "V", for "Victory".

In the 1960's, the "Little Man" symbol became taller, clean-shaven, and he got away from the "rain" of "Hardtimes, Sickness," and "Financial Distress".

In 1964, CUNA Inc. began development of the HANDS & GLOBE design mark, which was registered in 1966. In 1968, its use was limited to credit unions outside the United States.

In 1937, they established the Norwood Study Group Number One. Their purpose was to create a small co-operative agency that would encourage thrift and, eventually, provide financial services to its members. Their motivation was strong; they knew that Manitoba needed a financial institution that was locally accountable, that would be shaped by the members for the members.

In that period of the Great Depression, their pledged contributions reflected the times; ten cents per member per week. Within a year they had 15 members and $4.50 in the treasury. One of those early recruits was barber Fred Thibodeau, whose shop became their office. Within two years they bought a building lot from the City of St. Boniface for $1 and they sawed boards and pushed barrows to assist with the construction of what became the Norwood Credit Union, the first in Manitoba.

As word spread that private citizens, of modest means, could gain control over an important element in their lives, many other local credit unions were formed. By 1994 there are 76 of them, with 1,400 employees. They serve 340,000 members from 165 office locations. Their combined assets are $3.4 billion. They have $2.6 billion on loan to Manitobans. Credit unions are very much a part of the community in which they are located. In 1993 they donated two per cent of their net in-

come, over $350,000, to charitable organizations, and a further $330,000 to community events.

In only 57 years, Manitoba's credit unions have come a long way from the basic services offered in the 1930's. Today they are as modern as the moment, interconnected by computer, serving both individuals and corporations with a complete range of financial services.

It is significant that even in recent recessionary times, the credit union movement continues to grow. The membership increases by 8,000 to 10,000 per year. In more than 50 Manitoba communities, a credit union is the only financial institution. Local control made it possible for service to continue after other financial institutions closed their doors. One-third of all non-governmental farm loans in Manitoba are made by a credit union.

A credit union float joins a parade celebrating the Canadian Snowmobile Championship Races in Beausejour, 1970.

In the century-plus of Manitoba history, some things have never changed. The agricultural pioneers were moved by a yearning for independence. Their great-grandchildren now know that one way of achieving this happy state is by sharing in the credit union experience.

Operating one of Canada's largest printers from a small Prairie town

D.W. Friesen

...w of the Main Street general store and post office, showing ...ueck, owner and founder D.W. Friesen, and clerk Peter Winter

...T DEPRESSION SOUNDED THE DEATH KNELL for ...Manitoba enterprises, but it had the opposite ...family-owned business of D.W. Friesen.

...Depression began in ...Friesen was a small ...re/post office opera- ...on the main street of ...ough most business- ...to retrench in an ef- ...p their operations ...Friesen's two eldest ...nd David (D.K.) were ...kle new challenges. ...sons from leaving, ...greed to expand the

...pansion got under- ...), when the firm en- ...he school supplies ...ot long after that, it ...handling office sup- ...then established a ...chool supplies and ...vision to serve retail

The most significant long-term impact on the company resulted from David's decision in 1933 to set up a print shop in the basement of the town's bookstore. Five years later, he bought another print shop in town and merged the two operations. In 1941, the printing division also began producing a weekly newspaper—the *Altona Echo*.

By 1950, two of D.W.'s other sons, Ray and Ted, were handling most of the work in the firm's stationery division, so they and David pooled their resources and purchased their father's interest in the company, renaming it D.W. Friesen & Sons Ltd. Soon after, the printing division began printing school yearbooks, and in 1959 bought its first offset printing press. Ten years later, the division purchased its first large, colour press and expanded into the colour-printing business. It was soon printing a wide variety of colour products, including textbooks, illustrated books, community history books and cookbooks.

In 1971, the company added a paperbox manufacturing division to its overall operations. And while the paper box and wholesale stationery divisions remain an important part of D.W. Friesen & Son's overall operations, it is the printing division

Friesen's printing operation began with the press shown here.

Friesens

that has become the backbone of business, evolving into one of the largest book printers in Canada and one of only two dozen printing plants in the world capable of doing large volumes of high-quality colour books.

Today, D.W. Friesen & Sons employs about 450 people and operates out of a six-acre complex in Altona that includes a large stationery warehouse and a 135,000-square-foot printing plant. ✸

One of Canada's largest trucking firms

Kleysen Transport

MANITOBA WAS STILL IN THE GRIPS of the Great Depression when a young Toronto couple packed their belongings into a truck and headed for Winnipeg to start up a small cartage company.

Harry and Marguerite Kleysen's new Winnipeg venture, called Kleysen Cartage Company Limited, was a modest operation. Harry handled the truck-driving duties and Marguerite looked after the corporate accounts. Their specialty was hauling construction materials.

While the Kleysens had high hopes for their fledgling business, it's

Hubert and Tom Kleysen stand beside the restored original of the company's first truck—a 1936 Diamond T, shown inset. Employees and suppliers located the truck, restored it and presented it as a gift to the Kleysen family in 1993.

unlikely that even they could have foreseen how successful it would become. In the nearly 60 years since then, their one-truck, two-person operation has evolved into one of Canada's largest trucking companies, employing more than 1,300 people and boasting 2,000 pieces of rolling equipment and more than $120 million in yearly revenues.

One of the first big breaks for the Kleysens came in 1940, when they began hauling sugar beets for the Manitoba Sugar Company, a contract the firm has retained to this day. Five years later, the company took another step forward with the founding of a bulk cement hauling operation. A few years later, it obtained new licences that enabled it to begin hauling machinery, structural steel and building supplies.

Then in 1958, Kleysen made the jump from being a provincial to a national carrier when it landed a cement-hauling contract from Canada Cement that included all of Manitoba and parts of Saskatchewan and Ontario. That necessitated the purchasing of 40 more trucks, 40 trailers and 20 bulk cement tanks to accommodate the additional work load.

During the 1960's, the fast-growing firm suffered two major setbacks with the death of Harry Kleysen in 1960, and the on-the-job death of Harry and Marguerite's second eldest son, Garry, in 1967. At the time, Garry was in charge of the company's aggregate hauling contracts. After Harry's death Marguerite stepped in to fill the president's post until 1963, when she turned over the reins to their eldest son, Hubert.

In the three decades since then, Hubert has continued to build Kleysen Transport Limited into the conglomerate that it is today —a conglomerate that has hauling authority from Quebec to British Columbia in Canada and in all 48 mainland U.S. states, and that includes a half-dozen other firms (Kayway Industries Inc., Kayway Manufacturing Limited, Kayway Grit Inc. Blanchard Transport Ltd., C.D.M. Enterprises Ltd., and K.T. Farms Ltd..

Today, satellites provide two-way communication between Kleysen Dispatch and any of its trucks throughout North America. A 4,000-square-foot Learning Centre dedicated to Marguerite Kleysen serves as an education hub for all employees. A mainframe computer ties the company's operations together and establishes electronic links (E.D.I.) with customers. Above all, the company's greatest strength is its drive to continuously improve everything the Kleysen team does.

KLEYSEN TRANSPORT

Promoting a thriving and competitive egg industry in Manitoba

Manitoba Egg Producers

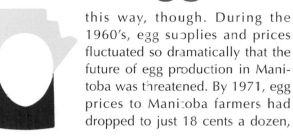

EGGS ARE EVEN
r and higher in
n they were 30
when just about
toba farm had a
n the yard.

neration ago,
be as much as
old by the time
ed consumers'
lay, the average
table egg to get
grocery store is
lays. Eggs are
aily and imme-
ed under refrig-
the farm until
grading sta-
e, the eggs are
r quality, sani-
acked for ship-
rocery stores,
processors.

rmers regularly
health of their
them in environmentally
onditions and feed them
balanced rations to en-
oduction of top quality
far cry from earlier times
cratched in the farm yards
ed and were exposed to
arasites and unpredictable

oba's egg farmers have
ted new tech-
wing them to
improve their
These gains in
have meant
able prices for
Between 1981
atistics Canada
t the average
ail price for all
se nearly four
t as that for

always been

this way, though. During the 1960's, egg supplies and prices fluctuated so dramatically that the future of egg production in Manitoba was threatened. By 1971, egg prices to Manitoba farmers had dropped to just 18 cents a dozen,

An early candling station, where Manitoba eggs were checked for shell quality

yet it cost up to 32 cents to produce a dozen eggs. In order to try to maintain incomes, farmers produced more eggs. But more supply meant even lower prices. Government and industry officials worried that ongoing low prices would push more and more farm families into bankruptcy.

Working co-operatively, Manitoba's egg farmers helped establish a national system of supply management for eggs in the early 1970's. The objective was to match egg supply with the demand for eggs in Canada. In return for agreeing to manage production, egg farmers were guaranteed a price based on a formula which would cover their cost of production plus a reasonable return on their labour and capital investment. The formula, updated regularly by an independent accounting firm, includes actual production cost data from efficient egg producers. This pricing procedure must be agreed to by representatives of government, consumers, egg producers and egg wholesalers. Grocery store prices are set solely by retailers.

To ensure the effectiveness of the national system of supply management, Manitoba Egg Producers (MEP) was established in 1971. MEP is actively involved in education and nutrition programs, egg quality monitoring and market development. MEP is not a government agency nor is it financed by taxpayers. It is managed and fully funded by the egg producers of Manitoba.

MEP partners with processor and consumer groups to ensure a thriving and competitive egg industry in Manitoba. In 1992 alone, egg production generated nearly $59 million at the farm gate, making Manitoba's egg farmers substantial contributors to our provincial economy. ❧

Today, eggs are scanned electronically for both interior and exterior quality, then undergo a final visual inspection by an operator using quartz candling lights.

Helping power Manitoba's growth for nearly 125 years

Manitoba Hydro

BY THE TURN OF THIS CENTURY, Winnipeggers were already familiar with some of the benefits electrical power had to offer. The first electric street light had appeared on the city's Main Street in 1873, and by early 1891, the first commercial electric street car system in Canada was providing regular service along Winnipeg streets.

It wasn't until after 1910, however, when competition within the province's burgeoning electrical industry made electricity more affordable for residential use, that residents of Winnipeg and Brandon began to fully appreciate the impact that electricity was to have on their lives. Between 1910 and 1920, a host of new electrical appliances became available in Manitoba—things like irons, toasters, cooking ranges and vacuum cleaners. This meant no more sweating over a hot, wood-burning stove and no more aching muscles from manually operating a washing machine.

But in addition to easing the burdens of home life, the advent of electrical appliances served another important role. It was the growing acceptance of electrical appliances that made it economically feasible for power companies to extend electrical service to Manitoba towns and farms. The province's rural electrification program officially got underway in 1920 with the construction of a transmission line between Winnipeg and Portage la Prairie. The following year, electrical service was extended to the Carman, Morden and Roland districts.

Although the rural and farm electrification efforts got off to a strong start, the forces of nature and finance were soon to intervene. A recession and crop failure in 1923, followed by the stock market crash of 1929 and the ensuing Great Depression, put a damper on the demand for

A department store showroom displayed the array of household devices powered by electricity.

Interior view of the Great Falls Power Station

electrical power.

By 1937, the picture began to brighten. New farm rates were established and every effort was made to reduce the cost of electrical service to individual farms. However, it took another disaster—the outbreak of World War II—for the farm electrification program to really take hold. That's because the war resulted in labour shortages on farms, and farmers realized they couldn't work without modern, electrical equipment. In 1942, the Manitoba Power Commission (a precursor to Manitoba Hydro) launched an ambitious Farm Electrification Program. By the time the program was completed

in 1955, 43,000 rural homes had electric power—a feat that earned Manitoba the distinction of being Western Canada's most electrified province.

In more modern times, Manitoba Hydro—the Crown corporation now responsible for the production and distribution of electricity in the province (except for the central area of Winnipeg)—continues to connect remote communities to electrical service. Examples of this are the farms on Peonan Point on the northern end of Lake Manitoba which began receiving electrical power in the fall of 1990; and the community of Herb Lake Landing, northeast of The Pas which was connected to the provincial power system in December 1993. ⚡

manitoba hydro

Seventy-five years of service to the public school system

Manitoba Teachers' Society

MODEST START in a base-
gymnasium, the Manitoba
Society has gone on to pro-
ars of service to Manitoba's
teachers and the public
tem.

ly, 1918, Belmont teacher
h gathered 17 teachers to-
he basement of the Normal
discuss forming a teachers'

school teachers were
dismissed for rejecting a
25 per cent salary cut.
The Federation's lobbying
failed to recover the teachers' jobs, but came to their
financial aid. As teacher
J.C. Wherrett noted: "We
felt that by taking a stand
we had perhaps saved oth-

1919 1994

teacher's contract which
closed the "trustees' es-
cape-hatch", the automat-
ic lapsing of contracts.

Up to and during
World War II, the MTF
lobbied for larger school
divisions to improve effi-
ciency. In 1942, the MTF
became the Manitoba
Teachers' Society (MTS) in
recognition of its responsibility for teachers' professional performances and ethical conduct.

In the 1950's, Manitoba teachers
lost the right to strike. In return they
gained binding arbitration, tenure
and a provincial certification board.
Baby boomers strained Manitoba's
schools throughout the 1960's, and
the Society continued its work towards the advancement of public
school education.

The 1970's saw improvements in
the teacher training and certification
processes and the MTS tackled the
issue of declining school enrolment.
Education finance, teachers' rights
and mainstreaming were addressed
during the 1980's.

New challenges such as underfunding, unequal access to programs,
school violence and education reform
face Manitoba teachers in the last
decade of the 20th century. The role
of public schools is under
debate and education re-
form proposals are being
closely scrutinized by the
MTS. Throughout its 75
years, the Manitoba Teachers' Society has protected
teachers' rights, advanced
public education and
fought for strong public
schools. It will continue to
champion excellence in
education as Manitoba en-
ters the 21st century. ✺

t to students has
a priority of the Manitoba
ociety.

on. Together, they pooled
rces to create the Manitoba
ederation (MTF).

pril 22, 1919, hundreds of
teachers met to examine
future. Some viewed the
iciously. As A.J. Struthers
We were not concerned
general public—anyway
le had shown themselves
indifferent to our doings.
businessmen, certainly
ol trustees, regarded this
as a revolutionary Bolshe-
oring on a general strike...".
ntley was chosen president
vart vice-president of the
MTF.

TF's first major test came in
nearly 80 Brandon's public

ers from such an ordeal."

Slashed teachers' salaries and in-
discriminate firings accompanied the
Depression. Membership in the MTF
fell dramatically during this period as
teachers left the profession. However,
in 1934, the MTF secured a new

The MTS serves over 13,000 teachers through
McMaster House, its central office in Winnipeg.

Serving the North from Alaska to Greenland

The North West Company

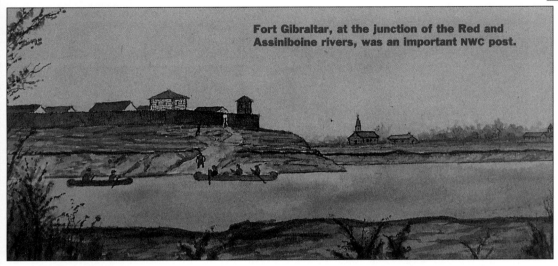

Fort Gibraltar, at the junction of the Red and Assiniboine rivers, was an important NWC post.

IN ITS BATTLE FOR FUR-TRADING SUPREMACY in the late 1700's and early 1800's, the North West Company established a host of small trading posts in remote locations throughout Canada's northwestern frontier. Those trading posts served as places where natives could trade furs for manufactured goods.

In the ensuing years, as European immigrants settled the West, some of those trading posts evolved into larger retail operations, albeit under a different name. That's because in 1821, the North West Company and its chief fur-trading rival, the Hudson's Bay Company, merged their operations. And although the North West Company was arguably the more aggressive of the two, it was decided that the new enterprise would operate under the Hudson's Bay name so that it could retain the land rights and guarantees in the Hudson's Bay Company's original charter from Britain.

The enterprise continued throughout the remainder of the 1800's and well into this century, first as the Northern Department, then as the Northern Stores division of the Hudson's Bay Company. In 1987, the Northern Stores division was acquired by a group of investors that included 415 employees. And three

Pangnirtung NT, typical of the remote communities served by Northern stores

THE NORTH WEST COMPANY

NWC has developed a wide variety of products, under the private label "Northern".

years later, the company renewed its links to the past and re-established its identity as an independent retailer when it changed its corporate name back to THE NORTH WEST COMPANY and named its retail operations NORTHERN.

Today, just as they did two centuries ago, The North West Company stores continue to serve as a place where residents of remote northern areas can go for everyday and special needs. Located in communities with populations of between 500 and 5,000, a typical Northern store offers a broad assortment of goods—everything from food to furniture.

In addition to its retail business, which now includes more than 150 stores in Canada and another 25 in Alaska, the Winnipeg-based company also operates a number of complementary businesses, including the largest Inuit art marketing service in the world, a Hudson's Bay Blanket Division, a Fur Marketing Division, and Transport Igloolik, a leading shipping service in the eastern Arctic.

The leading retailer in remote northern communities in Canada and Alaska, The North West Company is also Canada's largest employer of native people outside the federal government. And with yearly revenues of more than $548 million (1993), the firm is now one of the ten largest companies headquartered in Manitoba. ❦

Canada's largest private grain company

Pioneer Grain

RY OF PIONEER GRAIN can be
d back to 19th century colo-
io. In 1857, a Kingston tailor,
hardson, began accepting
payment from cash-strapped
omers. Soon he was buying
g grain and there was little
or tailoring. His historic deci-
ould leave the tailoring busi-
e more profitable grain trade.
0 years later, the Richardson
rain interests are still being
Pioneer Grain Company,
anada's largest private grain

Made of concrete, this is one of Pioneer Grain Company's newer grain elevators.

mes Richardson's Ontario
expanded, his
ge and Henry
and the firm
own as James
n and Sons.
lf-century of
including ex-
to the Prairie
—James Rich-
d Sons, Limit-
ied. Attracted
utation of the
at production
ies, Pioneer
npany Limited
d as a wholly-
ubsidiary to
the country
ystem, then
of 34 grain
Pioneer's first
was James A.
, grandson of
er, who upon
death of his
nator Henry

James Richardson and Sons shipped the first consignment of wheat to be transported via Hudson Bay.

, also assumed the presidency of the parent
ames Richardson and Sons, Limited.
er continued the growth initiated by JR, but if
crystallized the company's reputation as an
al grain handler, it was World War I. Grain be-
portant during the war that the company had to
ays of doing business. Company offices in Win-

nipeg and Kingston were connected by
wire service to each other, as well as to
the New York Produce Exchange and
the Chicago Board of Trade. So busy
was wartime that on a single day in
1916, Pioneer Grain's Winnipeg office
handled more grain than in any year
previous.

From the 1920's until the 1960's,
much of the leadership within Pioneer
Grain was provided by a hard-working
Scot named William McGillivray Rait.
Under Rait's direction, Pioneer expanded—despite the drought and the Depression of the 1930's—up to 250
elevators. In 1938, Rait was promoted
from general manager to president of
Pioneer Grain.

By the outbreak of World War II,
Winnipeg had become headquarters
for both James Richardson & Sons,
Limited and Pioneer Grain. Its present
day headquarters at the corner of
Portage and Main, built in 1969, has
become a Winnipeg landmark.

The continuous growth of the
Richardson family business interests
included impressive expansion in the
grain division. By 1939, the company
boasted ownership of 224 elevators. A
significant Pioneer acquisition came
about in 1951 when it took over operations of 146 Western Grain elevators.

Today, Pioneer is one of several
Richardson companies which operate
in the spheres of agriculture, real estate, investment securities, and oil and
gas. It is one of Canada's enterprising
agricultural firms. Together, with the
other companies comprising the Grain
Division of James Richardson and
Sons, Limited, Pioneer offers a complete and
innovative grain
merchandising pro-
gram and handling
services in the four
Western Canadian
provinces. ❧

THE PIONEER
PIONEER GRAIN COMPANY, LIMITED

Canada's largest bank, one customer at a time

Royal Bank of Canada

THE MERCHANTS' BANK OF HALIFAX was granted a federal charter on June 22, 1869. Throughout the 1870's and 1880's the bank cautiously expanded throughout the Maritimes, and in 1887 ventured into Montreal, Canada's emerging financial capital. The late 1890's saw several branches open in the Klondike gold fields, initiating the beginnings of a strong presence in the West.

In 1901, the bank changed its name to The Royal Bank of Canada, a change which heralded a program of rapid expansion to establish the bank as a national force. Manitoba's economy was enjoying unprecedented growth when the Royal Bank opened a Winnipeg branch in 1906. Outside Winnipeg, the influx of settlers saw new communities form along the growing network of rail lines of southern Manitoba. In 1906, the Royal Bank opened branches in Plumas, Lauder and Dominion City only to see the latter two close two years later as the branches did not flourish. Adopting a more prudent approach to expansion, the Royal Bank opened branches in Brandon and the Winnipeg Grain Exchange in 1908.

In Manitoba, the road to expansion lay through amalgamation. The purchase of the Quebec Bank (1917), the Northern Crown Bank (1918) and, especially, The Union Bank of Canada (1925), dramatically increased the number of Royal Bank branches in

Manitoba to 80. Royal Bank network expansion also followed Manitoba's resource development into the less populated north. Branches were opened in The Pas, Lac du Bonnet, Pine Falls, Flin Flon and Churchill.

The Depression years hit the agricultural industries of Manitoba es-

Royal Bank's Lauder, Manitoba branch was established in 1906

pecially hard. The number of Royal Bank branches in the province dropped from a pre-Depression total of 79 to 57 by the outbreak of World War II.

The 1950's were marked by unprecedented economic growth and change. The Royal Bank played an active role. Branches assumed a "friendlier" atmosphere as tellers were removed from their steel mesh cages and, one by one, branch premises were rebuilt or renovated. The 1950's

saw the Royal Bank emerge as the leader in the home mortgage market the "shopping centre branch" became commonplace in the 1960's. Winnipeg Branch and the district headquarters were moved to the tallest building in Winnipeg in 1966. The Royal Bank's Winnipeg-based Prairie Agricultural Department was expanded in 1972 to provide national service and a Data Processing Centre was built in 1980 for the bank's branches in Saskatchewan, Manitoba and Western Ontario.

Recently, the Royal Bank acquired both Dominion Securities (1988) and Royal Trust (1993). These two strategic acquisitions have transformed the Royal Bank, for many years Canada's largest chartered bank, into one of North America's most significant providers of integrated financial services. ▢

ROYAL BANK

A prominent Winnipeg landmark, the Royal Bank building at Portage and Fort

Winnipeg has a long history of professional sports teams

Tourism Winnipeg

THINGS COMBINE TO MAKE ng in—or visiting—a city e. Professional sports is a ddition to any community ipeg has been, and contin- home to a wide range of teams.

first professional game of in Winnipeg was played in 86, when a crowd of 1,500

INNIPEG *GREAT* **CITY!**

congregated in Winnipeg's park to watch a baseball ween the Metropolitans and The Metropolitan team in- veral professional players re- om a club in Hamilton, and delighted by the smooth pro's.

e more than 100 years since nnipeg has been home to a rofessional sports franchi- h have included the Cana- tball League's Winnipeg bers, the National Hockey Winnipeg Jets, the Northern League's Winnipeg Gold- National Basketball League's Thunder and the Canadian

Soccer League's Winnipeg Fury.

The sport with the oldest professional roots in Winnipeg is baseball. The city's teams have included the Maroons of the Class D Western Canada League (1909 to 1913), the Maroons of the Northern League (1933 to 1941), the Goldeyes of the Northern League (1954 to 1964), the Whips, which operated as a farm team of the Montreal Expos in 1970 and 1971, and the Goldeyes, which joined the independent AA-Class Northern League in the spring of 1994.

The city's first professional hockey team was the Winnipeg Strathconas, which played from 1906 to 1910 in the Professional League. It wasn't until 1926 that professional hockey returned with the Winnipeg Maroons of the North American Hockey Association. That team folded after two seasons, and was followed 28 years later by the Winnipeg Warriors of the Western Hockey League. Major-league hockey arrived in 1972, when the Avco Cup-winning Jets played in the World Hockey Association. In 1979, the WHA was disbanded and the Jets were accepted into the National Hockey League.

Another professional sport that

has enjoyed a distinguished history in Winnipeg is football. The community-owned Winnipeg Football Club, which became known as the Blue Bombers in 1936, was founded in 1930 and has won the Canadian Foot-

Blue Bomber Trevor Kennerd kicked the winning field goal in the 1988 Grey Cup game in Ottawa.

ball League's Grey Cup on eight occasions (1936, 1958, 1959, 1961, 1962, 1984, 1988 and 1990).

These sports, along with soccer and basketball, have added to the quality of life for Winnipeg sports fans over the years. They have also contributed to Winnipeg's attraction as a tourist destination for sports fans from around the province and neighbouring American states. ❧

as the attraction, Wesley Park play, c.1920

The beginning of tourism in Manitoba

Travel Manitoba

EXPLORE MANITOBA
TOURISM · INITIATIVE

THE YEAR 1878 WAS A MILESTONE in the development of Manitoba's tourism industry. It was the year the first train arrived in St. Boniface from St. Paul, Minnesota—establishing an important tourism link between Canada and the United States.

As railway lines criss-crossed the province, tourists started travelling throughout Manitoba. Europeans and Americans were attracted by the opportunity to hike, hunt and fish through the more remote areas of the province.

Later, automobile travel became very popular, although early road conditions were poor. The Winnipeg Automobile Club (later to become the Manitoba Motor League) demanded road improvements so their members could explore the province. Manitoba's first highway stretched from Emerson, near the U.S. border, to the town of Selkirk. By 1926, a numbered highway system had been developed and many vacationers took to the road

The bandstand at Assiniboine Park, c.1910

Moose and elk calves delight Riding Mountain National Park visitors, c.1933

for their holidays. The opportunity for recreation increased when new labour laws reduced working hours, providing more leisure time.

Street cars transported people to parks while inexpensive rail service took them to the beaches. On Saturdays, thousands of passengers would board the romantic "Moonlight Special" to Winnipeg Beach and return to Winnipeg at midnight. A similar train also travelled to the white sandy shores of Grand Beach, now considered one of North America's top ten beaches.

The creation of Winnipeg's Parks Board led to the development of the first city parks. In 1904 the rolling wooded lawns of Winnipeg's largest park were created. Named Assiniboine Park, its gardens and other attractions are still enjoyed by thousands today. Great family entertainment started in 19__ when the first Red River Exposition, a fun summer tradition that continues to the present.

Manitoba has a long and strong history of tourism development—a valuable resource that Travel Manitoba is committed to maintaining into the next century. ❧

Winnipeg Beach in the early teens was a popular place for strolling and people-watching.

Twenty farmers put up $20 each to start a Canadian insurance giant

Wawanesa Insurance

O FOWLER KEMPTON eamed of creating a mutual e company owned by and rmers. A travelling salesman vestern Manitoba, Kempton hand how poorly farmers ng served by the big stock companies. He was sure a better way.

vever, Kempton needed the cf a prominent farmer if o attain his goal. He ap- Wawanesa farmer Alex . The respected Naismith rvations about Kempton's ng reputation, but he liked

surance or their steam-powered threshers. Within a few years—as word spread about the fair dealings of Wawanesa—the company expanded to offer coverage on homes and com-

Our roots are small town but our branches cover Canada.

amorg the premier insurance companies in Canada. Steady growth through the following decades emboldened the company to move into life insurance and, in 1961, The Wawanesa Mutual Life Insurance Company sold its first policy. The opening of a Wawanesa office in San Diego, California in 1975 marked the first successful entry of a Canadian general insurance company into the United States.

Today, Wawanesa continues its tradition of fairness while reliably meeting the insurance needs of its customers in Canada and the United States. As an industry leader, Wawanesa uses the latest technology and business practices to provide fast service and accurate record-keeping on more than one million policies.

Wawanesa's eight branches in Canada and the American operation employ approximately 1,400 people, while the company is in partnership with as many independent brokers. As a full service insurer, Wawanesa meets a range of needs in residential, commercial, farm and automobile insurance. The company also offers individual life insurance and savings plans as well as group life and health products through its life subsidiary.

Founder Alonzo Fowler Kempton, centre, standing with staff in front of first Wawanesa building

f a mutual. The deal struck Kempton, Naismith and 19 ers gave birth in 1896 to The a Mutual Insurance Compa- ovided the foundation for a dian success story.

vanesa's first customers were who had tired of paying stock company rates for in-

mercial dwellings, and eventually on automobiles.

By the 1930's, the "farmer's mutual" that had begun humbly enough in a small Manitoba village, was writing business coast to coast and stood

An established corporate citizen, Wawanesa's commitment to Manitoba is as strong as ever. Although virtually every other aspect of the business has changed, the ideals that gave rise to the Wawanesa Mutual—fairness and accountability—are still central to its business today.

Setting an agricultural standard for more than a century

Winnipeg Commodity Exchange

WESTERN CANADIAN GRAIN production increased rapidly in the late 1880's. A new organization was needed to provide standards for the trading and exporting of grain. As a result, the Winnipeg Grain and Produce Ex-

Winnipeg Grain Exchange members on the trading floor

change was established in 1887 by a group of local grain merchants. The Exchange provided a meeting place for business transactions, a uniform set of rules, as well as a facility for communication with the markets of the world. The Exchange became the heartbeat of a system that provided a competitive "open-auction style" market for Canadian grains.

The Winnipeg Grain and Produce Exchange played an important role in the development of Winnipeg as a major business and financial centre. A major player in the Canadian agricultural industry, the Exchange contributed to the success of many local businesses. The Exchange was also instrumental in establishing a more efficient grain inspection system and improved transportation facilities.

More than 107 years later, the former Winnipeg Grain and Produce Exchange, now known as The Winnipeg Commodity Exchange, is one of the

The Exchange, Winnipeg's core business district, is named after the Grain Exchange Building on Lombard Avenue.

oldest, most vibrant international exchanges in the world. It is the only agricultural cash, futures and options exchange in Canada and provides facilities for trading in six major agricultural commodities, including flaxseed, canola, rye and oats, as well as feed quality wheat and barley for use within Canada.

The main purpose of the Exchange is to provide the facilities for price discovery, price protection, information dissemination and market information. It provides a mechanism for growers, users and marketers of Canadian grains and oilseeds to manage the price risks associated with growing and marketing these crops. It contributes to the efficient movement of grain from prairie farms to consumers throughout the world.

The Winnipeg Commodity Exchange

Current market participants include virtually all the major international grain trading companies, country and terminal elevator companies, domestic merchants, exporters, oilseed processors, feed manufacturers, malting companies, brokerage firms, banks, farmers and individuals.

The futures markets at The Winnipeg Commodity Exchange are among the most important commodity markets in North America. They remain the major price discovery mechanisms for handlers and processors of grains and oilseeds grown in western Canada.

The Winnipeg Commodity Exchange is committed to providing the agricultural industry with effective marketing tools and will continue the research and development of new trading instruments that can be used by Canadian industry. ◆

Western Canada's national newspaper

Winnipeg Free Press

The Free Press complex houses the largest colour presses of any newspaper in Canada.

WINNIPEG FREE PRESS has had many firsts in its illustrious 122-[yea]ry in Manitoba. One of the [lesser kn]own but still significant firsts [of p]ublication occurred in 1920, [when th]e Manitoba Free Press, as it [was the]n known, became the first [newspap]er in Canada to use an air-[plane to] cover a news event.

[On] October 13, 1920, three bank [robbers] blew open the vault in the [Union Ba]nk at Winkler. The Free Press [quickly a]rranged for a local aviation [firm to fl]y reporter Cecil Lamont [to] Winkler in a small Avro bi-[plane. Th]e plane landed in a field out-[side Wi]nkler after a 42-minute flight, [and Lam]ont hurried over to interview [bank em]ployees while the plane's [pilot too]k photographs of the bank's [wrec]ked interior. The men then [flew ba]ck to Winnipeg with their ex-[clusive s]tory.

[Th]e following year, the Manito-[ba Free] Press established another first [and] put Canada's first commercial [radio sta]tion, CJCG, on the air. Modest [by toda]y's broadcasting standards— the station's

transmitter had a rating of only ten watts—CJCG provided Manitobans with noon-hour news, grain, stock market and sports reports; a two-hour evening program of local musical talent; and, on Sundays, church music programs.

The Free Press was also the first Western Canadian newspaper to have an editor who advised prime ministers and had a direct influence on the shaping of public policy. John Wesley Dafoe served as the newspaper's editor from

1901 until his death in 1944 at the age of 78.

In 1917, Prime Minister Robert Borden praised Dafoe as "far above the class which our Western newspapers command". It was this respect that earned Dafoe an invitation to the 1919 Paris peace conference. He also served as an advisor to Prime Minister Mackenzie King at the Imperial Conference of the British Empire in 1923.

In the years since then, the Winnipeg Free Press, as the newspaper is now called, has continued that tradition of "firsts". In 1991, for example, it built a new $150-million printing plant and office complex that included the largest colour presses of any newspaper in Canada. As well, the Free Press has been recognized as having the highest-quality colour reproduction of any North American newspaper.

239

ORIGINS OF MANITOBA PLACE NAMES

Arizona Named after the U.S. state, due to its isolation from other settlements.

Atikameg Lake A Cree word for "whitefish".

Austin Originally known as Three Creeks, the village was renamed by the Marquis of Lorne in 1881 in honour of Sidney Austin, a correspondent with the *London Graphic*. The community of Sidney is also named after him.

Baldur Named after Baldur, a god in Norse mythology who represented the nobler qualities of human nature.

Balmoral Takes its name from the royal residence Balmoral Castle in Aberdeenshire, Scotland.

Beulah Named after a book of the same name at the suggestion of postmaster W.A. Doyle. The novel was written by Augusta J. Evans.

Binscarth Named after a stock farm established in the area by the Scottish, Ontario and Manitoba Land Co., which was founded and managed by William Bain Scarth.

Blumenort German name for "flower place" or "flower nook".

Bowsman Named by geologist J.B. Tyrrell after the bowsman of his canoe.

Brochet French name meaning "pike".

Calico Island Attributed to an 1872 shipwreck. When a steamer broke up in the rapids, the cargo of calico was taken to the island to dry.

Cranberry Portage The translation of the Cree words *wasagami sakahigan*.

Dallas Seems to be an anglicized version of the Polish name Dalaszynski, a family which settled in the area in the early 1900's.

Dominion City Once known as Losseau Crossing, it was renamed during the real estate boom of 1878, as were other ambitious towns like Crystal City and Rapid City.

Ebb and Flow Translation of the Cree *kizae-wakwepanik*. The local water rises and falls with the water in Lake Manitoba.

Eden Comes from the Charles Dickens novel *Martin Chuzzlewit* where the "thriving city of Eden" is mentioned.

Edwin Originally the Fox Post Office, it was later renamed after Canadian Northern Railway manager Edwin James.

Emerson Named by one of the settlement's founders, W.N. Fairbanks, in honor of American philosopher and writer Ralph Waldo Emerson.

Fannystelle A compound name: fanny and stella (star). The Countess of Alberufe, a Parisian philanthropist, founded the village in 1890 and named after her late friend Fanny Rieves.

Flin Flon Named by prospector Tom Creighton after Flintabbatey Flonatin, the protagonist of the dime novel *Sunless City*.

wood Once known as Kreuzburg, the ... renamed during World War I and is a ... of an early settler's name, Wood, and ...ife's maiden name.

...one A community for which the origin ... disputed. One story says the town was ... W.E. Gladstone, the British prime minis-... ...ccount says the town is named after a ... by local C.P. Brown.

...Isle During the 1852 Red River flood, ...sought refuge on the high ground of ... west of Winnipeg. Surrounded by ...the settlers named the area "big island".

... Originally called Hamilton, the post ... ...was changed to avoid confusion with ... ...mmunity of the same name. The name ... ...t of an early postmaster, Thomas ... ...he Cree word *ota,* meaning "at this ...

...Named in honour of Bret Harte, ...*ck of Roaring Camp.*

... The post office was located on a ... ...e was an abundance of hazelnuts.

...elandic for "uneven land". The CPR ... ...ally named Jellicoe.

...nes French name meaning "oak ...

...ace name from Western Ukraine, ...derived from the Urkainian Prince ...

...en from the Greek word for beauti-... ...f the striking scenery in the area.

...man for "cloverfield", the village ... ...nnonite village in south Russia.

...ainian name meaning "full of ... ...e suggested by early settler ...

...Name given by Archbishop Taché ... ...uncle Joseph B. de La Broquerie.

...let was originally called ... ...er Julius Kreiger. The name was ... ...eflect a Baltic town.

...known as Little Britain and later ... ...e village's name now reflects ... ...which opened in 1910.

...ed for *Montreal Gazette* edi-... ...ned and farmed land in the ... ...deputy minister of agriculture.

...d after Mafeking, South Africa, ...by Col. Baden Powell during ...

...ree word for "bad throat".

...Named for D. Matheson, ...eeper.

Melita Transplanted from Europe where Melita was the ancient name for the modern day island of Malta. The idea arose after a church service which discussed the shipwreck of the apostle Paul on an island called Melita.

Miniota Sioux name meaning "much water"; it was suggested by postmaster W.A. Doyle.

Minnedosa Originally called Tanner's Crossing, after the area's first settler, a one-armed Métis who ran the store and post office. With the arrival of Ontario settlers, the name changed to Minnedosa, from the Sioux words *minne* (water) and *duza* (rapid).

Morris Once known as Scratching River, the town takes its name from Alexander Morris, the first chief justice of Manitoba.

Napinka From the Sioux word meaning "equal to two".

Narcisse Suggested by Russian settlers, after the popular flower *narcyz.*

Norway House Named after Norwegian workers brought out to build a winter road between Hudson Bay and Lake Winnipeg. The project was abandoned.

Otterburne From a noted battle ground, Otterburn, in Northumberland, England.

Pilot Mound Takes its name from an area butte which is visible for miles and acted as a pilot for travellers. Local Indians called it *Mepawaque-moshen* or "Little Dance Hill" for the ceremonial dances they held there.

Plum Coulee Named after Plum Creek, which ran through the village.

Polonia Originially known as Huns Valley when it began as a Hungarian settlement initiated by G. De Dory in 1887. An influx of Polish settlers led to its name change in 1921.

Ponemah From Longfellow's *Hiawatha,* named after "the kingdom of Ponemah in the land of the 'Hereafter'."

The Pas From the French Fort du Pas (fort of the narrows).

Tolstoi Once called Oleskow, it was renamed in 1905 after Russian writer Count Leo Tolstoi.

Transcona Name was chosen in a contest, and is a combination of Transcontinental and Strathcona.

Wabowden Named after W.A. Bowden, chief engineer with the Department of Railways and Canals in Ottawa.

Waldersee Named after Field Marshall Alfred, Count Waldersee of Germany, who led the Allied troops in China during the Boxer uprising in 1900.

Wampum Named by the cook of a construction gang who used Wampum Baking Powder.

Zhoda Ukrainian for "agreement" or "harmony".

SIGNIFICANT DATES IN MANITOBA HISTORY

May 12, 1870	Parliament passed Manitoba Act, creating new province of Manitoba
July 15, 1870	Province of Manitoba officially admitted into Confederation. Winnipeg became capital of both Manitoba and the Northwest Territories.
August, 1870	The Red River Expedition, led by Col. Garnet J. Wolseley, arrived at Fort Garry and took possession of the fort. Riel fled to the United States. Wolseley asked HBC Commissioner Donald A. Smith to administer the government pending the arrival of the lieutenant-governor.
September 2, 1870	Lieutenant-Governor A.G. Archibald arrived at Fort Garry.
December 30, 1870	First election held for the province's Legislative Assembly.
March 15, 1871	First session of the first Legislature held in a house bought from A.G.B. Bannatyne. Twenty-eight members were present.
May 3, 1871	First Manitoba Public School Act passed.
August 3, 1871	Lieutenant-Governor Archibald and native leaders gathered at Lower Fort Garry to sign Treaty 1. Treaty 2 was signed August 21.
October 5, 1871	Fenians from the United States entered Manitoba and seized the HBC post at Pembina. Later they were captured by a corps of United States troops whom Lieutenant-Governor Archibald had given permission to cross the border.
November 9, 1872	First edition of the *Manitoba Free Press* appeared.
November 8, 1873	City of Winnipeg incorporated, with four wards and 12 aldermen.
July 31, 1874	First Russian Mennonites arrived at Winnipeg on the steamer *International*.
October 10, 1874	Ambroise Lepine found guilty of aiding Riel in the murder of Thomas Scott and sentenced to hang on January 29, 1875. His sentence was later commuted to two years' imprisonment.
October 11, 1875	First Icelandic immigrants arrived in Winnipeg.
October 7, 1876	Northwest Territories Act passed, separating them from Manitoba. Winnipeg would no longer be capital of the Territories.
October 21, 1876	First shipment of wheat from Manitoba to Ontario, some 857 bushels valued at $835.71.
February 28, 1877	Law Society of Manitoba incorporated. University of Manitoba chartered.
October 10, 1877	Manitoba's first railway locomotive—the *Countess of Dufferin*—arrives in St. Boniface via steamer.
November 2, 1878	John McBeth, last member of the first group of Selkirk settlers, died at Kildonan.
December 24, 1878	First freight by rail reached St. Boniface. Two days later, the first freight for export was shipped by rail from St. Boniface to St. Paul.
March 21, 1881	Manitoba Boundaries Act passed in Parliament, providing for an extension of the province's borders.
December 11, 1883	Standard time adopted throughout the province.
August 11, 1884	Boundary dispute between Manitoba and Ontario settled by a decision of the judicial committee of the Privy Council.
March 17, 1885	Louis Riel elected president of the Provisional Government in the Northwest Territories, launching the Northwest Rebellion.

May 9–12, 1885	Battle of Batoche, Métis leader Louis Riel's last stand. He was taken prisoner May 15.
mber 16, 1885	Louis Riel executed at Regina.
March, 1890	Denominational (separate) school system abolished in Manitoba.
October, 1892	First Ukrainians reached Winnipeg.
1906	Manitoba enacted legislation for a government-run telephone system. By January 15, 1908, Manitoba Government Telephones was operating the first such public utility in North America.
May 10, 1910	The steamer *Victoria* passed through the new St. Andrew's Locks. The Locks were formally opened July 15.
ary 26, 1912	Manitoba's new boundaries announced, increasing its size to present day borders.
May 12, 1915	Government of Rodmond P. Roblin resigned over Legislative Buildings scandal, and T.C. Norris becomes Premier.
ary 27, 1916	Women's Suffrage Bill adopted by the Manitoba Legislature. Manitoba women become first with right to vote and hold provincial office.
ch 13, 1916	Prohibition introduced and bars banished under the Manitoba Temperance Act.
ugust, 1916	Compulsory Education Act came into effect.
er 11, 1918	Ban placed on all public gatherings due to the Spanish Influenza epidemic.
ril 5, 1919	Greater Winnipeg Aqueduct completed, and soft water from Shoal Lake turned on in Winnipeg.
y 15, 1919	Winnipeg General Strike began as street car workers walked off the job.
e 21, 1919	Winnipeg General Strike culminated as Mounties charge a crowd of strikers and shots are fired. Two men die as a result of the struggle.
25, 1919	Winnipeg General Strike leaders who have not been taken into custody vote to end the strike. Services restored throughout the city.
21, 1919	Golden Boy placed on the dome of the Legislative Building.
29, 1920	Edith Rogers became first woman elected to Manitoba Legislature.
2, 1922	Canada's first commercial radio station, CJCG, was introduced by the *Free Press*.
ne, 1923	Provincial government repealed prohibition and established the Liquor Control Commission.
ch, 1926	Winnipeg's James A. Richardson formed Western Canada Airways Incorporated.
3, 1929	Last spike driven on the Hudson Bay Railway at Churchill. By August, 1931 the terminal elevator dock and other port facilities were in operation.
4, 1929	The value of stocks plummeted on North American stock exchanges, signaling the beginning of the Depression.
, 1930	The Diamond Jubilee of Manitoba's entry into Confederation was celebrated.
5, 1930	Control over Manitoba's natural resources was transferred from the federal government to the province.
1935	Federal government created the new Canadian Wheat Board.
1939	Canada declared war on Germany.

RECOMMENDED READING

Akenson, Donald H., *Canadian Papers in Rural History*. Ontario: Langdale Press, 1978.

Anderson, Charles W., *Grain: The Entrepreneurs*. Winnipeg: Watson & Dwyer Publishing Ltd. 1991.

Artibise, Alan F.J., *Winnipeg: A Social History of Urban Growth, 1874-1914*. Montreal: McGill-Queen's University Press, 1975.

Artibise, Alan F.J., *Winnipeg—An Illustrated History*. Toronto: James Lorimer & Company, Publishers, 1977.

The Beaver (magazine). Winnipeg: Canada's National History Society, 1920-19—.

Bellan, Ruben, *Winnipeg's First Century—An Economic History*. Winnipeg: Queenston House Publishing Co. Ltd., 1978.

Bercuson, David Jay, *Confrontation At Winnipeg: Labor, Industrial Relations and the General Strike*. Montreal: McGill-Queen's University Press, 1990.

Berry, Virginia, *150 Years of Art in Manitoba—Struggle for a Visual Civilization*. Winnipeg: The Winnipeg Art Gallery, 1970.

Berton, Pierre, *The Great Depression, 1929-1939*. Toronto: McClelland and Stewart, 1990.

Broadfoot, Barry, *Ten Lost Years—Memories of Canadians Who Survived the Depression*. Markham, Ontario: PaperJacks, 1980.

Bruno-Jofie, Rosa del C., *Issues in the History of Education in Manitoba: From the Construction of the Common School to the Politics of Voices*. Queenston, ON: E. Mellen Press, 1993.

Bumstead, J.M., *The Winnipeg General Strike of 1919—An Illustrated History*. Winnipeg: Watson & Dwyer Publishing Limited, 1994.

Canadian Journal of Native Studies. Brandon University: The Society for the Advancement of Native Studies, 1981-19—

Carter, Sarah, *Lost Harvests: Prairie Indian Reserve Farmers and Government Policy*. Montreal: McGill: Queen's University Press, 1990.

Chafe, J.W., *Extraordinary Tales From Manitoba History*. Toronto: McClelland and Stewart Limited, 1973.

Clark, Lovell, *Manitoba School Question: Majority Rule or Minority Rights*. Toronto: Copp Clark, 1968.

Coates, Ken, and McGuinness, Fred, *The Keystone Province: An Illustrated History of Manitoba Enterprise*. Burlington: Windsor Publications (Canada), 1988.

Coates, Ken, and McGuinness, Fred, *Manitoba: The Province and The People*. Edmonton: Hurtig 1987.

Dawson, C.A., and Younge, Eva R., *Pioneering the Prairie Provinces: The Social Side of the Settlement Process*. Millwood, N.Y.: Krauss Reprint Co., 1974.

Dictionary of Canadian Biography. Toronto: University of Toronto Press, 19—.

Ellis, Frank H., *Canada's Flying Heritage*. Toronto: University of Toronto Press, 19—.

Friesen, Gerald, *The Canadian Prairies: A History*. Toronto: University of Toronto Press, 1987.

Gibson, Dale, *Substantial Justice: Law and Lawyers in Manitoba 1670-1870*. Winnipeg: Peguis Publishers Limited, 1972.

Gillies, Ian et al, *Manitoba and its Great Resources: An Illustrated History of Resource Development in Manitoba*. Winnipeg: Natural Resources Institute, University of Manitoba, 1975.

Gleave, A.P., *United We Stand: Prairie Farmers, 1901-1975*. Toronto: Lugus Productions, 1990.

Gray, James H., *Booze*. Toronto: Macmillan of Canada, Ltd., 1972

Gray, James H., *Red Lights on the Prairies*. Toronto: Macmillan of Canada, 1971

Gray, James H., *The Roar of the Twenties*. Markham, ON: Paperjacks Edition, 1982

Gregor, Alexander, and Wilson, Keith, *The Development of Education in Manitoba*. Dubuque, Iowa: Kendall/Hunt Publishing Company, 1984.

Hackett, Chris, editor, *A Bibliography of Manitoba Local History: A Guide to Local and Regional Histories Written About Communities in Manitoba*. Manitoba Historical Society, 1989

Penny, *Place Names of Manitoba*. Sas-
Western Producer Prairie Books, 1980.

lton, F.W., *Service At Cost: A History of
vators, 1925-1975*. Saskatoon: Modern

ic and Scientific Society of Manitoba,
 in Manitoba: A Key to Places, Districts,
 Transport Routes*. History Committee,
Scientific Society of Manitoba, 1976.

Michael, editor, *The Dirty Thirties:
 Great Depression*. Toronto: Copp

Mary, editor, *First Days, Fighting
 in Manitoba History*. Regina: Cana-
search Centre, 1987.

Mary, and Fast, Vera, *Planting the Gar-
ated Archival Bibliography of the His-
 in Manitoba*. Winnipeg: University of
, 1987.

ames A. *Centennial History of Mani-
McClelland and Stewart Ltd., 1970.

llan, *The Exchange—100 Years of
 Winnipeg*. Winnipeg: Peguis Pub-
1987.

R.C., *Swords and Ploughshares: War
 in Western Canada*. Edmonton: Uni-
 Press, 1993.

s, Margaret, *Manitoba Milestones*.
nt, 1928.

ulture, Heritage and Citizenship,
nnipeg: Historic Resources Branch,

istory* (magazine). Winnipeg: Man-
ciety, 1980-19—.

geant* (magazine). Winnipeg: Man-
ciety, 1956-1979.

mes David, *The Political Econ-
evelopment: Governments and
lanitoba's Resource Frontier,
sity of Manitoba PhD dissertation,

r S., *History of Prairie Settle-
ersity of Toronto Press, 1975.

Morton, Desmond, and Granatstein, J.L.,
*Marching to Armageddon: Canadians and the Great
War, 1914-1919*. Toronto: Lester and Orpen Dennys,
1989.

Morton, W.L., *Manitoba: A History*. Toronto:
University of Toronto Press, 1967.

Paterson, Edith, *Tales of the Early West*. Winnipeg: Canadian News, 1978.

Rea, J.E., *Parties and Power: An Analysis of
Winnipeg City Council 1919-1975*. Winnipeg, 1976.

Ross, Lois L., *Harvest of Opportunity: New
Horizons for Farm Women*. Saskatchewan: Western
Producer Prairie Books, 1990.

Rudnyckyj, J.B., *Manitoba Mosaic of Place
Names*. Winnipeg: Canadian Institute of Onomastic
Sciences, 1970.

Sealey, D. Bruce, *The Education of Native Peoples in Manitoba*. Winnipeg: University of Manitoba,
1980.

Smith, Doug, *Let Us Rise: A History of the
Manitoba Labor Movement*. Vancouver: New Star
Books, 1985.

Stanley, George, *The Birth of Western Canada:
A History of the Riel Rebellions*. Toronto: University
of Toronto, 1960.

Stuart, E. Ross, *The History of Prairie Theatre—
The Development of Theatre in Alberta, Manitoba
and Saskatchewan, 1833-1982*. Toronto: Simon and
Pierre, 1984.

Thompson, John Herd, *The Harvests of War:
The Prairie West, 1914-1918*. Toronto: McClelland
and Stewart, 1978.

Warkentin, John et al, *Manitoba Historical
Atlas: A Selection of Facsimile Maps, Plans and
Sketches From 1612-1969*. Winnipeg: Historical and
Scientific Society of Manitoba, 1970.

Wells, Eric, *Winnipeg: Where the New West
Begins*. Windsor Publications (Canada) Ltd., 1982.

Wood, Louis Aubrey, *A History of Farmers'
Movements in Canada*. Toronto: University of
Toronto Press, 1975.

PICTURE CREDITS

Cover Settler, c. 1880's, PAM/N7934

Page iv: *Grain Elevator at La Salle*, 1931, Walter Joseph Phillips, PAM/A25/13 p.v: Lombard Avenue, WCPI/170-5331

Chapter 1 p.12-13: *The Dakota Boat*, n.d., by W. Frank Lynn (1835-1906), Collection of the Winnipeg Art Gallery/G-71-94; gift of Mr. and Mrs. Sam Cohen, photo by Ernest Mayer p.14: *The Forks*, n.d., by W. Frank Lynn (1835-1906), WCPI/15039 p.15: Louis Riel, PAM/N5733 p.15: Colonel Garnet Wolseley, WCPI/371 p.16: Wolseley Expedition, WCPI/725 p.17: Saloon at Portage and Main, c. 1872, PAM/Red Saloon 1 p.18: *The Marquette*, PAM p.19: First Class Lounge of *The Winnipeg*, PAM p.19: *The Selkirk*, PAM p.20: Lieutenant-Governor Adams Archibald, c. 1889, PAM/N12595 p.20: *The Fenian Excitement in Manitoba—The Commandant Addressing the Troops at Fort Garry*, Glenbow Archives/NA-1406-73 p.21: First Legislative Assembly of Manitoba, 1870, PAM p.22: Yellow Quill, PAM/Yellow Quill p.22: Cree Warrior beside teepee, WCPI/1788 (background) p.22-23: Chief addressing group at Red River, from *L'Opinion Publique*, September 14, 1871, Glenbow Archives/NA-47-41 p.23: Early survey map of Manitoba, PAM p.24: *The Treaty Line*, 1933, by George Agnew Reid 1860-1947, Collection of the Winnipeg Art Gallery/G-72-75; gift of Mrs. Carol Elliott, photo by Ernest Mayer p.24: Border mound, National Archives of Canada, Ottawa/C73304 p.24-25: Mounties en route, WCPI/665 (background) p.25: Stampede, from *L'Opinion Publique*, July 30, 1874, Glenbow Archives/NA-47-3 p.26: Lord Gordon Gordon, PAM/N5815 p.28: Ox cart on Winnipeg's Main Street, PAM N1424 p.29: *Mayor Cornish*, 1901, by Victor Long (1888-1938), WCPI/14996 p.30: *Winnipeg from St. Boniface, August 8, 1881*, by Frederick Boley Schell, National Archives of Canada, Ottawa/C120519 p.30: Winnipeg's Main Street, Collection of Winnipeg Transit p.31: 1884 Map of Winnipeg, PAM p.32: *The International* at Fort Garry, WCPI/2848 p.33: Mennonite barn, c. 1875, WCPI/1029 p.34: Arrival of Icelandic settlers at Willow Point, WCPI/5404 p.36: Settler and plough, PAM/Plough 1 p.36: Charlotte Ross, WCPI/15044 p.37: Settler and sod hut, Mennonite Heritage Centre Archives p.39: John Norquay, WCPI/ 39014 p.40: Troops at Winnipeg's CPR station, Glenbow Archives/NA-4967-7 p.40-41: *Battle of Fish Creek 1885*. Lithograph from a sketch by F.W. Curzon in *Illustrated War News*, PAM/A24/2 p.41: Louis Riel's trial, Glenbow Archives/NA-1081-3 p.41: Gabriel Dumont, WCPI/381

Chapter 2 p.42-43: Immigrants and CPR train, c. 1890, WCPI/09-276 p.44-45: *A Settler's Home Near Carberry*, Edward Roper, National Archives of Canada, Ottawa/C11030 p.44: Train, n.d., Glenbow Museum/NA-33-26 p.45: Trestle bridge, c. 1885, Canadian Pacific Limited Archives/A-688 p.46-47: Brandon's Pacific Avenue, WCPI 14274; The Canadian Pacific Railway. Traversing the Great Wheat Region of the Canadian Northwest, c. 1883, Canadian Pacific Limited Archives/GR 374 A p.48: General Thomas Rosser, PAM/Rosser 1 p.48: Sir William Van Horne, n.d., Canadian Pacific Limited Archives/A-5235 p.50: Chinese restaurant and laundry, Glenbow Archives/NA-1978-1 p.51: Thomas Greenway, PAM/Greenway 1 p.52: Settlers, Glenbow Archives/NA-1255-30 p.53: Log house with sod roof, WCPI/14266 p.54: Winnipeg Electric Street Railway, 1892, PAM/N7600 p.55: Immigration Hall in Winnipeg, c. 1890-1910, National Archives of Canada, Ottawa/PA122676 p.55: CPR immigration brochure, Canadian Pacific Limited Archives p.55: "Men Wanted" poster, 1883, Canadian Pacific Limited Archives/A-6419 p.56: Immigrants in CPR car, WCPI/7474 p.58: Clifford Sifton, PAM/Sifton 2 p.59: James Allen Smart, PAM/Smart 1 p.60: Aboriginal farmer, n.d., WCPI/1765 p.61: Cree farmers with machinery and farm instructor, Glenbow Archives/NA-929-1 p.61: Washakada Indian Industrial School, Elkhorn, c. 1896, Glenbow Archives/NA-4101-23 p.62: Emerson flood, 1897, PAM/N13980 p.62: Manitoba Hotel fire, 1899, WCPI/24912 p.62-63: Farewell to Manitoba Transvaal Contingent, 1899, Manitoba Museum of Man and Nature/5001 p.65: "The Golden Northwest" poster, Canadian Pacific Limited Archives/A-6418

Chapter 3 p.66-67: Labour day parade, Portage and Main, n.d., PAM/ N10342 p.68-69: Colourized postcard, Winnipeg market and city hall, c. 1908, PAM/N15970 p.69: Wagon accident, 1916, PAM/Foote 963, N2563 p.70: *Manitoba Free Press* ad, August 2, 1913, Manitoba Legislative Library p.70: Theatre Marquee, October 19, 1913, PAM/Foote 1622, N2718 p.71: Postcard of St. Boniface Cathedral, 1908, National Archives of Canada, Ottawa/PA29404 p.71: James Ashdown, WCPI/ 10107 p.72: Hugh John MacDonald, 1885, PAM/N3480 p.72: Augustus Nanton, WCPI/10129 p.72-73: Hunting in Charleswood, c. 1912, PAM/Foote 1124, N2085 p.73: Douglas C. Cameron's home, c. 1910,

PAM/N15529 p.73: Kilmorie, 1905, PAM/ Nanton 26 p.74: Colourized postcard of Ogilvie Flour Mill, 1907, PAM p.75: Roman Catholic Berlin, c. 1910, PAM/N10540 p.76-77: Portage and Main, collection Winnipeg Transit p.76: Telephone operators, 1907, WCPI/08 p.76: Hudson's Bay Company liquor store, 1909, PAM/N9728 p.78-79: Ball players, Manitoba Museum of Man and Nature/3766 p.78-79: Cock fighting (insert) and men standing near car, 1915, PAM/Foote 3 (background) p.80: John McRae, WCPI/53332 p.80: Winnipeg Police Department motorcycles, 1912, PAM/Foote 1557, N26 p.81: Winnipeg firemen, WCPI/16793 p.82-83: Winnipeg slum mission, National Archives of Canada, Ottawa/C30953 p.83: Kim square, 1904, PAM/N13261 p.83: Young criminals, 1914, PAM/Foote 35, N2651 p.84: David Morosnick's market, c. 1910, PAM/Jewish Historical Society 759 p.85: L. Meltzer's store, Selkirk Avenue, c. 1910, PAM/Jewish Historical Society 669 p.85: "Evil Eye" store, 60 Main Street, 1901, PAM/Jewish Historical Society 1325 p.86: Margaret Scott, PAM/Scott p.86-87: Assiniboine Park Pavilion, c. 1910, PAM/N4741 p.88: St. Andrew's Locks, National Archives of Canada, Ottawa/PA335 p.88: Interior of the *Winnipeg Telegram*, 1914, PAM/Foote 113-1, N234 p.88-89: Telegram Printing Company Building, PAM/Foote 1336, N233 p.89: Winnipeg garment factory, Manitoba Museum of Man and Nature/59 p.89: Striking electric railway workers, WCPI/271 (background) p.90: The Fort Garry Hotel, c. 1912, PAM/Foote 135, N4 p.90-91: Union Bank Building, PAM/N1484

Chapter 4 p.92-93: Manitoba Harvesting crew, c. 1910, WCPI/271 p.94: *Field Irrigation*, by Charles W. Simpson, Canadian Pacific Limited Archives/A-5143 p.95: Wheat field, courtesy Winnipeg Commodity Exchange p.96: Cora Hind, WCPI/61992 p.98: Dauphin, 1904, PAM/ Thomas Hoy Collection 1 p.99: Welcome sign near Hartney, 1915, National Archives of Canada, Ottawa/ PA119425 p.100: Ontario oven 1916, PAM/N9601 p.101: Billy Beal, courtesy Robert Barrow 2401 Farmer at Bender Hamlet, PAM/Jewish Historical Society 737 p.102: *Princess*, Manitoba Marine Museum (Selkirk) p.103: Cutting ice white Mud River, 1916, PAM/N3212 p.103: *Summer Afternoon—The Prairie*, 1921, by Lionel LeMoine FitzGerald, reproduced by permission Patricia and Earl Green, photo by Ernest Mayer, Winnipeg Art Gallery p.104: Settler, c. 1880's, PAM/N7934 p.106-107: Manitou, PAM/ Manitou 3, N1333 p.106: Dutch immigration book, 1884, Glenbow Archives/NA-1083-1 p.107: Alonzo Kempton and others, Wawanesa Mutual Insurance Company Archives p.108: *Massel Hawk*, 1903, by Ernest Thompson Seton, courtesy Philmont Scout Ranch, Seton Memorial Library, Cimarron, New Mexico and The Seton Centre, Carberry Manitoba p.109: Boy ploughing, 1930, National Archives of Canada, Ottawa/PA117285 p.109: Threshing outfit, PAM/N13 p.110: Lengruth school, 1918, PAM/N12525 p.110: Harvest at Winnipeg CPR Station, c. 1900, PAM/N7874 p.111: Catalogue page, courtesy Eaton's p.112: Ogilvie Mills Elevator, courtesy Winnipeg Commodity Exchange p.113: Downtown Brandon, WCPI/262-8358 p.113: Medora suburb 1905, PAM/Thomas Hoy Collection 20 p.115: Cattle, 1916, PAM/N3219 p.115: *The Grain Grower's Guide*, 1909, Glenbow Archives/NA-4C7 p.116: Curling team, 1913, PAM/N975 p.117: Current Geographic Boyne River, c. 1907, PAM/Carman churches 3

Chapter 5 p.118-119: *Battle of Ypres*, courtesy Regimental Headquarters Princess Patricia's Canadian Light Infantry p.120: *Library of Legislative Assembly*, c. 1912, Frank W. Simon, PAM/A17 p.121: Suffragettes' cartoon, Manitoba Museum of Man and Nature/9 p.121: Child's funeral, c. 1914, PAM/Foote 183, N178 p.123: Nellie McClung, PAM/N7694 p.124: *The Path of Progress*, 1911, by Eric Gundlach, Collection of George T. Williamson, with thanks to the Mendel: Saskatoon's Art Gallery, photo by AK Studio p.125: Winnie the Pooh, WCPI/52580 p.126: Tobias Crawford Norris, PAM p.127: Political Equality League, PAM/N9905 p.128: J.S. Woodsworth, WCPI/ 22959 p.129: Recruitment trench, PAM/N2 p.129: Battle trench, n.d., Fort Garry Horse Museum/02-259 p.131: Riflemen at Cambrai, Fort Garry Horse Museum/61502-800 p.131: Red Cross train, Fort Garry Horse Museum/61502-900 p.132: Wrecked large, PAM/H9 p.133: Billy Barker, PAM/N14765 (background) p.134: Nurses and babies at Grace Hospital, 1914, PAM/Foote 15, N34 p.134: Shoal Lake Aqueduct, PAM/Foote 851, N2451 p.135: Soldiers medic postcard, Fort Garry Horse Museum/61503-500 p.135: Battle postcard, Fort Garry Horse Museum/61502-700 p.137: Jack Krafchenko, 1914, PAM p.137: Jack Krafchenko's signature (background), PAM p.138: Swan River Farm, 1916, PAM/N3202 p.138: Manitoba Free Press, November 11, 1918, Manitoba Legislative Library p.139: Soldiers and train, n.d., Fort Garry Horse Museum/02-231 p.140: "Deal with the Alien Enemy" marchers, National Archives of Canada

p.140-141: Horses charging, National Archives of
C26782 p.141: Mob overturning streetcar, National
ada, Ottawa/C34024 p.142: Girls on roller skates,
s of Canada, Ottawa/C35638 p.143: C.A.S.C. trucks
hine guns, National Archives of Canada, Ottawa/
Winnipeg Free Press carrier boys, WCPI/38757 p.145:
ountain Penitentiary, 1919, National Archives of
39558

147: Worker at the Mandy Mine, WCPI/5079 p.148:
aving Lower Fort Garry, 1909, 1931, by Charles F.
s Bay Company Archives/PAM/P395 p.149: Norway
nal Archives of Canada, Ottawa/C652 p.149: Nah-
ak-Yash (Jacob Berens), 1909, by Marion Nelson
/4 p.150: Logging operation, 1901, PAM/N941
ts at Warren's Landing, 1920, PAM/N3573 p.151:
npany store Churchill, 1919, National Archives of
147457 p.153: Trapper's camp, PAM/N15191
urchill, c. 1920, Glenbow Archives/NA-1964-4
g old and new locations of Peguis Indian Reserve
school fire at Norway House, 1913, Glenbow
25 p.155: Portaging, PAM/N15014 p.156-157:
ent at York Factory, PAM/JG Jones 59 p.156: Jail
M/N12511 p.157: Dog race, c. 1915, Glenbow
p.158: Map of "Roblin City", 1912, PAM p.158-
Glenbow Archives/NA-2471-10 p.159: Log road,
g 1 p.160: Laying tracks near Churchill, 1929,
Canada, Ottawa/PA147455 p.160-161: Train
PAM/N1309 p.161: Driving the last spike on The
1928, PAM p.162: Open pit mine at Flin Flon,
14 p.163: Tractor train, PAM/N12046 p.163:
PAM/Weber 91 p.166: G-Casp Fokker, 1929,
Canada, Ottawa/PA88708 p.166: Vickers
e, c. 1921-34, Manitoba Museum of Man and
Group by airplane, 1938, PAM/C.A.I. coll. 1727
tern Canada Aviation Museum /OS-249 p.168:
any at Pine Falls, 1927, PAM/Foote 744, N14532
lopment, 1929, PAM/Foote, 494, N2094

Portage Avenue, Collection of Winnipeg Transit
nd, 1922, PAM/Foote 288, N1888 p.173: The
, WCPI/38957 p.174: Lombard Avenue, WCPI/
toba Club banquet, May 14, 1921, PAM/Foote
woy group at CJGX, February 20, 1932, PAM/
6: Interior of the Grain Exchange, September
6, N2036 p. 177: Train, WCPI/62937 p.178:
9051 p.179: Wheat pool tents, 1928, WCPI/
Institute, June, 1926, courtesy Manitoba
Frederick Philip Grove, PAM/Grove, Philip 1
Department of Archives and Special Collec-
Manitoba p.181: Domestic science class,
p.182: Safe at Assiniboine Park, May 27,
2536 p.183: Still on Boyd Avenue, Septem-
62, N2262 p.184: Act at Orpheum Theatre,
N3046 p.184: Ectoplasm, Department of
ctions, the University of Manitoba/PC 12-
c Society c. 1915, PAM/Virden Groups 1
mstead, 1934, by Walter Joseph Phillips,
nlight Special, 1914, National Archives of
188: James H. Ashdown's cottage, Collec-
ods Museum p.188-189: Girls playing on
(background), PAM/Foote 1206, N2182
eg Beach, 1927, PAM/Cripps Collection 23
9012 p.193: Scottish crofters, 1914, WCPI/
edding dance, Oakburn, 1921, Glenbow
John Bracken's radio address, October 7,
8 p.195: Woolworth fire, May 27, 1929.

bowl area, Manitoba, 1938. Glenbow
99: Grain Elevator at La Salle, 1931, Wal-
13 p.199: Cranberry Portage forest fire,
ction 17 p.199: Homemade windmill,
onal Archives of Canada, Ottawa,
Dafoe, courtesy Winnipeg Free Press
tmas, 1931, PAM/N14238 p.203: Horse
McAdam Collection 37 p 204: Deanna
23642 p.204: Portage Avenue looking

Artwork and other visual material graciously provided by:

ROB BARROW
CANADIAN WHEAT BOARD
CANADIAN PACIFIC LIMITED ARCHIVES
EATON'S
FORT GARRY HORSE MUSEUM AND ARCHIVES INC.
GLENBOW ARCHIVES
HUDSON'S BAY COMPANY ARCHIVES
JEWISH HISTORICAL SOCIETY OF WESTERN CANADA
LAKE OF THE WOODS MUSEUM
MANITOBA LEGISLATIVE LIBRARY
MANITOBA MARINE MUSEUM (SELKIRK)
MANITOBA MUSEUM OF MAN AND NATURE
MANITOBA WOMEN'S INSTITUTE
THE MENDEL: SASKATOON'S ART GALLERY
MENNONITE HERITAGE CENTRE ARCHIVES
NATIONAL ARCHIVES OF CANADA
PRINCESS PATRICIA'S CANADIAN LIGHT INFANTRY ARCHIVES
PROVINCIAL ARCHIVES OF MANITOBA (PAM)
THE SETON CENTRE, CARBERRY/SETON MEMORIAL LIBRARY,
CIMARRON, NEW MEXICO
UNIVERSITY OF MANITOBA ARCHIVES AND SPECIAL COLLECTIONS
WAWANESA MUTUAL INSURANCE COMPANY ARCHIVES
WESTERN CANADA AVIATION MUSEUM
WESTERN CANADA PICTORIAL INDEX (WCPI)
WINNIPEG ART GALLERY
WINNIPEG COMMODITY EXCHANGE
WINNIPEG FIRE FIGHTERS HISTORICAL SOCIETY
WINNIPEG POLICE MUSEUM
WINNIPEG TRANSIT
STUART JAMES WHITLEY

Special thanks to the following for permitting the reproduction of images:

The Artist, *Political Discussion, Depths of the Depression,
Winnipeg, 1932*, by Caven Atkins
Patricia and Earl Green, *Summer Afternoon—The Prairie, 1921*,
by Lionel LeMoine FitzGerald
John Phillips, *Grain Elevator at La Salle*, 1931; and *Manitoba Farmstead*,
1934, by Walter Joseph Phillips
George T. Williams, *The Path of Progress, 1913*, by Reinhold Gundlach

west from Donald, 1930, PAM/McAdam Collection 442 p.205: Manitoba Provincial Police, 1883, Collection of The Lake of the Woods
Museum p.206: *Political Discussion, Depths of the Depression, Winnipeg, 1932*. Caven Atkins, with thanks to The Mendel: Saskatoon's Art
Gallery, photo by AK Photos p.206-207: Protest march, Winnipeg, c.
1932, Manitoba Museum of Man and Nature/3777 p.207: Soup
kitchen, 1933, WCPI/1461 p.209: Road construction near Russell, September, 1931, PAM/Foote 1028 p.210: Aberdeen School, 1938, PAM/
N2664 p.210: Grey Owl, PAM/N8624 p.212: Unemployed men riding
in box car, 1935, WCPI/1457 (background) p.213: Mennonite coal,
1931, PAM/Altona Farms 4 p.213: Honey wagon, 1933, PAM/Flin Flon
40 p.214: Bennett buggy, 1934, WCPI /1427E p.214: Best bread adver-
tisment, 1937, courtesy Canadian Wheat Board p.214-215: Barns at
Indian Industria School at Brandon, 1935, National Archives of
Canada, Ottawa/PA41423 p.215: Charles Lindbergh at Churchill,
1931, Manitoba Museum of Man and Nature/3363 p.217: Unemployed at The Pas, 1931, Glenbow Archives/NA-1650-1 p.218:
Drewry's beer truck at the St. James Hotel, WCPI/229-7368 p.219:
Clark Gable in Portage la Prairie, 1938, WCPI 38834 p.219: Prince of
Wales' hunting trip to Delta Marsh, 1919, PAM/Foote 321, N1921
p.220: Crowd at the *Winnipeg Free Press*, October, 1939, WCPI/38280
p.221: Population table by ethnicity

Pages 240-241: *Manitoba: Fort Garry, Winnipeg, St. Boniface*, by
Roberts and Reinhold, National Archives Canada, Ottawa, C2823
p.242: Downtown Brandon, WCPI/262-8358 p.250: Group of immigrants at the CPR station in Winnipeg, 1928, PAM/Foote 466, N2066

INDEX